A WORLD IN CRISIS?

A World in Crisis?

Geographical Perspectives

Edited by

R. J. JOHNSTON
and
P. J. TAYLOR

Basil Blackwell

86-352

© Basil Blackwell Ltd 1986

First published 1986

Basil Blackwell Ltd
108 Cowley Road, Oxford OX4 1JF, UK

Basil Blackwell Inc.
432 Park Avenue South, Suite 1505,
New York, NY 10016, USA

British Library Cataloguing in Publication Data

Johnston, R. J.
  A World in crisis?: geographical perspectives.
  1. Geography, Economic
  I. Title   II. Taylor, Peter J. (Peter James) 1944–
  330.9′048   HF1025
  ISBN 0-631-13466-2
  ISBN 0-631-13524-3 Pbk

Library of Congress Cataloging-in-Publication Data

Main entry under title:
  A World in crisis?

  Includes index.
  1. Geography, Economic – Addresses, essays, lectures.
  2. Space in economics – Addresses, essays, lectures.
  3. Natural resources – Addresses, essays, lectures.
  4. Economic history – 1971–   – Addresses, essays, lectures.
  I. Johnston, R. J. (Ronald John)   II. Taylor, Peter J. (Peter
  James), 1944–
  HC59.W658   1986   337′.09′048   85-13440
  ISBN 0-631-13466-2
  ISBN 0-631-13524-3 (pbk.)

Phototypeset by Dobbie Typesetting Service, Plymouth, Devon
Printed in Great Britain by T. J. Press Ltd, Padstow, Cornwall

Contents

The crisis through which international relations and the world economy are now passing presents great dangers, and they appear to be growing more serious.

(Brandt Commission, *North–South: A Programme for Survival*. Cambridge, Mass.: MIT Press, 1980, p. 30)

Preface

The word 'crisis' is frequently used today to characterize some difficulty – local, national or international; particular or general – relating to human societies and their interrelationships with the environment. Indeed, the word is used too frequently, often as a synonym for 'problem', so that its proper definition – 'time of acute danger or difficulty' – is forgotten among so much indiscriminate usage. Perhaps this is understandable: many of the problems called 'crises' are very severe, suggesting to contemporary observers that they might be major turning-points in the course of world history – and the observers won't know whether they were or not until much later.

As with so many aspects of human society and the ways in which it operates, if something is identified as a crisis then crisis it is – at least to the identifiers. Thus we feel justified in using the word in the title to this book. Many people do perceive a *world* in *crisis* – with the dual emphasis indicating that the crisis is believed to be global, not national or local.

Assuming that there is a perceived crisis, what is the justification for offering a series of geographical perspectives on it? That it is recognized as a global crisis is almost sufficient justification in itself, for the portrayal of global processes and patterns is central to the geographer's activity. Further, as the chapters in this volume show, many aspects of the crisis are intrinsically geographical, relating as they do to both society–environment relationships and society–society interrelationships over space. Geographical perspectives provide insights into some of the main parameters of the crisis.

This book has been written for a wide audience. It is especially suited to university courses on global problems, courses which are becoming increasingly popular throughout the social sciences and not only in geography. Through it, we hope to sensitize students to the nature and extent of the problems and difficulties that go to make up the crisis, and to show them the value of geographical perspectives on those issues.

In producing this book, we are grateful to the authors for readily agreeing to contribute and for producing such stimulating essays. We are also very grateful to John Davey for his encouragement and assistance.

R.J.J.
P.J.T.

1

Introduction: A World in Crisis?

R. J. JOHNSTON and PETER J. TAYLOR

At some time during the late 1960s and early 1970s the world we live in seemed to change. The clearest, most abrupt sign of that change was the trebling of oil prices by OPEC in late 1973, an action which sent political and economic shock-waves right through the western world. With hindsight, we can see that this action was more a consequence than a cause of the new situation. It was the culmination of many tendencies which destroyed post-war optimism and replaced it with a 'new realism'. At the most general level, this book is itself a consequence of that destruction, a reaction of geographers to the need for a 'new realism'.

For most of the 1950s and 1960s, economic, social and political policies were based on an assumption of continuous economic growth; any outstanding problems – underdevelopment, for example – were seen as temporary aberrations, since it was only a matter of time before they would be solved by a combination of rational planning and political goodwill. (The market would triumph, freedom, democracy and prosperity would be achieved for all, and the forces of evil – i.e. communism – defeated.) The only cloud on the horizon for the western world was the USSR and the cold war, but at least that never hotted up. The future was rosy, and crisis was very far from the minds of all but a few diehard Marxists who refused to bring their analyses 'up to date'.

Then things began to go wrong. This was shown in myriad ways. Most fundamentally, the economic growth on which the whole optimistic edifice was built began to show signs of faltering; perhaps the post-war good times were not infinitely sustainable after all. Student unrest, city riots and wars in south east Asia and the Middle East all illustrated the increasing fragility of the world. Suddenly crisis seemed to be the word on everybody's lips, and the adjectives applied to it (ecological, environmental, demographic, urban, rural, debt, food, energy, etc.) were so wide-ranging that they contributed to a general sense of despondency. A number of reports was issued proclaiming one crisis after another, and it was but a short step to put them together and identify a general, or global, crisis.

It is, of course, extremely disconcerting to shift rapidly from a sure world full of optimism to an uncertain one full of pessimism and thoughts of crisis. But it is also exciting, especially to students of the world. Such a major shift throws up new opportunities and challenges. Scientists and scholars are forced to revise their thinking. Inevitably, this leads to academic debate and infighting, as society's crisis is reflected in the disciplines that study society. Hence the social sciences have suffered internal turmoil in the last decade as they tackle the new questions – 'Is there a crisis?'; 'What brought it about?'; 'What are the likely consequences?'; 'Can we get out of it? How?' In human geography the optimistic certainty of the 1960s has been replaced by diversity. After more than a decade of this, we need to assess our situation. We cannot expect to eliminate the current diversity – nor do we want to – but we should be able to map out some of the main parameters of the 'world in crisis', both empirically and in the revision of theory. This book is a modest contribution by geographers to that task.

WHAT KIND OF CRISIS? WHAT KIND OF RESPONSE?

Use of the word crisis does not imply a consensus definition of that term. In general usage 'crisis' implies something more severe than a 'problem' (or even a cluster of problems), in which the whole is greater than the sum of the parts. For every problem there is a solution, although we may not be able either to find it or to put it into operation. A crisis implies something qualitatively different (Frank, 1982). In its original Greek form, 'crisis' means 'decision' and so identifies a critical juncture in a process when a critical decision must be made. Its original application was in medicine. A breathing problem becomes a crisis when breathing stops; it is transformed from a problem of the lungs to a crisis of the whole organism, and the point of decision is reached when the existence of the organism itself is in the balance.

It is the technical definition of *crisis as a decision-point* that is used by writers, Marxist and non-Marxist, when they refer to a 'world in crisis'. A world that has not adapted to a new pattern of energy production faces an energy problem: a world that is running out of energy faces an energy crisis. In this context, Marxists use the term crisis to describe the point when the contradictions of the capitalist mode of production finally prevail and the system that it supports collapses, to be replaced by socialism. Wallerstein (1982), for example, is very careful to distinguish the long-term crisis of capitalism from the current phase of economic stagnation, as he describes it. Our problems are part of the long-drawn-out crisis of capitalism, but they do not constitute *the* crisis. Wallerstein fully expects the current problems to be resolved in a new era of growth during the 1990s, but believes that capitalism itself will remain terminally ill.

Within the present book, the authors have interpreted the term 'crisis' in a variety of ways. In general, their emphasis is on the current situation rather than on the long-term perspective implied by Wallerstein. This is entirely valid, for as social scientists we can only analyse the recent past as a guide to the future. Hence it is the vernacular use of the term 'crisis', reflecting the shock stimulated by the severity of recent changes, which predominates in these chapters. From Wallerstein's perspective, they emphasize just one phase of the genuine crisis of the world-system.

In identifying a crisis we are, implicitly at least, assuming the existence of a system, just as those who write about an 'urban crisis' assume that there is an 'urban system' which is breaking down in some sense. Today, it is common to refer to a wider, global crisis; there is no urban crisis *per se* because there is no independent urban system; rather there is a global crisis which is manifested in cities. Hence there are urban problems, but not urban crises. Such a perspective is part of a very strong tendency in modern social science to analyse social change at a much larger scale than heretofore. The move from optimism to the 'new realism' has involved a distinct shift in the geographical scale of emphasis, from national to global, which characterizes social science as a whole, and increasingly the discipline of geography in particular.

In the optimistic social science of the first three post-war decades most analysts, Marxist and non-Marxist alike, assumed that national society and the nation-state should be the basic unit of change. Probably the best-known of such analyses was Rostow's (1971) 'stages of growth' model, in which every country could be allocated to a rung on a ladder leading to 'high mass consumption'. This and similar models have been criticized, as part of the general critique of a modernization school that advances the comparative study of societies (i.e. nation-states) in terms of their 'modernity' (Taylor, 1986). That school of thought assumes the existence of 100–200 separate societies in the world, and assumes that change in those societies occurs autonomously. Such a premise has been a major casualty of the critique of the modernization school by social scientists, for it is obvious to all but the most myopic of observers that the current changes have no respect for national boundaries; they are spread, albeit in different manifestations, across the whole face of the earth, with states almost powerless to influence them (Johnston, 1985). Hence we have global problems, a world recession, international stagnation – perhaps even a world in crisis.

Global thinking is not new, of course, so the new perspectives are basically a shift of emphasis. The classification of countries into three types – First World (or developed/advanced/western/industrial); Second World (or communist/socialist/command economy); and Third World (underdeveloped/developing) – has always indicated an awareness of circumstances affecting change beyond the bounds of individual countries, although as a typology it is rigid and inconsistent. An even more explicit formulation of such cross-boundary links was the early post-war work of Latin American economists, with their identification of core and periphery at a transnational scale. Such themes have been consolidated and expanded in recent years to produce what may prove to be a major qualitative shift in social science.

Currently, that shift is expressed in a variety of forms, and the simplest way to view them is to place studies on a continuum ranging from recognition through to systematic. Close to the first pole are studies which are not far removed from their nation-state-oriented predecessors. The individual states remain the basic unit of analysis and the only emphasis extending beyond national boundaries is one on inter-state links. Change is viewed as a state-level process, but outside influences are allowed a stronger role than hitherto. This is explicitly demonstrated in recent political and welfare geography books (e.g. Coates, Johnston and Knox, 1977; Smith, 1977; Cox, 1979) where the 'international scale' is added to studies at national and local scales, but with little effort at developing links among the three (see Taylor, 1981, 1982). In short, the importance of global analyses has been recognized but it has not altered the overall form of the work.

Moving away from that pole, more sophisticated studies emphasize the linkages between states and particular types of social relations. The best-known examples can be found in the dependency school of development studies, in which core–periphery linkages are the fulcrum of the process of change. Within geography, as a reaction to this emphasis on a single type of link, the concept of interdependence has been used to indicate a much more complex set of relations between countries (e.g. Brookfield, 1975; Reitsma, 1982); but change is still channelled through countries. These studies go beyond simple recognition of global processes but they fall far short of conceptualizing the world as a system.

At the other end of the continuum the focus is on some form of world-system (Thompson, 1983). Change is presented as a property of the system as a whole, and so what happens in any one place can only be understood within a holistic framework. In such a schema, individual countries are no more than parts of a much larger whole; it is impossible to understand, for example, economic decline in Britain by considering Britain alone outside the context of general global processes. There is a great variety of perspectives on the 'world-system'. Among them, a particularly relevant distinction is between those which present the current situation as a new global phase of capitalism, distinct from those that have gone before, and those which argue that this is not a transient phase; to the proponents of this view, the capitalist world-system is by its nature transnational. The former group emphasizes the new features of the current situation (such as the industrialization of the Third World, presented as the 'new international division of labour') and builds an argument that the situation is a unique modern expression of capitalism (Ross, 1983). The other group, following Wallerstein (1974), views the 'modern world-system' as about 500 years old, as international throughout that period, and as global since about 1900. According to that argument, the current situation involves a further set of structural changes that have been continual since the modern world-system was initiated in the sixteenth century; such changes are manifested in different ways at different times and in different places. Both of these perspectives, despite their important theoretical differences, emphasize a *holism* that is lacking from the studies of interconnections among states. For the 'interconnectionists', the world may be in crisis because of a failure in the connections – as in the distribution of food; for the 'holists', the world will be in crisis because of the contradictions involved in its operation as a system.

The holism of the world-systems approaches implies much more than just a change of geographical scale in the study of social change. World-system ideas can be traced back to the political economy perspective which pre-dates the specialization tendencies within the social sciences. Wallerstein calls his project 'historical social science', for example, so as to repudiate the separation of history from social inquiry, and he offers a 'unidisciplinary' approach rather than the ubiquitous call for multi-disciplinary studies; 'historical social science', for Wallerstein, is a single discipline.

Geography shares some of the holistic heritage of the world-system analysts (Taylor, 1985b). As an organized body of knowledge it pre-dates the specialization trends within the social sciences, although latterly it has largely succumbed to this general tendency of modern science. The 'subdisciplines' of human geography are mirror images of the basic trilogy of the social sciences, for example, with social, economic and political geography reflecting sociology, economics and political science respectively. Nevertheless, many of the extremes of myopic thinking in the social sciences (does politics matter?; there is no alternative to monetarism) appear to have been avoided in modern human geography. Despite the pressures for intra-disciplinary specialization, human geographers have just about maintained a holistic viewpoint. Good geographical perspectives on the world in crisis are less narrow than those produced from other social sciences, as the chapters in the rest of this book demonstrate.

GEOGRAPHICAL PERSPECTIVES

The chapters in this book have not been written to a detailed brief and are not structured within any single approach to the study of the world in crisis; indeed, some of the authors are less certain that there is a crisis than others. The selection of topics and authors reflected editorial decisions on the important issues that should be covered in such a book, and experts in the field were invited to contribute, interpreting the general brief as they believed the topic should be studied. All are geographers, by training if not by current affiliation, and they bring geographical perspectives to bear on crucial world issues.

For many people in the core of the world-economy, the clearest evidence of a crisis is the level of unemployment and the apparent inability of governments, except that of the United States, to produce policies that will stimulate employment growth. (To some analysts, it is the policies adopted by the United States, and the consequent massive budget deficit and very high interest rates, that prevent governments elsewhere from stimulating employment.) Thus it is with the geography of employment and unemployment that the book starts, in Nigel Thrift's chapter on international economic disorder. In this wide-ranging survey, with much detail on the nature of the issue, he sets employment change in the context of capital restructuring at the international scale. As stressed already, the issue is one of the world-system as a whole, and Nigel Thrift identifies many of its ramifications, in all parts of the world.

Perhaps the clearest statement of the onset of international economic disorder, at least in the popular mind, came in late 1973 with the OPEC actions to raise oil prices and use that vital natural resource as a political bargaining tool. These actions brought to an end the complacent, optimistic years of cheap, apparently plentiful energy and stimulated much debate about and investigation into alternative sources. But is the world being drained of energy, so that a crisis is rapidly rising over the horizon? Peter Odell, an experienced analyst of the energy field and for long a trenchant critic of public and private sector energy policies, argues not. We have recently passed through a period of unparalleled growth in demand for energy, as a consequence of a particular conjuncture of causal factors, but that period is now over and we have returned to a manageable rate of growth. There are still problems of distribution and access, but his prognosis is much less pessimistic than many. If the crisis does come in the next few years it will not, it seems, be for a lack of energy supplies.

Through the late 1970s and the early 1980s the focus of 'crisis attention' shifted away from energy and towards food. In particular, the problems in Africa where several famines were linked to environmental deterioration (drought in the Sahel and the desertification of large tracts of land) were highlighted; these were forcibly emphasized in western Europe and North America by television reports from Ethiopia, where famine on a very large scale was linked to a continuing civil war (see chapter 10). The spectre of a food crisis loomed large: not for the first time, it was argued by many that the world could not support its population at even a bare subsistence level, that it was raping its natural resource base, and that the only solution – as practised by the Indian government in the mid-1970s – was a massive programme of birth control. And yet there were paradoxes in the situation, for the countries of the EEC were producing much more than they could eat or drink, United States farmers were being paid not to produce, and yields were being increased in many farming regions. So what is the real situation: is there a food crisis, an environmental crisis and a population crisis?

In chapter 4, Phil Bradley tackles the issue of hunger, focusing particularly on Africa. He contrasts peasant subsistence agriculture with capitalist, capital-intensive agriculture and shows how the latter is replacing the former through much of the Third World. He argues that the problems of feeding peoples in those countries stem from the reorientation of local agriculture to the external markets of the core of the world-economy. This is a process initiated four centuries ago in the Caribbean, and slowly spread through much of the rest of the periphery. The condition of subjugation of periphery by core is now virtually complete, and the food problems of the former have become endemic. There is a crisis – not so much of productive capacity as of the orientation of production and the distribution of the output.

And what of the pressures on the environment? Are we raping the earth of its resource base, and are there better ways of managing natural resources? Piers Blaikie finds much evidence of irresponsible use of resources, particularly in the Third World (chapter 5); there, the infiltration of capitalist values – paralleling the agricultural changes outlined by Phil Bradley – has led to rapid deterioration of the resource base in many areas. With regard to the future, Blaikie identifies many problems in developing more appropriate strategies. Those being applied in the Third World at present focus on the relative levels of technical expertise in the host countries and the multi-national corporations which wish to exploit the resources there; political control allows the host government to exert some leverage on the potential users, but the users themselves have considerable leverage in situations where there are more potential suppliers than the market can currently support. Capitalist enterprises can contribute to responsible resource use, but will they? And would an alternative, socialist, mode of production lead to less destructive exploitation? From the evidence of the contemporary Second World Blaikie identifies much environmental decline. Are human societies, whatever their mode of production, bound to destroy, eventually, that which sustains them?

Problems involved with the depletion of natural resources – especially those used in agriculture – and with the provision of food together suggest a population problem which, if insoluble within the present world-system, should lead inexorably to a population crisis. Is there such a crisis looming, with too many people in the world? This question has been asked many times before, and is reviewed in chapter 6 by Bob Woods. He focuses on the opposing views of Malthusians and Marxians on the resource–population equation. The former see the problem as stemming from the pressure on resources generated by rapid population growth, and identify a reduction (at least) in that rate of growth as the solution. The evidence presented by Bob Woods, both historical and contemporary, suggests that the required response does come, and that (in the same way that Peter Odell notes a return to previous rates of growth in energy use – chapter 3) in a longer time perspective the present century will be seen as a unique period of above-average growth. That is not to deny that there are places still experiencing the consequences of very rapid growth, and with little apparent ability to alleviate them. For Marxians, however, there will always be a condition akin to overpopulation in the world under the capitalist mode of production, because of the need to ensure the existence of an industrial reserve army – a pool of underutilized labour power. Thus, according to the latter view, there will always be population problems, verging on crisis proportions at certain times and places, whereas for neo-Malthusians any potential problems can be countered, within the mode of production, by social action (incorporating individual action – perhaps coerced).

Social action implies decision-taking by society as a whole, and by its individual members. What is the context for such action? The first chapters of the book focus on the economic base of society, and pay little attention to the milieux within which economic decisions are made and implemented. It could be deduced from such an approach – and indeed has been in many simplistic analyses – that the capitalist mode of production is a singular form of social organization. But it is not; contemporary capitalism in the First and Third Worlds is characterized by a great variety of social formations, separate organizational forms within which the imperatives of capitalism are interpreted and reinterpreted. (The same is true, though to a lesser extent, in the self-ascribed socialist countries of the Second World.) The world is a mosaic of regional cultures, each the outcome of the interaction of past and present modes of production and each with its characteristic social and political forms (see Massey and Allen, 1984).

This cultural variability is to some extent a hindrance to the spread of capitalism, and as a result powerful forces have sought to erode it and replace it by a 'world culture'. This process of erosion is the subject of chapter 7, where Dick Peet defines culture and investigates the central role of religion within it. Further, he looks at the commodification of culture, and the replacement of local modes by universal, media-based forms. The result is what he terms *ultra-culture*, elements of life 'launched on the market of minds in the pursuit of individual profit'.

The concept of ultra-culture implies the development of the capitalist monolith, the replacement of local variability and variety by standard uniformity as all aspects of life become subject to the forces of the market place and the core-dominated world-economy. What, then, is the position of the individual in such a situation; is there a crisis of individuality? Capitalism is associated in much popular rhetoric with freedom, to choose, to control one's own life and to influence the ways in which society makes its decisions. This is the basis of the concept of liberal democracy, a method of political organization which Ron Johnston shows (chapter 8) is closely associated with the core of the capitalist world-economy. Some models of economic and social development suggest that as the Third World periphery countries progress through the stages of economic growth (as outlined in Rostow's model: see pp. 182,194) so their citizens will achieve greater freedoms; in this way capitalism is presented as a liberating mode of production. Ron Johnston's analyses suggest otherwise, however, for the freedom is tenuous, not only in the Third World countries but also in those of the First. Liberal democracy has been created by states to legitimate the capitalist mode of production, which is an alienating form of economic and social life. But its ability to allow democracy to flourish is fragile, and the freedoms it permits are, at best, constrained.

Ron Johnston's chapter is the first in the book to pay explicit attention to the role of the state in the capitalist world-economy, though government policies are referred to in earlier essays. The state is an increasingly important element in the operations of the capitalist world-economy, and much attention is now being paid by social scientists to the nature and role of the state apparatus (among geographers, see Johnston, 1982; Clark and Dear, 1984; Taylor, 1985a). In those forms of economic organization that preceded the capitalist world-economy – the *world empires* in Wallerstein's terminology – political control by the state was the key element. With the transition to capitalism, and the dominance of markets, the state's role changed; it was needed to support and to promote, but in a secondary (partly ideological) role. Nevertheless, states were necessary components of capitalism, providing the secure environment (including territorial definitions) within which it could prosper. Thus the creation of states was part of the creation of the geography of capitalism (Harvey, 1985).

A strong ideological link has developed between state-building (the process of creating territorially defined units) and nation-building (the creation of popular identification with the state), and the two processes were the focus of the classic work of the Norwegian social scientist Stein Rokkan (see Urwin and Rokkan, 1983). In some parts of the world, the processes were initially more successful than they were in others, providing 'stable' springboards for some 'national' capitals in the competitive world-economy. But state and nation were not always spatially coincident – the newly defined territories were being overlaid on the pattern of pre-existing regional cultures, in some places with a better fit than in others. The consequence has been a tension between nation and state where the fits are poor, as illustrated by Colin Williams (chapter 9). Nationalism would seem to be a major problem today in many parts of the world; is it a necessary concomitant of a growing economic crisis?

In the process of state-building, some states have become much more powerful than others, producing a sequence of hegemonies according to John O'Loughlin's analysis (chapter 10). The powerful states seek to extend their political and economic influence, but their ability to do this declines, as they face economic competition from others and have to invest more in the military support needed for their global organizations. At times, the tensions between the declining superpower and the burgeoning would-be replacements have led to major wars. At others, the tensions are played out in a cold war, with no major conflicts but with many smaller ones in the periphery, as the hegemonic protagonists ally themselves with local forces – in some cases those fighting issues of national congruence, and in others linked to issues relating to economic organization. These are clearly illustrated in John O'Loughlin's chapter.

AND THE FUTURE?

So is there a crisis? Who knows? – yet! Clearly there are problems, many of them – and all of them intertwined in the operations of a capitalist world-economy, which is hell-bent on annihilating space and place. Those problems are severe now at a global scale, and life-destroying in some places. How, then, are they to be countered? Can they be used as the elements to create an intellectual crisis, as the stimuli to a turning-point, to a new set of decisions on how the world should be organized economically, socially and politically?

Change can be brought about in a variety of ways, one of which is a determination to do something new in the future because of the conclusions reached from analyses of the past and present. How should such analyses be conducted? The clear message of this book is that the approach must be holistic. It must not separate out the parts and treat their problems as curable independent of the other parts. We must take a global view, not only spatially but also through the adoption of a unified historical social science. This is Peter Taylor's conclusion in chapter 11, where he outlines in detail Wallerstein's world-systems project, and locates the geographical perspective within it. This is not a call for a narrow orthodoxy, but for a realistic framework within which to analyse the problems of the world and work towards the removal of its many inequities. We are entering a period of ideological confusion in which the epistemological and historiographical premises of the social sciences are facing their severest challenge since their creation in the nineteenth century. This intellectual crisis is part of a wider set of political opportunities which, Taylor argues, we must grasp for our construction of a new world.

And the task is urgent. Time may be running out, as we are reminded in Bill Bunge's epilogue (chapter 12). We possess the awesome power to destroy the world as we know it (and for all time, in all probability), through actions which may take only a few seconds. By such actions we would eradicate an environment in which, if we have the will, we could live in peace and universal prosperity. To make sure that this never happens, we must contribute to the creation of a better world order so that, to paraphrase one of Bill Bunge's earlier (1973) and memorable phrases, the world will be full of happy regions.

References

Brookfield, H. C. 1975: *Interdependent Development*. London: Methuen.

Bunge, W. 1973: Ethics and logic in geography. In R. J. Chorley (ed.), *Directions in Geography*, London: Methuen, 317–31.

Clark, G. L. and Dear, M. J. 1984: *State Apparatus*. London: Allen & Unwin.

Coates, B. E., Johnston, R. J. and Knox, P. L. 1977: *Geography and Inequality*. Oxford: Oxford University Press.

Cox, K. R. 1979: *Location and Public Problems*. Chicago: Maaroufa.

Frank, A. G. 1982: Crisis of ideology and ideology of crisis. In S. Amin, G. Arrighi, A. G. Frank and I. Wallerstein, *Dynamics of Global Crisis*, New York: Monthly Review Press, 109–66.

Harvey, D. 1985: The geopolitics of capitalism. In D. Gregory and J. Urry (eds), *Space and Social Structure*, London: Macmillan.

Johnston, R. J. 1982: *Geography and the State*. London: Macmillan.

Johnston, R. J. 1985: The state, the region and the division of labour. In M. J. Storper and A. J. Scott (eds), *Production, Work, Territory*, London: Allen & Unwin.

Massey, D. and Allen, J. (eds) 1984: *Geography Matters*. Cambridge: Cambridge University Press.

Reitsma, H. J. A. 1982: Development geography, dependency relations and the capitalist scapegoat. *The Professional Geographer*, 34, 125–30.

Ross, R. S. J. 1983: Facing Leviathan: public policy and global capitalism. *Economic Geography*, 59, 144–60.

Rostow, W. W. 1971: *The Stages of Economic Growth: A Non-Communist Manifesto*, 2nd edn. Cambridge: Cambridge University Press.

Smith, D. M. 1977: *Human Geography: A Welfare Approach*. London: Edward Arnold.

Taylor, P. J. 1981: A world-system perspective on the social sciences. *Review*, 5, 3–11.

Taylor, P. J. 1982: A materialist framework for political geography. *Transactions, Institute of British Geographers*, N.S.7, 15–34.

Taylor, P. J. 1985a: *Political Geography: World-Economy, Nation-State and Locality*. London: Longman.

Taylor, P. J. 1985b: The value of a geographical perspective. In R. J. Johnston (ed.), *The Future of Geography*, London: Methuen.

Taylor, P. J. 1986: The error of developmentalism in human geography. In D. Gregory and R. Walford (eds), *New Horizons in Human Geography*, London: Macmillan.

Thompson, W. R. (ed.) 1983: *Contending Approaches to World Systems Analysis*. Beverly Hills: Sage Publications.

Urwin, D. and Rokkan, S. E. 1983: *Economy, Territory, Identity: Politics of West European Peripheries*, Beverly Hills and London: Sage Publications.

Wallerstein, I. 1974: The rise and future demise of the capitalist world-system. *Comparative Studies in Society and History*, 16, 387–418.

Wallerstein, I. 1982: Crisis as transition. In S. Amin, G. Arrighi, A. G. Frank and I. Wallerstein, *Dynamics of Global Crisis*, New York: Monthly Review Press, 11–56.

2

The Geography of International Economic Disorder

NIGEL THRIFT

The 1970s will long be remembered as the decade in which the world economy entered a prolonged period of economic crisis. The economies of the industrialized market countries dipped into recession first in 1974–5. They recovered slightly but then in 1979–80 plunged into recession once again, a recession from which a slow recovery is only now under way. The economies of the developing countries followed those of the industrialized market countries into recession, at least in part because of linked effects such as the depressed demand for their goods from the industrial market economies (World Bank, 1983). Even the economies of the socialist countries of eastern Europe were not immune from the general downturn. In the last five years their overall economic performance has declined, and again, in part, this decline can be traced to international factors (Neuberger and Tysson, 1980). Only some of the oil-exporting countries seemed likely to weather the storm, but even their economies have recently taken a turn for the worse, hit by declining real oil prices.

The world economy in crisis has presented an unhappy prospect for each of the three principal groups of actors on the world stage – the multinational corporations, the banks, and the governments of countries. They have all been forced to adjust their roles in the general atmosphere of greatly heightened competition. The result has been a reshuffling of the world economy as certain of the actors in each group have proved more successful than others. Out of this reshuffling has come a new world-economic order which, after the period of turmoil in the 1970s, it now seems possible to outline. That is what this chapter attempts to do.

The first part of the chapter gives a highly compressed and necessarily selective account of the main changes that have taken place in the world-economy as a result of the crisis. The emphasis is very much upon the role of the multinational corporations and the banks in bringing about a new world-economic order, although the power of the governments of industrial countries is not forgotten. The second part looks at what has happened to people's jobs as a result of all the changes. It looks at the rise of unemployment and at new kinds of jobs. Particular consideration is given to the way employment opportunities in some parts of the world have become more closely tied to employment opportunities in other areas through the rise of the so-called 'new international division of labour' (its growth facilitated by state action), through international migration and the rise of a new international services economy. There is no need to stress that the chapter is geographical. All the changes described are inherently geographical. Indeed, they depend upon the existence of geography.

It is important first to clarify a number of issues. In this chapter the phrase 'world-economy' refers to the capitalist world-economy and the phrase 'new world-economic order' refers to the new capitalist world-economic order. No consideration is given to the socialist countries which some commentators (e.g. Wallerstein, 1979, 1983) place within the orbit of the capitalist world-economy and the capitalist world-economic order. Such countries are certainly increasingly linked to it (see, for example, Bora, 1981; Kortus and Kaczerowski, 1981; Gutman and Arkwright, 1981), but the case has yet to be convincingly made that they are an integral part of it. Second, since what follows is such a compressed account it is inevitable that changes in the world-economic order will be presented as remorseless, unitary movements forming an ordered and coherent whole. The reality, of course, is rather different. The changes taking place are still, even now, quite tentative processes which can conceivably be reversed. This is no surprise, for they are organized by humans. And the new world-economic order is not an ordered whole. Certainly, it has some semblance of order. Otherwise it would not work. But it is not 'an order established *in order* to be coherent' (Lipietz, 1984b, p. 92). Third, and following from the second issue, it is important to stress that no attempt is made in what follows to give one determinant of the change to a new world–economic order absolute priority at the expense of any other. In particular, many writers have been guilty of emphasizing the role of one or two of the groups of actors on the world-economic stage to the detriment of others. For some writers, for example, the multinational corporations and the banks have fused into an overarching 'world capital' which transcends all national barriers (e.g. Harris, 1982). For others, what goes on inside national barriers must be given priority and multinational corporations are a sideshow (e.g. Aglietta, 1982; Lipietz, 1984b). Each of these reactions is equally incorrect. The world-economy is the outcome of a whole series of countervailing forces operating at a whole series of scales, no one of which makes sense without the others.

Finally, some questions of definition. In this chapter the phrase 'developed countries' generally refers to the 24 countries that belong to the Organization for Economic Co-operation and Development (OECD), namely Australia,

Austria, Belgium, Canada, Denmark, Finland, France, West Germany, Greece, Iceland, Ireland, Italy, Japan, Luxemburg, the Netherlands, New Zealand, Norway, Portugal, Spain, Sweden, Switzerland, Turkey, the United Kingdom and the United States. The phrase 'developing countries' generally refers to those designated as low-income or middle-income developing countries by the World Bank in its annual *Development Report* (World Bank, 1983).

THE WORLD-ECONOMIC CRISIS AND
THE NEW WORLD-ECONOMIC ORDER

Economic experts are still arguing about the reasons for the world-economic crisis of the 1930s (see, for example, Kindleberger, 1973; Bruner, 1981). It comes as no surprise, then, to find that they cannot agree on the causes of the present crisis. Perhaps the only thing they *are* willing to agree on is that it is not simply the result, to cite the conventional mid-1970s wisdom of the McCracken report, of 'an unusual bunching of unfortunate events' (OECD, 1977, p. 103). As the immediate recession of the mid-1970s has lengthened into a period of prolonged crisis, so most economists have seemed more willing to agree that 'something fundamental happened' (International Labour Organization, 1984, p. 36).

So what is this fundamental something? It is important here to distinguish between, on the one hand, certain temporally contingent factors which have the effect of triggering periods of recession and, on the other hand, the set of processes – that fundamental something – which meant that a crisis would happen at some time. Among the temporally contingent factors, the most important was undoubtedly the 'oil shock'. In 1973–4 petroleum prices quadrupled. They fell by a sixth between 1974 and 1978 and then increased again, by 80 per cent in real terms, during 1979–80. Some perspective on the magnitude of this shock can be gained from just two facts. First, world trade in fuels increased from $29 billion in 1970 to $535 billion in 1980. Second, paying for the 1970s fuel-price increases was equivalent to the countries of the world having to find the money to buy all the exports of another United States (Mitra, 1983).

But, important as the oil shock was in triggering the period of crisis and then sustaining it, it seems likely that it would have happened quite soon because of other fundamental processes. More particularly, it seems that in the late 1960s the rates of profit of many firms operating in the industrialized market economies began to fall. This general fall, which was essentially a *national* phenomenon, can be traced to the breakdown of a particular 'intensive' regime of capital accumulation (Aglietta, 1979) which had become typical of the economies of many of the industrialized market countries and which reached its peak in the 1960s. This was based on massive increases in productivity, brought about through widespread mechanization and sustainable by equally massive increases in demand for the goods produced, generated by the linking of wages to productivity through the regulation (Aglietta, 1979; de Vroey, 1984) of state or state-mediated institutions such as collective bargaining and systems of welfare. For all effects and purposes, this system of mass consumption – the 'powerhouse of demand' as it has often been called – excluded countries other than those of the industrialized core: 'Capitalism had temporarily resolved the question of markets on an internal basis. One could even say that the exports of manufactured goods to the periphery were only just covering the cost of raw materials' (Lipietz, 1984b, p. 99). Certainly, the 1950s and 1960s saw a large increase in the number of multinational corporations in the world, mainly those of North American extraction, but their attentions tended to be restricted to the other developed countries.

With the general fall in the rate of profit two things happened. First, many firms were forced to reorganize in order to make a profit again. They might, for example, have had to change their production techniques, consider new products, reorganize their administrative and financial structures, and, in particular, think about producing and marketing in new locations. Not the least of the many stimuli behind this reorganization were the heightened conditions of competition brought on by the recession. Second, as these firms have groped towards a new regime of capital accumulation, so a new system of regulation, based upon new national and international institutions, has shown signs of coming into being. Out of the old order comes the new.

To summarize, that fundamental something underlying the economic crisis has been capitalism 'putting its books in order' (Magirier, 1983, p. 61). Whereas the world-economic crisis was brought on by essentially *national* phenomena (albeit triggered by an international event), the solution adopted by many corporations and banks was essentially *international*.

At the heart of the new world-economic order, then, is a very simple process – the internationalization of capital. Faced with falling rates of profit, firms were forced to 'automate, emigrate or evaporate' (*New York Times*, cited by Frobel, 1983). Many nationally based firms chose the path of emigration (usually mixed with a strategy of automation as well), for an obvious reason. Multinational corporations have been more profitable than other enterprises in the crisis and the gap between the rate of profit of multinational corporations and that of nationally based firms has actually grown during the years of the crisis (Andreff, 1984). This is not to say that the profits of existing multinational corporations were not hit by the crisis. But the rate of profit of these corporations has recovered, not least because many of them have become even more international than before. Thus the internationalization of capital describes the processes of both nationally based firms becoming multinational and multinational corporations becoming more multinational.

The Internationalization of Capital

What does the 'internationalization of capital' mean? Above all, it means the export of capitalist relations of production, not just of money. Capitalist relations of production are created on a world scale through direct investment by firms which create subsidiaries abroad, organized on capitalist lines. Multinational corporations are the main vehicles of this capital export and as they have increased in both number and size so they have taken on much greater importance in the world-economy than they had in the 1950s or 1960s.

The total flow of foreign direct investment abroad increased by about 15 per cent per annum (in current US dollar terms) in the 1970s and more than trebled between 1970 and 1980. In spite of the economic crisis, outflows of foreign investment continued to increase year by year. Indeed, the pressures of competition from the economic crisis stimulated the multinational corporations to channel direct investment in new ways, most especially through the internationalization of production and through the formation of global profit strategies which led to some of the larger international corporations being transformed into a new species – 'the global corporation'.

The export of capitalist relations of production can take three main forms, each of which has been important at a particular stage in the development of the world capitalist economy but all of which are still important now (Michalet, 1976; Brewer, 1980). First, capital export can be aimed mainly at obtaining raw materials. This has often meant that capitalist social relations were only formed in the mining and agricultural sectors of the developing countries. This kind of capital export was extremely important up until the second world war and continues to be so, although it is of declining relative importance. For example, table 2.1 shows the relative ownership of world aluminium, alumina and bauxite capacity in 1982. The six biggest transnational corporations (Aluminium Company of America (United States), Pechiney-Ugine-Kuhlmann (France), Swiss Aluminium (Switzerland), Aluminium Company of Canada (Canada), Reynolds Metal Company (United States) and Kaiser Aluminium (United States)) between them controlled 44.5 per cent of world aluminium capacity, 50.4 per cent of world alumina capacity and 46.3 per cent of world bauxite capacity (United Nations, 1983). Figure 2.1 shows the extent of Pechiney-Ugine-Kuhlmann operations outside France at the end of 1973. Currently, Pechiney-Ugine-Kuhlmann is involved in prospecting or exploiting all the large bauxite deposits in the world (apart from those in the Caribbean where North American companies prevail). It has a share in all the main aluminium complexes near strategic bauxite deposits (Guinea, Greece and Australia) and it has smelting plants in Europe, America and Africa (Savey, 1981). But increasing competition from the big North American producers in the recession has meant that the corporation has had to seek out new markets. The purchase of a smelter in South Korea in 1973 marked its entry into the south-east Asian market and the corporation is now also active in the USSR.

The subject of markets leads to consideration of the second form of capital export, which is aimed at penetrating the markets of countries that cannot be effectively penetrated by exports, for example because of tariff barriers. This form of capital export, which is oriented towards the manufacturing sector, was the dominant form even before the second world war and is still dominant today. It leads to a spatial structure in which production facilities are replicated

Table 2.1 Ownership of world aluminium, alumina and bauxite capacities, 1982

Owner	Aluminium		Alumina		Bauxite	
	Total capacity[a]	Share world capacity (%)	Total capacity[a]	Share world capacity (%)	Total capacity[a]	Share world capacity (%)
Big six multinational corporations	7,962	44.5	20,113	50.4	51,789	46.3
Other multinational corporations and investors	3,801	21.2	8,642	21.7	22,606	20.4
Governments of developed countries	1,497	8.4	1,571	3.9	323	0.3
Governments of socialist countries	3,730	20.9	7,026	17.6	15,600	13.9
Governments of developing countries	893	5.0	2,523	6.3	21,622	19.3
Total	17,883	100.0	39,785	100.0	111,940	100.0

[a]In thousands of tons.
Source: United Nations, 1983, p. 210

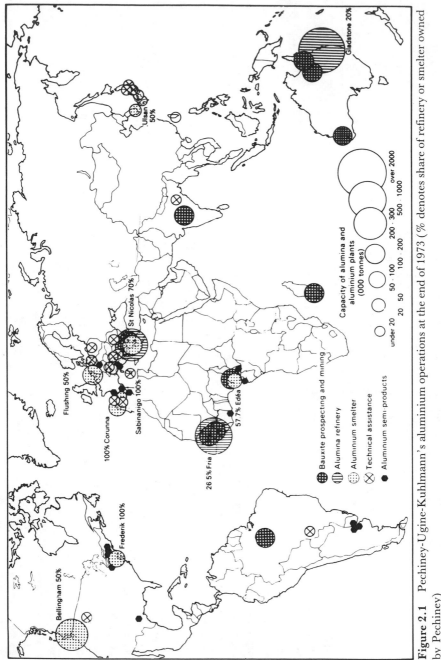

Figure 2.1 Pechiney-Ugine-Kuhlmann's aluminium operations at the end of 1973 (% denotes share of refinery or smelter owned by Pechiney)

Source: Savey, 1981, p. 309

in several countries. The reasons why a multinational corporation will almost certainly decide to internalize production in order to obtain entry to the market of a country, rather than license a local firm to make its products, are threefold (see Buckley and Casson, 1976; Dunning, 1981; Rugman, 1982; Caves, 1983). For example, a multinational corporation may find it impossible or too expensive to arrange with a local firm a contract which affords the multinational corporation effective protection from legal action. Such a reason is often invoked when new technology is involved or if the local producer is likely to make an inferior product and so damage the multinational's corporate image. Or the multinational may be unable to persuade the local firm to pay a price for making a product better than the price which can be obtained if the multinational makes the product itself. But the most usual reason is that other multinational corporations making a similar product have already established themselves in the same country. Rivalry with them becomes a very serious consideration (see Knickerbocker, 1973). Rees (1978) documented just such imitative rivalry among the five largest American tyre-producing multinationals – Goodyear, Firestone, Uniroyal, BF Goodrich and General Tire – in the 1960s and 1970s. In particular he showed how three of these corporations – Goodyear, Firestone and General Tire – fought each other with a move–counter-move strategy. Figure 2.2 shows the pattern of expansion of Firestone, Goodyear and General Tire in Asia. In several cases, each corporation set up plants in the same country within a few years of one another. In the Philippines, Firestone and Goodyear set up in the same year.

Finally, and of particular importance since the late 1960s, capital export has been aimed at exploiting cheap labour to produce goods for re-export to the home country or to third markets (including not only other countries but also other plants in the corporation). This strategy leads to the creation of integrated hierarchical production organizations which cut across national boundaries and is often called the 'internationalization of production'. An example of this most recent form of capital export can be found in the actions of the British multinational, Coats Patons, over the last ten years. Coats Patons is prominent in textiles, a fiercely competitive industry. In the 1970s its profits in the developed countries were threatened by imports from firms in the developing countries who could hold their unit costs down because labour costs were so much cheaper. Coats Patons' response was to move many of its production facilities to such countries, where they too can take advantage of the lower labour costs (see table 2.2), and by 1979 it had built up a sizeable labour force in the developing countries (see figure 2.3).

These are the main forms of capital export, but it is important to point out that, in reality, they are difficult to separate from one another. Thus parts of the operations of Pechiney-Ugine-Kuhlmann and even of the tyre companies may be aimed at obtaining raw materials whereas other parts are aimed at penetrating markets for the products made from the raw materials. Similarly, multinational corporations may be simultaneously seeking out reserves of cheap labour and new markets.

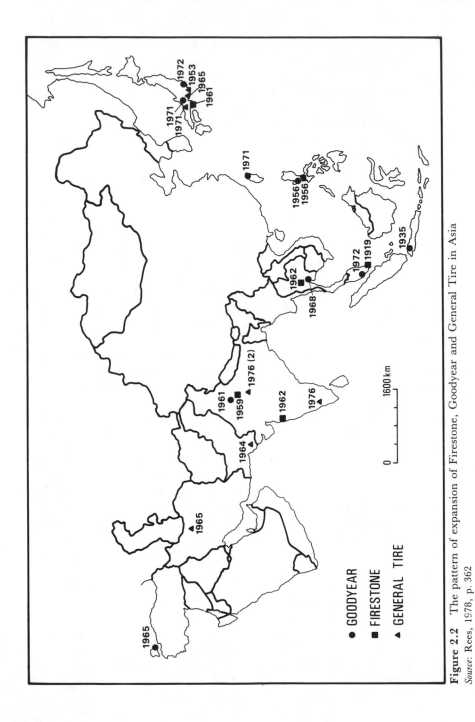

Figure 2.2 The pattern of expansion of Firestone, Goodyear and General Tire in Asia

Source: Rees, 1978, p. 362

Table 2.2 The Coats Patons table of comparative labour costs at 21 April 1981

	Single shift		Double shift		Treble shift	
	Total cost per hour (£)	Index	Total cost per hour (£)	Index	Total cost per hour (£)	Index
UK (base)	2.678	100	3.186	100	3.481	100
Italy	3.259	122	3.499	110	4.943	121
West Germany	3.561	133	3.696	116	3.913	115
Canada	3.596	134	3.564	112	3.613	109
United States	3.134	117	3.134	98	3.157	90
Portugal	1.076	40	1.177	37	1.799	42
Colombia	0.950	36	1.121	35	1.304	26
Brazil	0.840	31	1.009	32	1.065	31
Peru	0.611	23	0.620	19	0.637	19
India	0.342	13	0.345	11	0.416	11
Philippines	0.276	10	0.276	9	0.282	8
Indonesia	0.166	6	0.169	5	0.168	5

Source: Financial Times, 29 June 1981, p. 11

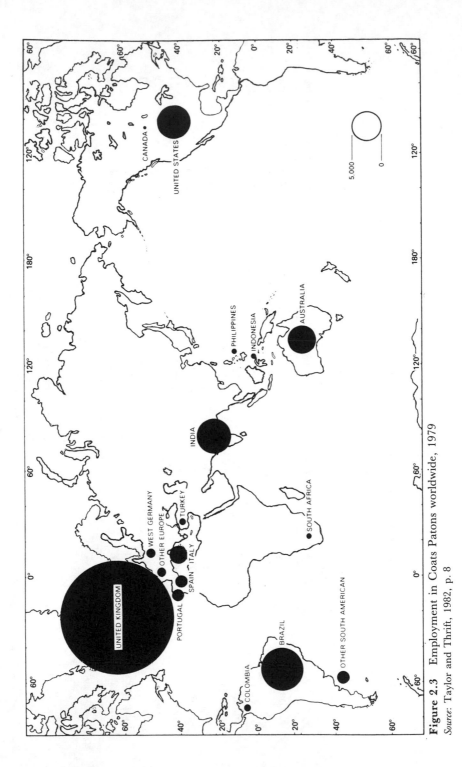

Figure 2.3 Employment in Coats Patons worldwide, 1979
Source: Taylor and Thrift, 1982, p. 8

The integration of the three different forms of capital export under the one corporate roof has become more and more common because the largest multinational corporations have become even larger, adding on more and more subsidiaries. Indeed, some of the larger multinational corporations now operate in the markets of virtually every country in which it is possible to make a profit. For them the challenge is no longer expansion into the markets of new countries. Rather, it has become how to organize their world network of subsidiaries in such a way as to make the best possible profit. Until the late 1960s the challenge of organizing and putting into effect such a global profit-making strategy would have been formidable. But technical developments, most notably in telecommunications and data-processing, organizational developments, especially the setting up of 'regional headquarters offices' (see Dunning and Norman, 1983; Grosse, 1982), and the rise of an international capital market have enabled this challenge to be met by some of them at least. The result has been the growth of a new type – the global corporation (Hunt, Parker and Rudden, 1982; Taylor and Thrift, 1982; *Economist*, 1984) – which will often carry on all three forms of capital export at one and the same time in an integrated way. They tend to promote global brand names, and production within them is organized on a regional or even global basis. The result of this integration of production, and of the constant shifting of materials, components and information that is entailed, is the dramatic enlargement of markets internal to the corporations (see Rugman, 1981, 1982). Just how widespread these internal markets now are can be traced through figures on intra-firm trade across national boundaries. For example, for the United States in 1977, 39 per cent of total imports and 36 per cent of total exports could be classified as intra-firm trade. The proportion of intra-firm exports in the total exports of the UK increased from 29 per cent in 1976 to 31 per cent in 1980. One UNCTAD estimate is that as much as *30 per cent* of world trade is now within corporations (United Nations, 1983).

A good example of how a global corporation came into existence and now goes about its business is provided by the European operations of the automobile manufacturers, Ford, currently the third largest company in the world and for long a multinational corporation. Even in 1930 the corporation was assembling its cars in 20 countries (Bloomfield, 1981; Maxcy, 1981; Ballance and Sinclair, 1983; Cohen, 1983). In 1950 Ford's European organization consisted of three main and quite separate manufacturing and assembly plants serving the three main retail markets of France, the UK and West Germany and four more 'completely knocked down' (CKD) assembly plants serving the subsidiary markets of Belgium, the Netherlands, Denmark and Ireland (see figure 2.4). The company's organization in 1960 was mainly an elaboration on this theme of national market concentration but with France abandoned as a market and the number of component manufacturing plants increased in the UK and West Germany. However, in 1967 Ford of Europe was created in an attempt to integrate the corporation's European operations. Among the factors involved in this decision were the desire to spread investment (especially

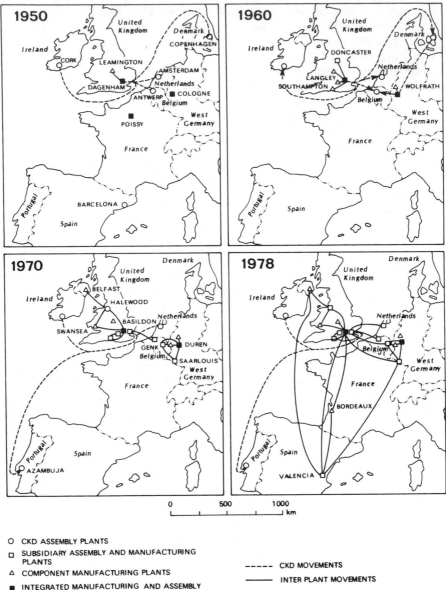

Figure 2.4 The changes in the organization of production at Ford Vehicles in Europe from 1950 to 1978

Source: Bloomfield, 1981, p. 284

because the British subsidiary was prone to labour unrest), the shortage of labour near the existing plants, the high cost of separate model development in a number of markets and the new market opportunities created by the founding of the EEC. By 1970, signs of this new kind of integration were already apparent and by 1978 integration of the European operations was becoming a reality. For example, the introduction of the Ford Fiesta created new and complex patterns of movement within the corporation, integrating plants such as Belfast (carburettors and distributors) and Bordeaux (transmission and axles) with the assembly centres in the UK, Germany and Spain (Bloomfield, 1981).

Prominent among the changes between 1970 and 1978 was the opening of a plant at Valencia, Spain, in 1972. This shows the risks of greater integration for the workers employed in a global corporation. Such corporations can choose a location for a new plant which, if it is successful, becomes the measure for all the other plants in the corporate network. Ford invested in Spain for two reasons: to gain access to the growing Spanish car market – import duties into Spain were prohibitive – and to take advantage of low labour costs. The success of plants like the one at Valencia now threatens other older plants at Dagenham in the United Kingdom and Cologne in West Germany, which find it hard to reach the new corporate norm that Valencia has set because their labour costs are inevitably higher (Cohen, 1983).

Changes in the Origin and Destination of Foreign Direct Investment

The advent of a new form of capital export and of the global corporation should not be allowed to obscure some far-reaching and important changes in the origins and destinations of direct investment during the crisis (see table 2.3). For, although the total flow of foreign direct investment increased at about 15 per cent per annum (in US-dollar terms) in the 1970s and, indeed, more than trebled between 1970 and 1980 (United Nations, 1983) there were very significant changes in the direction of flow.

Before 1970, US-based multinational corporations accounted for nearly two-thirds of the outflow of foreign direct investment. But by the end of the 1970s the US corporations' share of the total had dropped to less than half (see Table 2.3). The corollary of this decline was a rise in the relative position of corporations based elsewhere. In particular, Canadian, West German and Japanese corporations stepped up their rate of foreign direct investment. Of these three the Japanese case is probably the most significant, especially if accumulated direct investment is considered (see table 2.4). Already by the 1960s Japan had become a major economic power in the world, but in general its corporations produced at home and exported abroad. However, in the 1970s Japanese corporations went multinational as never before, spurred on by the state of the home market, by the accumulation of the international resources of capital needed to pay for expansion, by the threat of protectionism in many countries to which Japanese exports were directed, and by the active

Table 2.3 Foreign direct investment by selected countries, 1970–2 and 1978–80

	Outflow				Inflow			
	1970–2		1978–80		1970–2		1978–80	
	US$ million	%	US$ million	%	US$ million	%	US$ million	%
Developed market economies								
Australia	113	0.8	344	0.8	1,030	9.1	1,820	5.3
Austria	25	0.1	90	0.2	84	0.7	197	0.5
Belgium	171	1.3	699	1.7	384	3.4	1,371	3.9
Canada	316	2.4	2,617	6.3	807	7.1	1,138	3.3
Denmark	76	0.6	11	0.0	131	1.1	64	0.2
Finland	53	0.4	106	0.3	27	0.2	30	0.0
France	455	3.4	2,359	5.6	612	5.4	2,902	8.4
West Germany	1,161	8.7	4,262	10.2	1,220	10.8	1,257	3.6
Italy	242	1.8	42	0.1	976	8.6	42	0.3
Japan	481	3.6	2,552	6.1	155	1.4	173	0.5
Netherlands	564	4.2	2,210	5.3	575	5.1	1,038	3.0
Norway	21	0.1	120	0.3	93	0.8	315	0.9
South Africa	22	0.1	89	0.2	237	2.1	− 204	− 0.6
Spain	35	0.3	221	0.5	231	2.0	1,270	3.7
Sweden	217	1.6	551	1.3	86	0.7	145	0.4
United Kingdom	1,597	11.9	5,756	13.8	982	8.7	3,756	10.9
United States	7,649	57.4	19,547	46.9	929	8.2	10,205	29.6
Developing countries								
South-east Asia	20	0.1	152	0.4	530	4.7	2,389	6.9
Latin America	17	0.1	229	0.5	1,130	10.0	4,902	14.2
Total[a]	13,245	100	42,245	100	11,151	100	33,878	100

[a]Totals do not add up owing to the number of countries which have been omitted.
Source: from United Nations, 1983, p. 19

Table 2.4   Accumulated direct investment overseas by country, 1970 and 1978

	1970		1978		
	US$ bn	*Share (%)*	*US$ bn*	*Share (%)*	*Increase (%)*
United States	78	52	168	42	115
United Kingdom	20	13	35	9	75
West Germany	7	5	29	7	314
Japan	4	3	27	7	575
Switzerland	8	5	25	6	213
Others	33	22	116	29	252
World total	150	100	400	100	167

Source: Kirby, 1983, p. 40

involvement of government through the offices of MITI (the Ministry for International Trade and Industry) (Yoshihara, 1976; Franko, 1983).

Another significant outflow of foreign direct investment has come from the increasing number of multinational corporations based in the developing countries (see Lall, 1984; Wells, 1983). Its significance is not based upon the actual proportion of foreign direct investment in total – which is still small – but upon the fact that such investment exists at all. Up to 50 developing countries now have some direct overseas investment. As might be expected most of this comes from the 12 or so newly industrializing countries, the developing countries were the other recipients of foreign direct investment. But this growth has been concentrated in a small number of such countries – are Hong Kong, Brazil, Singapore, South Korea, Taiwan, Argentina, Mexico and Venezuela. Nearly 10 per cent of the top 500 non-US-based corporations in the world are now based in the developing countries, and most of these are multinational. Hyundai, the South Korean shipbuilding firm, is now bigger than Michelin or Rio Tinto Zinc. Taiwan's Walsin Likwa, an electronics group, is bigger than Distillers or De Beers.

The important changes in the destination of foreign direct investment during the crisis can be neatly summarized as a double capital movement (Teulings, 1984), towards both the United States and the developing countries. Before 1970, the United States accounted for only about 8 per cent of the total world inflow of direct investment. But, by the end of the 1970s, its share had increased to almost 30 per cent (see table 2.3) (see Dicken, 1980; McConnell, 1981, 1983). The developing countries were the other recipients of foreign direct investment. But this growth has been concentrated in a small number of such countries – again, those with a developed industrial base, the newly industrializing countries. Of the total inflow of foreign direct investment into the developing countries, just six (Argentina, Brazil, Hong Kong, Malaysia, Mexico and Singapore) accounted for between one-half and two-thirds of the total.

Within these flows of direct investment into particular centres, multinational corporations based in particular countries still tended to have particular regional biases. Thus US-based corporations are still biased towards Europe; Japanese-based corporations are still biased towards Asia, and are the largest investors in South Korea, Thailand, Malaysia and Indonesia. Developing-country multinational corporations are biased towards other developing countries.

The Internationalization of Finance

The expansion of production overseas in the 1970s and 1980s, whether as a result of the search for new markets or for cheap labour, has been matched by a parallel and complementary expansion of producer services, especially finance (Versluyen, 1981; Brett, 1983; Coakley, 1984). The expansion of finance cannot be seen as simply an enabling factor. Rather it is part and parcel of the whole process of internationalization of capital that has been caused by the world economic crisis. It has three main components, which will be considered in turn.

The internationalization of domestic currency. The modern international financial system is based upon the creation of a number of new international markets for domestic currency which can be borrowed and lent. These markets have become possible because of the advent of floating exchange rates and the creation of a series of 'pseudo currencies', especially Eurodollars. In 1944 the Bretton Woods agreement was signed, setting up what was essentially a US-run international financial system with three poles – the World Bank, the International Monetary Fund and, most important of all, fixed exchange rates, with the US dollar serving as the convertible medium of currency with a fixed relationship to the price of gold. This system worked only so long as sufficient international reserves of currency could be found to finance the growth of world trade through the 1950s and 1960s, and so long as the United States was the dominant economic power in the world (Daly, 1984). But by the 1960s the system was under pressure. Countries and companies could not find sufficient international reserves and the United States was no longer such a dominant economic power. In 1950 the United States produced 62 per cent of the total manufacturing output of the ten major western economies and 26 per cent of world exports. But by the beginning of the 1970s the figures were respectively 44 per cent and 19 per cent (Parboni, 1981). The result was that the Bretton Woods system crumbled. In particular, by the late 1960s fixed exchange rates effectively disappeared and every domestic currency became convertible into every other. Exchange rates 'floated' and, as a result, all domestic currencies could themselves become a medium that could be bought and sold and out of which a profit could be made. Soon exchange rates began to change far more frequently than other prices, and now exchange rates are changing in Tokyo when London businessmen are abed and then in London before New York businessmen wake up.

The establishment of a pool of Eurodollars, which are simply dollars held in banks located outside the United States, has been the other crucial factor in the development of the modern international financial system (see Aliber, 1979; Mendelsohn, 1980; Sampson, 1981; Coakley and Harris, 1983). The origins of the Eurodollar market are shrouded in mystery. It is thought to have started when, in the late 1940s and early 1950s, the Chinese and the Russians doubted the safety of holding dollar reserves in the United States (where they could be confiscated) and so transferred them to banks in Paris and London. Later, towards the end of the 1950s, as the United States government began to run a balance-of-payments deficit, paying out more than it was receiving and doing so in dollars, so the newly created dollar owners deposited their dollars in banks in Europe rather than in New York. Because the European banks were far away from any potential United States jurisdiction and (increasingly importantly) away from United States control over interest rates they were able to pay higher interest rates on these dollar deposits than the American banks. Then three things happened which made the market in Eurodollars take off (see figure 2.5). First, during 1963 and 1964 President Kennedy, worried by the increasing flow of dollars abroad, announced an Interest Equalization Tax and a Voluntary Credit Restraint Programme, which were intended to reduce capital outflow. Instead, international borrowers looked to Europe and the Eurodollar market. (Prominent among these borrowers were United States

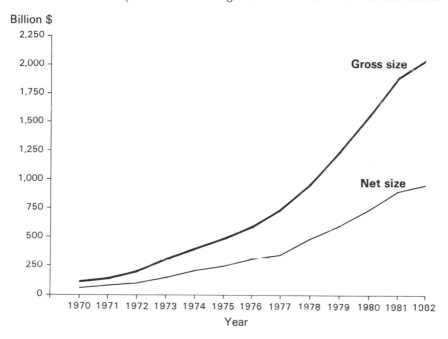

Figure 2.5   Eurocurrency market size, 1970–82
Source: *World Financial Markets*, Morgan Guaranty, New York

multinational corporations raising loans on the Eurodollar market so that they could continue to expand abroad.) Second, from 1971 the United States government began to finance its budget deficit by paying in its own currency, flooding the world with dollars and helping to fuel the inflationary process worldwide. It is estimated that world monetary reserves increased *twelvefold* between 1970 and 1980 (see Parboni, 1981). Finally, there was the 'oil shock'. When the members of the Organization of Petroleum Exporting Countries (OPEC) simultaneously raised the price of oil they also acquired huge reserves of dollars from their sales of oil, reserves which had to be invested. Many of these dollars were invested not in government bonds but in banks outside the United States, dramatically swelling the banks' Eurodollar deposits.

The international banks, and other institutions, had to find somewhere to put all the money they suddenly found in their coffers. This was no easy task. It was difficult to find borrowers in the shape of existing governments, government-backed corporations and multinational corporations willing to take out new loans and soak up the surplus. One outlet was to create new markets. For example, the Eurodollar market became considerably more sophisticated in order to allow a greater range of borrowers to participate. Three distinct categories of lending can now be found (Coakley and Harris, 1983). There are short-term loans (often overnight) called interbank loans which are made between one bank and another and by multinational corporations. There are medium-term (three to ten years) syndicated dollar credits; these are loans of dollars from banks outside the United States, made by syndicates of banks. And there are loans which can be long term. These are Eurobonds, IOUs issued by a borrowing state or corporation to raise Eurodollars which can be sold and resold. Another development in the Eurodollar market has been the inclusion of other Eurocurrencies, domestic currencies like Japanese yen, British pounds sterling or German marks held in banks outside the country of issue. But the dollar still reigns supreme in the Eurocurrency market – about 80 per cent of which will be in dollars in any one year. Other financial markets have also been created such as the *futures* market, which trades in contracts. The main futures markets are, in their order of importance, in treasury bonds, in soya beans, in corn, in gold, in stock index controls and – in Eurodollars.

Another outlet the banks found to soak up their surplus was the 'better-off' developing countries. The problem was that these countries could not, for a number of reasons, pay off the debts that they incurred in borrowing from the banks and there is now a widespread crisis of debt among them, especially those in Central and South America like Mexico, Brazil and Argentina (see figure 2.6). For example, by 1982 Brazil's debt service had reached the level of its total exports. This crisis of debt is not likely to be solved so long as interest rates continue at their present high levels. For example, the Bank for International Settlements estimates that to get the ratio of Latin American debts to exports down to the 1973/4 level will now take 15 years. It is no surprise that the governments and populations of many Latin American countries are beginning to balk. As one banker put it, 'Somehow the conventional wisdom

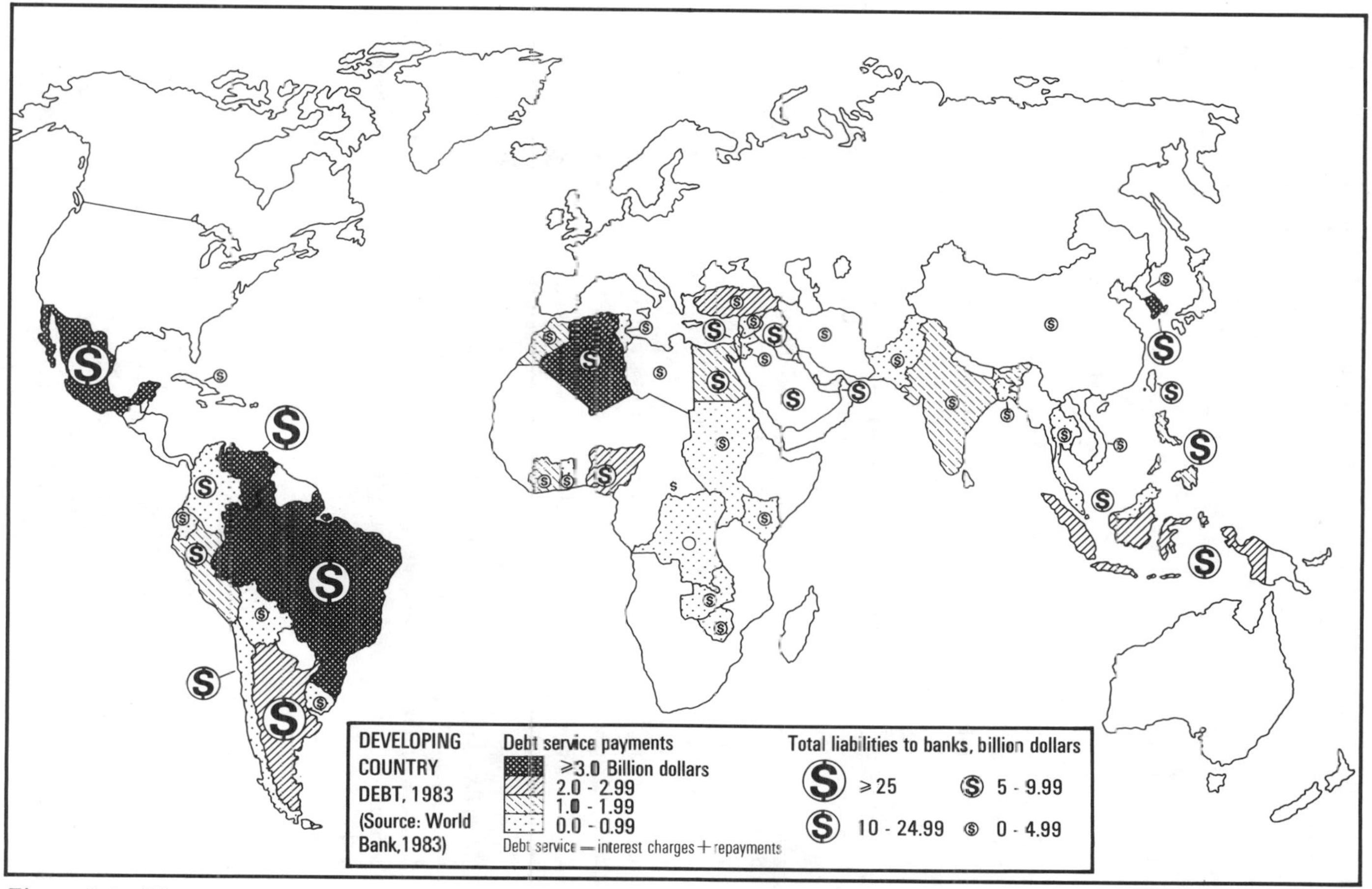
DEVELOPING
COUNTRY
DEBT, 1983
(Source: World
Bank,1983)
Debt service payments
≥3.0 Billion dollars
2.0 - 2.99
1.0 - 1.99
0.0 - 0.99
Debt service = interest charges + repayments
Total liabilities to banks, billion dollars
≥25
5 - 9.99
10 - 24.99
0 - 4.99

Figure 2.6 The crisis of debt, 1983

Source: The Banker, May 1984

of 200 million sullen South Americans sweating away in the hot sun for the next decade to earn interest on the debt so Citicorp can raise its dividend twice a year does not square with my image of political reality' (Delamaide, 1984, p. 123).

The internationalization of the banks. With all the money that was being pumped into them, the international banks became truly global in the 1970s, aided by advances in telecommunications and data-processing. In the race to become global the United States banks were the most successful. The number of foreign branches of US-based banks increased from 124 to 723 between 1960 and 1976 and their assets grew by 1,816 per cent (Sampson, 1981). But the United States banks were soon followed by the British and French banks (with their experience of dealing with former colonial countries) and later by the German, Italian, Arab and Japanese banks. Like Japanese multinational corporations, the Japanese-based banks have become a major force in global banking, first by forming Japanese companies abroad as they went multinational and then by competing for other business and especially the Eurodollar market (Fujita and Ishigaki, 1985). They are now second only to the US-based banks (see figure 2.7).

But a problem now affecting the internationalization of the banks is developing-country indebtedness. For the banks, having lent so much money, are now themselves locked into the problem of debt. If the Latin American countries were to renege on their debts, a number of the global banks could fail. This, in turn, might halt the further internationalization of banking and even put a question-mark over the further internationalization of capital (Lipietz, 1984a).

The internationalization of the capital markets. Occurring in parallel with the internationalization currency and banking has been the internationalization of the capital markets. All the infrastructure necessary to sustain the new international financial system, from stock exchanges through futures exchanges to tax havens, has proliferated (Gorastraga, 1983). The result has been that the international financial system is now a 24-hour-a-day business, with dealing in currency, shares and bonds migrating around the world with the passage of the sun.

The Internationalization of the State

The influence of the state is the final pole in an explanation of the economic crisis of the 1970s and 1980s. It is, of course, quite possible to build up a theory which either gives the state an undue amount of power to resist capital or reduces the state to an agent of capital. The reality is rather different. States are the result of a long-drawn-out conflict between different social groups to wrest different elements of power from one another. At different times and in different countries states play different roles. Four such roles can be identified, each of which has had some influence on the course of the world economy in the

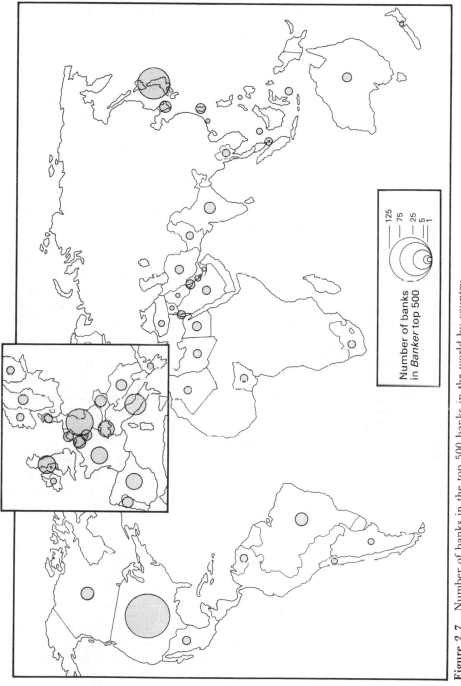

Figure 2.7 Number of banks in the top 500 banks in the world by country
Source: The Banker, May, 1985

Number of banks
in *Banker* top 500

125
75
25
5
1

1970s and 1980s, and has both contributed to the internationalization of production and finance and hastened the integration of states into the new world-economic order.

One role has been as a market. For example, a considerable part of the move of multinational corporations towards the United States in the 1970s, especially those involved in the electronics industry, can be explained by their desire to obtain lucrative United States government defence contracts. Another role has been restrictive: as the crisis has deepened, so it has touched off a rising tide of protectionism – the erection of new tariff barriers, the insistence on local labour, and so on. It has been argued that this increasing protectionism is one of the main reasons why Japanese corporations went abroad in such numbers in the 1970s. It was realized that the protectionist policies would make it more and more difficult for Japanese corporations simply to export. Instead they would have to produce within them. Certainly, this has been one of the motives behind Japanese expansion in a number of industries in Europe and the United States, most notably in the automobile industry.

A third role has been enabling. States can and do provide packages of measures to attract foreign direct investment. The activities of foreign investment agencies in nearly every country of the world are legion. The battle in 1983 and 1984 to attract a Japanese (Nissan) automobile plant into Britain is only one notable example. Then again, the state can act to help multinational corporations based in their country to expand into other countries, either indirectly by providing export advice and insurance, or directly through an explicit internationalization strategy as in the case of the Ministry of International Trade and Industry (MITI) in Japan and the efforts made by the South Korean government. Finally, the state can act as a competitor to other foreign direct investors. For example, it can compete for funds from the banks. The United States does this so effectively, in order to finance its budget deficit, that it has pushed up real interest rates around the world. Or the state can compete even more directly through state-owned multinational corporations. Thus in 1978, out of the largest 483 industrial companies in the developed market economies, 37 were state-owned and nearly all were multinational (Dunning and Pearce, 1981); the French state-owned Renault corporation now has over a quarter of its affiliates in developing countries (United Nations, 1983).

Finally, it is important to remember that states do not have to be restricted to their own boundaries. A number of international state organizations exist, all the way from the United Nations, with its various industrial bodies, through the 24-member OECD to the IMF and the World Bank. These international organizations can be used to extend a country's economic power abroad, promoting its exports or the influence of its multinational corporations. Thus it is difficult not to see the IMF as an explicit arm of United States economic policy, there to open up the economies of recalcitrant countries to United States exports and to United States multinational corporations, to discipline the economies of these countries to the needs of 'the market'.

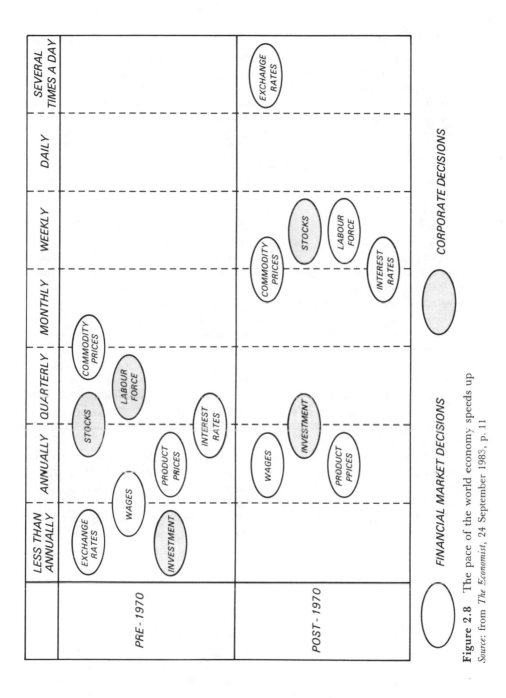

Figure 2.8 The pace of the world economy speeds up
Source: from *The Economist*, 24 September 1983, p. 11

Summary

Three main net effects of these changes will continue in the 1980s and beyond. The first is the acceleration of capital movement. Capital has become more footloose, both in time and space. Take the case of time first (see figure 2.8). Before the 1970s, exchange rates changed only once every four years on average, interest rates moved perhaps twice a year, companies reviewed the prices of their products once a year and made decisions on investment even less frequently. But in the 1970s and 1980s all this has changed. Exchange rates change every four hours, interest rates change more frequently, prices can be adjusted much more swiftly, companies make investment decisions every year. In other words, the whole economic system has speeded up. Capital has also become more footloose in space. Because of the speed-up in time multinational corporations now review the productivity of their plants much more frequently and if plants do not produce the required level of profit they are likely to be shut down. At the same time multinational corporations can, through the medium of acquisition, move more swiftly into new markets or production, gaining control over existing plants or opening up new plants as they go along. Thus there is a constant process of strategic rationalization in which plants are set up and shut down more frequently than before, with all the consequences this has for the countries in which these plants are located.

The second net effect is the growing interpenetration of capital as multinational corporations based in different countries have spread worldwide. To take but two examples, the largest amount of Japanese direct investment still goes to the United States, and European multinational corporations have increasingly channelled their direct investment into the United States as well (Dicken, 1982). On a smaller scale, European direct investment has increasingly been directed to the UK and vice versa (Dicken, 1980). Thus the core industrialized economies have become more tightly integrated. In the process the world-economy has moved from being an economy with but a single economic pole – the United States – to one that is multipolar.

The third net effect is that the borders of capitalist production have moved a little further out. There has been no wholesale industrialization of the Third World, as the increasing poverty of most of Africa attests. Rather the border of capitalism now encompasses a few developing countries – the newly industrializing countries – partly through their own efforts and partly through the attention of the multinational corporations. And the international debt crisis could still block even this small advance. This is hardly:

a picture of ascendant Southern industrial power. Rather local governments in the [newly industrializing countries] have attempted to maximize the possibilities for their indigenous capitalists, within a set of international economic and political constraints which makes preserving a space for indigenous capital a delicate business. This is not possible without permanent struggle. Perhaps South Korea has succeeded: probably Brazil, Taiwan, the Philippines, Argentina and Chile have not. (Roddick, 1984, pp. 126–7)

THE WORLD MARKET FOR LABOUR

These changes in the structure of the world economy have brought prosperity to some people and agony to many others (literally, in the case of some people working in developing countries with authoritarian regimes). The main cause of these mixed fortunes has been the changes in people's chances of getting a job.

There is still a very real difference between employment opportunities in the developed and the developing countries; there is little point in trying to play it down. Therefore, initially, the very different circumstances that can be found in each bloc will be enumerated. But it is a consequence of the form of internationalization of capital that has taken place during the crisis that some new links have now been forged between employment opportunities in the developed and the developing countries respectively: I will discuss four of these below.

The Developed Countries

The world-economic crisis of the 1970s and 1980s took place against the background of some quite important changes in the characteristics of the labour forces in the developed countries. The most important was the number of women (especially married women) joining the labour force. The proportion of women increased in nearly all the OECD countries over the period of the crisis. A second important factor was the 'baby boom' that lasted from the end of the second world war until 1960. The generation born then entered the labour market at the very time that opportunities for employment started to plummet.

By far the most visible effect of the world-economic crisis on the structure of opportunities for employment in the developed countries has been unemployment, which has increased dramatically. As firms restructure or go out of business in the climate of fierce competition which is typical of an economic crisis, so workers are laid off.

From 1960 to 1973, unemployment rates in North America varied between 4 and 7 per cent. In Europe and Japan they were never higher than 2 or 3 per cent. But after the first oil shock in 1973 unemployment rose quickly in nearly all countries until the end of 1975 (see figure 2.9). Then it remained relatively stable in most countries until 1979, when it again rose rapidly. In the UK the total number of unemployed is now more than 3 million and in France it is more than 2 million, while in West Germany the 2-million mark was passed at the end of 1982. By that time the unemployment rate exceeded 10 per cent in the United States, a statistic shared with Canada, the United Kingdom, Spain, Belgium and the Netherlands (see figure 2.10). In all, in the 24 OECD countries there were about 30 million persons out of work in 1983

(International Labour Organization, 1984), and 31 million in 1984. The OECD *Employment Outlook* reckoned that some 20 million jobs would have to be created in the OECD countries by 1990 just to keep unemployment at today's rates and as many as 35 million jobs to get back to the levels of unemployment of 1979. There were some breaks in the cloud. The United States' rate, in particular, was falling in response to that country's recovery but the OECD thought it likely that unemployment trends would actually drift up again in 1985 as the recovery slows down.

Added to this general upward trend in rates of unemployment and the numbers unemployed, disturbing enough in itself, are three other trends which have caused great concern. First, the numbers of long-term unemployed have been increasing in nearly all the developed countries. For example, in Britain the number of people unemployed for over a year has risen to over 1 million; 37 per cent of the jobless total. Second, in many countries unemployment is not only underestimated, which is generally the case with official figures, but it is thought that the number of those who are unemployed but not counted in the official figures is increasing. Third, unemployment has had particularly severe effects on certain social groups. Those who are least likely to be unemployed are men between 24 and 54 years of age who have a good education or training. These people tend to fill what is often called the primary segment of the labour market, the segment with full-time jobs, promotion opportunities

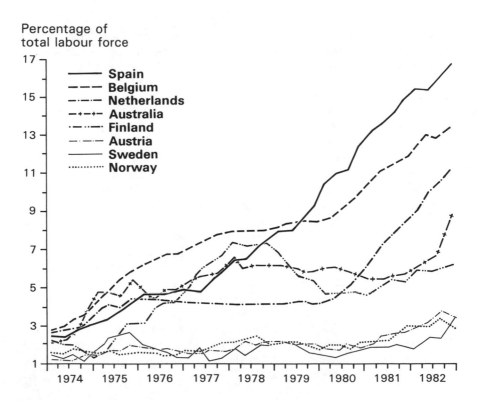

Percentage of
total labour force

and incomes steadily rising with age. In contrast the young, the old, women and minorities are more likely to be members of the secondary labour market – the segment with unskilled, poorly paid, insecure jobs – that is, if they are employed at all. The young and the old are more likely to be unemployed in every developed country. So are women. So are minorities. And any combination of these characteristics drastically reduces a person's chance of being employed. In short, on the average in every developed country:

> ten persons out of 100 are unemployed. Of these ten persons, five are young and three of these are women. [Further] among the unemployed queuing up for unskilled jobs, the successful applicants will first be adult males (between 24 and 54 years of age), then women of the same age, followed by young persons; the last will be minorities and older workers. (International Labour Organization, 1984, p. 46)

If unemployment is the most clearly visible effect of the world economic crisis this does not mean that the crisis has had no other effects on the structure of

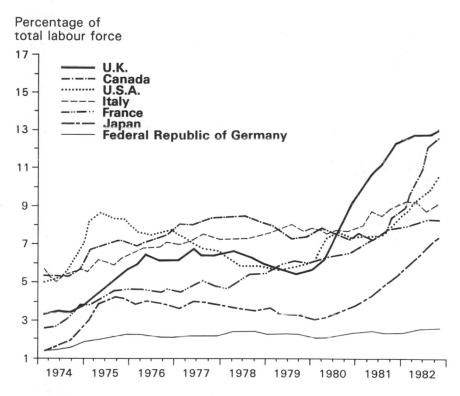

Figure 2.9   Standardized unemployment rates in 15 OECD countries (quarterly data, seasonally adjusted)

Source: International Labour Organization, 1984, pp. 38–9

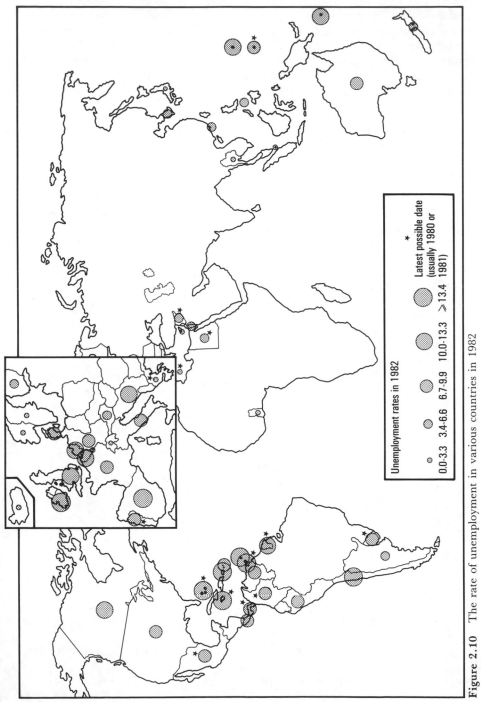

Figure 2.10 The rate of unemployment in various countries in 1982

Source: International Labour Organization, 1983

opportunities for employment. In fact, the economic crisis has undoubtedly hastened the demise of manufacturing employment and the rise of service employment. Manufacturing employment has declined in nearly all the developed countries since the oil shock of 1973. The main exception has been the electronics sector, where demand for computers, office equipment and videos has kept employment up. Employment in services has grown in nearly all the developed countries since 1973. In the OECD countries, for example, employment in services, on average, had risen to 63 per cent of total employment by 1981. Employment in services in the United States and Canada is now as high as two-thirds of total employment and well above 50 per cent in most other countries. Part of this increase is, of course, a relative effect of the decline in manufacturing employment but there has also been an absolute increase in numbers employed in some parts of the service sector since 1973, most particularly in government and in financial and business services.

Of course not all the growth in the services sector has been a direct result of the world-economic crisis. The role of the service sector in the economies of developed countries was increasing before the 1970s. But the crisis has hastened its growth – employment in the services sector grew much more rapidly in the OECD countries between 1973 and 1980 than from 1960 to 1973. And in some cases it has had more direct impact. For example, in many countries the greatest growth in government employment has been in social services concerned with promotion of employment: 'Owing to slower economic growth and a rise in unemployment, many governments have expanded activities in the field of employment promotion, vocational guidance, training and security' (International Labour Organization, 1984, p. 49). Similarly, although much of the growth in employment in financial and business services during the 1970s was the result of banks and other financial institutions expanding their branch networks, some of the growth in employment was also the result of the rise of international banking and the increase in the information-gathering and other producer services demanded by multinational corporations.

It is important to note that much of the increase in service employment consisted of an increase in the number of part-time workers. By 1981, part-time work accounted for more than a quarter of all employees in employment in Sweden, 20 per cent in the UK and more than 10 per cent in most of the other OECD countries. Most of this part-time work is concentrated in service-sector industries which need flexibility from their employees to meet their peaked patterns of business activity during the day (for example, in banks and restaurants) or during the week (for example, in shops). The majority of this part-time work is done by women. Nowhere is the figure for female part-time employment below 60 per cent and in a number of the developed countries it is well above this figure. In the United States, for example, by 1981 the figure was nearly 70 per cent and in the UK it was over 90 per cent for the same year. Further, the proportion of women in part-time work is increasing.

The second effect which the world-economic crisis has had on the state of employment opportunities has been to hasten the rise of an informal economy. According to Pahl (1980) the informal economy has two major components.

The first is the household economy. Production in the household has increased enormously in the last 20 years in the developed countries as households have switched from buying services to producing their own. More precisely, households now increasingly buy goods, which are in effect capital equipment, to which they then add their own labour. So there has been a rise in do-it-yourself, in vegetable gardening, and so on. We no longer go to the laundry or employ servants; instead we use washing machines and vacuum cleaners which we operate ourselves. This is the rise of the so-called 'self-service economy' (Gershuny, 1978). The second component is the underground or clandestine economy (de Grazia, 1984), which consists of the production of goods and services that evade systems of public regulation and taxation. It takes three main forms. The first is the undeclared employment of workers, especially illegal immigrants (to be found among outworkers in the clothing industry and workers in building, agriculture, the hotel and catering trades, housework, etc.). The second is undeclared self-employment (to be found among workers in dressmaking, in car repairs, in household repairs, among those running a market stall, etc.). The final form is undeclared multiple jobholding (to be found especially now among teachers, businessmen and policemen). The numbers employed in each of these forms of employment are all on the increase.

This might not matter if the underground economy were small, but it is not. Figure 2.11 shows estimates of the percentage of GNP taken up by the underground economy for selected countries. The proportions are large, and the numbers employed in the underground economy are large. Clandestine employment is, of course, the only job that many workers have, especially for the unemployed, migrant workers, pensioners and housewives. There are, it must be remembered, over 500,000 clandestine immigrant workers in Europe and 5 million in the United States. Estimates vary concerning the number of the unemployed who have jobs, from 80 per cent in some *départements* of France to very few in parts of the UK (see Pahl, 1984). If the figures of those who have a clandestine second job are added in to the total then the numbers become very large indeed. In West Germany it is reckoned that 2 million workers, or 8 per cent of the workforce, have a second undeclared job. In France, Sweden and Belgium the proportion of the workforce so employed varies from 5 to 15 per cent. In the United States and Canada some estimates are as high as 25 per cent (International Labour Organization, 1984).

It is difficult to know precisely how the world economic crisis has affected the informal economy but it has almost certainly fuelled its growth. Faced with competition, many firms have resorted to clandestine employment to reduce labour costs, and there are many more unemployed who are prepared to work at what they can find in order to eke out a living.

The Developing Countries

In the developing countries employment problems are far more serious because of the massive expansion of the labour base which makes the post-war baby

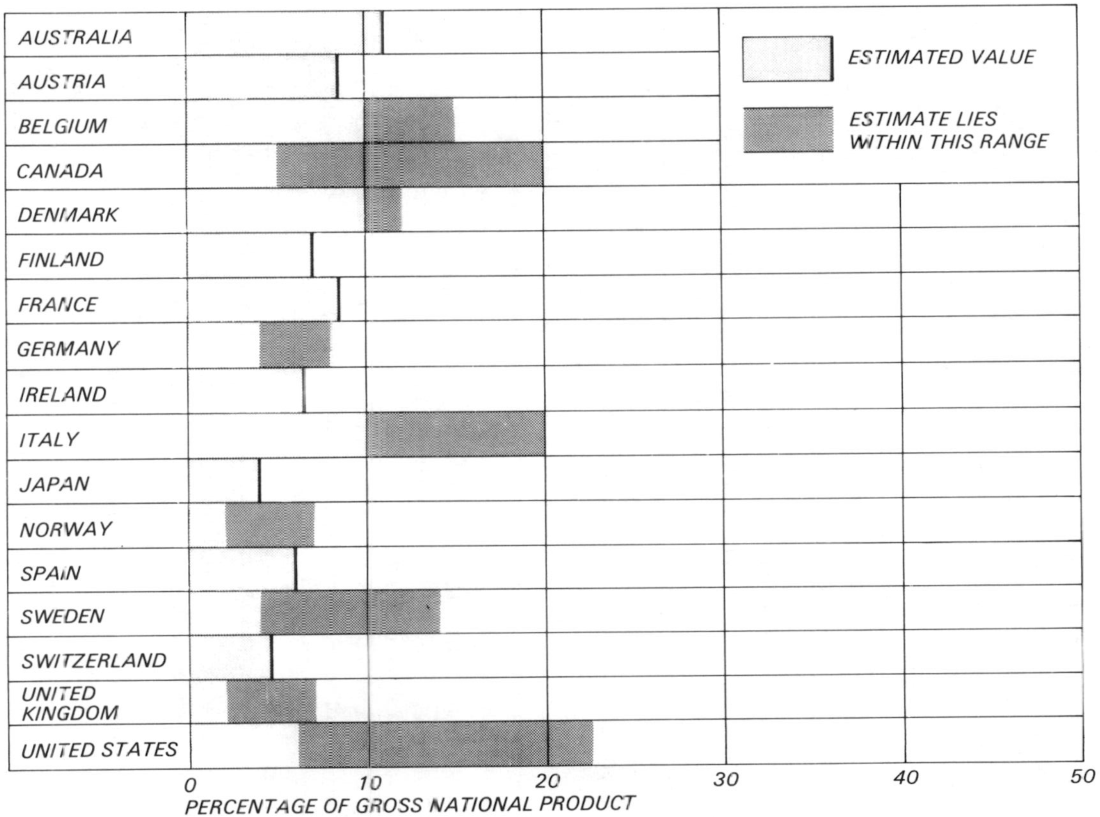

Figure 2.11 Informal sector estimates of the underground economy in selected countries

Source: Tanzi, 1982

boom in the developed countries seem insignificant. Demography reigns supreme. Take the case of the Asian region. The International Labour Organization (1980) has estimated that the labour force in the developing Asian region will have increased by 139 million between January 1980 and December 1987. China will account for some 46 per cent of this increase but Indonesia alone needs to find *2 million* jobs a year just to stand still.

Undoubtedly the world-economic crisis has had some effect on employment opportunities but in the face of figures like these it is rather difficult to identify. Certainly, it seems clear that the crisis did have an impact on the labour forces of the newly industrializing countries, which are more tightly linked to the world-economy. In these countries the crisis was transmitted through the manufacturing sector in the shape of labour demand for manufactured goods from the developed countries. But there are countervailing trends, in particular the related shift of manufacturing industry into developing countries, which make the exact effects difficult to quantify.

The truth is that figures on unemployment in the developing countries are hard to come by, difficult to compare because of differing definitions and applicable only to the wage labour force. These figures are summarized in figure 2.10. In general, the unemployment rate does not seem particularly high by comparison with rates in the developed countries. However, the *underemployment* rate (those who are in employment of less than normal duration) is very high. In the Asian economies, for example, it is estimated that 40 per cent of rural workers are underemployed, as are 23 per cent of urban workers.

As in the developed centres, so in the developing countries, the world economic crisis has had some effects on the structure of employment opportunities, as well as provoking the simple lack of employment opportunity through unemployment and underemployment. The first important effect has a close parallel with the growth in the developed countries of the so-called *urban informal sector* of employment (Bromley and Gerry, 1979; Sethuraman, 1981). It seems certain that the world economic crisis has speeded the expansion of this sector.

The urban informal sector consists of what is often the largest part of the urban labour force in the developing countries, workers who carry on their livelihoods outside the domain of public regulation and taxation. The activities that are included in this sector are too diverse to itemize one by one, but they include small-scale commodity production (for example, of bicycles) and repair shops, street vending (the selling of food, cigarettes and drink), the operation of low-income forms of transport (such as tricycles, scooter-based three-wheelers and jeeps), and a whole range of activities that are often illegal, such as prostitution and running drinking dens. The urban informal sector has come about, in part at least, because the activities that it comprises are the only activities that many rural–urban migrants – who stream into the cities of so many developing countries – can gain access to. Since the urban population of the developing countries is expected to double over the next two years, in great measure owing to rural–urban migration, it seems highly unlikely that the sector will diminish in size and highly likely that it will continue to grow. The world economic crisis has directly affected this growth, especially through increasing the rates of migration into the cities in many countries as agricultural poverty has become more severe.

The second way in which the world economic crisis has had effects on the structure of employment opportunities has been through manufacturing employment. Manufacturing has continued to grow as a proportion of total employment in nearly all developing countries and it has grown particularly fast in the newly industrializing countries. This growth has come about in part through the expansion of indigenous industries trying to satisfy new levels of consumer demand, in part through the demands of a thriving local construction industry, in part through aggressive (and usually state-led) export strategies, and in part through decisions made by many foreign-based multinational corporations to relocate some of their unskilled assembly production to the dozen or so newly industrializing countries, thus apparently providing the beginnings of a new world spatial division of labour often called the 'new international division of labour'.

The Global Effects of the World Economic Crisis on Employment Opportunities

This new spatial division of labour is the first of four direct effects on employment of the economic restructuring that has taken place during the world economic crisis which are truly global in character – that is, they are effects which span both the developed and developing countries and which have effects on the employment opportunities of both simultaneously. The other three effects are the growth of free trade zones, the growth of international migration and the growth of 'world cities'. Each of these effects will be considered in turn.

The new international division of labour. By 1980, 44 million workers were in jobs directly provided by multinational corporations (International Labour Organization, 1981). Much of this employment is provided by US-based multinational corporations. Thus the 500 largest United States corporations now employ an international labour force almost exactly the same size as their national labour force. In the period from 1960 to 1980 manufacturing employment outside the United States directly controlled by US-based multinational corporations increased from 8.7 per cent to 17.5 per cent of the total, a 169 per cent increase compared with a 20 per cent increase in the United States (Peet, 1983) (see figure 2.12). But, as would be expected, multinational corporations based in other countries have taken an increasingly larger part of the total; in 1978 Japanese company subsidiaries employed about 650,000 people around the world (Nakase, 1981).

A new aspect of this pattern of employment by multinational corporations is that so much of it is in developing countries. Multinational corporations now employ 4 million workers, or 9 per cent of their labour force, in the developing countries, and the number of these workers has been growing much faster in

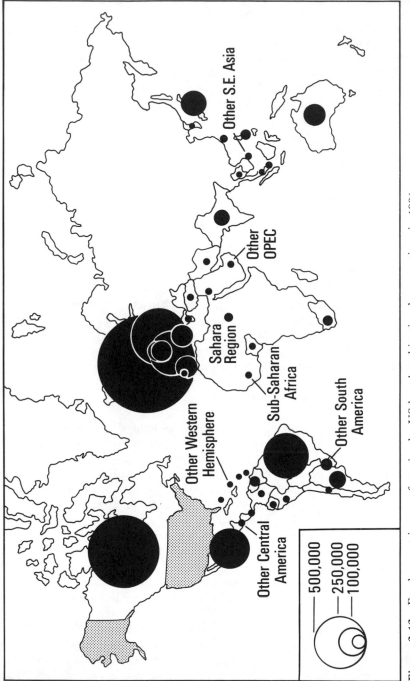

Figure 2.12 Employment in manufacturing by US-based multinational corporations in 1981
Source: Peet, 1983, p. 141

these countries than in most of the developed nations. For example, from 1960 to 1980 manufacturing employment in the developing countries controlled by US-based corporations increased from 1 per cent to 5.3 per cent (Peet, 1983). Some countries' multinationals employ even more of their labour force in the developing countries; in 1978 the figure for Japanese multinationals was 72 per cent of their labour force outside Japan. The increasing presence of workers employed by multinational corporations in developing countries (in manufacturing in particular) has led some writers to posit the existence of a new international division of labour (Frobel, Heinrichs and Kreye, 1980; Tharakan, 1980) – in which the parts of the production process which require cheap, unskilled labour are relocated to the Third World. One reason why this new international division of labour has taken root has been the breakdown of traditional economic and social structures in many developing countries, leading to an inexhaustible supply of cheap labour. Another reason has been that the production process has become more fragmented and more homogenized, making it possible for many sub-processes to be spatially separated and carried out by unskilled workers after very short training periods. A third reason is that as transport and communications technology have developed so it has become possible to carry out complete or partial production processes at many new sites around the world without prohibitive technical, organizational or cost problems.

The trouble with this simple explanation of the new international division of labour is that it is difficult to sustain the argument that it exists as a significant *global* tendency (Thrift, 1980). The most important component to this argument is that there is only limited evidence for the actual *relocation* of employment, that is for the direct physical movement of a plant from a location in a developed country to another in a developing country. Certainly such cases exist, but not in profusion. For example, Gaffikin and Nickson (1984) looked at all the redundancies announced by ten major British multinational corporations in the West Midlands region of Britain from September 1979 to October 1983: not one involved the direct relocation of plants to Third World locations. Another component is that there are real difficulties in interpreting the new international division of labour as simply the result of a search for low-cost wage locations by multinational corporations. Certainly wage levels *are* an important determinant, but other commentators (e.g. Faire, 1981) have argued that the need to control markets within developing countries is an equally important or even more important determinant of relocation even when this relocation is then accompanied by a significant growth of imports from plants located in these countries (Jenkins, 1984). Yet other commentators have argued that the higher level of labour discipline in developing countries, especially the fact that trade unions are outlawed or incorporated, is an important determinant.

It is clear that the new international division of labour is, in any case, limited in its impact, both by country and by industry. The redeployment of manufacturing employment by multinational corporations in the developing countries has generally been restricted to a very few countries, mainly the newly industrializing ones. Even in the latter the part played by multinational corporations in stimulating employment varies enormously. In Singapore, for example, the share of employment in both foreign-owned and joint-venture firms rose from 33 per cent in 1963 to 69 per cent in 1978. In the Republic of Korea and Hong Kong, however, the proportions were much smaller, at 10 per cent in 1978 and 11 per cent in 1971/2, respectively (see International Labour Organization, 1984; Jenkins, 1984; United Nations, 1983).

Moreover, the new international division of labour is restricted to a few industries, especially textiles and clothing (Clairmonte and Cavanagh, 1981) and electronics (Morgan and Sayer, 1983; Economist Intelligence Unit, 1984), where the economic and technological considerations of making particular products make it more difficult to increase mechanization with existing technologies and much easier to relocate production abroad. The difference between the worldwide patterns of employment in the two industries shown in figures 2.13 and 2.14 is that in the textile and clothing industry there is strong indigenous industry in the newly industrializing countries. (Local firms accounted for 42 per cent of the clothing and footwear exports of the 318 largest enterprises in Brazil in 1973, for 75 per cent of Mexico's total exports of clothing and footwear in 1979 and for 88 per cent of textile and apparel exports by the Republic of Korea in 1978.) While multinational corporations' involvement in production abroad in textiles and clothing is considerable, in the electronics industry – where the newly industrializing countries have severe problems in terms of gaining access to technology, and sufficient capital for research – multinational corporations' involvement in production is all but total. In the electronics industry the tendency for multinational corporations to shift the assembly and simple testing stages of production to developing countries has been almost irresistible. A sample of 37 leading United States, Japanese and western European companies, which by 1979 accounted for more than 90 per cent of world semiconductor production, had 23 ventures in developing countries in 1971 and 87 in 1979. Most of these ventures were located in the newly industrializing countries of south-east Asia and in Mexico (United Nations, 1983).

So, seen in the narrow sense as the relocation of elements of the production process to developing countries by multinational corporations searching for low wages, the new international division of labour is of less importance than originally thought. Indeed, some writers have gone so far as to suggest that the phenomenon may even be temporally limited if the costs of automation of these elements of the production process reach the point where they offset the advantages which peripheral low-wage locations may now give (see Jenkins, 1984).

However, the new international division of labour is of much greater significance if to the direct shift in employment from developed to developing countries is added the relative shift in employment between the countries of the world, a shift which favours the developing countries. Seen in this light,

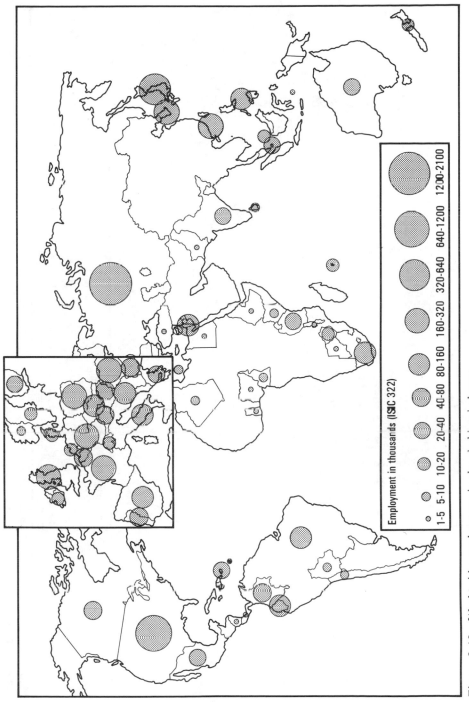

Figure 2.13 Worldwide employment in the clothing industry
Source: International Labour Organization, 1983

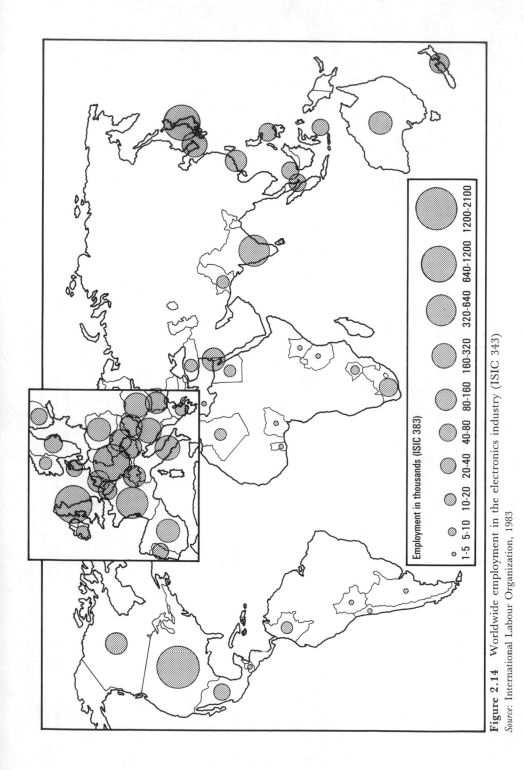

Figure 2.14 Worldwide employment in the electronics industry (ISIC 343)

Source: International Labour Organization, 1983

Employment in thousands (ISIC 383)

1-5 5-10 10-20 20-40 40-80 80-160 160-320 320-640 640-1200 1200-2100

the concept has very considerable merit in describing the employment outcomes of the strategies pursued by multinational corporations as they have restructured during the world-economic crisis. Then the spatial pattern of employment more or less follows the spatial pattern of direct investment outlined above.

In particular, there is a general fall-off in the labour force of most multinational corporations in response to the restructuring needed to weather the world-economic crisis. But within this trend of a general decline there is a shift in where the remaining employment is concentrated because employment falls more in certain countries and falls less, if at all, in others. Specifically, employment decreases more in the home countries of multinational corporations, and decreases less, or even expands, in other countries and especially in some of the developing countries.

For example, among European multinational corporations there has been a greater tendency for employment to fall in the home country's plants and offices, while staying static in Europe and expanding in North America and some of the developing countries. A number of corporate studies have made the picture clearer, for example the study by Teulings (1984) of the operations of the Dutch-based multinational corporation Philips, and the study by Clarke (1982) of the British-based multinational corporation, ICI.

The case of ICI in the years from 1970 to 1983 is indicative. ICI was originally formed in 1926. A large number of products are made and marketed by the corporation, including fertilizers, fibres, general chemicals, organic chemicals, industrial explosives, paints, petrochemicals, pharmaceuticals and plastics. In the 1970s ICI ran into trouble. Too many of its products were in declining markets like fibres, petrochemicals and plastics. The result was that the corporation was forced to restructure its operations worldwide, in the process making the transition from a multinational to a global corporation. It now has factories in more than 40 countries and selling organizations in more than 60.

In the process of restructuring a very different division of labour was produced within the corporation, which is reflected in the employment figures for its regional divisions. In general, there was a decrease in employment within the corporation. Employment rose from 190,000 in 1970 to 192,000 in 1975 but then fell to only 117,900 in 1983, so that over the 1970–83 period there was a 38 per cent drop in the workforce. However there was a particularly massive drop in employment in the United Kingdom, from 137,000 in 1970 to 132,000 in 1975 to only 61,800 in 1983, a 55 per cent decrease, which contrasted with a relative increase in employment elsewhere. In fact, most regional divisions recorded an absolute loss of employment but a relative increase. However, two divisions – the Indian subcontinent, and Australia and the Far East – also recorded an absolute increase (most of the employment increase in the Australian and Far East division was in south-east Asia).

Reinterpreted in this more general light the new international division of labour is a general tendency which has undoubtedly had serious repercussions on employment prospects of workers in developed countries, particularly in those countries with 'open' economies. These are countries like the Netherlands,

Sweden and the United Kingdom whose corporations have historically carried out much of their production overseas (see Houston and Dunning, 1976; Dunning, 1981; Taylor and Thrift, 1981) and which are themselves extensively penetrated by multinational corporations. In these countries the behaviour of just their 'own' multinational corporations has led to extensive job loss.

Export-processing zones. Governments have not stood idly by as the refurbishing of the world economy has taken place. They have been active participants in all the ways mentioned in the first part of this chapter. But one relatively new phenomenon whose period of growth coincides with the world-economic crisis has been the export-processing zone, an adaptation of the free trade zone which has been common around many ports for some time (Currie, 1979; Marsden, 1980; Salita and Juanico, 1983; Wong and Chu, 1984), and now a response by governments, especially the governments of the developing countries, to the new international division of labour. In the words of Frobel, Heinrichs and Kreye (1980, p. 283):

> World market production cannot be undertaken at every location in the developing countries where there happens to be an unemployed workforce. Profitable industrial production for the world market requires an adequate provision of industrial inputs and a sophisticated infrastructure as well as a labour force. These factors are not necessarily available at those sites where there is an abundant supply of unemployed labour. In addition, profitable industrial production requires the lifting of the national restrictions on international transfers which exist in most developing countries as a result of their chronic balance of payments deficit. In fact, it is the function of [export processing zones] to fulfil the requirements for profitable world market-orientated industrial production in those places in the developing countries where unemployed labour is available and suitable for industrial utilisation.

The United Nations Industrial Development Organization (UNIDO) defines export-processing zones as 'small closely definable areas within countries in which favourable investment and trade conditions are created to attract export-oriented industries, usually foreign-owned'. Within export-processing zones four conditions are usually found. First, import provisions are made for goods used in the production of items for duty-free export and export duties are waived. There is no foreign exchange control and there is generally freedom to repatriate profits. Second, infrastructure, utilities, factory space and warehousing are usually provided at subsidized rates. Third, tax holidays, usually of five years, are offered. Finally, abundant, disciplined labour is provided at low wage rates.

The first successful implementation of an export-processing zone was in 1956 at Ireland's Shannon International Airport. Puerto Rico (in 1962) and India (in 1965) were the first two developing countries to follow suit followed by Taiwan, the Philippines, the Dominican Republic, Mexico, Panama and Brazil in the period from 1966 to 1970 (Wong and Chu, 1984). The great expansion in the number of such zones came after 1970. By 1975 there were 31 zones in 18 countries. By the early 1980s at least 68 zones were established in 40 (principally developing) countries. The major world regions in which they are found are in the Caribbean, Central and Latin America, and Asia, although there are also a few in Africa. In the rest of this section particular attention will be given to the cases of Mexico and Asia (see figure 2.15).

Export-processing zones have three chief characteristics connected with the type of industry to be found in the zones, the number in the labour force and labour-force composition. Each of these characteristics will be examined in turn.

Most of the industry in the export-processing zones is owned by foreign-based multinational corporations and, not surprisingly, most employment in export-processing zones is in the two industries that have expanded strongly in developing countries (partly as a result of multinational corporations' intervention), namely electrical and electronic goods and textiles and clothing. In Mexico in 1978, 60 per cent of the *maquiladoras*, the assembly plant factories located in special zones near the United States border with Mexico, were concerned with electronics and electrical assembly, while 30 per cent were in textiles and clothing (Hansen, 1981). In Asia, approximately 60 per cent of employment is in the electronics industry with the clothing and footwear industries second. The advent of electronics companies is fairly recent, which makes the build-up even more impressive. For example, in 1975 the Philippines export-processing zones were almost entirely given over to textiles and clothing, but then, in 1976, multinational electronics companies started to move in.

The numbers employed in the export-processing zones' labour forces are modest, with a few exceptions. The case of Mexico is well known. In 1980 *maquiladora* employment was estimated to be over 110,000. Juarez alone accounted for 115 plants and 40,000 workers, including major United States corporations such as RCA, Ford, General Motors, Chrysler and General Electric, as well as Japanese companies. Some of the zones in Asia have also generated considerable employment. There are about 500,000 workers directly employed in export-processing zones in Asia. But, of this number, nearly 50 per cent are employed in the zones of Singapore (105,000) and South Korea (121,700). Zone employment is also comparatively high in Malaysia (73,000) and Hong Kong (70,000).

Most employment in the zones, usually over 75 per cent, is of young, unmarried women aged between 17 and 23; in Mexico about 85 per cent of *maquiladora* employment is of young women. In some of the zones in Asia the figures are even higher. In Sri Lanka young women account for 88 per cent of zone employment, in Malaysia and Taiwan 85 per cent, in South Korea 75 per cent and in the Philippines 74 per cent (Morello, 1983).

Young women are employed because their wages can be lower than men's and because they are considered 'dexterous' and 'more able to cope with repetitive work'. Very little skill is required of them, certainly, and wages are very low, often less than 50 US cents per hour. Overtime and incentive

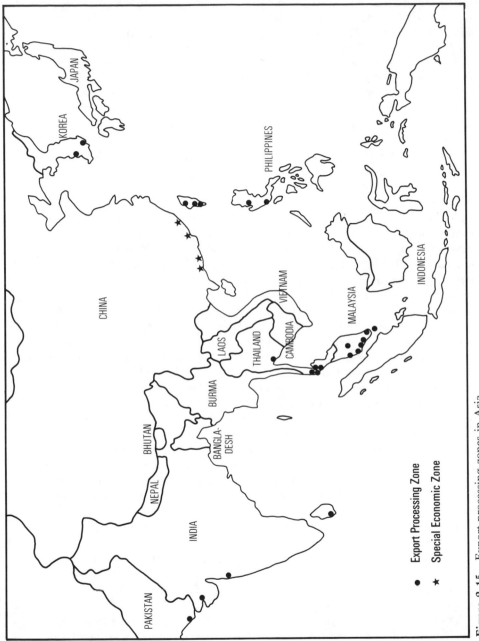

Figure 2.15 Export-processing zones in Asia
Source: Wong and Chu, 1984, p. 4

payments account for a high proportion of wages. Working weeks range from 45 to 55 hours. What is more, in some zones the iniquitous trainee system is used, in which 'trainees' are paid only 60 to 75 per cent of the local minimum wages and are constantly fired and rehired so as to obtain a permanent 40 per cent reduction in the wages bill.

Weighing up the advantages and disadvantages of export-processing zones to the centres in which they are located is no simple task. There is the matter of employment creation. In some areas, the employment advantages have been substantial. For example, since their establishment export-processing zones have accounted for at least 60 per cent of manufacturing employment expansion in Malaysia and Singapore and for about 10 per cent in Hong Kong, the Philippines and South Korea. But except in these few cases the impact of the zones on joblessness has been marginal and even in the successful cases most of the employment created has been temporary and lowly paid; in 1980, measured against the average hourly earnings in Japan's electronics and clothing industries of US $5.97 and US $3.56 respectively, comparable export-processing zones' figures were 97 US cents and US $1.03 in Hong Kong, 90 US cents and 80 US cents in Singapore, 91 US cents and 59 US cents in South Korea and 30 US cents and 17 US cents in the Philippines. Then there is the matter of the generation of foreign exchange. This can be high; the foreign exchange generated by the *maquiladora* industries in Mexico is fourth after oil revenues, remittances and tourism. But the figures can be deceptive: in 1981 the value of the Philippines' three export-processing zones export total was US $236.2 million but the figure for exports minus the imports into the zones was only US $62.5 million, and this was *before* interest payments and repatriation of profits was taken into account (Morello, 1983).

It is arguable that export-processing zones, through their linkages to local firms, might create extra employment outside. But in fact links to local economies are generally minimal; for example, a survey of 33 firms operating in export-processing zones in Malaysia and the Philippines found that these firms bought less than one-tenth of their raw materials, components and parts locally. Another survey concluded that in 1978 enterprises in the Penang (Malaysia) processing zone purchased 87 per cent of their materials from *abroad*, 9.6 per cent from firms *within* the zone and only 3.2 per cent from Malaysian suppliers outside. The only real local linkages were through service sector activities such as banking, transport, electricity and maintenance. Finally, other advantages have been mooted such as transfer of technology and upgrading of workers' skills; little evidence of these can be found. Indeed, the export-processing zones' concentration on electronics assembly and textiles and clothing limits worker training to simple, quickly mastered skills. The more complex production processes remain in the developed countries.

To sum up, export-processing zones are marginal in most, although not all, cases. For example, one study of the Indonesian export-processing zone on Batam Island, located so as to take advantage of Singapore's need for cheap labour, found that benefits only outweighed costs when bribes were taken into account! Further, competition between zones is now undermining what benefits there were. Competitive bidding for firms between prospective sites has resulted in more and more incentives having to be offered. Tax holidays are now being extended from five to ten years in many zones as evidence mounts that multinational corporations will simply relocate when these holidays come to an end – about 20 of the 68 firms in the Philippines Bataan zone had closed down by 1982 (Morello, 1983). So export-processing zones are, on the whole, a much commented upon but relatively unimportant outgrowth of the new international division of labour. Estimates vary, but it is unlikely that they currently employ more than a million workers worldwide – this is a drop in the ocean.

International migration. The export-processing zone represents an attempt to bring work to the workers. Another solution is for workers to go to the work. International migration has been an important part of the world-economic system since before the turn of the century, but the world-economic crisis has influenced international migration in new ways (Portes and Walton, 1981; Petras and McLean, 1981).

The International Labour Organization (1984) estimates the stock of economically active migrants in the world today as between 19.7 and 21.7 million (plus a similar number of dependants living with them). In general, the flow of migrants is from the less economically successful countries to the most economically successful. Thus the United States had some 5 million legal immigrants in 1979, half of whom were in the labour force and two-thirds from developing countries, with a further 2.5 to 4 million illegal immigrants, most in the labour force and nearly all from Mexico. Canada also has a large immigrant workforce. Western Europe has numerous economically active immigrants, perhaps as many as 6.3 million (see table 2.5). The Arab countries employ some 2.8 million foreigners, nearly all of whom are from developing countries (see table 2.6). But many developing countries also have substantial migrant-worker labour forces; those of South America have 3.5 to 4 million migrant workers and those of West Africa have 1.3 million (International Labour Organization, 1984).

This migration has considerable economic importance for all the countries concerned, increasing the interdependence of the world-economy. For example:

> In 1978, the flow of migrant workers' savings (remittances) to major migrant-sending countries amounted to US $24,000 million. This provided a notable element of international financial flexibility and much-needed hard currency for many developing countries. On the part of migrant-receiving countries, for example, one in six cars made in the Federal Republic of Germany in 1980 can be attributed to the work of Mediterranean migrants and the ratio would be higher if only production-line workers were counted. On the part of migrant-sending countries, for example, the inflow of remittances in the Yemen Arab Republic since

Table 2.5 Recorded number of migrant workers in selected western European countries, 1980 ('000s)

Out-migration country	In-migration country									
	Austria	Belgium	France	W. Germany	Luxemburg	Netherlands	Sweden	Switzerland	UK	Total
Algeria	–	3.2	322.7	1.6	–	–	–	–	–	327.5
Finland	–	–	–	3.7	–	–	108.0	–	1.0	112.7
France	–	38.5	–	54.0	8.5	2.0	–	–	14.0	117.2
Greece	–	10.8	3.0	138.4	–	1.2	7.5	–	6.0	166.9
Italy	–	90.5	146.4	324.3	11.2	12.0	–	301.0	73.0	958.4
Morocco	–	37.3	116.1	16.6	–	33.7	–	–	–	203.7
Portugal	–	6.3	430.6	59.9	13.7	4.2	–	–	5.0	519.7
Spain	–	32.0	157.7	89.3	2.3	10.4	–	85.7	17.0	394.4
Tunisia	–	4.7	65.3	–	–	1.1	–	–	–	71.1
Turkey	28.2	23.0	20.6	623.9	–	53.2	–	20.1	4.0	773.0
Yugoslavia	115.2	3.1	32.2	367.0	0.6	6.6	24.0	62.5	5.0	616.2
Other	31.3	83.2	192.4	490.1	15.6	70.2	94.6	237.0	804.0	2,018.4
Total	174.7	332.6	1,487.0	2,768.8	51.9	194.6	234.1	706.3	929.0	6,279.0

No figure given if no migrants recorded or estimated, if magnitude less than 500, or if not applicable.

Source: International Labour Organization, 1984, p. 100

Table 2.6 Estimated number of migrant workers in Arab countries, 1980 (actual figures)

Out-migration country	In-migration country										
	Bahrain	Jordan	Iraq	Kuwait	Libya	Oman	Qatar	Saudi Arabia	UAR	Yemen	Total
Democratic Yemen	1,125	–	–	9,500	–	120	1,500	65,000	6,600	–	83,845
Egypt	2,800	68,500	100,000	85,000	250,000	6,300	5,750	155,100	18,200	4,000	695,650
India	12,300	500	2,000	45,000	32,000	35,600	11,850	29,700	109,500	2,000	280,450
Iraq	310	–	–	40,000	–	–	–	3,250	1,200	–	44,760
Jordan (incl. Palestine)	1,400	–	7,500	55,000	15,000	2,250	7,800	140,000	19,400	2,000	250,350
Lebanon	300	–	4,500	8,000	5,700	1,500	750	33,200	6,600	500	61,050
Oman	900	–	–	2,000	–	–	1,150	10,000	19,400	–	33,450
Pakistan	26,160	4,000	7,500	34,000	65,000	44,500	220,770	29,700	137,000	3,000	371,630
Somalia	–	–	–	500	5,000	400	–	8,300	5,000	500	19,700
Sudan	900	–	500	5,500	21,000	620	750	55,600	2,100	2,250	89,220
Syrian Arab Republic	150	–	–	35,000	15,000	600	1,000	24,600	5,800	1,000	83,150
Yemen	1,125	–	–	3,000	–	120	1,500	325,000	5,400	–	336,145
Other Arab	–	–	–	300	65,600	120	–	500	–	–	66,520
Other Asian	10,000	1,000	1,500	10,000	27,000	–	4,500	93,500	20,700	300	168,500
Other	10,250	2,000	2,000	45,900	44,200	4,670	22,930	49,800	54,100	1,450	237,300
Total	67,720	76,000	125,500	378,700	545,500	96,800	80,250	1,023,250	411,000	17,000	2,821,720

No figure given if migrants recorded or estimated, if magnitude less than 500, or if not applicable.

Source: Birks and Sinclair, 1980

the early 1970s has covered the country's growing trade gap or – which amounts to the same thing – migrants' transfer payments have enabled the country to increase its imports correspondingly, amounting to about 600 times the level of exports at the end of the 1970s. (International Labour Organization, 1984, pp. 102–3)

Conventionally, international migration is split into four categories; settlement migration, irregular migration, contract migration, and official and business migration. In each of these categories there has been some response to the world-economic crisis and the restructuring it has brought about. However, it is among contract migration and official and business migration that the most important responses can be found (see Petras and McLean, 1981).

Contract migration has grown swiftly during the period of the crisis, involving migration for a period of time which is dependent upon the issue of a contract by an employer in the country concerned. Indeed quite often a group of workers are admitted under a collective contract for the span of a particular project or part of a project. Thus a group of workers may be brought into a country on contract to build factories and infrastructure and they are then replaced by another group who specialize in operations and maintenance. The contract for Riyadh University was won by a consortium – Bouyges-Blount – dominated by the French Bouyges corporation. The joint venture acts as a kind of broker, subcontracting each part of the project. So a consortium of companies from South Korea holds the general construction contract and is bringing in Korean workers to do most of the work. An Italian group has the electricity contract and will bring in Italian workers, and so on. The number of subcontract workers will reach 10,000 at the height of the project (International Labour Organization, 1984). This kind of project, offering a complete package, is becoming more common and, as it does so, it is possible to see how flows of migrants and the objectives of multinational corporations can become much more closely integrated.

Official and business migration has also become more important in the period of the crisis as a result of increasing activity by multinational corporations, and especially of their 'globalization'. This category of migrants includes many types of temporary migrant, in particular the subcategory of businessmen and intra-company transferees. As businessmen have been forced to go from country to country more frequently, and as intra-company transfers of personnel have had to be made more often as multinational companies have grown larger and established themselves in more countries, so these subcategories have increased in proportion. Here patterns of migration closely mirror the internationalization of capital.

However, international migration has also produced problems as the world-economic crisis deepened. The potential number of international migrants is increasing in the poor countries of Asia, Central and Latin America and Africa but the opportunities for employment in the developed countries are falling away. It is no surprise, then, that many developed countries are now trying to rid themselves of the 1950s and 1960s boom who originally formed a useful substratum of the working class but in the recession have formed the leading ranks of the unemployed; in West Germany, for example, there are now 2.5 million unemployed of whom 274,000 are foreign, and of these foreigners 40 per cent are Turks (International Labour Organization, 1984). The West German government has even started a scheme to pay foreign workers to leave the country.

The growth of the international service economy. The final global effect of the crisis on employment opportunities has been the growth of a new international service economy based upon corporate activities. This growth can be traced to the internationalization of production and especially the growth of global corporations with their large internal markets which require considerable administration. Much of this administration is carried out *within* corporations, especially through new innovations like the regional headquarters office (see Heenan, 1977; Grosse, 1982; Dunning and Norman, 1983). (Regional headquarters offices provide the intermediate tier of management between the administration, much of it strategic, carried out by the head office of a corporation and the administration, much of it routine, carried out by regional branch offices. They are responsible for definable regions of the world such as Asia and the Pacific, and are intended to reduce the internal transactions costs of moving information and making decisions within the global corporation.) However, the growth of the administrative load has been such that it has also stimulated the growth of more and more producer services. These are services which could, no doubt, be produced within the corporation but which, for various reasons, especially because they can be obtained more cheaply outside are externalized and bought in. Producer services, then, are 'activities that assist user firms in carrying out administrative, developmental (research and development, strategic planning), and financial functions, banking, insurance, real estate, accounting, legal services, consulting, advertising and so forth' (Noyelle, 1983a, pp. 117–18). All these services have internationalized too, sometimes following in the wake of the multinational corporations, but sometimes expanding independently of them as well (see Thrift, 1985). For example, banks have internationalized to meet the financial needs of their corporate customers but also in order to search for new customers.

The most important result of the growth of corporate administration and related producer services has been the growth of a complex of corporate activities, which has had important results for employment. For example, in 1977 Noyelle and Stanback (1983) reckoned that this complex of corporate activities accounted for 12 per cent of full-time employment in the United States and 20 per cent of GNP. In the United Kingdom Daniels (1985) estimated that by 1981 as much as 22 per cent of services employment was in producer services.

The main result of the worldwide growth of this complex of corporate activities has been the formation of the so-called world cities (Cohen, 1981; Friedmann and Wolff, 1982; Noyelle, 1983a, 1983b; Soja, Morales and Wolff,

1983; Thrift, 1983, 1985). For various reasons, producer services have tended to develop in a very selective hierarchy of key urban centres round the world in which they have come to dominate economic life. The world cities occupy the top of this hierarchy, and can be divided into three (Daly, 1984). First, there are the truly international centres – New York, London, Paris, Zurich and Hamburg. These contain many head offices, branch offices and regional headquarters offices of the large corporations, and include the head offices or representative offices of many banks. They account for most large business dealings on a world scale. Second, there are the *zonal* centres – Singapore, Hong Kong, Los Angeles. These also have many corporate offices of various types and serve as important links in the international financial system but they are responsible for particular zones rather than for business on a world scale. Finally, there are the *regional* centres – Sydney, Chicago, Dallas, Miami, Honolulu and San Francisco. These host many corporate offices and foreign financial outlets but they are not essential links in the international financial system. Some specialize in providing space for corporate regional headquarters serving particular regions. Thus Miami is a regional headquarters node for US-based multinational corporations operating in Latin America (with at least 150 such offices) and Honolulu is a regional headquarters node for US-based multinational corporations operating in Asia (with at least 50 such offices).

The importance of employment in producer services in these cities should not be underestimated. London, for example, is now a massive corporate complex with 24 per cent of the United Kingdom's office space. In 1977 525 out of the *Times* top 1,000 companies had their headquarters there (Goddard and Smith, 1978); 72 of the largest US-based multinational corporations and 11 of the largest Japanese-based multinational corporations had their regional headquarters in London. In 1983, in keeping with the city's role as a corporate complex and the chief node of the Eurocurrency market, there were 391 foreign banks directly represented in London. A further 69 were indirectly represented, and there were 94 foreign securities houses. In all 38,020 people were directly employed in these financial institutions in 1983 (*The Banker*, 1983) and Daniels (1985) has calculated that in 1981 467,000 workers were employed in Greater London in banking, finance, insurance, business services and leasing. London is only one such case. In 1982, Hong Kong received 26 per cent of its GDP from financial services and more than 5 per cent of its employment was in finance, insurance, real estate and business services. In the same year, Singapore received 20 per cent of its GDP from financial services, and producer services accounted for nearly 8 per cent of the island's employment.

But the trend towards greater centralization of corporate complexes – which still seems to be going on (see Noyelle, 1983b) – has some negative effects. In particular, while some privileged cities can derive prosperity from being the location of corporate complexes, other cities get only the leftovers, the manufacturing jobs and the lowlier service jobs. Thus the international services economy increasingly bypasses many cities and many workers.

CONCLUSIONS

Perhaps the most important conclusion to draw from this chapter is that, as a result of the world-economic crisis, the world-economy has become more integrated than ever before. There are new links between multinational corporations, banks and countries and the old links have been strengthened.

Take, first, the interconnections between the multinational corporations and the banks. The internationalization of production and finance has forged much closer links between the two. Company finance and profits now depend on interest rate and currency swaps, on Eurobond issues, on financial futures and on foreign exchange options, all usually arranged by the banks. Banks advise on corporate finance, on mergers, on acquisitions. And banks are increasingly the shareholders of the multinational corporations (see Fennema, 1982; Grou, 1983; Andreff, 1984). Second, the ties between multinational corporations and countries have been strengthened. In nearly every nation of the world the level of foreign direct investment has increased and national economies have consequently become more 'open'. Indeed, country action to prevent import penetration by the use of tariffs and other barriers has only hastened this process. In a few countries like the United Kingdom and the Netherlands, which have particularly high levels of foreign direct investment and which conduct much of their production abroad, it is possible to ask whether a coherent national economy still exists (Radice, 1984). Finally, there are much greater connections now between countries and banks. The present international debt crisis is simply the most extreme illustration of this fact (Lipietz, 1984a).

The greater level of integration of the world-economy should not be overemphasized. The rise of a new world-economic order does not give overwhelming power to the multinational corporation, it does not give the banks total control, and it does not mean the end of national sovereignty. The internationalization of capital, understood in its broadest sense, is a very messy business. It is, as Michalet (1976) has pointed out, a process which produces partial outcomes; it is not an economic apocalypse. But it is still the most important economic event taking place in the world at present and it is having crucial reverberations – economic, social and cultural – on many countries. Yet, even now, few human geographers seem willing to come out of their national shells and take the wider view which would enable them to understand what is going on *within their own countries*. They still seem quite willing to document the national effects of international processes. This insular view of the world cannot continue, because the world is no longer like that.

References

Aglietta, M. 1979: *A Theory of Capitalist Regulation. The U.S. Experience.* London: New Left Books.

Aglietta, M. 1982: World capitalism in the eighties. *New Left Review*, 136, 25–36.

Aliber, R. Z. 1979: *The International Money Game.* New York: Basic Books.

Andreff, W. 1976: *Profits et structures du capitalism mondiale.* Paris: Calmann Levy.

Andreff, W. 1983: *Les Multinationales hors la crise.* Paris: Le Sycamore.

Andreff, W. 1984: The international centralization of capital and the re-ordering of world capitalism. *Capital and Class*, 22, 58–80.

Ballance, R. J. and Sinclair, S. W. 1983: *Collapse and Survival. Industry Strategies in a Changing World.* London: Allen & Unwin.

Beenstock, M. 1983: *The World Economy in Transition.* London: Allen & Unwin.

Birks, J. S. and Sinclair, C. A. 1980: *International Migration and Development in the Arab Region.* Geneva: International Labour Office.

Bloomfield, G. T. 1981: The changing spatial organisation of multinational corporations in the world automative industry. In F. E. I. Hamilton and G. J. R. Linge (eds), *Spatial Analysis, Industry and the Industrial Environment*, vol. 2: *International Industrial Systems*, Chichester: Wiley, 357–94.

Bora, G. 1981: International division of labour and the national industrial system: the case of Hungary. In F. E. I. Hamilton and G. J. R. Linge (eds), *Spatial Analysis, Industry and the Industrial Environment*, vol. 2; *International Industrial Systems*, Chichester: Wiley, 155–84.

Brett, E. A. 1983: *International Money and Capitalist Crisis. The Anatomy of Global Disintegration.* London: Heinemann.

Brewer, A. 1980: *Marxist Theories of Imperialism.* London: Routledge & Kegan Paul.

Bromley, R. and Gerry, C. (eds) 1979: *Casual Work and Poverty in Third World Cities.* Chichester: Wiley.

Brunner, K. (ed.) 1981: *The Great Depression Revisted.* Boston: Kluwer Nijhoff.

Buckley, P. and Casson, M. 1976: *The Future of the Multinational Enterprise.* London: Macmillan.

Caves, R. E. 1983: *Multinational Enterprise and Economic Analysis.* Cambridge: Cambridge University Press.

Central Statistical Office 1983: *UK Balance of Payments 1983.* London: HMSO.

Clairmonte, F. and Cavanagh, J. 1981: *The World in Their Web. Dynamics of Textile Multinationals.* London: Zed Press.

Clarke, I. M. 1982: The changing international division of labour within I.C.I. In M. J. Taylor and N. J. Thrift (eds), *The Geography of Multinationals*, London: Croom Helm, 90–116.

Clarke, I. M. 1984: 'The spatial organisation of corporations'. Unpublished Ph.D. thesis, Department of Human Geography, Australian National University, Canberra.

Coakley, J. 1984: The internationalisation of bank capital. *Capital and Class*, 23, 107–20.

Coakley, J. and Harris, L. 1983: *The City of Capital.* Oxford: Basil Blackwell.

Cohen, R. B. 1981: The new international division of labour, multinational corporations and urban hierarchy. In M. J. Dear and A. J. Scott (eds), *Urbanisation and Urban Planning in Capitalist Society*, London: Methuen, 287–315.

Cohen, R. B. 1983: The new spatial organisation of the European and American automotive industries. In F. W. Moulaert and P. B. Salinas (eds), *Regional Analysis and the New International Division of Labour*, Boston: Kluwer Nijhoff, 135–43.

Currie, J. 1979: Investment: the growing role of export processing zones. *Economist Intelligence Unit Special Report* 64. London: Economist Intelligence Unit.

Daly, M. T. 1984: The revolution in international capital markets: urban growth and Australian cities. *Environment and Planning A*, 16, 1003–20.

Daniels, P. 1985: Producer services and the post-industrial economy. In R. L. Martin and R. Rowthorne (eds), *Deindustrialisation and the British Space Economy*, Cambridge: Cambridge University Press.

Delamaide, D. 1984: *Debt Shock*. London: Weidenfeld & Nicolson.

Dicken, P. 1980: Foreign direct investment in European manufacturing industry: the changing position of the United Kingdom as a host country. *Geoforum*, 11, 289–313.

Dicken, P. 1982: Recent trends in international direct investment, with particular reference to the United States and the United Kingdom. In B. T. Robson and J. Rees (eds), *Geographical Agenda for a Changing World*, London: Social Science Research Council, 118–61.

Dunning, J. H. 1981: *International Production and the Multinational Enterprise*. London: Allen & Unwin.

Dunning, J. H. and Norman, G. 1983: The theory of the multinational enterprise: an application to multinational office location. *Environment and Planning A*, 15, 675–92.

Dunning, J. H. and Pearce, C. D. 1981: *The World's Largest Industrial Enterprises*. Farnborough: Gower.

Economist 1984: Multinationals vs. globals. *The Economist*, 5 May, 67.

Economist Intelligence Unit 1984: How to make offshore manufacturing pay. *Economist Intelligence Unit Special Report* 171. London: Economist Intelligence Unit.

Faire, A. 1981: The strategies of economic redeployment in the West. *Review*, 2.

Fennema, M. 1982: *International Networks of Banks and Industry*. The Hague: Martinus Nijhoff.

Franko, L. G. 1983: *The Japanese Multinational*. Chichester: Wiley.

Friedmann, G. and Wolff, G. 1982: World city formation: an agenda for research and action. *International Journal of Urban and Regional Research*, 6, 309–44.

Frobel, F. 1983: The current development of the world economy: reproduction of labour and accumulation of capital on a world scale. *Review*, 5, 507–55.

Frobel, F., Heinrichs, J. and Kreye, O. 1980: *The New International Division of Labour*, Cambridge: Cambridge University Press.

Fujita, M. and Ishigaki, K. 1985: The internationalisation of Japanese banking. In M. J. Taylor and N. J. Thrift (eds), *Multinationals and the Restructuring of the World Economy*, London: Croom Helm.

Gaffikin, F. and Nickson, A. 1984: *Jobs Crisis and the Multinationals. The Case of the West Midlands*. Nottingham: Russell Press.

Gershuny, J. 1978: *The Self-Service Economy*. London: Frances Pinter.

Gershuny, J. I. and Miles, I. 1983: *The New Service Economy*. London: Frances Pinter.

Goddard, J. B. and Smith, I. J. 1978: Changes in corporate control in the British urban system, 1972–1977. *Environment and Planning A*, 10, 1073–84.

Gorastraga, X. 1983: *International Financial Centres in Underdeveloped Countries*. London: Croom Helm.

De Grazia, R. 1984: *Clandestine Employment*. Geneva: International Labour Office.

Grosse, R. E. 1982: Regional offices in multinational firms. In A. M. Rugman (ed.), *New Theories of the Multinational Enterprise*, London: Croom Helm, 107–32.

Grou, P. 1983: *La Structure financière de capitalisme multinational*. Paris: Presses de la Fondation Nationale des Sciences Politiques.

Gutman, P. and Arkwright, F. 1981: Tripartite industrial cooperation between East, West and South. In F. E. I. Hamilton and G. J. R. Linge (eds), *Spatial Analysis, Industry and the Industrial Environment*, vol. 2: *International Industrial Systems*, Chichester: Wiley, 185–214.

Hansen, N. 1981: Mexico's border industry and the international division of labour. *Annals of Regional Science*, 15, 1–12.

Harris, N. 1982: The road from 1910. *Economy and Society*, 12, 347–62.

Harris, N. 1983: *Of Bread and Guns. The World in Economic Crisis*. Harmondsworth: Penguin.

Heenan, D. A. 1977: Global cities of tomorrow. *Harvard Business Review*, 55, 79–92.

Houston, T. and Dunning, J. H. 1976: *U.K. Industry Abroad*. London: Economists Advisory Group.

Hunt, T., Parker, M. E. and Rudden, E. 1982: How global companies win out. *Harvard Business Review*, 60, 98–108.

International Labour Organization 1980: *Asian Development in the 1980s. Growth, Employment and Working Conditions*. Geneva: International Labour Office.

International Labour Organization 1981: *Employment Effects of Multinational Enterprises in Developing Countries*. Geneva: International Labour Office.

International Labour Organization 1983: *Yearbook of Labour Statistics 1983*. Geneva: International Labour Office.

International Labour Organization 1984: *World Labour Report 1. Employment, Incomes, Social Protection, New Information Technology*. Geneva: International Labour Office.

Jenkins, R. 1984: Divisions over the international division of labour. *Capital and Class*, 22, 28–57.

Kindleberger, C. P. 1973: *The World in Depression 1929–1939*. London: Allen Lane.

King, A. D. 1985: Capital city: physical and social aspects of London's role in the world economy. *Development and Change* (forthcoming).

Kirby, S. R. 1983: Towards the Pacific Century. Economic Development in the Pacific Basin. *Economic Intelligence Unit Special Report* 137. London: Economist Intelligence Unit.

Knickerbocker, F. T. 1973: *Ologopolistic Reaction and Multinational Enterprise*. Cambridge, Mass.: MIT Press.

Kortus, B. and Kaczerowski, W. 1981: Polish industry forges external links. In F. E. I. Hamilton and G. J. R. Linge (eds), *Spatial Analysis, Industry and the Industrial Environment*, vol. 2, *International Industrial Systems*, Chichester: Wiley, 119–54.

Labour Research 1983: Multinationals and manufacturing employment. *Labour Research*, May, 123–5.

Lall, S. 1984: *The New Multinationals. The Spread of Third World Enterprises*. Chichester: Wiley.

Lipietz, A. 1984a: How monetarism has choked third world industrialisation. *New Left Review*, 145, 71–87.

Lipietz, A. 1984b: Imperialism or the beast of the apocalypse. *Capital and Class*, 22, 81–109.

Lloyd, P. and Reeve, D. E. 1982: North West England 1971–1977: a study in industrial decline and economic restructuring. *Regional Studies*, 16, 345–59.

Lozano, B. 1983: Informal sector workers: walking out of the system's front door. *International Journal of Urban and Regional Research*, 7, 340–62.

McConnell, J. G. 1981: Foreign direct investment in the United States. *Annals of the Association of American Geographers*, 70, 259–70.

McConnell, J. G. 1983: The international location of manufacturing investments: recent behaviour of foreign owned corporations in the United States. In F. E. I. Hamilton and G. J. R. Linge (eds), *Spatial Analysis, Industry and the Industrial Environment, vol. 3: Regional Economies and Industrial Systems*, Chichester: Wiley, 337–58.

Margirier, G. 1983: The eighties: a second phase of crisis? *Capital and Class*, 21, 61–86.

Marsden, J. 1980: Export processing zones in developing countries. *UNIDO Working Papers on Structural Change* 19.

Maxcy, G. 1981: *The Multinational Motor Industry*. London: Croom Helm.

Mendelsohn, M. S. 1980: *Money on the Move*. New York: McGraw Hill.

Michalet, C. A. 1976: *Le Capitalisme mondiale*. Paris: Presses Universitaires de France.

Michalet, C. A. (ed.) 1981: *Internationalisation des banques et des groupes financières*. Paris: Centre Nationale de la Recherche Scientifique.

Mitra, P. M. 1983: World Bank research on adjustment to external shocks. *World Bank Research News*, 4 (3), 3–14.

Morello, T. 1983: Sweatshops in the sun? *Far Eastern Economic Review*, 15 September, 88–9.

Morgan, K. and Sayer, A. 1983: The international electronics industry and regional development in Britain. *University of Sussex, Urban and Regional Studies, Working Paper* 34.

Nakase, T. 1981: Some characteristics of Japanese-type multinationals today. *Capital and Class*, 13, 61–98.

Neuberger, E. and Tysson, L. D. (eds) 1980: *The Impact of International Economic Disturbances on the Soviet Union and Eastern Europe*. Oxford: Pergamon.

Noyelle, T. J. 1983a: The implications of industry restructuring for spatial organisation in the United States. In F. Moulaert and P. W. Salinas (eds), *Regional Analysis and the New International Division of Labour*, Boston: Kluwer Nijhoff, 113–33.

Noyelle, T. J. 1983b: The rise of advanced services. Some implications for economic development in U.S. cities. *Journal of the American Planning Association*, 25, 280–90.

Noyelle, T. J. and Stanback, T. M. 1983: *The Economic Transformation of American Cities*. Totowa, N. J.: Allanheld, Osmun.

OECD 1977: *Towards Full Employment and Price Stability*. Paris, OECD.

Pahl, R. E. 1980: Employment, work and the domestic division of labour. *International Journal of Urban and Regional Research*, 4, 1–19.

Pahl, R. E. 1984: *Divisions of Labour*. Oxford: Basil Blackwell.

Parboni, R. 1981: *The Dollar and its Rivals*. London: Verso.

Peet, J. R. 1983: Relations of production and the relocation of United States manufacturing industry since 1960. *Economic Geography*, 59, 112–43.

Petras, E. and McLean, M. 1981: The global labour market in the world economy. In M. M. Kritz, C. B. Keely and S. M. Tomasi (eds), *Global Trends in Migration*, New York: Centre for Migration Studies, 44–63.

Portes, A. and Walton, J. 1981: *Labour, Class and the International System*. New York: Academic Press.

Portes, R. 1984: The effects of the world economic crisis on the East European economies. *The World Economy* 3.

Radice, H. 1984: The national economy – a Keynesian myth? *Capital and Class*, 22, 111–40.

Rees, J. 1978: On the spatial spread and oligopolistic behaviour of large rubber companies. *Geoforum*, 9, 319–30.

Roddick, J. 1984; Crisis, Seignorage and the modern world system; rising third world power or declining US hegemony. *Capital and Class*, 23, 121–34.

Rugman, A. M. 1981: *Inside the Multinationals*. London: Croom Helm.

Rugman, A. M. (ed.) 1982: *New Theories of the Multinational Enterprise*. London: Croom Helm.

Salita, D. C. and Juanico, M. B. 1983: Export processing zones: new catalysts for economic development. In F. E. I. Hamilton, and G. J. R. Linge (eds), *Spatial Analysis, Industry and the Industrial Environment*, vol. 3: *Regional Economies and Industrial Systems*, Chichester: Wiley, 441–61.

Sampson, A. 1981: *The Money Lenders*. London: Hodder & Stoughton.

Savey, S. 1981: Pechiney Ugine Kuhlmann: a French multinational corporation. In F. E. I. Hamilton and G. J. R. Linge (eds), *Spatial Analysis, Industry and the Industrial Environment*, vol. 2: *International Industrial Systems*, Chichester: Wiley, 305–27.

Sethuraman, S. V. (ed.) 1981: *The Urban Informal Sector in Developing Countries*. Geneva: International Labour Office.

Soja, E., Morales, R. and Wolff, G. 1983: Urban restructuring: an analysis of social and spatial change in Los Angeles. *Economic Geography*, 59, 195–230.

Tanzi, V. 1982: *The Underground Economy in the United States and Abroad*. Lexington, Mass.: Lexington Books.

Taylor, M. J. and Thrift, N. J. 1981: British capital overseas: direct investment and firm development in Australia. *Regional Studies*, 15, 183–212.

Taylor, M. J. and Thrift, N. J. (eds) 1982: *The Geography of Multinationals*. London: Croom Helm.

Teulings, A. W. M. 1984: The internationalisation squeeze: double capital movement and job transfer within Philips worldwide. *Environment and Planning A*, 16, 565–706.

Tharakan, P. M. 1980: *The New International Division of Labour and Multinational Companies*. Farnborough: Saxon House.

Thompson, A. 1983: The prospects for establishment-level databanks. In M. J. Healey (ed.), *Urban and Regional Industrial Research*, Norwich: Geo Books, 65–89.

Thrift, N. J. 1980: Frobel and the new international division of labour. In J. R. Peet (ed.), *An Introduction to Marxist Theories of Underdevelopment*, Australian National University, Department of Human Geography, HG14, 181–9.

Thrift, N. J. 1983: World cities, world property market. *Australian National University, Department of Human Geography, Seminar Paper*.

Thrift, N. J. 1985: The internationalisation of producer services and the integration of the Pacific Basin property market. In M. J. Taylor and N. J. Thrift (eds), *Multinationals and the Restructuring of the World Economy*. London: Croom Helm.

United Nations 1983: *Transnational Corporations in World Development: Third Study*. New York: United Nations.

Vernon, R. 1979: The product cycle hypothesis in a new international environment. *Oxford Bulletin of Economics and Statistics*, 41, 255–68.

Versluyen, E. 1981: *The Political Economy of International Finance*. London: Gower.

De Vroey, M. 1984: A regulation approach interpretation of contemporary crisis. *Capital and Class*, 23, 45–66.

Wallerstein, I. 1979: *The Capitalist World Economy*. Cambridge: Cambridge University Press.

Wallerstein, I. 1983: *Historical Capitalism*. London: New Left Books.

Wells, L. T., Jr 1983: *Third World Multinationals. The Rise of Foreign Investment from Developing Countries*. Cambridge, Mass.: MIT Press.

Wong, K. and Chu, D. K. Y. 1984: Export processing zones and special economic zones as generators of economic development: the Asian experience. *Geografiska Annaler*, Series B, 66, 1–16.

World Bank 1983: *World Development Report 1983*. Oxford: World Bank/Oxford University Press.

Yoshihara, H. 1977: The Japanese multinational. *Long Range Planning*, 18, 41–5.

3

Draining the World of Energy

PETER R. ODELL

Each and every society's capability of development, or indeed its ability to survive, depends on continuing access to energy in appropriate forms and quantities, and at acceptable levels of costs (Cook, 1976). There is a relationship, which changes over time, between the degree of development in a society (economy) and the use of energy. This is illustrated in figure 3.1. The relationship has, until very recently (when a small number of wealthy and highly industrialized countries have started to use less energy), been one of an increasingly intensive use of energy as development occurred. Thus the gradual transformation of the world over the last 200-plus years, from a world in the mid-eighteenth century made up of primitive and peasant societies which were largely subsistence in their structure and organization to a world consisting mainly of post-industrial, industrial and industrializing economies, has led to a global use of energy which is now over 20 times greater than it is estimated to have been in 1860 – the earliest date for which world energy use can be estimated with any degree of confidence (Marchetti and Nakicenovic, 1979). Even by 1860, however, world energy use was probably about twice what it had been at the beginning of the industrial revolution in the third quarter of the eighteenth century so that the world in 1985 is probably using energy at a rate which is about 40 times greater than it was in 1785. Figure 3.2 shows the evolution of energy use over the 125 years back to 1860. It demonstrates what a remarkably consistent rate of growth there has been over the whole of the period since then (at just over 2 per cent per annum), except for the years between 1950 and 1973 when the rate more than doubled to almost 5 per cent per year. It is, however, the very long-term consistent 2-plus per cent per annum growth rate in energy use against which the availability and potential availability of the world's energy supplies need to be measured when looking at the energy prospects on a global scale for the medium- to long-term future.

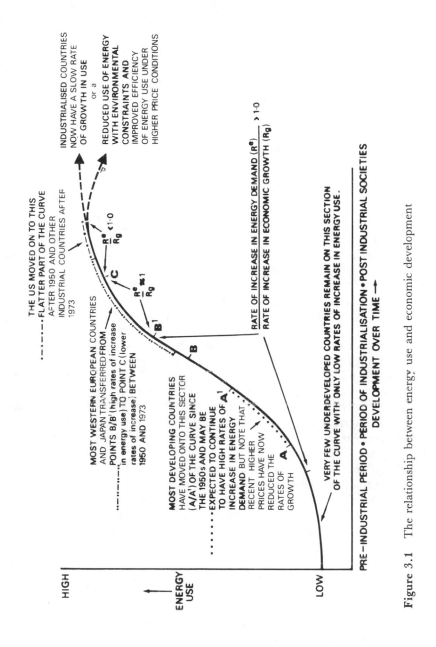

Figure 3.1 The relationship between energy use and economic development

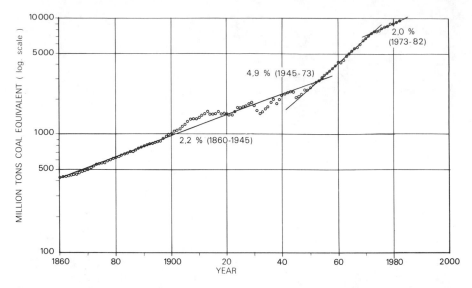

Figure 3.2   Trends in the evolution of world energy use since 1860

THE DEMAND FOR ENERGY

The near 5 per cent per annum energy-use growth rate of the years between 1945 and 1973 is important because current attitudes to the world energy situation and its outlook are heavily dependent on the idea that this exceptionally high rate of growth in energy use represents the 'norm' – the 'required' rate of increase to match a continuation of population increase and desirable economic progress. This is unlikely to be the case, however, as the 1945–73 period rate of increase can be shown to be the result of a temporally unique set of factors, involving virtually all of the world's nations. At that time the world's nations were almost all on the steepest part of the curve shown in figure 3.1: in a situation, that is, in which their economies were going through the most heavily energy-intensive period of development.

   First, the small number of the western economic system's rich countries were then in the later stages of the traditional industrialization process; a stage marked by an emphasis on products with high energy inputs, such as motor vehicles, household durable goods and petrochemical products (Schurr and Netschert, 1977). As a result, the use of energy on the production side of such economies greatly increased. At the same time, the increase in the per-capita use of energy on the consumption side of these countries' economies was even more dramatic. This arose from the mass use of motor cars, the suburbanization of cities and the increasing length of the journey to work, the switch from public to private transport, the expanded availability of leisure time and the 'annihilation of space' in the public's use of such time, the mechanization of households by the use of electricity-powered equipment, and the achievement of much higher standards of comfort (by heating and/or cooling) in homes and other buildings (Leach et al., 1979). Cheap energy was one of the main bases for the 'revolution of rising expectations' on the part of the populations of the rich countries. The progress of that revolution in the 1950s and the 1960s was thus marked by a very rapid increase in energy use in the industrialized world.

Second, many of the same factors positively influenced the rate of growth in energy use in the centrally planned economies of the Soviet Union and Eastern Europe, in spite of the differences of ideology and of economic and political organization between east and west (Park, 1979). This was particularly the case in respect of the industrialization process in which all these countries participated as a matter of deliberate policy – and with a special emphasis on the rapid expansion of heavy, energy-intensive industry. To a smaller but, nevertheless, a still significant extent, consumers in the centrally planned economies also increased their levels of energy use in this period as a result of higher real living standards and of changes in lifestyles. Electrification, a particularly energy-intensive process, was moreover a declared central aim of such planned economies – not least because Lenin had specified it as a necessary part of the evolution to communism (Lenin, 1966). Thus all these countries were also moving up the steepest part of the curve shown in figure 3.1 during this period.

Meanwhile, in the Third World of poorer countries, most nations moved off the lowest part of that curve as these (for the large part) newly independent nations pursued policies of deliberate industrialization (viewed as the panacea for, and the *sine qua non* of, economic progress), and found that such policies were necessarily accompanied by rapid urbanization with its much enhanced energy requirements. The sorts of industry which were established were, moreover, either energy-intensive, heavy industry – such as iron and steel, metal fabricating, vehicles and cement – or relatively energy-intensive industry such as textiles and household goods. The concurrent urbanization process meant that peasants and landless agricultural labourers were transferred from their low-energy ways of living (in which situation, moreover, most of the energy required was collected rather than purchased) to lifestyles in the city or urban environment which, no matter how poor the living standards achieved turned out to be, were nevertheless much more demanding in their use of energy generally – and, in particular, in their use of electricity and petroleum products (Dunkerley, 1981).

It was essentially the temporal coincidence of these fundamental societal developments in most countries of the world in the 1950s and 1960s which caused the abnormally high rate of growth in energy use over that period. It is not without significance that, as the United States moved off the steepest part of the curve in the late 1960s and early 1970s, so its rate of growth in energy use started to fall away and, because of the importance of the United States in total world energy use, this also started to exercise a downward pull on global rates at that time – some years, that is, prior to the first oil-price shock of 1973. There was, however, another powerful factor at work in influencing

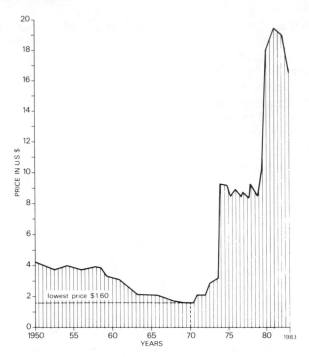

Figure 3.3   The price of oil 1950–83 (Saudi Arabian light crude in 1974 US$)

the rate of increase in energy use in the more than 20 years before that price shock. This was the long-continuing decline in the real price of energy after 1950 (Adelman, 1972). This is shown in the left-hand part of the curve in figure 3.3 in which the evolution of the (real price) of Saudi Arabian light crude oil over the years from 1950 is illustrated. It shows how the market value of a barrel of this oil fell between 1950 and 1970 by over 60 per cent from $4.25 to $1.60 under the impact of the technologically efficient and politically powerful oil companies which, at that time, were able both to ignore the interests of the oil-producing countries in the exploitation of their resources and to persuade the importing countries of the continuity of these low-cost oil supplies (Odell, 1983).

This decline in the oil price brought about a falling market price for all other sources of energy throughout the world during this period, though not to the same degree as the fall in the price of crude oil when calculated in terms of the reduction in price to the final consumer of energy. This fall in energy prices was especially important in the western industrial countries with their open – or relatively open – economies under their post-second-world-war liberal trading regimes. In these countries local energy production – such as coal in western Europe and Japan, and oil and natural gas in the United States – either had to be reduced in price to enable it to compete with falling-price imported oil, or else the industries concerned were cut back or eliminated (Manners, 1971).

Thus both the actual decline in the cost of energy over this period and the perception among energy users that energy was cheap and getting cheaper – so hardly worth worrying about in terms of the care and efficiency with which it was used – created conditions in which the careless and wasteful consumption of energy became a hallmark of both technological and behavioural aspects of societal and economic developments. There was a consequential emphasis on systems of production, transport and consumption which were quite unnecessarily energy-intensive (Odell, 1975) and against which a reaction of significant proportions could be expected once the real price curve started to move up. This phenomenon dates from 1970, but in 1973–4, as shown in figure 3.3, it took a massive upward leap with the so-called 'first oil-price shock'. By the time of the second price shock in 1979–81 structural changes in the energy-careless and wasteful systems described above were already well under way, and they have since both intensified and become geographically much more diffuse.

STRUCTURAL CHANGES IN THE ENERGY SYSTEM SINCE THE MID-1970s

In other words, the order-of-magnitude jump in oil and other energy prices in the 1970s has terminated the perception of energy as a near-costless input to economic and societal developments in most parts of the world. Thus, as shown in figure 3.2, the rate of increase in energy use has now been brought back to its historic, long-term figure of about 2 per cent per annum: to date, the most important element in the change has been the quite dramatic decline in the energy intensity of economic activities in the western industrialized countries, where the motivation to achieve energy savings has been greater than elsewhere and the ability so to do has been higher (Fritsch, 1982). Both behavioural and technological components have contributed to this development.

Behaviourally, users have responded to the higher prices by taking steps (such as turning down thermostats and by 'trip combinations' in the use of motor vehicles) which save energy. They have, moreover, been subjected to 'Save It'-style energy-conservationist campaigns which have imparted knowledge whereby energy-using behaviour could be adjusted appropriately. The technological component has, however, been much more effective, largely because there was so much 'fat' to work out of the system from the energy-careless and thoughtless technology of the pre-1970 period. More efficient energy processes in factories, more efficient lighting in offices, better insulation in buildings, the development of motor vehicles, planes and ships which give more kilometres per litre (or ton) of fuel, and the expansion of inherently more energy-efficient systems of electricity production have jointly combined to produce significantly lower rates of energy use per unit of output of goods and services. Overall in western Europe, for example, the energy intensity of energy growth from 1973–80 was less than half that of the preceding ten years, and since 1980 the ratio has fallen still further (International Energy Agency, 1982).

In spite of the already considerable reductions in the intensity of energy use over the last decade, both the behavioural and the technological components involved in reducing energy use still have a long way to go before the energy-inefficient systems which were the norm in the period of low- and decreasing-cost energy are finally replaced. This is true even in the world's rich countries where the required investment funds and the other necessary inputs of knowledge, managerial and technical expertise and know-how are available so rendering the changes simply a matter of time (Darmstadter et al., 1977 and 1983).

The diffusion of more efficient energy-using systems and infrastructure to the modern sectors of most Third World countries will be a slower process, because of the relative scarcity in such countries of the inputs that are required to implement the changes – notably the lack of investment capital and of expertise. Such diffusion is, however, taking place under the powerful stimulus of the very high foreign exchange costs of energy (particularly oil) imports on which Third World countries depend to a larger degree even than most industrialized countries (Dunkerley, 1981). The alternative to more efficient energy use in such cases is, indeed, too little energy to keep the systems going, because a limit has to be placed on the amount of oil that can be imported. Thus enhanced levels of energy-utilization efficiency will eventually be achieved in the Third World. This is an important conclusion in relation to the longer-term evolution of global energy demand as the percentage of world energy used in these countries must increase steadily under the joint impact of their high population growth and of economies which are going through their most energy-intensive period of development (as illustrated in figure 3.1). The countries of the north, which already use much more energy per capita, will meanwhile experience a slow or even a negative growth rate in energy use (Hoffman and Johnson, 1981).

The countries with centrally planned economies lie somewhere in between the industrialized and the Third World nations in respect of their energy-use pattern and the prospects for their development (Dienes and Shabad, 1979; Park, 1979). To date they have done significantly less well than the market economies in saving energy – partly for economic (price) reasons, and partly for technical and organizational reasons. The importance of energy conservation has now, however, become much more generally recognized by the governments concerned so that, given the opportunities which exist in such 'command' economies for the speedy implementation of policies, measures to save energy are now being accorded a much higher priority than hitherto.

Given these structural changes in attitudes and policies towards the energy sectors of the economies of countries in all parts of the world, there are now long-term prospects for a slow rate of increase in energy demand – even in the event of a renewal of economic growth in the western system. The massive differences in the quantities of energy which will be used as a result of these

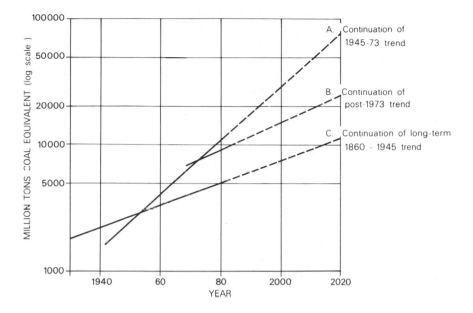

Figure 3.4 World energy use 1980–2020 with the extrapolation of different historic trends in energy use

changes are illustrated in figure 3.4. Thus, for example, a continuation of the abnormally high growth rate in energy use of the years between the late 1940s and the early 1970s would, by 2020, have required an annual supply of energy of almost 70,000 million tons of coal equivalent. With a continued growth rate of 2.2 per cent per annum from the 1973 base, the 2020 use of energy will be only a little over 20,000 million tons; and if the high 1945–73 rate of growth is compensated by a rate of growth in the meantime that by 2020 brings the curve back to its 1860–1945 trend, then energy use in 2020 will be of the order of 11,000 million tons coal equivalent. As the latter development would imply an average annual growth rate of less than 0.6 per cent from 1973 it would seem overly optimistic to reckon on such a 'good' result from increasing efficiency of energy use. This sort of increase would, moreover, imply a failure of the world-economy to expand at a high enough rate to improve living standards in the Third World, and would thus indicate a situation of increasing economic conflict between 'north' and 'south'. If this is to be avoided then enough energy will have to be used to sustain an adequate development of the world's economy. Assuming this can be achieved (this is a question beyond the scope of this chapter – it is considered elsewhere in the book (see chapter 1); here we are concerned with the energy demand – and supply – aspects of an assumed continued adequate growth in economic activities), then my best guess for global energy demand by 2000 is 12,000 to 14,000 million tons coal equivalent (compared with a use of 1983 of about 10,500 mtce); and for 2020, between 16,000 and 18,000 mtce.

These are formidable totals – compared with what has been achieved to date – but they are very much lower expectations than those which are still related to an extrapolation of the high rates of growth in energy use between 1945 and 1973 – in spite of the experience since then in the achievement of greater efficiencies in energy use, and the impact of much higher energy prices. The more modest expectation of the demand for energy over the next critical 35 years or so (after which the world seems likely to be in a position to turn increasingly to the utilization of renewable and benign energy sources – notably the direct use of the sun's energy) is highly significant in relation to the potential for increasing the supply of energy. In particular, it adds to the significance of the world's available fossil-fuel supplies, because it is these which offer the best prospects for a relatively safe and the lowest-possible cost supply for the world's energy using systems. This eliminates both the potential dangers from a too-rapid rate of development of relatively untested and still unproven nuclear energy (Lovins, 1977) and the need that would otherwise arise for the expenditure of too high a proportion of the world's wealth and its available scientific and technical expertise on a 'crash programme' of development of non-conventional energy sources (Pryde, 1983).

THE SUPPLY AND PRICE OF FOSSIL FUELS

Oil and Natural Gas

In the 1948–73 period of low and declining energy prices the geography of energy production gradually became dominated (outside the United States and the Soviet bloc) by a rapidly increasing flow of oil from the Middle East and a small number of countries elsewhere in the world – as shown in figure 3.5. The prolific and extremely low-cost-to-produce oil resources of this small group of countries undermined the economic production of most other sources of energy in most of the rest of the world. Indeed, the survival of energy production elsewhere, in the face of low-cost oil from the Middle East and a few other countries, where it was efficiently produced and from where it was equally efficiently transported by the seven major international oil corporations and a number of somewhat smaller, but still large, other oil companies (Odell, 1983; Sampson, 1975; Blair, 1976), depended largely on protectionist legislation. In spite of such protectionism many pre-existing energy-supply industries were closed down or were severely cut back; as in the case of the coal industries in Britain, and the exploitation of relatively cheaper but still somewhat higher cost energy resources was undermined. This was particularly important in the industrializing countries of the Third World where, generally, local energy sources had not hitherto been developed because of the lack of demand. Now they could not be developed because capital could not be attracted to enterprises unable to compete with low-cost imported oil (Odell and Vallenilla, 1978).

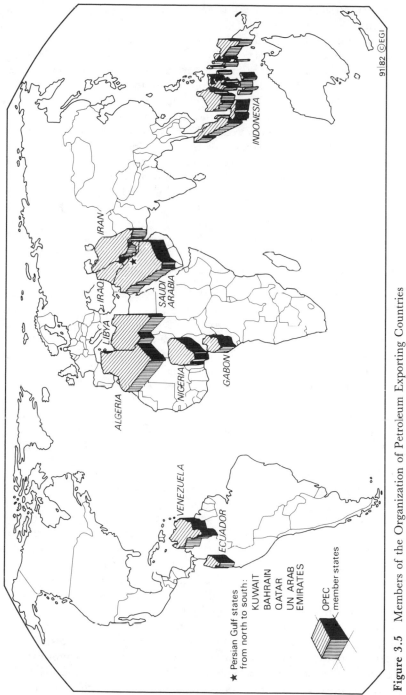

Figure 3.5 Members of the Organization of Petroleum Exporting Countries

Those countries, such as the United States, which tried to protect their own indigenous energy production (of coal, oil and natural gas) and so had to pass on the higher prices to the consumers of energy, found that they then suffered adverse economic consequences in the form of competition for markets for industrial goods from countries such as Japan and many countries in western Europe which enjoyed the cost advantages given to them by their use of low-cost oil imports from the Middle East. Thus in the early 1970s even the United States had to open up its markets to international oil (Blair, 1976), although by then prices of such oil were already beginning to rise (see figure 3.3) under the impact of the initial successes of the organization which the main oil exporting countries had formed (viz. the Organization of Petroleum Exporting Countries – OPEC), and its collusion at that time with the major international oil companies. The latter were then also seeking higher prices in order to enhance their profitability, and their ability to go on finding the increasing volumes of new oil required to satisfy a market which was expanding at about 7.5 per cent per annum (Anderson, 1984).

Table 3.1   Sources of energy used in the non-communist world (excluding the OPEC countries) in 1973 and 1983

	mtoe[a]	% of total	mtoe[a]	% of total
Total energy use	4,045	100	4,005	100
Imports of OPEC oil	1,480	36.5	780	19.5
Other energy imports[b]	100	2.5	225	5.6
Indigenous production	2,465	60.9	2,990	74.8
Oil	760	18.8	1,115	27.8
Natural gas	765	18.9	685	17.1
Coal	805	19.9	955	23.8
Other	135	3.3	245	6.1

[a]mtoe = million tons oil equivalent.
[b]Oil, natural gas and coal from the centrally planned economies.

By 1973, as shown in table 3.1, oil exports from the OPEC countries accounted for 36.5 per cent of total energy production in the non-communist world: oil, natural gas and coal, in the whole of the non-communist world outside the OPEC countries, were each only a little over half as important as OPEC oil: 25 years earlier (in 1948) oil exports from the countries that were later to become the members of OPEC had satisfied less than 10 per cent of the non-communist world's demand for energy.

The order-of-magnitude increase in oil prices since 1973 and the enhanced uncertainty over the willingness of OPEC countries to produce sufficient oil to meet the world's demand for energy produced a general reappraisal of the prospects for the indigenous production of energy in most countries. These were significantly heightened in both economic and political terms and, as a result, there has already been a marked fall in the contribution of OPEC oil to world energy supplies. This can be seen in table 3.1 in the contrast between the 1973 and the 1983 division of the non-communist world energy market between oil imported from the OPEC countries on the one hand and, on the other hand, other sources of energy supplies.

Table 3.1 shows how dramatically OPEC's contribution to the non-communist world's energy supply has fallen compared with total energy production elsewhere in the non-communist world and, on a smaller scale, with imports from the centrally planned economies. In particular, oil production in the western world excluding OPEC now comfortably exceeds OPEC's oil exports, whereas in 1973 the latter were almost twice as important as the former. OPEC's oil exports in 1983 were, moreover, little more than gas production in the western world and well below the contribution from indigenous coal.

In other words a geographically much more diffuse pattern of world energy production has been developing rapidly under the post-1973 conditions: this diffusion is set to continue as long as the price of OPEC oil remains so far above the cost of producing alternatives – and as long as OPEC oil is perceived to be unreliable as a source of supply. This is a strong perception, given not only the continuing interruptions from time to time in the flow of oil from OPEC countries (for example, as a result of the Iran–Iraq war), but also the policy of OPEC deliberately to restrain supplies through the quota system which it first established in 1983 as a means of holding up prices (Odell, 1983).

Oil and/or natural gas is already being produced in significant quantities in 75 countries – compared with under 60 a decade ago – and the number will continue to increase as exploration becomes more widespread and more successful. Most countries are, indeed, aiming for self-sufficiency – or better – in terms of oil and gas. This includes the countries of the industrialized world, where a number, such as Norway, Britain, the Netherlands, Denmark and Australia, have already been successful and will continue to build up their production potential. There are also good prospects geologically in many Third World countries, but these are often thwarted by financial and other problems in their exploration and exploitation efforts so that the process of increasing production in most of these countries will be gradual rather than spectacular (United Nations, 1982). Figures 3.6 and 3.7 show how much work remains to be done in trying to find and to develop the oil and gas resources of Latin America, Africa and Asia (World Bank, 1983; Odell and Rosing, 1983).

Thus, over the rest of the century – and into the first quarter of the twenty-first century – the importance that the major oil-exporting countries hitherto managed to achieve in terms of their dominance of the oil-supply pattern seems likely to continue to diminish. Moreover, in spite of their very considerable resources, their natural gas production will be constrained by the difficulties of finding markets in the rest of the world where indigenous production will generally be sufficient to meet expanding needs and will certainly be the preferred source of supply.

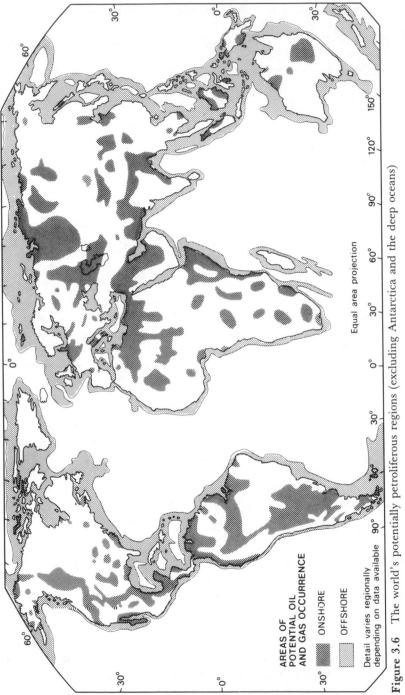

Figure 3.6   The world's potentially petroliferous regions (excluding Antarctica and the deep oceans)

AREAS OF
POTENTIAL OIL
AND GAS OCCURRENCE

ONSHORE

OFFSHORE

Detail varies regionally
depending on data available

Equal area projection

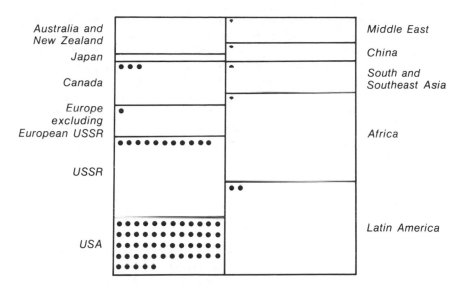

Figure 3.7   The regional distribution of potentially petroliferous areas
shown in proportion to the world total

Within each region the number of exploration and development wells which have been drilled
is shown – each full circle represents 50,000 wells drilled by the end of 1980. Segments of circles are
included only for regions in which the total number of drilled wells to 1980 is less than 50,000.
Relative to the US, all other parts of the world, but especially the regions of the Third World,
are very little drilled for their oil.

Source: Grossling, 1976, p. 83 (updated by author)

There will, however, be a penalty involved in this changing global pattern
of world oil and gas production – with a greater emphasis on the development
of reserves within consuming countries, and a reduced emphasis on the
exploitation of oil and gas from areas with relatively little demand for energy,
so that export markets are essential. Success in achieving exports was, as shown
above, a function of the low-cost nature of producing oil in these areas. In so
far as much of this low-cost production is being replaced by higher-cost energy
production from other parts of the world, the inevitable consequence will be
a reduction in the overall potential for economic growth in the western world's
economic system – so ensuring that fewer of the world's people achieve an
adequate standard of living. This will be the penalty for failing to produce and
use the world's lowest-cost energy resources.

   On the other hand, the much reduced rate of growth in demand for oil and
gas resulting from higher prices, and the enhanced supply potential which is
created by the diffusion of exploration and production activities, will together
have the effect of postponing for several decades the occurrence of peak volumes

of oil and gas output. Conventional oil and gas will be available in the quantities demanded until well into the second quarter of the twenty-first century and, thereafter, oil from non-conventional habitats (such as tar-sands and oil shales as well as heavy oil from relatively shallow horizons) will be developed and thus ensure the continued slow expansion of the oil industry until some time in the second half of the twenty-first century (Odell and Rosing, 1983). Similarly – and even more emphatically – with natural gas: the expansion of conventional supplies from an increasing number of locations will enable this industry to increase its contribution to world energy needs over many decades into the future – as has, for example, happened in western Europe over the last 20 years and which is now beginning to take place in many countries of Latin America, south and south-east Asia, and even in parts of Africa (Halbouty, 1983). Moreover, the prospects for additional gas from non-conventional habitats are even brighter than are those for oil. For example, deep gas dissolved in a saline solution offers a vast potential on which work is already under way in the United States (Hodgson, 1978); deep ocean and Arctic gas hydrates offer a longer-term prospect; and beyond these is the possibility of a new infinite source of natural gas arising from the hypothesis of an abiogenic origin for most of the world's methane (Gold and Soter, 1980). Based on resources which are already known and exploitable, plus a 50-year period during which one or other of the sources of non-conventional gas can be proven and commercialized, natural gas could well provide a steadily increasing proportion of the world's slowly increasing needs throughout the twenty-first century. The attractiveness of the prospects for natural gas are, indeed, more a function of the geography of resources' development, relative to the geography of demand, than of the global aggregate of the resources available or potentially available. The internationalization at best, or at least the regionalization, of the natural gas industry is required for an effective use of the world's resources of this largely non-polluting source of energy: and this, of course, is an essentially geopolitical question.

Coal

Meanwhile, high oil prices have stimulated the exploitation of the world's low-cost coal reserves so that, as shown in table 3.1, production of coal in the non-communist world increased by about 20 per cent between 1973 and 1983. Coal's share of total energy use over the decade grew from under 20 per cent to almost 24 per cent. In the centrally planned economies over the same period coal production rose by a somewhat higher percentage – about 26.5 per cent – and by 1983 these countries used rather more coal than in all the rest of the world (about 1,700 million tons compared with 1,500 million tons). In the aftermath of the oil-price increases – and the fears at that time of the inadequacy of oil reserves – there was a great deal of enthusiasm and optimism over the prospects for developing the world's production and use of coal (WOCOL Report, 1980). However, rapid expansion has, to date, proved to be neither possible nor necessary (because of the dramatic decline in the rate of increase in energy use), so that the net global expansion of the coal industry has been relatively modest.

Nevertheless, it should be noted that the net increase emerges out of a more rapid growth in some areas which has, in part, been offset by continuing stagnation or decline in the traditional deep-mined coal industries of western Europe, Japan and a few other countries. Though there are plenty of remaining coal reserves in countries such as Britain, West Germany, Belgium and France, their exploitation has proved to be much too costly, largely because of the high price of the main component in the overall production costs: labour costs account for between 50 and 60 per cent of the total costs of traditional deep-mined coal. The prospects for any significant change in this respect are poor, particularly in circumstances in which much lower-cost coal can be produced elsewhere, both from deep-mines in countries with lower wage costs (such as South Africa, India, Taiwan and Poland), and from open-cast coal production in countries with vast reserves of good-quality coal at or near the surface. This is possible in, for example, western Canada, the US mid-west and Australia where major developments have already taken place or are planned (International Energy Agency, 1984). In addition, however, large new surface-mines are under development or planned in a number of other countries such as Colombia, Botswana and Indonesia.

These, and other developments elsewhere in the Third World (as well as in China), will over the next 20 years provide much of the increasing supply of coal for international trade. This is currently dominated by Australia, the US and South Africa, but the new suppliers will gradually add to the complexity of such trade. The importance of internationally traded coal in total world energy supplies is likely slowly to increase – in part at the expense of traditional deep-mined production from traditional areas, but in greater part as a result of the increasing use of coal, particularly for power generation as a lower-cost alternative to both the continued use of oil and the expansion of capital-intensive nuclear power. In supply/demand terms there is no reason why the cost of coal in real terms should increase above its present levels for at least the rest of the century so that, given its current price advantage over oil (and over natural gas where, as in western Europe, its price is related to that of oil), it should be able to find expanding markets to serve, providing that the air-pollution problems associated with its use can be controlled and reduced (James, 1982).

ALTERNATIVE ENERGY SOURCES

The high oil/energy prices and the supply problems from time to time arising from political – military events since 1973, together with the increasing concern for environmental problems caused by the use of fossil fuels (European Environment Bureau, 1981), have created enthusiastic lobbies and pressures for the rapid expansion of benign energy systems based on solar, wind, water, waste and biomass energy potential (Foley, 1976). To date, however, there has only been a modest official response to this enthusiasm in most parts of the world. This is largely a result of the difficulties which are involved in incorporating such dispersed energy-producing systems into the highly centralized and bureaucratic energy systems which were developed in most parts of the world in the period before 1973 and which most governments have assumed, for purposes of energy-policy planning, must be the basis for organizing future energy supplies. In addition, of course, the technology of producing benign energy has remained underdeveloped as there was little motivation for governments or private firms to invest in the necessary research at a time when fossil fuels (plus nuclear power) were thought to be more than sufficient to sustain future energy needs. So there are formidable problems to overcome before the production of benign energy sources can be much increased. The relative contribution of such sources of energy to total world energy needs thus remains small (even including the long-developed hydro-electricity component) and it seems unlikely to grow very much at all until after the turn of the century. Even these longer-term prospects, moreover, still depend on the investment of increased amounts of research and development funds. This is a development which seems likely to depend more on the private sector in respect of improving prospects for commercial solar power (through so-called solar ponds and as a result of developments in photo-voltaics) than on governments, most of which have decided to concentrate their investment in the alternative to fossil fuels in the nuclear power industry (Pryde, 1983).

Nuclear power, indeed, has secured the support of most governments – and of all intergovernmental energy organizations – as the best means of reducing dependence on fossil fuels in general, and on oil in particular. This expansion has thus been generously, even extravagantly, funded – in part, at least, because it is linked to the development of the major powers' military interests and their military–industrial establishments. Nevertheless, nuclear power remains less than half as important as hydro-electricity in global terms and it still contributes less than 0.25 per cent to the world's total use of energy. (This is measured, as by the United Nations in its Energy Statistics, in terms of the heat value of the electricity produced by nuclear power. The pro-nuclear governments and intergovernmental agencies measure nuclear power's contribution, on the other hand, in terms of the amount of fossil fuels which would have been required to produce an equal amount of electricity: this has the effect of more than doubling the apparent importance of nuclear power.) Officialdom generally remains convinced of nuclear powers' potential (with Sweden and Denmark as notable exceptions), but cost escalation in building nuclear power stations, public concern for safety (whether justified or not is irrelevant), and the lack of fast enough growth in base-load electricity demand to justify large expansions of nuclear generating capacity (which has to be used in base-load configuration to be economic) have severely restricted its rate of growth in most of the non-communist world, and have even more severely undermined its prospects for rapid development. So it, too, seems destined to make only a very limited

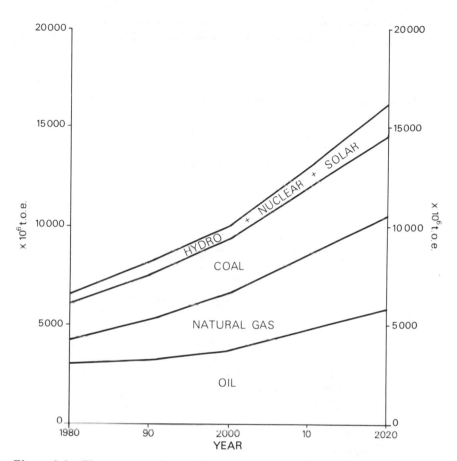

Figure 3.8   The prospects for supplies of the main sources of world energy to 2020

additional contribution to world energy supplies over the rest of the century –
and beyond.

Figures 3.8 and 3.9 summarize the outlook for world energy developments
(except for so-called non-commercial energy which is dealt with in the final
section of this chapter) over the period of the next 35 years or so to 2020. Growth
in use will be modest as the historic trend in the evolution of energy use reasserts
itself after the short abnormal period of high growth between 1948 and 1973.
The contribution of fossil fuels will remain dominant in the world energy picture
though (as shown) oil, which enhanced its position very markedly in the 25
years prior to 1973, will lose part of its share of the total market to natural
gas and to coal. Alternative energy sources, taken together, seem unlikely to
be very much more important by 2020 (relative to the increased amount of
energy used) than they are at the present time. Indeed, in so far as the
maintenance of the around 8 per cent contribution of alternative energy sources

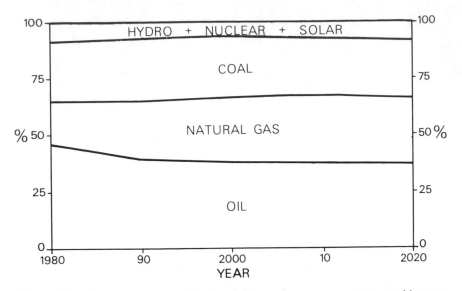

Figure 3.9   The percentage contributions of the main energy sources to world energy use, 1980–2020

to total energy used depends on the expansion of nuclear power, then this share is at risk. This is because an accident of serious dimensions to a nuclear power station anywhere in the non-communist world will very likely lead to the closure of similar nuclear power stations everywhere, and so dramatically reduce the total contribution of alternative energy to the world total for at least a decade.

THE POOR WORLD'S ENERGY PROBLEM

One important element in the world's energy situation and prospects has so far been excluded from the framework of the analysis as presented in this chapter. Nevertheless, it is of central importance for very large parts of the world with even larger populations, viz. the supply and use of locally available energy in societies which remain largely or mainly subsistence in their economic and social organization.

The per-capita energy use in such societies is small (it is measured in *kilograms* of oil equivalent rather than in *tons* of oil equivalent, as in the most industrialized countries) and it depends essentially on the locally available supply of combustible materials for cooking and lighting (and, sometimes, heating) needs. In total, however, this form of world energy use is still large because of the numbers of people involved. It is estimated to account for about 20 per cent of total world energy supply overall, but in some parts of the Third World (most notably in the poorest countries of Africa and Asia) its contribution reaches over 90 per cent of the total energy consumed by the populations (Smil and Knowland, 1980). In many such regions the local scarcity of firewood is becoming a pressing problem – a problem which is related to the increasing distances which have to be covered, and hence to the increasing time and effort required, to collect the volume of wood required for basic survival purposes. A solution to this basic development problem requires the implementation of effective 'energy-farming' practices whereby wood becomes an annual crop), and new, albeit simple and low-cost, technological developments for enhancing efficiencies in the utilization of wood, etc. This is a world energy problem about which little is known (even though it has its parallels in seventeenth and eighteenth century Europe when there was a similar wood-scarcity problem), and about which even less is being done; compared, that is, with the attention that is being given to the problems of oil and the other energy sources required for intensive use – often for non-essential purposes – in the developed world, both capitalist and communist, and in the modern sectors of the economies of the developing countries.

References

Adelman, M. A. 1972: *The World Petroleum Market*. Baltimore: The Johns Hopkins University Press.

Anderson, J. 1984; *Oil: The Real Story behind the Energy Crisis*. London: Sidgwick & Jackson.

Blair, J. M. 1976: *The Control of Oil*. London: Macmillan.

Cook, E. 1976: *Man, Energy and Society*. San Francisco: Freeman.

Darmstadter, J., Dunkerley, J. and Alterman, J. 1977: *How Industrial Societies Use Energy*. Baltimore: The Johns Hopkins University Press.

Darmstadter, J., Landsberg, H. H., Morton, H. C., and Lodu, M. 1983: *Energy Today and Tomorrow: Living with Uncertainty*. Englewood Cliffs: Prentice-Hall.

Dienes, L. and Shabad, T. 1979: *The Soviet Energy System*. Washington: Winston.

Dunkerley, J. 1981: *Energy Strategies for Developing Nations*. Baltimore: The Johns Hopkins University Press.

European Environment Bureau 1981: *The Milano Declaration on Energy, Economy and Society*. Brussels.

Foley, G. 1976: *The Energy Question*. Harmondsworth: Penguin.

Fritsch, B. 1982: *The Energy Demand of Industrialized and Developing Countries until 1990*. Zurich: Institute of Technology.

Gold, T. and Soter, S. 1980: The deep earth gas hypothesis. *Scientific American*, June 1980, 154–61.

Grossling, B. 1976: *Window on Oil: a Survey of World Petroleum Sources*. London, Financial Times.

Halbouty, M. T. 1983: Reserves of natural gas outside the communist block countries. *11th World Petroleum Congress*, London. Winchester: Wiley.

Hodgson, B. 1978: Natural gas: the search goes on. *National Geographic*, November 1978, 132–51.

Hoffman, T. and Johnson, B. 1981: *The World Energy Triangle*. Cambridge, Mass.: Ballinger.

International Energy Agency 1982: *The World Energy Outlook to 2020*. Paris: OECD.

International Energy Agency 1984: *Coal Prospects and Policies in I.E.A. Countries*. Paris: OECD.

James, P. 1982: *The Future of Coal*. London: Macmillan.

Leach, G. et al. 1979: *A Low Energy Strategy for the United Kingdom*. London: IIED.

Lenin, V. I. 1966: Report of the work of the Council of People's Commissars and the Eighth All-Russia Congress of Soviets – December 22 1920, *Collected Works of V. I. Lenin, 31, April–December 1920*, Moscow: Progress Publishers.

Lovins, A. B. 1977: *Soft Energy Paths*. Harmondsworth: Penguin.

Manners, G., 1971: *The Geography of Energy*. London: Hutchinson.

Marchetti, C. and Nakicenovic, N. 1979: *The Dynamics of Energy Systems*. Laxenburg: IIASA.

Odell, P. R. 1975: *The Western European Energy Economy, Challenges and Opportunities*. London: Athlone Press.

Odell, P. R. 1983: *Oil and World Power*, 7th edn Harmondsworth: Penguin.

Odell, P. R. 1984: Energy issues. In A. M. Kirby and J. R. Short (eds), *The Human Geography of Contemporary Britain*, Harmondsworth: Penguin.

Odell, P. R. and Rosing, K. E. 1983: *The Future of Oil; World Resources and Use*, 2nd edn London: Kogan Page.

Odell, P. R. and Vallenilla, L. 1978: *The Pressures of Oil: A Strategy for Economic Revival*. London: Harper & Row.

Park, D. 1979: *Oil and Gas in Comecon Countries*. London: Kogan Page.

Pryde, P. R. 1983: *Non-Conventional Energy Resources*. New York: Wiley.

Sampson, A. 1975: *The Seven Sisters: the Great Oil Companies and the World They Made*. London: Hodder & Stoughton.

Schurr, S. and Netschert, B. 1977: *Energy in the American Economy, 1850–1975*. Baltimore: The Johns Hopkins University Press.

Smil, V. and Knowland, W. E. 1980: *Energy in the Developing World: The Real Energy Crisis*. New York: Oxford University Press.

United Nations 1982: *Petroleum Exploration Strategies in Developing Countries*. London: Graham & Trotman.

WOCOL Report 1980: *Coal, Bridge to the Future*. Cambridge, Mass.: Ballinger.

World Bank 1983: *The Energy Transition in Developing Countries*. Washington D. C.

4

Food Production and Distribution – and Hunger

P. N. BRADLEY

INTRODUCTION: THE MAGNITUDE OF THE FOOD CRISIS

In 1961, Africa's food sufficiency ratio stood at 98 per cent. By 1971 it had declined to 89 per cent, and by 1978 it had fallen as low as 78 per cent. The corollary was that, between 1970 and 1980, food imports for the continent showed an annual increase of 8.4 per cent. Cereal imports for human consumption cost $5 billion per annum. Excluding South Africa, only 7 of the remaining 47 states increased per-capita food production during that period, and these states represented only 5 per cent of the continent's total population (again excluding South Africa). Throughout this period, various parts of the continent experienced a succession of disasters: the sahelian drought of the early 1970s, the catastrophe in the Horn which continues to the present day, and the recent droughts of the south and east of the continent. Television news coverage and documentaries brought these crises into the living rooms of the developed world in 1984, which focused on the famine in parts of Ethopia and adjacent countries. A combination of factors meant that millions were starving, and many more were convinced that the world could not feed itself.

While these tragedies were unfolding, the world production of major cereals was constantly increasing (see figure 4.1). According to FAO (Food and Agriculture Organization) annual reports, world production levels for wheat, maize and rice increased from 1970 to 1980 by 40, 50 and 30 per cent respectively. At the global scale, then, there would seem to be an adequate level of food production, with (according to a wide range of opinion) a considerable reserve capacity for further expansion (at least in the USA, Canada, the EEC and Australia). The promising global situation does not seem to have resulted in improved nutrition levels for the poor families of the Third World. Without

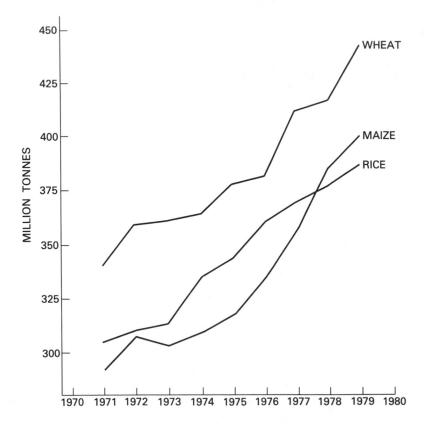

Figure 4.1   World production of major cereals, 1970–80 (three-year moving means)

doubt the worst-affected continent has been Africa. At the aggregate level it has performed consistently worse than either South America or Asia (see figure 4.2), and at the level of individual states, or even sections of the population within states, food supply has become an increasingly acute problem. Table 4.1 indicates the extent to which this food crisis is affecting a selection of African states.

Two issues emerge from these statistics. The first is that, at a global level, the production of food has increased considerably, and at a greater rate than the corresponding growth in population (see figure 4.1). The second is that for individual continents and states, the global improvement may not be reflected at this smaller scale. In fact for Africa the situation is particularly grim, for it has failed to keep its food production in line with an increasing demand (see figure 4.2). There is a third issue, to which table 4.2 draws attention, that is concerned with the problem of distribution. In this sense distribution is related to poverty. Put crudely, those who are poor cannot buy what food there is on the market. As a consequence, the absolute level of supply has little bearing on their nutrition.

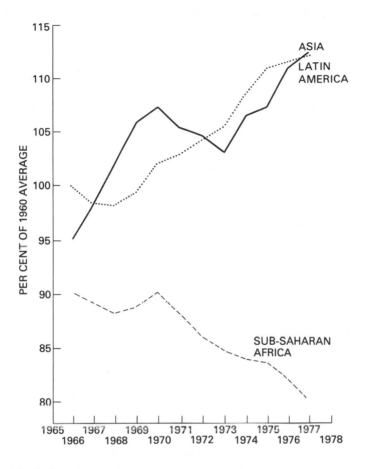

Figure 4.2   Index of per-capita food production for sub-Saharan Africa, Asia and Latin America, 1965–78 (three-year moving means based on 1960 index of 100)

As subsistence economies give way to those founded on commerce, the pattern of income distribution becomes a critical factor in the provision of food.

Additional data could be presented to reveal the growing dimensions of the problem. Such data would merely reinforce the impression that global hunger seems to be increasing inexorably, with the result that every year we see more and more countries of the Third World, with ever-increasing urgency, appealing to the First World relief agencies for help. As I have observed, the problem is particularly acute in Africa, for it is there that we see both insufficient aggregate production (see figure 4.2) and inequity in distribution. The subsequent discussion focuses principally on Africa, but the arguments should not be seen as unique to that continent. In fact the forces that have generated Africa's current crisis operate throughout the periphery. I merely identify their

Table 4.1   Selected indices of the food crisis as it affects Zambia, Mali, Nigeria and Tanzania (%)

	Zambia	Mali	Nigeria	Tanzania
Increase in volume of wheat imports 1971–81	260	508	495	1,004
Increase in value of wheat imports 1971–81	790	2,133	2,130	4,300
Increase in consumer food-price index 1968–78	NA[a]	65	436	163
Change in per-capita food production index 1969/71 to 1977/9	– 1	– 12	– 13	– 6
Population with calorie intake below 1.2 basic metabolic rate	34	49	NA[a]	35

[a]Data not available.

Sources: Food and Agriculture Organization, 1981; International Labour Organization, 1978; World Bank, 1981; United Nations, 1980

Table 4.2   Pattern of income distribution (share of total household income) in a selection of states from Africa, Latin America and Asia (%)

	Accruing to poorest 20% of population	Accruing to richest 20% of population
India (1975/6)	7.0	49.4
Indonesia (1976)	6.6	49.4
Phillipines (1970/1)	5.2	54.0
Malaysia (1970)	3.3	56.6
Malawi (1967/8)	10.4	50.6
Tanzania (1969)	5.8	50.4
Peru (1972)	1.9	61.0
Mexico (1977)	2.9	57.7
Brazil (1972)	2.0	66.6
Argentina (1970)	4.4	50.3

Source: World Bank, 1981

particular expression in Africa as illustrative of the fundamental processes that govern the global food situation.

Before examining some of these processes, I must first devote a little more attention to some of the questions posed by the figures and tables so far presented, for a mythology has developed around such statistical presentations. Such myths need to be dispelled if the underlying causes of world hunger are to be revealed. As they are currently presented, the 'liberal' explanations of the global food crisis do little more than rephrase the questions that they seek to answer. Far from offering a genuine explanation, they draw yet more attention away from the cause towards the symptoms. It is not the intention here to examine these explanations in depth, for they have been adequately considered elsewhere (George, 1976; Lappe and Collins, 1980). Instead the brief review serves to indicate their general inadequacy, at the same time leading on to the discussion of more fundamental issues.

Overpopulation

A popular explanation for the food crisis is overpopulation, but there is in fact no shortage in the supply of food at the global level, even allowing for overconsumption in the core. There are not too many people in the world. For certain regions, and in certain states, it has been argued that the principal cause of the general insufficiency of food is overpopulation, coupled with excessively high population growth rates. Efforts to reduce such growth rates (through birth-control policies, education and so on) are urged on less developed countries by international agencies and core states, but the truth is that for much of the Third World population policies (meaning birth control) are both irrelevant and misguided. They are irrelevant because with one or two exceptions (perhaps Bangladesh, Java, Egypt and parts of India) the Third World is not 'overpopulated': 'The most obvious and final example is, of course, China which experienced famine somewhere nearly every year when it was a country of 500,000,000 people. Now it furnishes over 2,300 calories a day to a population of 800,000,000' (George, 1976, p. 59). They are misguided because such policies are addressed to the problem of food consumption and not food production. We have seen that at the global level production is adequate, but we have also noted that for certain regions and states of the Third World, production is failing to increase sufficiently, if not actually declining. Reducing population (in any event an extremely long-term objective) will do nothing to arrest the decline in food production in Africa. Certainly its current popularity as the universal panacea is totally ill-founded. However, the purpose here is not to discuss the overpopulation debate at length; for a full critique readers are referred to George (1976) and others.

Maldistribution

A second myth, that of the poor allocation and transportation of available food, and consequent undernourishment in those areas outside existing distribution patterns, is also inadequate as an explanation. We can divide distributional problems into two categories. The first is easily dealt with. It concerns the physical transfer of food from one area or region to another: the transport infrastructure. While there is little doubt that, at a technical level, the transport systems of the Third World lack the speed and efficiency of those in the core, there is nevertheless a wide range of goods that circulate through peripheral states. Even states such as Niger, frequently diagnosed as too remote from the coast to allow development, somehow manages to export uranium from deep within the Sahara desert. It seems that raw materials inevitably find a route out, while consumer imports are able to penetrate to the most isolated regions. Torch batteries, matches and carbonated drinks can be found in even the smallest shops in the hinterland. It is false therefore to claim that food cannot circulate in the same fashion. Where we see the most sweeping assertions of transport failure is in the context of emergency relief, in which massive quantities of food need to be transported at great speed. Obviously such extreme demands cannot be accommodated, but it would be wrong to argue that unusual circumstances of this nature demonstrate a more general failure. The fact remains that at a more continuous and steady level, transport networks are able to cope with demand. For average conditions, then, we can argue that the lack of modern transport technology is not a significant impediment to the transfer of commodities, still less an acceptable explanation of the 'food distribution problem'.

There is, however, a second aspect to the distribution problem, that of the inequitable allocation of food. It is argued that with more egalitarian state policies, the existing and adequate food supplies would reach the needy and avert the crisis. I shall address this issue in more detail below. Here it is sufficient to state that inequitable allocation of the results of production is a necessary, functional component of the present world economic system. It cannot be wished, or even programmed, away. Without it the world economy would be totally transformed.

Other Explanations

Even the briefest glance at the literature on the subject would yield many other putative explanations: desertification and disasters, underinvestment and a lack of modernization, peasant conservatism, administrative inadequacy, etc. The point to be made about them all is that, almost without exception, they fail to get to the root of the problem. Their focus is the visible 'face' of the food crisis, not the cause. Thus when the wretched overcrowding and evident malnutrition in the slums of Calcutta or São Paulo claims public attention, the quick answers are that there are too many people for too little food, that food is not getting to those who need it most, that a 'western-style' agricultural modernization programme is needed, and so on. But these are not explanations, and such pronouncements fail to get to grips with the problem. Assuming that gifts of food aid are at best a short-term palliative, there are two ways by which people can obtain food. They can either grow it or buy it. We shall see below that for the people of the Third World, the workings of the world-economy make it increasingly difficult to pursue the former course, while dispossessing them of the means to follow the latter.

THE FAILURE OF FOOD PRODUCTION

To see Third World farming as an undeveloped and 'primitive' version of the modern industrial agriculture of the core (and therefore capable of being 'upgraded' to match the productivity of its mentor – the modernization argument) is to compound an essential dichotomy.

Discussions of global agriculture inevitably draw attention to the grain-producing regions of the temperate latitudes, as indeed we shall do later. The production of wheat, barley, maize and other bulk grains in the USA, Canada and the EEC has for its first and fundamental rationale that it is a commodity to be sold on the open market. The agribusinesses of the core operate just as if they were producing industrial consumer goods. Indeed, if we forget for a moment that people cannot eat light bulbs, there is no real difference in motivation, and the commercial decisions that go with it, between an electrical-components company and a large-scale farm enterprise. The products of both are for exchange, and the profit that goes with it, rather than for immediate and essential use. In the context of the North American wheat belt, the product has value above all else because it can be sold, or exchanged, on the market, and not at all because it can be eaten. The fact that it will eventually be consumed as food plays no part in the commercial decisions governing its production.

A different situation confronts the peasant smallholder of the periphery. While the concept of total subsistence agriculture is no longer tenable in the modern world-economy, there is nevertheless a more immediate hunger for food that pervades the agricultural economies of the periphery. Hyden (1980) in particular argues that a 'peasant' mode of production still pertains, at least in Africa, and that a central feature is food production for internal consumption. Whether or not his argument is acceptable in its entirety, there is nevertheless a distinction to be drawn between capital-intensive and market-orientated systems in the core and labour-intensive agriculture in the periphery, with its emphasis on food production. Thus in the periphery agriculture is characterized by a retention of traditional values: undercapitalized, with low output, and geared towards self-sufficiency. In the core it is business: modern, dynamic, capital-intensive and staggeringly productive. On the one hand we see a vestige of the past, the peasant mode of production. On the other the modern replacement, market-orientated and profit-based: a capitalist mode of production.

We should note that while in appearance and motivation the two are distinctly different, they nevertheless have certain functional qualities in common. When viewing the two as farming systems there is a tendency to treat agriculture as a singular and distinctive enterprise, somehow different in intent and ethics from other sectors of activity. It is none of these. For those in the periphery it is the means of existence, for those in the core it is another form of business, no different in motivation from any other industrial enterprise. In both cases agriculture takes place in a wider sphere of economic activity, and cannot be considered in isolation. This is increasingly true for the less advanced systems of the periphery, just as it is for the core. In the 1950s writers spoke of a dual economy (Boeke, 1953): a modernized urban–industrial sector, counterposed to a functionally isolated, archaic rural agriculture. Such a view can no longer be sustained. Just as in the core, so too in the periphery; the independence of the two systems is illusory. A functional articulation is seen to exist. Frank (1969) speaks of a cascade of relations, in which surplus is extracted from the peasantry (in the form of products, cash or direct labour power) through a sequence of intermediaries, to the urban centres. A chain of linkages, of which the most obvious is the dramatic migration of rural workers to the shanty towns, ensures a close integration between the two erstwhile elements of the dual economy.

We may go further. The articulation of the economic activities of a society does not stop at national frontiers. The concept of a national economy, certainly the notion of its independence, is hard to justify in the context of the world-economy. The periphery is a necessary component of a capitalist world system, and the sovereignty of individual nations is subordinate to the exigencies of this global system. There is no denial of the fact that the concrete circumstances, and individual histories of these peripheral states gives them specific social formations, but there is also no doubt that, to a greater or lesser extent, they are all controlled by the politico-economic determinants of the core. The terms of trade, the wages of labour, the use of the dollar as a global currency standard, the monopolistic control of transnational companies, all bear witness to this integration. All of these global processes limit the freedom of individual states to pursue their own internal policies. Simply because rural societies are often physically remote from the centres of economic and political power, there is no reason to suppose that they are somehow structurally removed from these global influences. There is, in fact, no such thing as a 'dual economy'. The rural sector is functionally bound to its urban overlord, which in turn is locked into a global process emanating from the core. We see then that Third World farmers are participants in the continuing evolution of this capitalist world-economy, and to that extent the visible differences between modern agribusiness and traditional farming cloak a more fundamental unity. We must therefore search for an explanation of the global food crisis within this context.

THE TWO POLES: AGRIBUSINESS IN THE CORE,
PEASANT SMALLHOLDING IN THE PERIPHERY

I will argue that the source of the global food crisis lies in the workings of the capitalist world-economy. In pursuing this argument I will focus on the two ends of the spectrum. The 'top', to which I have already drawn attention, is exemplified in the grain belt of the temperate latitudes – specifically the North American agrisystem – as representative of the most advanced situation in the core. The 'bottom' is peasant agriculture in the periphery, with its varied historical development, and its diverse present circumstances. While social relations within individual states must condition the impact of world forces, with the result that each state is in some way different from the others, nevertheless I can illustrate general conditions with a few, selected examples. Just as North America does not encapsulate all facets of industrial agriculture in the core, but nevertheless portrays the essential process, so Kenya provides us with a vivid illustration of the manner in which food production is being undermined in the periphery.

Modern Agriculture in the Core

A recurrent theme of discussions dealing with the global food crisis is, of course, the 'bread-basket' of the core: the grain belt of North America. Much is made of the role of US wheat production in feeding the world's hungry, and more particularly in exerting a level of control over the global food market. Robbins and Ansari (1976), George (1976, 1979), and Lappe and Collins (1980) all point to the fact that wheat production in the USA, and now in the EEC, is determined by both profit-motivated decisions and domestic and foreign-policy political considerations. As we have observed, in the core agribusiness is, as the term suggests, business. More so than by climatic or other environmental variables, fluctuations in production are determined by US price-support policy, which is predisposed to ensure a high world market price.

Thus in 1972, the crisis year of the sahelian drought in which starvation was widespread, the US government paid farmers $3 billion to take 50 million hectares out of production (Robbins and Ansari, 1976). The intent was quite clear. In order to remedy the 'glut' of previous years, which saw the grain reserve rise to 49 million tons by 1972 with a commensurate fall in the world price, the US government determined to reduce production and create an effective shortage, and thus raise again the world price. In this case the price of wheat (US No. 2 Fob Gulf) on the world market increased by 236 per cent between 1971 and 1974. Corresponding figures for rice (Thai White Fob Bankok), maize (Yellow No. 2 Fob Gulf) and soya bean (US Cif Rotterdam) were 347, 117 and 464 per cent respectively (data from Robbins and Ansari, 1976). It has been estimated that the lost production through this policy would have averted the sahelian crisis with plenty to spare. The deliberately induced shortage was exacerbated by commercial sales to the Soviet Union; not, it seems, through deliberate government action, but via the combined efforts of a number of individual Russian buyers and the sales pitch of the controlling corporations in the USA. The wheat that could not be made available to the starving sahelians, instead went to feed cattle so that the supply of meat to the urban centres in the Soviet Union could be increased.

It is worth drawing attention to several key issues in this now infamous episode, for they are constantly recurring elements in this discussion. Firstly we can observe the extent to which agricultural production and distribution is determined (through control of marketing, and transportation) by a small number of giant corporations (in this instance the 'big six': Cargill, Continental, Bunge, Archer-Daniels-Midland, Peavey and Cook handle 90 per cent of all the grain shipped in the world – Hightower, 1975). Monopolistic tendencies exist in agriculture just as they do in industry, again indicating their essential synonymy. Secondly, the level of production was determined by government policy. In essence it was a clear attempt to buy votes, through ensuring a pricing structure designed to satisfy mid-west farmers. The shortage had little if anything to do with environmental forces, or with the so-called workings of 'the free market economy'. Thirdly, and in spite of an apparent shortage, adequate supplies were made available to meet an economic rather than physical demand, in this case Russian feedstocks. Fourthly, the destination of this supply remained in the core, which by global standards is already more than adequately nourished. Moreover this extra supply was destined for luxury meat (an acknowledged inefficiency in the utilization of grain-based protein and energy). The wider context is that, in part if not *in toto*, these observations might equally apply to dairy, sugar and meat production in the EEC throughout the 1970s and 1980s, or sugar, tea, coffee in tropical Africa, or beef production in Amazonia. In all these cases the driving force is the capitalist nature of the world-economy. The provision of food for the hungry has little to do with such global processes.

Peasant Agriculture in the Periphery

As an initial premise, we can conceive of Third World farming as being essentially concerned with small-scale, labour-intensive food production. By extension it would appear that the commodification of agricultural production in the Third World has yet to reach the level and extent evident in the core. In fact the position is one in which traditional practices, derived from a peasant mode of production, are adhered to in the face of a rapid integration into a capitalist economic system. So far the stage has not been quite reached where food crops are indistinguishable from cash crops. Among the former we may include maize, sorghum, millet, rice (to a certain extent) and tubers. In the latter are cotton, groundnuts, coffee, tea, tobacco, vegetable oils and so on. Of course such a division is to a certain extent arbitrary, because it focuses on the product rather than the production process. Groundnuts, for example, are both commercial crops and food crops, as is rice. Furthermore, traditional foods such as maize are becoming increasingly commercialized (which of course they have been for a long time in the core). The difference is less in the nature of the crop itself, and more in the purpose and manner of its cultivation. What has been thought of as a difference between food and cash crops only holds so long as the production systems are different. Prior to the 1950s, at least in

East Africa, commercial crops were grown either on colonial estates or in plantations. In other parts of the continent, peasant production of cash crops (for example groundnuts in West Africa) had begun to emerge, but, within limits, peasant-based production systems were left more or less intact. Since the war, however, these very same peasants have been increasingly drawn into the market as capital has realized the potential of smallholder production. As a consequence we now witness the commercialization of even food crops such as maize, rice and horticultural produce. Much of this change in the food-production system is attributed to the state's need to generate foreign exchange through export crops. That these have come to include food crops as well as the more usual industrial crops has implications for domestic food production, but makes no difference as far as the needs of the market are concerned. We see the continuing expansion of industrial agriculture from the core to the periphery; modernization, no less. Capitalist relations of production are penetrating even the most isolated rural communities. It is through this process that we can best interpret the current food crisis, and translate the inanimate statistics of the FAO annual report to the concrete circumstances under which individual peasants labour. We shall see the means by which even the remotest of these peripheral peasant families is suborned to a global capitalist system, and in so doing we shall locate the real causes of hunger.

Smallholder production in Kenya. Firstly we must dismiss the notion that failing productivity is the disease. It is now well established that intensive smallholder production is highly productive, much more so than the large estates which characterized the 'White Highlands' of Kenya, or the 'Latifundia' of Latin America (World Bank, 1975). These and other examples clearly demonstrate that Third World agriculture has the potential to produce adequate supplies of food without being 'modernized'.

Rather than focusing on the technical question of productivity (as expressed in output per unit of labour, or on a cost-benefit determination based on the market), we should instead address the issue of autonomy on the part of the peasant. It is the contention here that in fact peasants have very little freedom of action over their own enterprise. The imperatives of the state have effectively removed from the farmer the control over his own means of production. He has become integrated into a global process on which he has little or no influence.

The specific processes through which Third World farmers have lost their independence is well documented elsewhere (for example Franke and Chasin, 1980, on West Africa; Leys, 1975, on Kenya; and Frank, 1969, on Latin America). At the risk of simplification we may mention: the enforced monetization of the peasantry by colonial taxes; the resultant need to grow commercial crops in order to generate that money; the control of credit and other inputs, and of marketing, first by chartered companies and later by transnational corporations; the burgeoning urban populations whose political quiescence is bought through a cheap food policy at the expense of rural people;

the requirement on the part of the state to earn foreign exchange through export crops; the alienation (and commercialization) of land, coerced labour, and later the development of wage labour and thus the transformation of peasants to proletarians; and so on. In fact we see the gradual commodification of all factors of production as well as the produce itself: of land, of labour and, of course, of crops. All of these pressures have been experienced in one way or another throughout the periphery (the particular sequence and combination dependent on individual histories and circumstances). The net result is that for the most part (but again dependent on the same individual circumstances) the agricultural societies of the Third World have been integrated into the capitalist world-economy. The question of whether individual farmers can themselves be considered as capitalists is not at issue. The fact remains that they operate in a social formation increasingly dominated by capitalist relations of production, and that these relations are expressed through national and international processes beyond their control.

As an example we may consider the smallholders of Kenya, where a number of factors combine to force the farmer's hand. For one thing, the state is almost totally reliant on agricultural products to pay or substitute for imports. As a proportion of Kenya's total exports, agricultural products averaged 64 per cent between 1976 and 1980. In one year, 1977, they contributed 78 per cent, with tea and coffee comprising 67.8 (Barve, 1984). Accordingly, through specific programmes of assistance, such as the Kenya Tea Development Authority, farmers are encouraged to cultivate such crops as tea, coffee, tobacco, sugar and pyrethrum. All of these export commodities divert resources from food production.

Further, Kenya has been a prime focus for capitalist modernization since the 1950s, with all that that entails in the way of the penetration of market forces. Land has been privatized following the Swynnerton Plan of 1953, thus making it a capital (and thereby commercial) asset. The intention, in addition to the obvious one of furthering the commodification process, was to enable the peasant to offer security for a loan, and so invest in his enterprise. By so doing one of the theoretical constraints on improved productivity is, in principle, removed. Of course the loan has to be repaid in cash, which obliges the peasant to cultivate commercial crops.

Finally, through the economic policies followed by the state (which actively facilitates the release of market forces, with little or no safeguards), modern Kenya is dominated by a rapid circulation of money, exchanged for virtually all material needs. In order to survive, Kenyans of all occupations (perhaps with the single exception of some of the pastoralist groups) have a pressing need to generate money. One of the principal means is to release labour from 'subsistence' agriculture on to the free labour market. Hence we see a classic case of active men deserting the rural areas in search of wage employment in the cities, leaving their families behind to maintain the farms. In order to reproduce this system, and particularly with the hope of improving on these dim prospects, education is perceived as the only available route. This too demands a considerable monetary outlay, and further deepens the crisis. At the cultural level, modernization also incorporates western attitudes, and thus we see the wholesale adoption of western clothes, corrugated iron roofs, and a whole panoply of consumer items, all available only through cash purchase.

All these processes of change bind the farmer to a system which requires the production of goods which can be sold on the open market, in this case involving the replacement of food crops for those with export potential. It is therefore not surprising that, when viewed at the national scale, the production of Kenya's staple food crop – maize – is failing to keep pace with population growth. Shortages of this nature have little if anything to do with technical incapacity, peasant conservatism or even environmental pressures such as declining soil fertility, soil erosion, desertification or whatever. The conclusion is that Kenyan peasants are less and less able to apply their resources to the production of food.

PURCHASE RATHER THAN PRODUCTION

The processes which I have briefly described, and which chart the integration of peripheral agriculture into the world-economy, suggest that the prospects for expanded food production (at least that which relates to the immediate provision for peasants) in the periphery are poor. Three issues have emerged in the discussion. There is a continuous and persistent diversion of agricultural activity away from the production of locally needed food crops. The cash-crop economies that have taken over are vulnerable to the dynamics of a wider market over which peasants have little if any control. And the underlying function of this transformation of peasant agriculture is the commoditization and proletarianization of the peasant economy itself; in short its greater articulation with the capitalist world-economy.

The starting-point of this history has been the independent self-sufficient farmer, providing largely for his own needs. Accordingly we have considered the problems related to food production and consumption at source. As we have observed, however, in its extreme form such a concept of subsistence agriculture is clearly outdated, even though a visible 'surface' still persists. Moreover, for many centuries these pre-capitalist formations had engaged in some form of exchange, both internally and to a limited extent with external trading partners. Nevertheless modern processes continue to force the pace of transformation. The few remaining elements of an autonomous economy are rapidly being replaced by a more complete array of capitalist relations of production and exchange.

If food production for immediate consumption continues to decline, the gap can only be filled by purchase. The issue of food can then be considered from a second perspective, which acknowledges the wider system of the world-economy, and which links the core and the periphery in terms of external supply and internal demand. It is here that we return to the distributional debate.

The second aspect, to which I referred earlier, is of greater interest, concerned with equity and trade. It relates not to the physical transfer of food, nor to the particular location it might be intended to reach, but to the fact that in an economic or commercial sense the markets for food products do not include the needy.

Thus we see the paradox of increasingly severe grain shortages in the Third World at the same time as we see an increasing proportion of total global grain production diverted to animal feeds. According to the FAO (1974) the expected requirement for cereal-based animal feedstocks in 1985 will amount to 66 per cent of total demand. Moreover we should not conclude that this proportion comes only from the intensive industrial systems of the core. Even the semi-periphery and periphery are involved. Thus in Mexico, 'more basic grains are consumed for animal forage than by 20 million peasants' (quoted in Frank, 1981, from *International Herald Tribune* of 9 March 1978). If not the product of agricultural land, then the land itself is diverted from food production to animal pasture. In Central America, beef production between 1962 and 1975 increased at an annual rate of 5 per cent whereas beef exports accelerated at a rate of 18 per cent per annum (George, 1979). In Costa Rica per-capita beef consumption declined from 49 lb in 1950 to 33 lb in 1971, yet in 1965 60 million lb of beef were exported to the USA (Lappe and Collins, 1980).

The literature is full of such examples. The conclusion is that food is destined for markets which can afford it, and not to where the nutritional need is most evident. The locus of product is immaterial so long as costs are minimized and a profitable sale can be made. As one US rancher commented on the costs of production, 'Here's what it boils down to – $95 per cow per year in Montana, $25 in Costa Rica' (quoted in Lappe and Collins, 1980, p. 203). Thus in the midst of hunger, food is exported for profit. If consumers in the core are prepared to pay more for meat than peasants in the periphery can afford for grain, then it should come as no surprise that the market fails to include the poor.

If we accept that rural communities, even whole regions, are no longer able to safeguard food supply by internal means, then we are forced to consider the processes determining food production in a wider, external arena. As Third World agriculture becomes increasingly capitalist, and thereby increasingly characterized by a greater degree of monetary exchange, it follows that more and more basic needs will have to be purchased rather than locally produced. To an increasing extent, then, the basic needs of a rural household are obtained by purchase (it goes without saying that urban families are already forced to purchase all their needs). In terms of the need, the demand exists, but in the context of the capitalist world-economy demand is only effective when expressed in terms of available purchasing power. As expressed in profit-based exchange relations the economic demand (i.e. that which is recognized by the global production system, and to which it can respond) is much more limited. Rural households are simply too poor: 'there is therefore nothing surprising in the combination of poverty, hunger and even starvation on the one hand and food exports on the other – a reality in many African countries. It shows once again that within the capitalist system food is grown for profit, not to feed people – especially hungry ones' (Bondestam, 1976, p. 207).

We have come full circle. As food is now a commodity, the forces which govern its production are those which relate to buying and selling at a profit. If the poor of the Third World cannot afford to purchase it, then its production and distribution will fail to adjust to their real needs, even though there may be widespread malnutrition and even starvation. Thus we observe a paradox, whereby a global production system has the capacity to feed the world, but does not do so because people are too poor. *In extremis*, such is the logic of capitalism that the very fact that the poor of the Third World are starving is the reason why they cannot be fed.

Nevertheless, although there appears to be an extremely limited market for the sale of foodstuffs to the periphery, capital is certainly interested in its land and labour. The recent and expanding penetration of agribusiness into the periphery has been well documented through a number of African case studies:

> At present, industrial countries import about 90 per cent of all traded horticultural products, of which Third World countries ship 30–40 per cent. Trade is dominated by citrus fruits, potatoes and tomatoes, but in Africa an increasing amount of land is being cultivated to supply European markets with a variety of fresh flowers and out-of-season vegetables and fruits – either dried or flown fresh. (Dinham and Hines, 1982, p. 30)

To this new product we can, of course, add those agricultural export crops that have continued to dominate African agriculture from the early colonial days (groundnuts, oil palm, cocoa, coffee, tea, etc.). Much of the renewed penetration of agribusiness into peripheral agriculture takes the form of 'contract' farming, whereby the farmer grows what the company requires. The whole process is tightly controlled. Effectively the farmer leases his land and labour. He bears the risks, and the company takes the profits. A classic example of this type of venture is described by Feder (1978), in his analysis of the strawberry scheme in Mexico. The process continues: as peasants are increasingly marginalized, and the peasant economy regresses to the point of extinction, agricultural resources are deployed in the service of a capitalist world-economy, a deployment that sees no gains to be made from food production.

CONCLUSION

By placing the food crisis within the context of the capitalist world-economy we have necessarily dealt with a far more complex set of relationships and processes than would have been the case had the discussion been confined to technical matters. Despite this complexity, a world-systems approach carries with it a logical structure that is denied to an idiographic technical approach. It is also more fundamental, in that it focuses on causes rather than symptoms.

Furthermore, because of its holistic framework, such an approach is less easily deflected to a reductionist perspective. Therefore the discussion is best considered in the context of the remaining chapters of the book, for they all deal with different aspects of the same base. Accordingly, we may summarize the discussion, and at the risk of oversimpliciation, itemize a number of central axes, or elements:

The first is that the present food crisis has a long history. Its origins can be traced back to the emergence of the capitalist world-economy in the sixteenth century. The first search for global pillage laid the foundations for the current problem. Perhaps the most telling example is that of the sugar economy of South America and the Caribbean in the seventeenth and eighteenth centuries. Even in those early times an agricultural crop was produced solely for profit. Such a production system contained within it all the elements that we can observe today in modified form: export and the transfer of surplus to the emergent core; transformation, and in that particular case, extermination of a pre-existing rural economy; the provision of displaced labour through the slave trade; the expropriation of resources in answer to external forces, and so on.

Secondly, and via a number of specific processes, which nevertheless have a common eventuality, we can trace the subjugation of what has become the periphery to the core. In this case we are concerned with food. The different processes: monetization, commoditisation, the manipulation of trade, control of the means of production through state apparatuses, penetration of foreign companies in allegiance with a *comprador* bourgeoisie, a global financial structure refereed by the IMF; all point to the same conclusion. We observe the transformation of rural societies, whose economies were based on some form of reciprocity in their exchange relationships, to a capitalist model of which the central characteristic is one of surplus value extraction and profit. The net result is that, by being more or less forcibly wedded to this capitalist suitor, peasant societies of the Third World have lost the freedom to determine their own futures. They are on an express train without the means to jump off. The power to grow food and ensure adequate nutrition has been wrested from them, while the meagre rewards they earn for accommodating to a profit-based exchange system leave them too poor to purchase the very commodities they have been obliged to produce.

Thirdly, we may assume with some confidence that remedial measures emanating from the core, such as aid and development schemes and trading cartels, have as their ultimate goal the preservation of the status quo. The central beneficiary of the global trading system is hardly likely to promote changes which lead to its demise. It is in this context that we can locate the north–south debate. It is merely an attempt to re-energize the dynamism that is so evidently lacking during the current global depression. By stimulating trade, it does no more than refuel a motor starved of energy. Technocratic solutions are part of the same process: watering the deserts, farming the seas, bacterial cultures and the like derive from the core. They are as remote as the sun to the peasantry of the periphery, and, like the green revolution, will only result in further immiseration of the hungry.

Finally, we can extend these processes into the future. It is now axiomatic that the nations of the south are unable to promote continued and reliable self-sufficiency in food production (this is particularly true of Africa). There is no logical reason to suppose that history can be reversed, and that the rising tide of food imports can miraculously be checked. In fact the opposite is the case. All reason points to a further deepening of the crisis. Short of a fundamental, structural change in the world system, we can expect the penetration of capitalist relations of production to intensify. Those corners of the periphery which have still to be fully incorporated will witness an erosion of their remaining autonomy. In this process of integration the 'trickle-down' salvation will benefit only a very small minority. For the majority little can be offered, for they can provide neither a market nor any other means of surplus extraction. They are an irrelevance. Accordingly we must assume that 'basket-cases' such as Bangladesh will be abandoned. Effectively, and like a worn-out mine, they have been exhausted.

References

Barve, A. G. 1984: *The Foreign Trade of Kenya. A Perspective*. Nairobi: Transafrica.

Boeke, J. H. 1963: *Economics and Economic Policy of Dual Societies*. New York: International Secretariat, Institute of Pacific Relations.

Bondestam, L. 1976: The politics of food in the periphery with special reference to Africa. *Political Economy of Food. Proceedings of an International Seminar*, Tampere: Peace Research Institute.

Dinham, B. and Hines, C. 1983: *Agribusiness in Africa*. London: Earth Resources Research.

Food and Agriculture Organization 1974: *Assessment of the World Food Situation, Present and Future*. Rome: FAO.

Food and Agriculture Organization 1981: *Trade Yearbook*. Rome: FAO.

Feder, E. 1978: *Strawberry Imperialism: An Enquiry into the Mechanisms of Dependency in Mexican Agriculture*. The Hague: Institute of Social Studies.

Frank, A. G. 1969: *Capitalism and Underdevelopment in Latin America*. Harmondsworth: Penguin.

Frank, A. G. 1981: *Crisis: In the Third World*. London: Heinemann.

Franke, R. W. and Chasin, B. H. 1980: *Seeds of Famine*. Montclair, N. J.: Allanheld, Osmun.

George, S. 1976: *How the Other Half Dies: The Real Reasons for World Hunger*. Harmondsworth: Penguin.

George, S. 1979: *Feeding the Few: Corporate Control of Food*. Washington, Amsterdam: Institute for Policy Studies.

Hightower, P. 1975: *Eat Your Heart Out: Food Profiteering in America*. New York: Crown.

Hopkins, R. F. and Puchala, D. J. 1978: *The Global Political Economy of Food*. Madison: University of Wisconsin Press.

Hyden G. 1980: *Beyond Ujamaa in Tanzania: Underdevelopment and an Uncaptured Peasantry*. London: Heinemann Educational Books.

International Labour Organization 1978: *Yearbook of Labour Statistics*. Geneva.

Lappe, F. M. and Collins, J. 1980: *Food First*. London: Abacus.

Leys, C. 1975: *Underdevelopment in Kenya: The Political Economy of Neo-Colonialism*. London: Heinemann Educational Books.

Robbins, C. and Ansari, J. 1976: *The Profits of Doom*. London: War On Want.

United Nations 1980: *Population Studies* 70. Department of International Economic and Social Affairs. New York.

World Bank 1975: *Ad Hoc Consultation on World Food Scarcity*. Washington.

World Bank 1981: *World Development Report*. Washington.

5

Natural Resource Use in Developing Countries

PIERS BLAIKIE

The editors of this book suggested that the title of this chapter should be 'The Rape of the Earth'. It would have been a dramatic title, and in keeping with the direction of the book as a whole, which I take to be the identification and explanation of regressive ill effects in the capitalist world-economy. That the title has turned out to be more ambiguous arises from my view that much of the radical critique of natural resource use has chosen to fight many crucial debates on uncertain ground. Except for the uncritically converted, it needs careful argument to distinguish 'rape' of natural resources from 'use'. In a nutshell, this chapter tries to show that many radical critiques have managed to expose the depredations of a developing capitalist world-economy upon pre-capitalist and peripheral capitalist societies. These ill effects have been felt from earlier mercantilist capitalist beginnings, through the industrial revolution, up to monopoly capitalism and the transnational company of today. They include waste, pollution, exhaustion of land and labour, loss of livelihood for local people who hitherto used natural resources, and systemic damage to the natural renewal of resources. This exposé has been useful, but it has not gone far enough. Specific programmes for alternative uses of natural resources along with more general strategies to further a socialist use of natural resources are both, by and large, still lacking. Many questions remain. In what alternative ways are natural resources to be used, and to what social ends in a capitalist world? To whom does, and should, a particular natural resource belong, and who should benefit? These and many more have to be answered if the critique is not to remain a romantic anti-capitalist indulgence.

The discussion starts with a review of the political implications of the victory of the right in academic debate over the Club of Rome reports and its 'Limits to Growth' thesis. The debunking of much of the substance of these reports undoubtedly was overdue on technical grounds, but was linked to an ideological offensive in which capitalist technology, an unfettered market mechanism and the necessity for resource-rich countries to open themselves up to the world market were presented as the best policies for all. The left, apart from some inadequate critiques which maintained that the problems of resource use in the world today were no more than the inevitable outcome of the contradictions of capitalism, showed itself unable to reply effectively.

The following section of this chapter deals with the role of radical critique in exposing the depredations of world capitalism upon natural resources, upon those who work them (e.g. miners, peasants, labourers), and upon those whose livelihoods have been taken away. This has been a useful exercise but a more realistic approach based on a clearly worked-out strategy for a transition to socialism is required. This strategy must recognize the retrogressive *and* progressive elements of capitalism. It is argued here that if a particular capitalist enterprise fulfils the criteria of increasing production, socializes labour, encourages unionization and training, and provides funds for development, there are good reasons for supporting it in the absence of sustainable socialist alternatives. A mechanistic 'one road to socialism' is avoided here for a more opportunistic and flexible one. Nonetheless, it is argued that for many countries, particularly small ones, the sustainability of socialist change must be very much open to doubt where there has been little development of the forces of production and the socialization of labour as a result of the development of capitalism. In each case, the problem arises in weighing up the likely impact of each new project, industry or policy. So often these do not fulfil even one of the criteria suggested above, and their impact is the subject of discussion below.

The spirit of the 'rape of the earth' theme is more evident later in the chapter where the deleterious effects of capitalist enterprise upon agriculture and forests are surveyed. Following this, a search for a progressive use of natural resources is made. Four preconditions for the use of natural resources are suggested – positive identification, the necessary technical expertise, political control of the natural resource, and the condition of the relative utility of the natural resource to others or other possible substitutes. The chapter concludes with discussion of the problems and possibilities of improving the preconditions for socialism in each of these preconditions of resource use.

GLOBAL RESOURCES – THE CURRENT DEBATE

The debate which followed the publication of the 'Limits to Growth' reports by the Club of Rome from 1972 is now more than a decade old, and it is not my intention to rehearse it here. However, it is a relevant starting-point since it has been the victory of the right over liberals, conservationists and advocates of no growth or redistribution, and the debunking of most of the 'Limits to Growth' theses, which must provide the ground for any effective critique today.

Full accounts of this debate can be found in Maddox (1972), Daly (1972), O'Riordan (1976), Freeman and Jahoda (1979), K. Smith (1979) and Sandbach (1980). Here the discussion will focus upon the aspects of the debate which deal with the impact of incorporation of economies and societies into the world-economy upon resource use, and of the growth of the world-economy itself.

Since the early computer simulations of the growth of the world-economy for the Club of Rome, by Meadows et al. (1972) and Mesarovic and Pestel (1975), there have been a number of thorough debunkings by Beckerman (1974), Kahn et al. (1976), Simon (1981) and others. The grounds on which these have been based are the failure of the simulations to specify multiple relations and feedback loops in the predictions of future populations, food supply, industrial production and pollution. For example, population growth can (and has) adjusted to changing economic and social conditions; pollution control can be initiated either through the operation of the free market or through state intervention. Also technological advances which enhance productivity per worker and per unit of natural resource (land, minerals, etc.) are insufficiently accounted for – indeed, 'there is no technical reason why technical advance should not continue indefinitely' (Hagen, 1972, p. 13). Further, the future availability of natural resources cannot be based upon known reserves, since these, for most of the widely used minerals at least, have almost consistently increased as a percentage of annual use over the past 150 years or so (Alexandersson and Klevebring, 1978, p. 17; Simon, 1981). In those cases where this has not been so, substitution or completely new technologies have been able to *create* new resources, and are confidently expected to do so in the future. The basic elements of this debate will be known to most readers (Du Boff, 1974, provides a good summary), and it is not these which directly concern us here. Instead, we focus upon the ideological grounding of this debate and the political implications for the transition to a socialist use of natural resources.

There is an enormous range of views on the issue of growth, equity and the use of natural resources within the world-economy, in which unexpected ideological bed-fellows abound on a variety of issues. Kahn et al. (1976, pp. 9–16) define the range of views by a number of categories, each of which have an internally consistent package of positions upon such issues as technology and capital, management and decision-making, resources, income gaps, innovation, industrial development and so on. While such a classification may be helpful in identifying broad categories of optimism and pessimism (the summary criterion for distinguishing the categories), it does so within a status-quo framework for two basic reasons. The first is that the optimist/pessimist criterion does not specify some fundamental differences between the various theories of social change which the so-called 'convinced neo-Malthusian', 'guarded pessimist', 'guarded optimist' and 'technology-and-growth enthusiast' all hold. Thus a 'convinced neo-Malthusian' (so called) can believe that natural resources, the heritage of poor countries, are being consumed by the rich countries, denying the poor any real hope for better living conditions (1976,

p. 14), but a Marxist can also do so. On the other hand, a convinced Malthusian can believe that 'future population growth will hasten and increase the magnitude of the future tragedy' while (very few) Marxists would do so. Lastly, many Marxists who may be most pessimistic about many of the shorter-term implications of capitalist growth may also feel there is no short cut to progress and that capitalist technology and growth offer the best long-term strategy for the socialization of the means of production and the growth of effective class consciousness (Hyden, 1983; Warren, 1973, 1980).

An alternative 'classification' of views with much more analytical power must start with a statement of strategic social objectives in the short and longer terms, and the means by which these are to be reached. These will both be based on the theory of social change. The theories of Beckerman (1974), Bauer (1976, 1981), Kahn et al. (1976) and Simon (1981), who have all addressed the 'Limits to Growth' debate, are built upon an affirmation of capitalism in which unfettered market forces should largely determine natural resource use and economic activity in general, without any significant intervention on the part of the state. Simon (1981, p. 154) shows, for example, how the price of many minerals has declined in real terms over the past 80 years; thus it will benefit resource-rich countries to open up their economies to exploit these resources as soon as possible so that maximum revenue can be gained from them. Conservation of mineral resources is considered wasteful and a missed opportunity, therefore incorporation into the world-economy *now* is the best path to development.

With regard to the issue of environmental degradation, for example soil erosion, alkanization, salination and water-logging of soils, much of the same 'optimistic' views can be found:

> Of course arable land in some places is going out of cultivation be-cause of erosion and other destructive forces. But taken as a whole the amount of arable land in the world is increasing year by year. (Simon, 1981, p. 81)

> The vague counter-argument that more intensive cultivation will ruin the soil is hardly convincing in view of the fact that soil has been farmed with increasing intensity in Europe for about 2000 years and there is still no sign that it is exhausted. Most of the world's cultivable areas, by comparison, have hardly been touched or not yet touched at all. (Beckerman, 1974. pp. 239–40)

It is worth mentioning in passing that subtropical soils bear so little resemblance to those in Europe as to render Beckerman's observations invalid on technical grounds alone. However, the ideological content is the same for their observations on other natural resources – that the free market should operate world-wide and resources are thereby never 'raped', merely used rationally, and 'rape' occurs only in cases of political or economic irrationality, and specifically of tinkering with the operation of the free market.

RADICAL CRITIQUE – EXPOSÉ WITHOUT ALTERNATIVES

Radical critiques of the 'Limits to Growth' debate have usually been content with an exposé of the evils of capitalism, although Ensenberger (1974) went further and pointed out the bourgeois origins of the reports in the sense that it was only when environmental deterioration started to foul capitalism's own backyard, and maybe even threaten the process of accumulation, that much attention was paid. However, he admits to a view which I share, when he says:

> The attempt to summarise the left's arguments has shown that the main intervention in the environmental controversy has been through the critique of ideology. This kind of approach is not completely pointless, and there is no position other than Marxism from which such a critical examination of the material would be possible. But, an ideological critique is only useful when it remains conscious of its own limitations. It is in no position to handle the object of its research by itself. As such it remains merely the interpretation of an interpretation of real conditions, and is therefore unable to reach the heart of the problem. . . . [Thus] Marxism [can become] a defensive mechanism, as a talisman against the demand of reality, a collection of exorcisms – these are tendencies we all have reason to take note of and combat. The issue of ecology is but one example.

Almost all critiques of capitalism until the 1970s paid little attention to the use of natural resources and environmental issues, with the possible exception of William Morris. Neither Marx nor Engels paid much attention to the environment, more interested as they were in the development of capitalism in the nineteenth century when the environment was seen to perform merely an 'enabling function' for rapid capitalist development (Redclift, 1983, p. 7). Marx did mention that 'all progress in capitalistic agriculture is a progress in the art, not only of robbing the labourer but of robbing the soil; all progress in increasing the fertility of the soil for a given time is a progress towards ruining the lasting resources of that fertility' (Marx, quoted in Bagchi, 1982, p. 213). However, it was not until later that major catastrophes in the developed world, such as the dust bowl in the USA in the 1930s, and writers on resource use at the periphery, particularly about the Sahel (discussed below), drew attention to the very serious problems of environmental use under capitalist agriculture (Malcolm, 1938; Jacks and Whyte, 1939; Glover, 1946; Rounce, 1949; Hyams, 1952, are some earlier examples of empirical accounts of environmental degradation).

There are two problems, however, which radical critiques of environmental degradation under world capitalism have to face. The first is that degradation occurs at the present time in China and the USSR too – quite disastrously so – and there is little evidence that any battle is being won to conserve soil, water and forest resources in Mozambique, Angola, Guinea or Vietnam. In the USSR there is widespread evidence of oil spills, extinction of fishing grounds, high levels of air pollution, and widespread loss of topsoils from the dry steppe [(for favourable accounts see Gerasimov and Armand, 1971, and Pryde, 1972, and for a swingeing critique, see Komarov, 1981).] Pryde observes that Marxian economics assumes that only labour produces value, and therefore all natural resources are considered 'free' inputs of production. However, the explanation of wasteful and harmful use of natural resource in the USSR probably derives more from the nature of the state and the context in which it evolved. The forced march to industrialization, insensitive and bungled centralized planning and also perhaps a careless optimism (MacEwan, 1984) all contributed. The ecological implications of the following extract from 'The Great Plan' (1929) – quoted by Burke (1956) – can be imagined: 'It is a tremendous country [referring to the USSR] but not yet entirely ours. Our steppe will truly become ours only when we come with columns of tractors and ploughs to break the thousand year old virgin soil. We must plough the earth, break rocks, dig mines, construct houses, we must take from the earth.' At the same time, set against a probable 'destruction of nature' (as Komarov, 1981, calls it) as a result of ignorance, incompetence and the suppression of the free flow of important information about pollution and other failures, must be the nation's tremendous successes in industrial production, raising the standard of living of its people, and making the nation secure against its enemies.

The record of the use of soil, water and forest resources in China has left a more mixed commentary, from the very favourable (e.g. Sandbach, 1980, ch. 6) to the unfavourable (Howard, 1981; Dequi et al., 1981; Delfs, 1982; Smil, 1983). Perhaps there was a tendency for Chinese achievements to stand for the sole instance of proof that socialist reconstruction was not a figment of the imagination and that it was going on right now – an onerous and overworked role that did not come through unscathed upon detailed examination. Smil's most recent account (1984) of environmental decline in China is marked by almost unrelieved pessimism:

> the magnitude of China's accumulated environmental problems owing to the legacy of ancient neglect and recent destruction is depressing. The dimensions of the future tasks in population control, food and energy supply and overall social modernisation are overwhelming, and the potential for further accelerated environmental degradation is quite considerable. (p. 198)

The author's unrelenting criticism of and cynicism towards *all* China's efforts in development, its institutions and its western admirers ('embarrassingly misinformed and naive') makes me hesitant in believing all I am being told. However, there are other less ideologically aggressive accounts of many of the unfortunate processes of environmental decline, and so a general conclusion that the revolution in China has not dramatically improved the situation is probably a safe one.

The problem, then, which radical critiques must face up to, is that there will always be struggles and contradictions over natural resources even in a 'socialist state', and that problem-solving is not the technocratic preserve of status-quo neo-classical economics. The directions that lead away from generalist calls to the barricades towards practical solutions and the art of the possible may seem less than revolutionary and sometimes make tame and reformist reading. In general terms, then, all that can be said is that directions towards socialism *should* make a less wasteful and more socially acceptable natural resource use possible.

The second problem is that it is not true in all cases that capitalist natural resource use is wasteful, polluting and socially irresponsible, although at the most abstract level capitalism undoubtedly is. As Baran and Sweezy (1966) have pointed out, competition between producers leads to chronic overproduction which itself is wasteful. Crises of overproduction are constantly resolved and reproduced by the creation of needs through advertising; the manufacture of arms whose built-in obsolescence and destruction in warfare both require constant replacement of the armaments themselves as well as of industrial equipment; and require the capturing of new markets (new consumers). In this general sense, then, capitalist resource use is wasteful. However, action to alter resource use is always 'contexted', and taken not only with abstract and global theories and objectives in mind. The questions which arise typically concern alternative and possible ways of using natural resources which are less wasteful, and more socially useful than at present. There are many capitalist farms and plantations, mines and hydro-electric stations which are not particularly wasteful and may in the longer term be socially progressive. Therefore rather less abstract criteria must also be established which can be used in individual cases, and these should be related to the type of capitalist development involved in each case, and also to a longer-term strategy of socialist transition. An examination of the problematic of underdevelopment theories and their major critics (Warren, 1973, 1980; Hyden, 1983; Kitching, 1983) is particularly relevant here.

One of the major problems with critics of underdevelopment theory such as Warren is that the role of struggle against *present* iniquities and inequalities, to better the quality of life for workers and peasants the world over, tends to be obscured. In the long term, the prodigious ability of capitalism to increase production can promote socialist transition by systematically social-izing the means of production; encouraging workers to organize into unions, and to move towards directing and controlling the means of production; and by using capitalist technology to provide an ample sufficiency of material goods for all. In such an analysis there is often, but not always, a conflict over the long-term objective of winning better working conditions, and more control over the way and rate of use of natural resources in any particular case. Therefore a socialist strategy for the use of natural resources in less developed countries (LDCs) has to be based upon a theory of socialist transition. There are three crucial elements which have been debated, all of which depend on whether the socialist transition is possible without a fully developed capitalist stage.

The first element is the need to increase production in less developed countries so that the population achieves its basic needs. A failure of a population to get enough to eat, clothe and house itself may lead to an irruptive gesture, a riot or uprising, but has seldom led to either successful *coups d'état* or to socialist government thereafter. Socialist construction has been extraordinarily difficult to secure when the population is preoccupied with finding enough to eat. Certainly the falterings of socialist initiatives in Tanzania and Mozambique (Coulson, 1982) were partly due to the failure of agriculture to feed their populations satisfactorily, although the successful efforts of destabilization by Pretoria were also involved in the latter failure. Therefore, as long as capitalist enterprises do not undermine the capability for future production (erode soils, deplete forests, pollute life-support systems) but lead to improvements in living standards, there seems little ideological and economic alternative but to accept them.

Secondly, capitalist enterprises can (under circumstances to be described) socialize the means of production, help to organize the workforce into unions and to involve workers in the experience of working in, and eventually taking over, the capitalist enterprises themselves. As long as the enterprise trains in a technical sense its workers at all levels, and provides the confidence that workers can run it with the required skill and discipline, then again the enterprise should be accepted. Thirdly, capitalist enterprises can provide funds for governments through royalties or concessions to build up physical infrastructure and encourage other enterprises through industrial linkages, which accelerates the two processes above.

The problem is that few capitalist enterprises fulfil even one of the elements which may be conducive to socialist transition. Many mining, timber and agricultural enterprises in less developed countries financed both by transnational and by indigenous capital have been responsible for widespread depletion of soil fertility, deforestation, pollution and the rapid working out of minerals with little in the way of royalties or taxes and the construction of port facilities, roads, railways, etc. They have often casualized the workforce, frequently awarding very short contracts to workers unused to factory conditions, whose contracts are terminated before unionization and a struggle for better wages and working conditions can begin. Furthermore, transnational companies can reduce royalties and taxes paid to government by a variety of means. That these cases form the majority, and struggle (or adept negotiation) cannot substantially reduce this majority, is of course the argument of underdevelopment theorists such as Frank (1980) and Amin (1974). This chapter takes the view that the experience of capitalist resource use is mixed, but that a variety of means including armed struggle, nationalization and bargaining over prices, training, participation and the like *can* be employed to raise living standards, and the experience and consciousness of the workforce. However, every case must be taken in context and evaluated for its advantages or disadvantages in furthering socialism. Such a cautious, longer-term and ambivalent view does not lend itself to rhetorical anti-capitalism, nor to the universal means of achieving socialist transition. The next section reviews some cases where world capitalism certainly has *not* provided the three conditions for progressive social change, and it is here perhaps that the analogy of 'rape' of the earth (and exhaustion of human labour) is most apposite.

Thus much of the left critique of natural resource use has been characterized by utopianism and neo-populism. There is an unwritten assumption in much radical writing about the world-economy that under socialism class contradictions would disappear, allowing a more far-sighted use of the natural environment. While critiques of the impact of world capitalism are useful, sins of omission leave the reader wondering whether pre-capitalist forms of resource use *can* manage to provide for a socialist future, and whether autarky, collectivization or co-operatives are on the agenda – or not. There will always be conflicts of interest and techno-administrative problems of natural resource management in every future social formation, and these have to be addressed alongside the political struggles of the day.

A strong neo-populist element can be detected in radical critiques, too, again by omitting what is really implied. Articles about the destruction of ethno-science by commercialization and the world economy (e.g. Richards, 1975, 1985; Brokensha et al., 1980; O'Keefe et al., 1977) resemble in this respect E. P. Thompson's *The Making of the English Working Class* and the writings in the *History Workshop Journal*, and the criticisms are similar to those made by Kitching (1983, pp. 68f.). In writings about both capitalist destruction of pre-capitalist technology and ethno-science, as in E. P. Thompson's work, the broader historical perspectives of the ambivalent nature of capitalism are not provided – that it is both progressive *and* destructive, developing *and* underdeveloping. It is not clear in the accounts of pre-capitalist social relations of production and technology whether these are to form the basis of socialism, or the basis of a more efficient capitalism. While Belshaw (1980) and other 'bottom-up' agricultural researchers (advocates of listening to farmers and learning from them) clearly see indigenous agricultural science as helping capitalist farming, most others (in Brokensha et al., 1980) leave out its political economic implications for future social change altogether.

There is also a strong neo-populist sentiment to new critiques of capitalist resource use. Here is one example:

> In economic policy the priority must be given to raising food production. This cannot be achieved by state direction of peasant producers, but only encouraging peasant initiative based on their experience and improving their own material well being and defending their own gains against the demands of even the revolutionary state. (Williams, 1976, p. 152)

In this example it is difficult to judge how a socialist transition is to be achieved, because it will not just occur after a call for government to get off the peasants' backs.

In this sense Warren's observation is relevant:

> Anti-capitalist ideology is not the same as socialist ideology; correspondingly, a moral critique . . . an anti-capitalist ideology can be backward-looking, reactionary or both. In principle a socialist ideology can only be forward-looking in that it builds on and does not attempt to negate the achievements of capitalism. (Warren, 1980, p. 20)

My own view is that monolithic theories of development with inflexible blueprints should be avoided. This does not mean an abandonment of theory altogether, but a recognition of the opportunities to further the cause of socialism when they arise, and also of constraints to achieving this end. Strategic and military considerations are frequently of crucial importance (e.g. as in Nicaragua, Mozambique and Angola today), but not in all instances. The size of the country itself and its natural endowment will also be most important. Where small size and military vulnerability endanger socialist objectives, the extent to which support from the Soviet Union is forthcoming and principled may be decisive (as in Cuba, for example). No one would propose that opportunities for a leftist government to achieve power in Africa, Asia or Latin America should wait for industrialization and/or modernization according to our uncritical 'application' of classical Marxism. It is just that, in the absence of capitalist development and a degree of development of state functions and infrastructure, further progress towards socialism will be very difficult, although my own view stops short of Kitching's (1983), which is that backward societies produce backward socialism. I disagree not so much because this may not be true, but because the 'backward' socialism *may* lead to something more progressive more quickly than backward capitalism.

It is in this light that utopian and neo-populist critiques are criticized. They cannot be condemned directly, however, since an exposé without an alternative is better than nothing, and it could be said that it is up to others to provide that alternative. Therefore the defect can only be applied to the genre as a whole. Further, some neo-populist policies are also not necessarily anti-socialist and may well be the only feasible alternative in some circumstances to the anarchic and destructive aspects of capitalist penetration. In the next section, this genre of critical research is drawn upon to provide just such an account of these aspects of the effect of world capitalism upon natural resource use, and of cases which even the most ardent advocate of either capitalism or classical Marxism would shrink from endorsing.

DESTRUCTIVE NATURAL RESOURCE USE
IN AGRICULTURE AND FORESTRY

One of the earliest and best critiques of the impact of capitalism upon natural resource use refers to the Sahel, where the radicalization of the 'drought issue' exposed the unfavourable effect of commercial expansion of beef, cotton and peanut production under the French colonial period and up to the present time upon pre-capitalist strategies of adequate storage, sophisticated cropping and pastoral techniques, risk-sharing and risk-aversion (Watts 1983, 1984). All were undermined by commercialization. This reduced the size of stored food reserves; increased reliance upon cash surpluses from the sale of commercial crops to buy in essential foods; substituted mono-cropping and deep-ploughing for inter-cropping and other moisture and soil retaining strategies; and broke up communal risk-sharing groups to replace them with mutually competitive entrepreneurs (Franke and Chasin, 1980; Meillassoux, 1974; Copans, 1975). Similar studies in Nigeria (Watts, 1983, 1984) and in Kenya (O'Keefe et al., 1977) show the destructive aspects of both commercial crops and commercial farmers who displaced and spatially marginalized indigenous crops and sometimes the cultivators themselves. Some of the most extreme cases have been carefully documented by Dinham and Hines (1983), who have shown how transnational companies (TNCs) have pillaged the soil, pushed farmers off their land and pressed the most outrageously one-sided agreements upon national governments in Africa; an example is summarized below. In many of these cases, local organizations for communal production, and mutual aid between households, villages and larger groups in times of food shortage were weakened or eliminated. It is a most important issue in socialist construction whether these organizations can transcend their frequently inegalitarian and feudal origins as well as provide a basis for increased production. The issue is similar to that faced by the mid-nineteenth-century Russian populists, such as Herzen and Chernyshevsky who saw the *obshchina* (or the institution which organized peasant labour and rent payments in favour of the landlord) as collectivist or proto-socialist, and capable of forming the basis for a progressive transition to socialism (Kitching, 1982, p. 35).

Another widely publicized case of destruction of natural resources by international capital is the logging of tropical and subtropical forests. Here the direct and indirect effects of capital upon deforestation must be spelt out: they are broadly similar to the effects upon agriculture, which can also lead to environmental degradation. There has been much debate about whether it has been the logging companies or the shifting cultivators which have been responsible for very rapid deforestation throughout the world (reported to be 10–12 ha per minute by FAO (the Food and Agriculture Organization), or up to 40 ha in the view of Myers, 1983). The problem is probably much more serious than was once thought. Satellite pictures and improved photo-interpretation have revised upwards the rate of deforestation and have often cut national estimates of remaining forests of various grades by as much as a factor of 30 per cent. For example, in the Philippines the actual percentage of forest of total land surface is only 38, as opposed to the official figure of 58 (Grainger, 1980). Smil (1984, p. 12) estimates that the actual forested area in China is only 35 per cent of the official one, and even existing forests are of lower productivity than claimed.

What is clear is that forests are disappearing fast (for global and regional surveys see Myers, 1983; Routley and Routley, 1980; Plumwood and Routley,

1982; Grainger, 1980). While local circumstances are bound to vary greatly, it is noticeable that the 'blame' for tropical and sub-tropical deforestation is placed either on indigenous cultivators or logging companies as a matter of ideological temperament rather than detailed local analysis. A comparison between Lanly (1982, for FAO) and Plumwood and Routley (1982) shows that whenever both papers refer to the same area they come to very different conclusions as to who is to blame. However, the connection between forest contractors and indigenous cultivators and pastoralists is strongly made by the loss of cultivators' land, and closure of common property resources by private ownership or private contracts and forest concessions, which *force* the latter to cut down the forest (for a fuller account, see Blaikie, 1985). Undoubtedly, rapid population growth of rural populations is also a contributory factor, given that other political economic determinants of production and reproduction are fixed, given and unexamined. Hence the implications of a large logging concession (or purchase of forest for clearing to start up cattle ranches) in a populated area spread beyond the boundaries of the concession itself and can set up complex and damaging 'knock-on' effects in other areas and parts of the rural economy.

Logging companies seek to reduce economic benefits from logging by neglecting or even blocking forward linkages such as sawmills, plywood or chipboard manufacturing. Second, they often pay very low prices for timber by a number of honest and dishonest strategies, among the most important being the use of superior knowledge of the details of timber resources. Third, they attempt to maximize the repatriation of profits, as do most TNCs, and avoid contributing to the cost of either reafforestation or training local personnel in forest management. Fourth, they 'cream' forests, and take little care over the conservation of other trees not valuable enough to fell. Lastly, they frequently fail to honour clauses in agreements once logging has been started, since local monitoring is difficult for many LDCs to carry out (Leslie, 1980).

The damage from indiscriminate logging, under the conditions implied above, is enormous. The loss of livelihood of local inhabitants, siltation of reservoirs, damage to hydro-electric plant and an increase in flash floods with consequent damage to property, crops and livestock are obvious ones, and documented in depth all over the world.

TOWARDS A PROGRESSIVE USE OF NATURAL RESOURCES

For a natural resource to be used at all, four conditions have to apply. There has to be positive identification of the natural resource as defined by existing technology and social relations of production. There has to be the technical expertise to use the resource. Political control by the would-be user appropriate to the resource itself and to the technology and social relations of production is necessary. Some resources do not require much political control: where a timber concession is signed, the timber is cut and the whole operation can be over in less than 18 months. Others such as minerals or estates and plantations require a longer-term political security of agreements, operation and profit-taking by the user. Last, the resource has to have relative utility to other occurrences of the same resource (or a substitutable one) elsewhere. This usually refers to the quality and location of the resource, but also to the political conditions which may help to determine the other three conditions (for a general discussion, see Blaikie, 1985).

The following paragraphs outline some of the most important areas of struggle to win some of the preconditions for future socialism and for a better standard of living for workers today. However, two qualifying remarks are necessary. First, it is through struggles across a wide area that a transition to socialism is made, and many of these will lie in different areas from struggles over natural resource use altogether. The areas of struggle in natural resource use are mostly aided and supported by other improvements in working conditions, material well-being, political consciousness and experience of workers and peasants, all of which come about through struggles which may have little to do with natural resource use itself.

However, it is also true that natural resources use *is* a very important element in realizing the general social objectives discussed in this chapter, as well as for other objectives which are desirable in themselves, whether or not they serve a longer-term strategy. For example, legislation for working conditions to prevent industrial diseases is a result of progressive organization of workers in the workplace, but is an achievement in itself. A second qualifying remark is necessary because little mention has been made of the class structure of the state, and therefore of internal struggles between contending classes. There must be no assumptions that a national government represents a benign and unified front fighting socialist or even nationalist battles over, say, mineral rights against a TNC. There are also present continuous struggles within all states on union representation, a free press, civil rights, women's rights and so on, which only indirectly concern international capitalist enterprises, institutions and governments. What is also clear is that there are immense variations in the form and strength of the state, and the relative importance of TNCs in the struggle over the use of natural resources (i.e. in primary industries). In sub-Saharan Africa, for example, the state as a rule is perhaps weaker than in, say, Morocco or Algeria, and 'has left representatives of international capital to exercise more influence than they have been able to do in other societies where an indigenous class structure has been in place' (Hyden, 1983, p. 195).

To return to the preconditions of resource use, the first is positive identification. The political economic circumstances of resource identification have largely to do with technical expertise (particularly geological survey, often with test drilling), aerial surveys of forests and sample botanical field surveys, and other natural resource surveys and assessments. The issue here is control over that information and sometimes, too, its ideological content. From early imperial times, 'trickery, deceit, astute lobbying and brute force' have been the means by which mining companies have secured concessions in developing countries (referring here to Rhodes's concessions from King Lobenghela in Southern Africa: Lanning and Mueller, 1979, p. 59). A part of the trickery and deceit was then, as it is now, a knowledge of the mineral resources of a country which is withheld by one party in a negotiation from another. Collection of data about minerals is notoriously expensive because it is also risky (Howe, 1979). Exploration for some minerals and particularly for ocean mining is so expensive that even large TNCs have to form consortia (United Nations, 1980c). Therefore, information about natural resources generated by exploration has extremely high value. In the same way, natural resource surveys often carried out in remote areas of developing countries are held only by the party wishing to negotiate the logging concession with government bureaucrats. On the one side of the negotiation there is a TNC with good information which it withholds completely, and on the other hand an imperfect but open administration where the inconsistencies and imperfect knowledge of the bureaucrat are already known by the TNC (Leslie, 1980). Furthermore, the level of technical knowledge about mining engineering, metal refining and possible environmental impacts (particularly pollution) has to be of a high standard, not necessarily possessed by negotiating teams of less developed countries.

Clearly technical training as well as training in management plus knowledge at the highest level are part (and only part) of the solution. The opening up of all information about the natural resources under negotiation, or the carrying out of alternative surveys, are other small but not insignificant ways with which information can be put more squarely at the service of national governments. This helps, but by no means assures, those governments of more reliable criteria on which national or local control and use of natural resources could be planned. This course of action also assumes that, in many cases, TNCs are a necessary evil:

> The point which is being made here is not a defence of multi-national corporations. They are, in the view of the present author, a necessary evil that Africa has to accept in the absence of any advanced economic structures of its own. (Hyden, 1983, p. 20)

This probably does not hold true for some Latin American countries or for India where there is much more evidence of these local economic structures, and therefore the need for a more complete knowledge of natural resources is less acute. But for many African countries their reliance on foreign expertise is considerable, as in the catastrophic decline in Angola's ability to produce diamonds after white technicians withdrew in 1975.

Turning now to the question of the expertise which is required to use natural resources, it is clearly in mining and ore-refinement that it is most crucial, because scarce. It is here that the inequality in bargaining power between national governments of the developing countries and TNCs is most acute, and therefore attempts to institute international legislation or codes of practice tend to fail in the bilateral details of negotiations. 'The need for an international code has been recognised by the international community and the Commission [on TNCs] has decided that, whatever its nature, the code should be effective' (United Nations, 1976, p. 39). Here is the response of a transnational company to the Chilean government's attempts at negotiating a joint interest in the production of plastics with the TNC (Gunnemann, 1975, p. 10): 'Our response was that we were interested in a joint venture if we could have a controlling interest so that we could protect our exceptional technology and ensure the proper efficient management of the business with co-operation between TNCs and governments.' It is logical that technical expertise is shared only when it is obsolete and of low value. This problem is the more intractable because TNCs are usually in a powerful position, and only training to an extremely high degree of expertise in developing countries will start to solve the problem. Also the experience of gaining expertise through lengthy foreign training has shown that those fortunate few naturally want to work for transnational companies themselves and not to be relatively poorly paid government negotiators.

Thirdly, the question of political control is perhaps one over which nationalized governments have the most leverage. In the past, extremely large revenues have accrued to many companies who are able to secure long agreements from puppet and other comprador leaders of national governments who found themselves in contractually inferior positions during negotiations. In some cases strong political domination of a national government has ensured extraordinary large benefits to flow to many companies up to the present day, and for TNCs to dominate the politics to the country and mould the labour market to their requirements. For example, Namibia has very large deposits of lead, cadmium, zinc, diamonds and uranium. Various transnational mining companies and the South African government have combined to plan an area of black homelands to provide labour for those mines (Lanning and Mueller, 1979, p. 455). However, political independence has given a very important extra leverage for national governments to secure a greater share of both revenues and control over production of mineral resources as well as agriculture (when farmed by white settlers in Central and Eastern Africa). Many mineral concerns require large capital outlays and high entry costs, which make it very difficult for local firms to compete in mining. It has also been difficult to persuade TNCs to commit themselves to backward- and forward-linking manufacturing undertakings, so much so that they have 'conspicuously failed' to accelerate local development (Girvan, 1976, p. 30).

The ability of a government to play one TNC off against another in these negotiations is lessened because there is colossal concentration of the share of production in many minerals (for example nickel and copper: United Nations, 1981b). In addition there undoubtedly exist unofficial 'fidelity' contracts and informal understandings between TNCs which enable them to deal more effectively with difficult national governments. There is also considerable vertical integration of TNCs in all stages of mineral extraction; this is so with bauxite in the Caribbean, enabling TNCs to control all stages of mining and refining of aluminium to such an extent that they control the political economy of the entire Caribbean region. Sometimes the United States itself becomes involved to assert control for its TNCs, as in the case of Chile (Girvan, 1976, ch. 2; United Nations, 1981b).

However, in spite of these difficulties the situation of the political control over minerals has gradually improved. Before the last war royalties (which were calculated on the level of production of refined metal) were the most common means of retaining revenue. This gave way in the 1950s to income tax, which many TNCs preferred because production costs and profit can be withheld or manipulated. Recently, there has been a tendency for many more joint ventures, often financed from sources other than the TNC itself, with considerable local participation up to a high level. Further developments have recently taken place in which TNCs withdraw to minority holdings and leave national governments to take the risks in production and in keeping down labour costs. In this way TNCs organize service contracts to provide technical services and marketing, while the national government is left with direct control of the workforce. The same problems of contractually unequal relations between the two parties still exist, and it is not clear that there is any clear advantage for workers of industrial concerns or peasant smallholders (growing crops for TNCs) in these new arrangements.

Turning now to the issue of political control over land and water resources in developing countries, some of the problems discussed in relation to the mining industry are similar, particularly with regard to highly mechanized plantation growing of commercial crops on a large scale. Displacement of peasants and pastoralists from what is usually the most fertile land from which they derived their livelihood, their partial or complete proletarianization (so that they have to work part- or full-time on the commercial farm or plantation), and frequent depletion of natural fertility, are all symptoms of many but by no means all capitalist agricultural enterprises. Dinham and Hines (1983) give one among many examples, of a TNC called Bud Antle Inc., a large Californian-based food conglomerate which negotiated a large-scale, highly capital-intensive scheme to grow quality vegetables in Senegal, which were flown to markets in Europe. By 1976 the project had virtually failed and the Senegalese government (which had formed a joint enterprise with Bud Antle Inc.) was left with eroded soils, imported machinery which could not be maintained and dispossessed pastoralists/peasants (p. 32). Surely one lesson to learn from this is that the Senegalese government was ill advised, in a legal sense, not to insist on clauses in the agreement which would have prevented this débâcle. Joint ventures with TNCs must be buttressed with hard-headed agreements, based upon reliable knowledge of the issues and resources involved.

This is one extreme case. Taking together all the circumstances of TNC involvement in land and water resources, there is a continuum of commitment to conserve these resources over a long period, through short-lease contracts of ten years or so, to very short-term logging contracts. Clearly, for reasons of resource conservation as well as for more general objectives of social change, longer leases with penalty clauses for running down natural resources (depletion of soil fertility, destruction of forest areas, etc.) are necessary, but require a well-developed bureaucracy with a considerable degree of technical training and sense of public duty. It is this latter development which is a necessary, although not sufficient, condition to implement a natural resource policy which avoids the depredation of TNCs and the expansion of commercial agriculture into unsuitable areas.

So far this chapter has concentrated upon national governments' relations with international capital. There is not the space here to enter into the debate about the use of soil and water resources by peasants and pastoralists in a transition to socialism. Clearly a discussion of crucial issues concerning the peasants and socialism would balance a rather 'top-down' and industrially biased treatment here, and a fuller one must include this whole issue too.

CONCLUSION

'Rape' of the earth, or *Raubwirtschaft* (Friedrich's term cited in Goudie, 1981, p. 5), is widespread. Exhaustion of land and labour and the working out of minerals and fish stocks without the advantages of modernization (which in my view should be still a 'respectable' concept in Marxian debate) has happened all over the world. The awesome problems of working outside the capitalist system altogether, and of developing a socialist system which would markedly reduce these ill effects, have at least been pointed out. It seems clear that no blueprint is possible, other than a general rhetoric of the socialist alternative, without specifying on how to get from here to there. Every national context and every new proposal for the working of natural resources have to be looked at separately to see what longer-term advantages can possible be gained. These advantages must include improvement in the standard of living of workers, technical training and experience of working and managing enterprises, and progressive socialization of the relations of production. If a capitalist enterprise can be made to do these things, so be it. Once these criteria are used, *Raubwirtschaft* can be distinguished from use.

Acknowledgement

I wish to acknowledge the help of Sheila Chatting, who acted as my research assistant and suggested many useful ideas.

References

Alexandersson, G. and Klevebring, B. I. 1978: *World Resources*. Berlin: Walter de Gruyterm.

Amin, S. 1974: *Accumulation on a World Scale: a Critique of the Theory of Underdevelopment*, vol. 1. New York: Monthly Review Press.

Amin, S. 1976: *Unequal Development: An Essay on the Social Formations of Peripheral Capitalism*. Brighton: Harvester Press.

Bagchi, A. K. 1982: *The Political Economy of Underdevelopment*. Cambridge: Cambridge University Press.

Baran, P. A. 1969: *The Longer View: Essays Towards a Critique of Political Economy*. New York: Monthly Review Press.

Baran, P. A. and Sweezy, P. M. 1966: *Monopoly Capital*. New York: Monthly Review Press.

Bauer, P. T. 1976: *Dissent on Development*. London: Weidenfeld & Nicolson.

Bauer, P. T. 1981: *Equality, the Third World and Economic Delusion*. London: Weidenfeld & Nicolson.

Bauer, P. T. and Yamey, B. S. 1957: *The Economics of Under-developed Countries*. Cambridge: Cambridge University Press.

Beckerman, W. 1974: *In Defence of Economic Growth*. London: Jonathan Cape.

Belshaw, D. 1980: Taking indigenous knowledge seriously. The case of inter-cropping techniques in East Africa. *IDS Bulletin*, 10, 24–7.

Bertelman, T. , et al. 1980: *Resources, Society and the Future*. Oxford: Pergamon Press.

Blaikie, P. M. 1981: Class, land-use and soil erosion. *ODI Review*, 2, 57–77.

Blaikie, P. M. 1984: *Natural Resources and Social Change*. Social Sciences: *Changing Britain, Changing World*. D205, Unit 7. Milton Keynes: The Open University.

Blaikie, P. M. 1985: *The Political Economy of Soil Erosion*. London: Longman.

Brokensha, D. W., Warren, D. and Werner, O. (eds) 1980: *Indigenous Knowledge Systems and Development*. Washington, DC: University Press of America.

Burke, A. E. 1956: Influence of man upon nature: the Russian view. In W. L. Thomas, et al. (eds), *Man's Role in Changing the Face of the Earth*, Chicago: University of Chicago Press.

Copans, J. 1975: *Qui le nourrit de la famine en Afrique and Sécherésses et famines du Sahel* (2 volumes). Paris: F. Maspero.

Coulson, A. 1982: *Tanzania: A Political Economy*. Oxford: Clarendon Press.

Daly, G. H. E. (ed.) 1972: *Towards a Steady-state Economy*. San Francisco: Freeman.

Delfs, R. 1982: The price of neglect. *Far Eastern Economic Review*, 20 August. p. 20.

Dequi, J., Leidi, Q. and Jusheng, T. 1981: Soil erosion and causation in the Winding River Valley, China. In R. P. C. Morgan (ed.), *Soil Conservation: Problems and Prospects*, Chichester: Wiley.

Dinham B. and Hines, C. 1983: *Agribusiness in Africa*. London: Earth Resources Research.

Du Boff, R. B. 1974: Economic ideology and the environment. H. G. T. Van Raay and A. E. Lugo (eds), in *Man and the Environment Ltd*, The Hague: Rotterdam University Press.

Ensensberger, H. M. 1974: A critique of political ecology. *New Left Review*, 8, 3–32.

Frank, A. G. 1978: *Dependent Accumulation and Underdevelopment*. London: Macmillan.

Frank, A. G. 1980: *Crisis in the World Economy*. London: Heinemann.

Frank, A. G. 1981: *Crisis in the Third World*. London: Heinemann.

Franke, R. and Chasin, B. 1980: *Seeds of Famine*. New York: Universe Books.

Freeman, C. and Jahoda, M. (eds) 1979: *World Futures: The Great Debate*. Oxford: Martin Robertson.

Gerasimov, I. P. and Armand, D. L. 1971: *Natural Resources of the Soviet Union: Their Use and Renewal*. San Francisco: Freeman (1st pub. Moscow, 1963).

Girvan, N. 1976: *Corporate Imperialism: Conflict and Expropriation*. New York: Monthly Review Press.

Glantz, M. H. (ed.) 1977: *Desertification*. Boulder, Colorado: Westview Press.

Glover, Sir. H. 1946: *Erosion of the Punjab: Its Causes and Cure*. Lahore, Pakistan: Feroz Printing Works.

Goudie, A. 1981: *The Human Impact: Man's Role in Environmental Change*. Oxford: Blackwell.

Graham, R. 1981: *The Aluminium Industry and the Third World*. London: Zed Press.

Grainger, A. 1980: The state of the world's tropical rain forests. *Ecologist*, 10, 6–52.

Gunnemann, J. P. (ed.) 1975: *The National State and Transnational Corporations in Conflict*. New York: Praeger.

Hagen, E. E. 1972: Limits to growth reconsidered. *International Development Review*, June, 10–12.

Howard, P. H. 1981: Impressions of soil and water conservation in China. *Journal of Soil and Water Conservation*, 36, 122–24.

Howe, C. W. 1979: *Natural Resource Economics Issues, Analysis and Policy*. New York: Wiley.

Hyams, E. 1952: *Soil and Civilization*, 2nd edn London: John Murray (1976).

Hyden, G. 1983: *No Shortcuts to Progress: African Development Management in Perspective*. London: Heinemann.

Jacks, G. C. and Whyte, R. O. 1939: *Vanishing Lands: A World Survey of Soil Erosion*. New York: Doubleday Doran.

Kahn, H., Brown, W. and Martel, L. (eds) 1976: *The Next 2000 years*. New York: William Morrow.

Kitching, G. 1982: *Development and Underdevelopment in Perspective: Populism, Nationalism and Industrialisation*. London: Methuen.

Kitching, G. 1983: *Rethinking Socialism*. London: Methuen.

Komarov, B. 1981: *The Destruction of Nature in the Soviet Union*. London: Pluto Press.

Lanly, H. P. 1982: *Tropical Forest Resources*. FAO Forestry Paper 30, Rome.

Lanning, G. with Mueller, M. 1979: *Africa Undermined*. Harmondsworth: Penguin.

Leslie, A. J. 1980: Logging concessions: how to stop losing money. *Unasylva*, 32 (129): 2–7.

MacEwan, M. 1984: The Greening of Britain. *Marxism Today*, July, 23–7.

Maddox, J. 1972: *The Doomsday Syndrome*. London: Macmillan.

Malcolm, D. W. 1938: *Sukumaland: An African People and Their Country*. London: Internatonal African Institute, Oxford University Press.

Meadows, D. H., Meadows, D. L. and Anders, J. 1972: *The Limits to Growth*. London: Earth Island.

Meillassoux, C. 1974: Development or exploitation: is the Sahel famine good business? *Review of African Political Economy*, 1, 27–33.

Mesarovic, M. and Pestel, E. 1975: *Mankind at the Turning Point*. London: Hutchinson.

Myers, N. 1983: The tropical forest issue. In T. O'Riordan and K. Turner (eds), *Progress in Resource Management and Environmental Planning*, vol. 4, pp. 1–28.

OECD 1972: *Problems of Environmental Economics*. Paris: OECD.

O'Keefe, P., Wisner, B. and Baird, A. (eds) 1977: *Kenyan Underdevelopment: A Case Study of Proletarianization*. London: International African Institute.

O'Riordan, T. 1976: *Environmentalism*. London: Pion.

Orr, D. W. and Soroos, M. S. 1979: *The Global Predicament*. Chapel Hill: University of North Carolina Press.

Plumwood, V. and Routley, R. 1982: World rainforest destruction – the social factors. *Ecologist*, 12, 4–22.

Pryde, P. R. 1972: *Conservation in the Soviet Union*. Cambridge: Cambridge University Press.

Qu Geping 1980: Deserts in China and their prevention and control. *Mazingira*, 4, 74–9.

Redclift, M. 1983: *Development and the Environmental Crisis: Red or Green Alternatives?* London: Methuen.

Richards, P. (ed.) 1975: *African Environment: Problems and Perspectives*. London: International African Institute.

Richards, P. 1985: *Peoples' Science: Ecology and Food Production in West Africa*. London: Methuen.

Rounce, N. V. 1949: *The Agriculture of the Cultivation Steppe of the Lake, Western and Central Provinces*. Capetown: Longmans.

Routley, R. and Routley, V. 1980: Destructive forestry in Melanesia and Australia. *Ecologist*, 10, 56–7.

Sandbach, F. 1980: *Environment, Ideology and Policy*. Oxford: Blackwell.

Simon, J. L. 1981: *The Ultimate Resource*. Princeton: Princeton University Press.

Smil, V. 1979: Controlling the Yellow River. *Geographical Review*, 69, 251–72.

Smil, V. 1983: *The Bad Earth: Environmental Degradation in China*. London: Zed Press.

Smith, V. (ed.) 1979: *Scarcity and Growth Reconsidered*. Baltimore: The Johns Hopkins University Press.

Stewart, F. 1977: *Technology and Underdevelopment*. London: Macmillan.

Thompson, E. P. 1968: *The Making of the English Working Class*. Harmondsworth: Penguin.

United Nations 1976: *Transnational Corporations: Issues involved in the Formulation of a Code of Conduct*. New York: UN Centre on Transnational Corporations.

United Nations 1980a: *Sea-Bed Mineral Resource Development: Recent Activities of the International Consortia*. New York: United Nations Department of Economic and Social Affairs.

United Nations 1980b: *The Activities of the Industrial Mining and Military Sectors of Southern Africa*. New York: United Nations Centre on Transnational Companies.

United Nations 1980c: *The Nickel Industry and the Developing Countries*. New York: United Nations Department of Technical Cooperation for Development.

United Nations 1981a: *Transnational Corporations in the Bauxite/Aluminium Industry*. New York: United Nations Centre on Transnational Corporations.

United Nations 1981b: *Transnational Corporations in the Copper Industry*. New York: United Nations Centre on Transnational Companies.

Wallerstein, I. 1979: *The Capitalist World-Economy*. Cambridge: Cambridge University Press.

Warren, B. 1973: Imperialism and capitalist industrialization. *New Left Review*, 81, 3–44.

Warren, B. 1980: *Imperialism: Pioneer of Capitalism*. London: New Left Books.

Watts, M. 1983: On the poverty of theory: national hazards research in context. In K. Hewitt (ed.), *Interpretations of Calamity*, London: Allen & Unwin, pp. 231–62.

Watts, M. 1984: The demise of the rural economy: food and famine in a Sudano-Sahelian region in historical perspective. In E. Scott (ed.), *Before the Drought*, Boston: Allen & Unwin.

Williams, G. 1976: Taking the part of peasants: rural development in Nigeria and . Tanzania. In P. Gutkind and I. Wallerstein (eds), *The Political Economy of Contemporary Africa*. London: Sage Publications.

Young, O. R. 1982: *Resource Regimes*. Berkeley: University of California Press.

6

Malthus, Marx and Population Crises

ROBERT WOODS

Malthus' principle implies, without explicitly stating, the existence of an optimum population, that is a population the size of which maximizes the level of real wages or income per head. It also suggests the possibility of sub- and supra-optimum populations which if excessively low or high will lead to population crises. Such crises may therefore result from either underpopulation or overpopulation. Malthus himself was concerned almost entirely with overpopulation, the geometrical rate of population growth, the arithmetic rate at which food supply could be increased, and the discrepancy between the two rates. Crises would be characterized by 'misery and vice' but also by substantial increases in mortality which would act to redress the imbalance between supply and demand by reducing the latter, thereby easing population towards the optimum size. But these Malthusian subsistence crises do not represent the only forms of population crises that are possible, nor were they in any sense inevitable for, according to Malthus, the tension between the rate of population growth and that of food supply would lead to other preventive checks to population increase.

Malthus' *First Essay* of 1798 and his *Second Essay* of 1803 were particularly influential among contemporaries and have proved so again in the late twentieth century when the problems of world overpopulation seem acute. (The literature on Malthus' principle of population and his political economy – Malthus, 1970, 1973 – is voluminous, but see especially Spengler, 1972; Petersen, 1979; and Dupâquier, Fauve-Chamoux and Grebenik, 1983.) In this chapter I shall first review the current state of the world demographic system using this neo-Malthusian perspective. Secondly, the notion of a crisis of numbers will be questioned in the context of other potential causes of population-related crises and the long-term recurrence of similar events. Thirdly, the chapter will examine the Malthusian principle at greater length by contrasting it with the notion of surplus population advanced in Marxian political economy.

Table 6.1 *World population growth since 1950*

	Populations in millions							% growth rate p.a.	1975–80		Projections in millions	
	1950	1955	1960	1965	1970	1975	1980		CBR	CDR	2000	2050
World	2,525	2,757	3,037	3,354	3,696	4,066	4,432	1.7	29	11	6,206	9,973
Africa	220	245	275	312	355	407	470	2.9	46	17	903	2,297
North America	166	182	199	214	226	236	248	1.0	16	9	286	320
Latin America	164	188	216	248	283	822	364	2.5	34	9	543	868
East Asia	673	738	816	899	994	1,096	1,175	1.4	21	7	1,443	1,709
South Asia	716	786	877	988	1,117	1,256	1,404	2.2	37	15	2,164	3,810
Europe	392	408	425	445	459	474	484	0.4	14	11	527	570
Oceania	13	14	16	18	19	21	23	1.5	22	9	28	37
USSR	180	196	214	231	242	253	265	0.9	18	9	312	362

Source: United Nations *Demographic Yearbook*, 1981; and for projections Demeny (1983, p. 110)

THE CONTEMPORARY WORLD DEMOGRAPHIC SYSTEM

The population of the world in the mid-1980s is approaching 5 billion: in 1950 it was 2.5 billion; in 2050 it may be 10 billion. In these circumstances it is obvious why Malthusianism is again influential and why population is believed to pose a 'global problem', yet as table 6.1 reveals there are extreme regional variations in the rate and character of population growth. During the late 1970s the rate of world population increase was about 1.7 per cent per annum but while in Africa, Latin America and South Asia it was 2 per cent or more, in Europe, the USSR and North America it was 1 per cent or less. One of the implications of these differential rates is illustrated in table 6.2, which shows the changing percentage of the global population in each region. The world may be divided into three. In Africa and South Asia growth is rapid and will remain so well into the twenty-first century, by which time this area will contain over 50 per cent of the global total. In Latin America and East Asia growth has been rapid, but its pace has slackened, especially in East Asia, and in consequence this area is likely to maintain its 30 per cent share. The remaining 20 per cent of the world's population will live in Europe, the USSR, North America and Oceania, but this area will contain only 8 per cent of world population growth between 1980 and 2000, compared with two-thirds and a quarter in the other two areas.

The immediate cause of these different growth rates is also obvious from table 6.1. The crude death rate (CDR) is now relatively low, but the crude birth rate (CBR) remains particularly high in many regions. Figure 6.1 illustrates international variations in CDR and CBR and thus the level of natural increase, which is shown on the diagonal lines as the annual growth rate in per cent. Figure 6.1 also classifies countries by their estimated or known life expectations at birth (e_0). The four classes of e_0 used there are also

Table 6.2   Percentage share of world population

	1950	1980	2000	2050	Increase 1980–2000
Africa	8.71	10.60	14.55	23.03	24.42
North America	6.57	5.60	4.61	3.21	2.14
Latin America	6.50	8.21	8.75	8.70	10.10
East Asia	26.65	26.51	23.25	17.14	15.12
South Asia	28.36	31.68	34.87	38.20	42.87
Europe	15.52	10.92	8.49	5.72	2.43
Oceania	0.51	0.52	0.45	0.37	0.28
USSR	7.13	5.98	5.03	3.63	2.65

Source: based on table 6.1

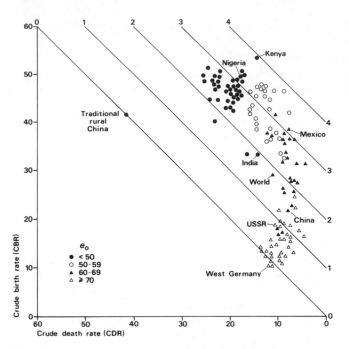

Figure 6.1 International variations in estimated crude birth and death rates 1975–80
Source: see table 6.1

illustrated in figure 6.2. Clearly there are substantial differences in the mortality levels experienced yet these differences are not as important as those in the pattern of fertility since it is the latter that largely determines the population growth rate. (The following provide important reviews of contemporary international demographic patterns: Tabah, 1980, 1982; Coale, 1982, 1983a; United Nations, 1979; Demeny, 1982. This chapter will not be particularly concerned with the general relationship between population and development; for which see Coale and Hoover, 1958; Simon, 1977; Cassen, 1976; and Birdsall et al., 1979.)

In the late 1970s the population of Kenya was growing by nearly 4 per cent per annum, CBR was higher and CDR lower than even African standards, of which Nigeria was more typical (Dow and Werner, 1983; Page and Lesthaeghe, 1981). In Mexico growth rates exceeded 3 per cent with mortality nearly as low as in Europe (in terms of CDR at least) (Hicks, 1974; Seiver, 1975). The case of India, which dominates the South Asia region, raises a number of interesting issues for while the growth rate was at about 2 per cent e_0 had probably only just reached 50 by 1980, and although the CBR had declined the pace of the fertility transition had not proved to be as rapid as in parts of east and south-east Asia (Cassen, 1978; Chaudhry, 1982).

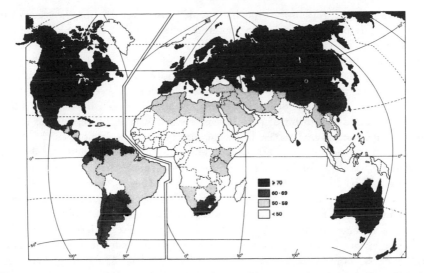

Figure 6.2 International variations in estimated life expectation at birth (e_0), 1975–80
Source: see table 6.1

These three countries – Kenya, Mexico and India – provide contrasting examples of areas which might be thought to be experiencing a population crisis, because of its rate of increase, or to be overpopulated, because of its density. But there are other areas with rather different demographic conditions where the terms 'population crisis' and 'overpopulated' are just as appropriate. In the late 1970s China appears to have had only a moderate growth rate yet in the two preceding decades the disparity between a rapidly falling death rate and a persistently high birth rate led the Chinese government to adopt an extreme neo-Malthusian policy. In western Europe, on the other hand, there are examples of national populations with death rates in excess of birth rates where depopulation is a legitimate fear (West Germany in figure 6.1, for example) (Bourgeois-Pichat, 1981; Kirk, 1981).

Apart from these countries, which in terms of the implied Malthusian definition of population crises may be appropriate candidates for the use of the term, there are other instances in which the phrase might be justified. Within the Soviet Union there are extreme differences between the contemporary demographic systems of European Russia (especially the Baltic states) and Soviet Central Asia. Whereas the latter is similar to south-west Asia the former is far closer to eastern and western Europe. One consequence of this demographic division will be the declining proportion of Russians in the Soviet population and the exacerbation of a nascent ethnic problem in Soviet society (Heer, 1965; Coale, Anderson and Härm, 1979; Jones and Grupp, 1983). In parts of Europe the problems of demographic ageing are particularly acute, while the age structures of most Latin American, African and Asian countries are such that the phrase 'youth revolution' has been widely used. In Europe the escalating cost of welfare payments to the elderly impose strains on the economically active; moreover, in the latter group the increased costs associated with child health care and education are immediate, and those linking with under- and unemployment in a rapidly expanding labour force are likely to prove critical to the prospects for political stability.

The term 'overurbanization' has been used in instances where it seems that there is a maldistribution of population towards a rapidly expanding urban sector whose employment base is not increasing in step (Gugler, 1982). Rural depopulation is not an automatic consequence, although even where the absolute size of the rural population also increases some relief from pressure may be experienced (Clarke and Kosinski, 1982; Grigg, 1980). Although these three additional examples – nationally divisive demographic subsystems, very unbalanced age structures, overurbanization and redistribution – all in their own ways create conditions that if extreme might be regarded as population crises, they are in a sense peripheral to the central issues in the Malthusian and even the popular conception of a population crisis. The central issues are rate of growth, size, and thus density, of population. Figure 6.1 shows that on at least one of these traditional criteria conditions appear ripe for a crisis of numbers in several countries, but for others in similar or only slightly better economic circumstances neither criterion is met or, if one is, then in not such an obvious manner. Has the population crisis been averted in China, for example? If so, by what means? Can these means also be applied in Nigeria, Kenya, Mexico or even India? Our ability to answer these questions depends upon an understanding of the processes which produce fertility decline. Given that a return to the former high levels of mortality is unacceptable, a fall in fertility is the only possibility for the reduction in the rate of population growth. (Bulatao and Lee, 1983, provide a review of the most recent work on the determinants of fertility.)

China and India

Figure 6.3 provides a summary of the recent changes in Chinese mortality and fertility in terms of the crude birth and death rates and the total fertility rate (TFR) (see Pressat, 1982, p. 300; Coale, 1981a). All three rates should be subjected to close scrutiny; they are estimates based on Chinese sources which may not always be checked and are likely to be revised in the light of both the population census and the Chinese State Family Planning Commission's fertility survey of 1982 (Aird, 1982; Pressat, 1982, 1983; Caldwell and Srinivasan, 1984). The graph (figure 6.3) appears to show both the substantial reductions in mortality and fertility that have occurred since 1949, and the effects of disruption and famine during the Great Leap Forward of the late 1950s and early 1960s.

The demography of traditional rural China has been reconstructed by Barclay et al. (1976) using survey data collected in 1929–31. Their estimates suggest

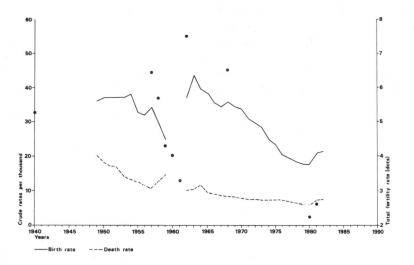

Figure 6.3 Changing estimated crude birth and death rates in the People's Republic of China
Source: from Pressat (1982)

a CBR of 41.2, a CDR of 41.5, an e_0 of 24.2 and a TFR of 5.50; and that the mean age at marriage for men was 21.32, for women 17.52, with virtually all women marrying before age 50 (I_m was 0.874). Marital fertility was of the natural fertility form with no evidence for parity-specific control, yet it was particularly low by most historical European standards (I_g was 0.510 and I_f was 0.446). Some of these measures are now available for the early 1980s, again in estimated form. Life expectation at birth (e_0) is probably in the low sixties and infant mortality is about 50 per thousand (see Banister and Preston, 1981). As figure 6.3 shows, TFR was 2.24 in 1980 and 2.63 in 1981, but in the urban areas it was only 1.15 and 1.39, respectively, in those years. It may well be that the fertility transition began in the mid-1950s in these urban areas. Its progress can be linked with the growing involvement of women in the labour force and perhaps the economic and social upheavals that followed the founding of a People's Republic.

The first birth-control campaign was probably largely ineffective and certainly ended when the Great Leap Forward was initiated in 1958. The second campaign, 1962–6, does not appear to have been very effective either, but the third, which began in 1968 and was re-emphasized in 1972–3 and 1979, has proved a most important vehicle for persuasion or coercion (Aird, 1978a, 1978b; Caldwell and Srinivasan, 1984). The aims of the present campaign as stated in 1979 were to reduce the growth rate of the Chinese population to 0.5 per cent by 1985 and to 0 by 2000; to increase the age at marriage of men to 25 and of women to 23 in rural areas, but 27 and 25 in urban areas; and to reduce the completed family size to one at best, two under certain circumstances, but certainly not three or more (Coale, 1981a, 1981b). Several attempts have been made to examine the long-term consequences were these goals to be achieved. Chen and Tyler (1982), for example, have made the necessary projections, which show that immediate adoption of the one-child family norm would stabilize the population by 2000, and that zero growth would be achieved by 2020 with the two-child family. A three-child family norm would ensure the doubling of population by 2030 at about 2 billion. The implication of these projections is clear: unless the TFR is reduced to, and maintained at, approximately 2 the accelerated growth of the Chinese population which has occurred in the period since the 1950s will not be curtailed.

Establishing the one- or two-child family norm has posed particularly difficult problems for the Family Planning Commission. First, it has been necessary to employ all the resources of the state's propaganda machinery to persuade couples that one child is sufficient when Chinese tradition lays particular emphasis on the family, children – especially boys – and the family economy (Baker, 1979; Watson, 1982). But the possession of a 'one-child certificate' (acquired after sterilization, or the elapse of four years from the birth of a first child and the couple's promise to have no more) entitles the child and parents to special educational and financial benefits. The penalties for breaking the terms of the certificate are severe, as are those imposed on couples who do have two or more children. The balance of carrot and stick has been such that nationally some 56 per cent of eligible couples were reported to have certificates in 1980, an increase from 34 per cent in 1979, but in Beijing the figure was 79 per cent (Goodstadt, 1982).

Second, couples have had to adapt to the use of new methods of birth control, to submit to sterilizations or abortions in a third or subsequent pregnancy. The results of the survey reported by Caldwell and Srinivasan (1984, p. 77) suggest that among married couples, where the wife was under 50, up to 25 per cent had been sterilized, 35 per cent used IUDs, 6 per cent used oral contraceptives, 1 per cent used the condom, but 31 per cent were not using birth-control methods. Many of the women in this last-mentioned group would be in their twenties.

Third, there are striking differences between the urban and rural sectors of Chinese society. Family-size targets are lower in the urban areas, the proscribed marriage ages are higher, and the family-planning programme more effective, yet only about 20 per cent of the Chinese population lives in towns. The problem is illustrated quite effectively in the following way: in 1981 86 per cent of all births to urban couples were first births while among rural couples the figure was 40 per cent, with only 44 per cent in China as a whole (Caldwell and Srinivasan, 1984, p. 79). In the rural sector in particular there is a lasting desire for early marriage, often arranged by parents, and for large families, so that the kin-related labour supply can be maintained, the wishes of grandparents fulfilled and some measure of security in old age guaranteed. But while these traditional and entirely rational objectives remain they represent the most important restrictions on the success of the family-planning programme and the general demographic strategy of which it is the major part (Qian Xinzhong, 1983).

Some of these remarks could also be applied to rural India. But there, as figure 6.1 suggests, the pace of demographic change has been relatively slow during the last two decades, with population growth at about 2.20 per cent per annum in the 1960s and 2.23 per cent in the 1970s. Although a family-planning programme has existed in India since 1952, and a much expanded one since 1966, only 24 per cent of couples in the reproductive age group were protected by some effective method of birth control in the late 1970s (Cassen, 1978). Of the 24 per cent, sterilizations represent by far the most important category. The impact of the programme has not been spectacular nationally, since between the 1960s and 1970s CBR fell by only 13–16 per cent from about 42 to 38–39, thereby only keeping pace with the decline in CDR (Jain and Adlakha, 1982, p. 595; see also Dyson and Crook, 1984).

Some of the reasons for the programme's limited influence are obvious on reflection. For example, Gwatkin (1979) provides an account of the government's difficulties in 'enforcing' a rigorous sterilization scheme during the mid-1970s and describes the state of national emergency to which it contributed. But the underlying causes are less obvious. There is considerable demographic diversity among the Indian states in terms of both mortality and, particularly, fertility variations (Woods, 1982, pp. 72–85). It is a diversity which is clearly not merely a function of economic development, levels of living or urbanization, but which seems to reflect cultural divisions between north and south (Dyson and Moore, 1983). In the north – Rajasthan and Uttar Pradesh, for example – mortality and fertility rates are well above the national average and the take-up rate for family planning is low, but in the south – especially Kerala – mortality and fertility are lower and the family-planning programme has been quite successful. These differences can be associated with, among other variables, regional differences in female social status. In the south marriage and kinship arrangements favour a higher level of female autonomy (female literacy is far higher for instance) and the interests of child and mother are of greater importance than appears to be the case in the male-orientated northern societies.

Too simple comparisons of China and India are not particularly helpful yet it is reasonable to observe certain apparently significant differences (Coale, 1983b). The ability and will of the state to enforce a rapid change in family-planning practice are certainly important. Both governments have acted in a neo-Malthusian fashion, but in China the political machine has been effective and the public supportive, or at least compliant, whereas in India the democratic institutions have been used to thwart excessive haste. However, it is possible that the fertility levels that pertain in rural south India are equivalent to those in many areas of contemporary rural China. In India the attainment of a stationary population must remain a long-term goal which will be achieved with economic development, social modernization and the encouragement of government planners. In China the same goal can be realized more quickly, but probably not as soon as is hoped for in government circles.

Latin America

The rate of population growth has been particularly rapid in recent decades in Latin America. Mortality has declined abruptly since the 1940s and 1950s (Palloni, 1981; see also United Nations, 1982), but fertility has remained persistently high in many of the larger countries and is only now beginning to decline. The reasons for the international and regional variations in fertility levels, together with the leads and lags in decline, have proved particularly difficult to explain. They are not simply and universally a reflection of socioeconomic differences, literacy, education, urbanization, or the availability of an effective family-planning programme (Beaver, 1975), but each of these influences can be important in certain circumstances. To illustrate the complex nature of the problem:

> The case of Costa Rica is of special interest because its fertility fell so fast despite the fact that in other respects it is more typical of Latin America. While its literacy levels have been unusually high for some time, the substantial improvements in post-primary schooling in the 1950s probably effected an educational breakthrough critical for fertility. The initiators of the decline were young couples, living in the more economically developed cantons, especially those undergoing the greatest reduction in agricultural employment. Such couples cut the number of their children by such means as *coitus interruptus* and the condom, methods unencumbered by legal restrictions. Information about contraception was diffused by freer communication than elsewhere between spouses – a product of higher educational levels in Costa Rica, and possibly of cultural norms more permissive of sex-related discussions. This set a favourable scene for the family-planning programme, which both stepped up communications and made new contraceptives available – IUDs and pills. Once the programme had been launched, older or less educated women were attracted to contraception, and the fertility of the more backward cantons began to decline. (Stycos, 1978, p. 424)

Despite these developments, Costa Rica still had a CBR of 31.1 and a CDR of 4.1 in the late 1970s (e_o was 68 and the annual growth rate 2.70 per cent), but in Mexico CBR was 38.3 and CDR was 7.8 (e_o was 66 and the growth rate 3.05 per cent).

From the Malthusian perspective Mexico appears to provide a classic example of a society experiencing a population crisis where the rate of growth is out of balance with economic growth or development (Coale, 1978). Until 1973 there was little or no effort on the part of the government to encourage family limitation although the provision of medical facilities was extended and, like other Latin American countries, mortality declined. Those analyses based on data for 1960 and 1970 have pointed to the perpetuation of high fertility (CBR was 45 and CDR was 9 in the early 1970s) despite rapid economic development, increases in literacy, education, urbanization and a rising female labour-force participation rate (Seiver, 1975; Hicks, 1974). Although many of these classical demographic transition theory variables did help to account for cross-sectional variations in fertility – especially the share of the labour force employed in agriculture (+) and the percentage of the population speaking an indigenous language (–) – fertility decline was limited and it appeared related, if to any variables, to reduction in the agricultural labour force and increase in life expectation. More up-to-date accounts await the availability of the 1980 census, yet even in Mexico there are some indications of the first stages of a fertility transition, one which may have elements in common with the experience of Costa Rica.

A CRISIS OF NUMBERS?

The governments of China, India and, rather more recently, Mexico have each identified a population problem in their respective countries. By this they affirm their belief in the need to keep population under control, the beneficial influence a slow rate of growth may have for economic development and their fear of the excesses which a crisis of numbers may bring for economic, social and political stability. Having reviewed the state of the contemporary world demographic system and the reactions of certain governments to their current position we may now turn to reconsider the notion of a crisis of numbers and population crises in general. This will be done in two ways: by examining the structure of demographic systems, and by reviewing the influence of crises in historical perspective.

Figure 6.4 places in order most of the important elements which must operate by definition in any demographic system. It should be read from the top downwards and outwards. A population may appear to have reached a crisis point if the rate of its growth or its size are out of balance with the prevailing economic and social conditions, yet a number of the elements in figure 6.4 are by the same token able to generate forms of crisis in their own right. The use of the word 'crisis' is appropriate at two levels, therefore. Firstly, one may distinguish a general crisis of numbers which will affect the nation or regions thereof. Secondly, more particular tensions may arise which are linked with sub-elements of the demographic system. It is also obviously the case that some of the general crises stem from imbalances between rates of change in the three major demographic components: mortality, fertility and migration.

A small number of examples must suffice to illustrate these distinctions. Contemporary international labour migration serves to redress the imbalance between levels of regional economic development since it is attuned to the most obvious spatio-temporal differentials, but it is also associated with political and social crises. In the United States the political reaction to illegal Mexican immigration has been substantial (Grebler, 1966; Dagodag, 1975) while the governments of France, Germany and Switzerland have all been faced with a new migrant ethnic minority problem to which they have reacted with a variety of restrictions designed to meet perceived national self-interest and political expediency (Castles and Kosack, 1973; White and Woods, 1983). In the Republic of South Africa the need for a pliant workforce together with the threat posed by extreme differences in rates of growth between white and non-white populations have encouraged the development of a strictly controlled system of internal circulatory migration (Smith, 1983). The crisis associated with the Sahel drought apparently provides a classic example of the consequences of overpopulation coupled with environmental degeneration. In this example we have a modern demographic crisis (see figure 6.4) of the subsistence variety having its origins in food shortages and ultimately overpopulation. But such a simple interpretation, which equates famine with natural disasters, conceals complicated arrangements for the allocation of food resources, termed entitlements by Sen (1981). Sen contrasts the 'food availability decline' interpretation, which emphasizes the production and supply of food, with the 'exchange entitlements' approach which dwells on the distribution of food to consumers and the relative position of those consumers in the market for food. Famines can thus occur when the exchange entitlements of a population decline and need not merely be a consequence of a reduction in the availability of food; Sen (1981) provides detailed examples of this phenomenon drawn from Bengal (1943), Ethiopia (1973), the Sahel (1968–73) and Bangladesh (1974).

These examples suggest, among other things, the variety of forms which a population crisis may take and, by implication, the imprecision of the phrase as a technical term in modern usage. In contrast, the use of the equivalent

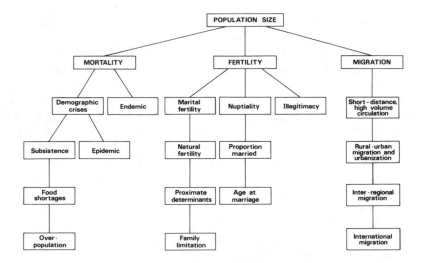

Figure 6.4   Elements of the general demographic system

phrase 'demographic crisis' in the historical literature is normally restricted to the direct consequences of a sharp, usually short-term, increase in mortality. As figure 6.4 shows there are two major sources for these demographic crises. The most straightforward relates to outbreaks of epidemic disease, such as bubonic plague, typhus, smallpox and influenza. The second source – often referred to as subsistence – is apparently coincidental with Malthus' notion of the positive check. Here food shortages are a direct effect of overpopulation; famine, or at least widespread malnourishment, and increased mortality are the inevitable consequences. However, absolute food shortages also arise when inclement weather affects the harvest or when livestock suffer from disease, while relative food shortages among certain social categories relate to the system of allocation and entitlement mentioned above.

It has proved particularly difficult to establish an empirical definition for demographic crises, to infer the most likely causes of particular events and to assess the importance of crisis-related mortality to historical demographic systems. Most of these difficulties are related to the vagaries of interpreting historical data. The key definitional variable for such demographic crises has been the extent to which crisis mortality exceeds the normal level of mortality. Crisis periods are therefore those in which mortality exceeds the normal by an arbitrarily determined amount (Schofield, 1972). The application of this definition is dependent upon the availability of reliable mortality statistics, but breaks down where and when one has only a general impression of high mortality or merely reference to famine, dearth or disease. For example, the return of bubonic plague to western Europe in 1348–9 represents a clear instance of a substantial demographic crisis yet the extent of mortality above the average is beyond accurate measurement, although it is generally presumed that from 25 to 50 per cent of the population died in the first outbreak (McNeill, 1977; Hatcher, 1977).

Where parish registers provide a more accurate means of identifying mortality crises – their intensity, frequency and cause – there is obviously scope for a more detailed assessment. Wrigley and Schofield's (1981, pp. 645–93) analysis of data from 404 English parishes in the period from the 1540s to the 1830s is a particularly important example in this respect. In only four years did more than a quarter of the parishes experience a mortality crisis. There was no national crisis of numbers during the three centuries in England although there were many localized crises – often associated with epidemic disease – and several regional crises. On the basis of this analysis there seems little reason to suppose that demographic crises played an important part in the general population system and even if they did locally or for short periods regionally then they were of the essentially random epidemic disease variety rather than of the subsistence kind.

However, England may not have been typical even of Europe. France suffered regional famine in the seventeenth century and severe food shortages in the eighteenth; Scandinavia was racked by severe mortality crises at the end of the eighteenth century and it has been argued that much of western Europe experienced a subsistence crisis in the early decades of the nineteenth century. (On France see, for example, Meuvret, 1977; on Scandinavia, Jutikkala, 1955; Jutikkala and Kauppinen, 1971; Sogner, 1976; and on Napoleonic Europe, Post, 1977; also Flinn, 1981, pp. 47–64.)

The impact of demographic crises certainly varies with period and place. Low rates of population growth in fifteenth-century England have been attributed to repeated attacks of bubonic plague (Gottfried, 1978). The stationary population of Tokugawan Japan is said by some economic historians to have been related to chronic famine conditions (Hanley and Yamamura, 1977). In general, however, the various pre-industrial demographic regimes may have been influenced more by the background level of mortality – especially high infant mortality – than by the dramatic but irregular additional element of crisis mortality. (Cassen and Dyson, 1976, provide an interesting illustration of the negligible long-term impact of demographic crises in their study of Indian population dynamics.) Bubonic plague is possibly the most significant exception to this general point.

But the scheme outlined in figure 6.4 also requires one to examine the significance of the balance between mortality and fertility for the changing rate of population growth. The north-west European marriage pattern, as defined by Hajnal (1965, 1982), developed from a number of interrelated social institutions among which the nuclear family system, the formation of new households at marriage and the necessity to ensure the independent household's economic viability before marriage may be contracted were the most important. Given the effective operation of these social 'rules' the consequent marriage pattern is likely to reflect prevailing economic conditions in the longer term. In the good years couples will marry relatively young, in their early twenties perhaps, but in the bad years marriage will be delayed to the late twenties or early thirties and celibacy will increase. By these means the demographic and economic systems will be linked via nuptiality since while natural fertility predominates the level of overall fertility will mainly be controlled by the age at first marriage and the proportion of the population marrying. After a short-run demographic crisis, opportunities for household formation would increase, marriage would be contracted at a younger age and the birth rate rise, thus replacing the lost population within a generation or two. The effective operation of this mechanism within an essentially agrarian society like Tudor England would tend to nullify the long-term impact of a single mortality crisis, but not the repeated recurrence of such events (see Wrigley and Schofield, 1981).

Taking this historical perspective on pre-industrial western societies helps us to appreciate the complex nature of the crisis concept and to see that while mortality crises were by no means rare they were not necessarily of great importance for the working of the population system. This is not to say that at certain times villages, towns and even whole regions were not devastated by epidemics or famines, but rather that the long-term influence of the dramatic and acute on population and economic growth must be brought into question.

OVERPOPULATION AND SURPLUS POPULATION

So far we have considered the incidence, nature and influence of population crises – variously defined – using an essentially Malthusian framework and largely within the terms of the demographic rather than the related economic, social or political systems. In this final section we turn again to reconsider Malthus' *Principle of Population* and to compare his term 'overpopulation' with Marx's concept of a 'surplus population'. This comparison will enable us to examine wider aspects of crises beyond those that stress rates of population growth, size and acute events in the relatively short term. The possibility of a 'permanent crisis' affecting subpopulations also needs to be considered.

Malthus' theories of population and political economy often appear unsophisticated in the 1980s yet the ideas contained therein are just as important and as debatable as they were over 150 years ago. Given a zero or negligible rate of technological progress in a predominantly agrarian society, the functional relationship between income per head or real wages and the size of a population will tend to be positive when densities are low and population growth stimulates effective demand for commodity production, but a turning-point will be reached above which diminishing returns will transform the positive to a negative relationship. An extra increase in population size will depress even further the level of income per head to a point at which the material necessities of life are in such short supply that life itself is endangered. Once that point is reached, overpopulation is apparent (see Grigg, 1980, p. 62; Wrigley and Schofield, 1981, p. 460; Schultz, 1981, pp. 9–61). Malthus himself (using the USA as his example) compared the possible geometric rate of increase of population and the known (in the absence of counter-examples) arithmetic rate of increase of agricultural production in order to illustrate his point that the former would inevitably outstrip the latter if there were no checks to the rate of population growth. Since it seemed that there was generally some balance between the rate of growth of subsistence and the level of real wages the effective checks must be in operation to make the balance possible and to avoid the excesses of overpopulation. These checks have come to be known as positive, mortality related (misery and vice), and preventive, nuptiality related (moral restraint).

In the *First Essay* of 1798 the positive check was especially emphasized, but the *Second Essay* of 1803 altered the balance of checks towards the preventive. As we have already seen, the preventive check appears to have worked in early – modern England and life was not in general endangered by the positive check, but elsewhere and in theory the positive check, via an increase in mortality, could effect a reduction in population size and a return to some form of resources/population equilibrium. In short, Malthus argues that overpopulation (simply an excess of population compared with food supply or a population an increase in the size of which will adversely affect the level of real wages or income per head) is an ever-present possibility in human society which when it occurs will be rectified by an increase in mortality (a mortality crisis), but

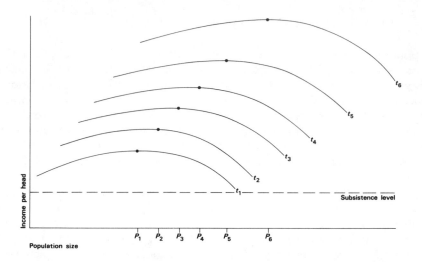

Figure 6.5   The influence of technological advance on the relationship between income per head and population size

which may be averted by delaying marriage, thus effectively reducing the growth rate of a population by lowering its fertility.

The logic of the 'ever-present possibility' seems inescapable, yet there are a number of other ways in which overpopulation can be avoided. Figure 6.5 illustrates one possiblity. The t_1 function shows the classic curvilinear relationship between income per head and population size where the former is low and relatively close to the level of subsistence. The optimum population under these conditions is P_1. If one now assumes, in contrast to Malthus, that technological advance is possible, that it even accelerates over time, then the functions t_2 to t_6 become appropriate. The related optima, P_1 to P_6, show an increase, as of course does income per head. Although the principle of diminishing returns and overpopulation is retained in the t_1 to t_6 functions, by t_6 population increase beyond P_6 must be massive before the subsistence level is reached and the material necessities of life are endangered. In these circumstances although the logic of the ever-present possibility remains unbroken, technological advance makes its direst consequences unlikely. In oversimplified form figure 6.5 portrays the experience of the western economies over the last two centuries save that marginally sub- or supra-optimum population sizes were actually involved (see Schultz, 1981, pp. 47–51).

An additional obvious method of avoiding overpopulation would be to employ alternative, more effective forms of the preventive check. Natural fertility began to disappear in France in the late eighteenth century and in the rest of Europe from the last decades of the nineteenth. The use of birth-control methods is now universal in the west, and even in underdeveloped countries, as we have seen, substantial numbers limit their marital fertility to the extent that completed family size varies from two to four children. This neo-Malthusian strategy has been favoured by western governments and international agencies in their dealings with underdeveloped countries, but it has also been freely adopted and made most effective in China.

These two ways of avoiding overpopulation can still be discussed within Malthus' original framework; they merely require the relaxation of one of his most important assumptions concerning the limited ability of the rate of subsistence to increase and the extension of moral restraint to cover what for Malthus represented an immoral act – the deliberate use of methods of birth control. Marx's 'law of population' is developed from a radically different perspective. (Once again the literature on Marx's economic and social thought is enormous, but relatively little has been written concerning his approach to the population question, which is to be found mainly in chapter 25 of *Capital* (Marx, 1976). Some interesting comparisons of Malthus and Marx are to be found in Hayes, 1954; Petersen, 1964; Daly, 1971; Harvey, 1974; Woods, 1983; but see also Meek, 1953, for Marx and Engels on Malthus.)

First, Marx was intent on countering the idea that the regulation of human population is controlled by a natural law. Rather, we should seek to understand the economic, political and thus social system which provides the context for changes in demographic patterns and structures. 'Capitalist production can by no means content itself with the quantity of disposable labour-power which the natural increase of population yields. It requires for its unrestricted activity an industrial reserve army which is independent of these natural limits' (Marx, 1976, p. 788). This emphasis on population as a dependent variable, albeit an important one, is particularly significant in the Marxian framework.

Second, in *Capital*, at least, Marx aims to unravel the laws that govern the development of capitalism and is thus especially interested in the problem of capital accumulation and its relation to the supply of labour. While the accumulation of capital feeds on appropriated surplus value the working population 'produces both the accumulation of capital and the means by which it is itself made relatively superfluous' (p. 783). The creation of a surplus population of unemployed:

> is a necessary product of accumulation or of the development of wealth on a capitalist basis, this surplus population also becomes, conversely, the lever of capitalist accumulation, indeed it becomes a condition for the existence of the capitalist mode of production. It forms a disposable industrial reserve army, which belongs to capital just as absolutely as if the latter had bred it at its own cost. (p. 784)

The inherent phases of production in the capitalist industrial system create, but also require, a pool of 'unemployed or semi-employed "hands"', the size of which relates to the current stage of the cycle. Within the working class – that section of the population that does not own or control the means of production, but gains its subsistence by selling its labour power – relations between members of the reserve and active armies, as well as the ratio of the former to the latter, have important consequences. 'The over-work of the employed part of the working class swells the ranks of its reserve, while, conversely, the greater pressure that the reserve by its competition exerts on the employed workers forces them to submit to over-work and subjects them to the dictates of capital' (p. 789). Marx also argues that the movement of wages will be determined by the ratio of members of the reserve army to those in the active army and not by variations in the absolute numbers of the working population. The higher the proportion of the working class in the reserve army, the lower will be the level of wages for those in the active army (see Junankar, 1982, p. 85). The extent of pauperism will also be influenced by this reserve/active ratio while those in the reserve army will obviously be most prone to poverty. There is a further claim: both fertility and mortality will be inversely related to the level of wages.

Marx concludes his discussion of the general law of capitalist accumulation by distinguishing four separate elements in the surplus population. The *latent* surplus population is to be found mainly in rural areas whence it is drawn, when need arises, into the towns to become part of the manufacturing proletariat. The *floating* surplus population emigrates as capital emigrates and its size may be increased by the laying-off of apprentices or female workers. The *stagnant* element suffers from extremely irregular employment often associated with the decaying branches of industry. This partially active population is liable to suffer from a maximum of working time but a minimum of wages. The fourth element, that is 'the lowest sediment of the relative surplus population, dwells in the sphere of pauperism'. Again, there are four divisions: the lumpenproletariat (vagabonds, criminals, prostitutes); those who are able to work; orphans and pauper children; and 'the demoralized, the ragged and those unable to work'. Accordingly, for Marx, 'Pauperism is the hospital of the active labour-army and the dead weight of the industrial reserve army' (Marx, 1976, p. 797).

Two additional points need to be examined a little more carefully before we turn to a more general evaluation of the implications of the Marxian model and its relation to the Malthusian principle. One of the most important features of Marx's economic thinking is the argument that short-run, trade cycle like crises are an inherent feature of the capitalist system. During a crisis the size of the reserve army increases as workers are laid off, wage rates are depressed, and eventually profits begin to rise again and the 'beautiful trinity of capitalist production', as Marx (p. 787) calls overproduction, overpopulation and overconsumption, can repeat itself. Economic crises, fluctuations in the absolute and relative size of the surplus population, and changes in the rate of capital accumulation are all closely linked in this scheme. The size and structure of the labour force responds to and affects in turn the system of economic change. Economic crises and population structures are thus closely linked.

Marx was further concerned to establish that 'in fact every particular historical mode of production has its own special laws of population, which are historically valid within that particular sphere' (p. 784). Of these laws he only outlined the one peculiar to the capitalist mode. We should be warned not to expect this 'capitalist law of population' to operate under the ancient slavery, feudal, Asiatic or socialist modes (see Marx, 1964).

The contrasting notions of overpopulation and surplus population can bear scrutiny from a variety of perspectives. Only two will be explored here and related to the contemporary world demographic system. It is obvious that overpopulation may actually be present (depending on the way one wishes to define the list of symptoms), but that it is *always* an 'ever-present possibility'. The principle from which it is derived is meant to be general and universally applicable, yet even in its original Malthusian form overpopulation is by no means inevitable. Within the capitalist system the creation of a surplus population is inevitable. The limits to its existence are determined by the creation and destruction of an entire economic framework. Further, Marx's scheme emphasizes the importance of divisions within society which are to be defined in essentially economic terms. Owners of the means of production are distinguished from sellers of labour power, but even within the working class the active and reserve armies are distinctive, as are subdivisions within the surplus population. Access and allocation are of crucial importance here, rather than the size of the labour pool or the total population. A fall in income per head (one form of pauperization) is not a simple function of the rate of population increase or its size, but stems from the tensions between employers, employees and unemployed. Certain individuals may remain permanent, or at best long-term, members of the surplus population while larger numbers will be temporary members, part of the stagnant reserve army perhaps. Whether an individual family lives in poverty will be determined by the length of time spent by its potential wage-earners as part of the surplus population.

It appears, therefore, that in Malthus' model population crises stem from excessive rates of population growth, but that in Marx's model crisis conditions exist for that alienated group whose economic position renders them socially and politically weak. The former would regard a population crisis as a severe, acute yet avoidable event, but the latter model envisages a permanent state of crisis for a subpopulation of varying size.

Do either of these models, laws, schemes bear any relation to contemporary or historical reality? One could justifiably claim that both models provide interesting interpretive frameworks, but that their emphasis, structure and scope differ radically. Neither is able to capture the complexities of any one particular situation. Malthus' model works best in pre-industrial western Europe. Marx's has specific value for early industrial capitalism. In approaching the population crisis in contemporary Africa, for instance, one would do well to advance via political economy (entitlement theory perhaps – Sen, 1981), while remembering the logic of the 'ever-present possiblity' and its apparent realization in large regions. It is also clear that many governments frame their population policies in an explicitly neo-Malthusian fashion and that in the case of China this is not regarded as counter-revolutionary.

CONCLUDING REMARKS

Five points are worth making by way of conclusion. First, the concept of a population crisis is particularly difficult to define: the forms it may take are various, and some of them are particularly conditioned by ideological stance. Second, it appears that the world is now passing through one form of population crisis, but, as Coale (1982, p.15) has remarked, 'if 2000 years from now a graph were made of the time sequence of the rate of increase of world population, the era of rapid growth that began a couple of centuries ago would look like a unique and narrow spike.' Third, there are clear signs that the rate of world population growth is now slackening, but also that there are many large countries with particularly high growth rates in which fertility is only just starting to be reduced. There are thus in certain places 'crises of numbers', but even in the west some structural characteristics are giving rise to economic and social problems. Fourth, the neo-Malthusian approach to population issues predominates in the late twentieth century, yet it owes only loose affiliation to Malthus' original principles. Fifth, the political economy of Marx, together with notions, of allocation and entitlement, offers an additional perspective on contemporary demographic issues which emphasizes the differential characteristics of classes together with the economic origins of what for some groups is a permanent population crisis.

References

Aird, J. S. 1978a: Population growth in the People's Republic of China. In Joint Economic Committee (Congress of the United States), *Chinese Economy Post-Mao*, Washington DC: US Government Printing Office, 439–75.

Aird, J. S. 1978b: Fertility decline and birth control in the People's Republic of China. *Population and Development Review*, 4, 225–53.

Aird, J. S. 1982: The preparations for China's 1982 census. *China Quarterly*, 91, 369–85.

Baker, H. D. R. 1979: *Chinese Family and Kinship*. New York: Columbia University Press.

Banister, J. and Preston, S. H. 1981: Mortality in China. *Population and Development Review*, 7, 98–110.

Barclay, G. W., Coale, A. J., Stoto, M. A. and Trussell, T. J. 1976: A reassessment of the demography of traditional rural China. *Population Index*, 42, 606–35.

Beaver, S. E. 1975: *Demographic Transition Theory Reinterpreted: An Application to Recent Natility Trends in Latin America*. Lexington, Mass.: Lexington Books.

Birdsall, N., Fei, J., Kuznets, S., Ranis, G. and Schultz, T. P. 1979: Demography and development in the 1980s. In P. Hauser (ed.), *World Population and Development: Challenges and Prospects*, Syracuse, N.Y.: Syracuse University Press, 211–95.

Bourgeois-Pichat, J. 1981: Recent demographic change in western Europe: an assessment. *Population and Development Review*, 7, 19–42.

Bulatao, R. A. and Lee, R. D. (eds) 1983: *Determinants of Fertility in Developing Countries*. Vol. 1: *Supply and Demand for Children*. New York: Academic Press.

Caldwell, J. C. and Srinivasan, K. 1984: New data on nuptiality and fertility in China. *Population and Development Review*, 10, 71–9.

Cassen, R. H. 1976: Population and development: a survey. *World Development*, 4, 785–830.

Cassen, R. H. 1978: *India: Population, Economy and Society*. London: Macmillan.

Cassen, R. H. and Dyson, T. 1976: New population projections for India. *Population and Development Review*, 2, 101–36.

Castles, S. and Kosack, G. 1973: *Immigrant Workers and Class Structures in Western Europe*. Oxford: Oxford University Press.

Chaudhry, M. 1982: Demographic transition theory and developing countries: a case study of India. *Demography India*, 11, 73–114.

Chen, C. H. and Tyler, C. W. 1982: Demographic implications of family size alternatives in the People's Republic of China. *China Quarterly*, 89, 65–73.

Clarke, J. I. and Kosinski, L. A. (eds) 1982: *Redistribution of Population in Africa*. London: Heinemann.

Coale, A. J. 1978: Population growth and economic development: the case of Mexico. *Foreign Affairs*, 56, 415–29.

Coale, A. J. 1981a: Population trends, population policy, and population studies in China. *Population and Development Review*, 7, 85–97.

Coale, A. J. 1981b: A further note on Chinese population statistics. *Population and Development Review*, 7, 512–18.

Coale, A. J. 1982: A reassessment of world population trends. *Population Bulletin of the United Nations*, 14, 1–16.

Coale, A. J. 1983a: Recent trends in fertility in less developed countries. *Science*, 221 (no. 4613), 828–32.

Coale, A. J. 1983b: Population trends in China and India (a review). *Proceedings of the National Academy of Science of the USA*, 80(6), 1757–1763.

Coale, A. J., Anderson, B. and Härm, E. 1979: *Human Fertility in Russia Since the Nineteenth Century*. Princeton: Princeton University Press.

Coale, A. J. and Hoover, E. M. 1958: *Population Growth and Economic Development in Low-Income Countries: A Case Study of India's Prospects*. Princeton: Princeton University Press.

Dagodag, W. T. 1975: Source regions and composition of illegal Mexican immigrants to California. *International Migration Review*, 9, 499–511.

Daly, H. E. 1971: A Marxian – Malthusian view of poverty and development. *Population Studies*, 25, 25–37.

Demeny, P. 1982: Population policies. In Faaland, J. (ed.), *Population and the World Economy in the 21st Century*, Oxford: Blackwell, 206–28.

Demeny, P. 1983: A perspective on long-term population growth. *Population and Development Review*, 10, 103–26.

Dow, T. E. and Werner, L. H. 1983: Prospects for fertility decline in rural Kenya. *Population and Development Review*, 9, 77–97.

Dupâquier, J., Fauve-Chamoux, A. and Grebenik, E. (eds) 1983: *Malthus Past and Present*. London: Academic Press.

Dyson, T. and Crook, N. (eds) 1984: *India's Demography: Essays on the Contemporary Population*. New Delhi: South Asia Publishers.

Dyson, T. and Moore, M. 1983: Kinship structure, female autonomy, and demographic behaviour in India. *Population and Development Review*, 9, 35–60.

Flinn, M. W. 1981: *The European Demographic System, 1500–1820*. Brighton: Harvester Press.

Goodstadt, L. F. 1982: China's one-child family: policy and public response. *Population and Development Review*, 8, 37–58.

Gottfried, R. S. 1978: *Epidemic Disease in Fifteenth-Century England: The Medical Response and the Demographic Consequences*. Leicester: Leicester University Press.

Grebler, L. 1966: *Mexican Immigration to the United States: The Record and its Implications*. Los Angeles: University of California Press.

Grigg, D. B. 1980: Migration and overpopulation. In P. E. White and R. I. Woods (eds) *The Geographical Impact of Migration*, London: Longman, 60–83.

Gugler, J. 1982: Overurbanization reconsidered. *Economic Development and Cultural Change*, 31, 173–89.

Gwatkin, D. R. 1979: Political will and family planning: the implications of India's emergency experience. *Population and Development Review*, 5, 29–59.

Hajnal, J. 1965: European marriage patterns in perspective. In D. V. Glass and D. E. C. Eversley (eds), *Population in History*, London: Arnold, 101–43.

Hajnal, J. 1982: Two kinds of preindustrial household formation system. *Population and Development Review*, 8, 449–94.

Hanley, S. B. and Yamamura, K. 1977: *Economic and Demographic Change in Preindustrial Japan, 1600–1868*. Princeton: Princeton University Press.

Harvey, D. W. 1974: Population, resources and the ideology of science. *Economic Geography*, 50, 256–77.

Hatcher, J. 1977: *Plague, Population and the English Economy, 1348–1530*. London: Macmillan.

Hayes, D. R. 1954: Neo-Malthusianism and Marxism. *Political Affairs*, 33, 41–57.

Heer, D. M. 1965: Abortion, contraception and population policy in the Soviet Union. *Demography*, 2, 531–39.

Hicks, W. W. 1974: Economic development and fertility change in Mexico, 1950–1970. *Demography*, 11, 407–21.

Jain, A. K. and Adlakha, A. L. 1982: Preliminary estimates of fertility decline in India during the 1970s. *Population and Development Review*, 8, 589–606.

Jones, E. and Grupp, F. W. 1983: Infant mortality trends in the Soviet Union. *Population and Development Review*, 9, 213–46.

Junankar, P. N. 1982: *Marx's Economics*. Oxford: Philip Allan.

Jutikkala, E. 1955: The great Finnish famine in 1696–7. *Scandinavian Economic History Review*, 3, 48–63.

Jutikkala, E. and Kauppinen, M. 1971: The structure of mortality during catastrophic years in a pre-industrial society. *Population Studies*, 25, 283–5.

Kirk, M. 1981: *Demographic and Social Change in Europe, 1975–2000*. Liverpool: Liverpool University Press.

McNeill, W. H. 1977: *Plagues and Peoples*. Oxford: Blackwell.

Malthus, T. R. 1970: *An Essay on the Principle of Population* (reprint of 1798 essay edited by A. Flew). Harmondsworth: Penguin.

Malthus, T. R. 1973: *An Essay on the Principle of Population* (reprint of 1803 essay, with amendments, edited by T. H. Hollingsworth). London: Dent.

Marx, K. 1964: *Pre-Capitalist Economic Formations*. London: Lawrence & Wishart.

Marx, K. 1976: *Capital*, vol. 1. Harmondsworth: Penguin.

Meek, R. L. (ed.) 1953: *Marx and Engels on Malthus*. London: Lawrence & Wishart.

Meuvret, J. 1977: *Le Problème des subsistances à l'époque Louis XIV*. Paris: Mouton.

Page, H. J. and Lesthaeghe, R. J. (eds) 1981: *Child-Spacing in Tropical Africa*. London; Academic Press.

Palloni, A. 1981: Mortality in Latin America: emerging patterns. *Population and Development Review*, 7, 623–49.

Petersen, W. 1964: Marx versus Malthus: the symbols and the men. In W. Petersen, *The Politics of Population*, London: Gollancz, 72–89.

Petersen, W. 1979: *Malthus*. London: Heinemann.

Post, J. D. 1977: *The Last Great Subsistence Crisis in the Western World*. Baltimore: The Johns Hopkins University Press.

Pressat, R. 1982: La population de la Chine. Bilan des trente dernières années. *Population*, 37, 299–316.

Pressat, R. 1983: Premiers résultats du recensement de la Chine. *Population*, 38, 403–9.

Qian Xinzhong 1983: China's population policy: theory and methods. *Studies in Family Planning*, 14(12), 295–301.

Schofield, R. S. 1972: 'Crisis' morality. *Local Population Studies*, 9, 10–21.

Schultz, T. P. 1981: *Economics of Population*. Reading, Mass.: Addison-Wesley.

Seiver, D. A. 1975: Recent fertility in Mexico: measurement and interpretation. *Population Studies*, 29, 341–54.

Sen, A. 1981: *Poverty and Famines: An Essay on Entitlement and Deprivation*. Oxford: Clarendon Press.

Simon, J. C. 1977: *The Economics of Population Growth*. Princeton: Princeton University Press.

Smith, D. M. (ed.) 1983: *Living Under Apartheid: Aspects of Urbanization and Social Change in South Africa*. London: Allen & Unwin.

Sogner, S. 1976: A demographic crisis averted? *Scandinavian Economic History Review*, 24, 114–28.

Spengler, J. J. 1972: Malthus's total population theory: a restatement. In J. J. Spengler (ed.), *Population Economics*, Duke, North Carolina: Duke University Press, 3–65.

Stycos, J. M. 1978: Recent trends in Latin American fertility. *Population Studies*, 32, 407–25.

Tabah, L. 1980: World population trends: a stocktaking. *Population and Development Review*, 6, 355–89.

Tabah, L. 1982: Population growth. In J. Faaland (ed.), *Population and the World Economy in the 21st Century*, Oxford: Blackwell, 175–205.

United Nations 1979: *World Population Trends and Policies, Monitoring Report*. Vol. 1: *Population Trends*; vol. 2: *Population Policies*. New York: United Nations Department of Economic and Social Affairs.

United Nations 1982: *Levels and Trends of Mortality Since 1950*. New York: United Nations Department of International Economic and Social Affairs.

Watson, J. L. 1982: Chinese kinship reconsidered: anthropological perspectives on historical research. *China Quarterly*, 92, 589–622.

White, P. E. and Woods, R. I. 1983: Migration and the formation of ethnic minorities. *Journal of Biosocial Science*, Supplement 8, 7–24.

Woods, R. I. 1982: *Theoretical Population Geography*. London: Longman.

Woods, R. I. 1983: On the long-term relationship between fertility and the standard of living. *Genus*, 39, 21–35.

Wrigley, E. A. and Schofield, R. S. 1981: *The Population History of England, 1541–1871: A Reconstruction*. London: Arnold.

7

The Destruction of Regional Cultures

RICHARD PEET

After centuries of unreality, after having wallowed in the most outlandish phantoms, at long last the native, gun in hand, stands face to face with the only forces which contend for his life – the forces of colonialism. And the youth of a colonized country, growing up in an atmosphere of shot and fire, may well make a mock of, and does not hesitate to pour scorn upon, the zombies of his ancestors, the horses with two heads, the dead who rise again, and the djinns who rush into your body while you yawn. The native discovers reality and transforms it into the pattern of his customs, into the practice of violence and into his plan for freedom.

(Frantz Fanon, *The Wretched of the Earth* (1963), p. 58)

The development of capitalism as the dominant world economic system has been paralleled by the spread of its culture into all regions of the globe. A thousand interactions have pitted local and regional cultures, related to local environments and forms of livelihood, against the power of the international culture founded on a dynamic capitalism. There are several dimensions to the resulting cultural interaction. Capitalist culture has absorbed elements from the regional cultures it has encountered – its conception of paradise on earth is strongly flavoured by the encounter with the Polynesians on 'unspoilt Pacific Islands'. Capitalism and regional cultures have merged into synthetic cultures – for example, Japanese culture contains strong elements from the islands' particular version of the feudal past. But a continuing theme, running through virtually all discussions of the encounter between world capitalist and regional non-capitalist cultures of the Third World, is the pervasive power of the first and the transformation of the second.

Thus multinationalization of industry has been linked with the global spread of international advertising agencies, the development of consumerism, and effects on the 'whole fabric of society' in the Third World (Janus and Roncaglio, 1979). International publishing, dominated by multinational corporations, has been examined in terms of 'cultural dependency as a complement to economic dominance' in the Third World periphery (Golding, 1978). There are many works on the international flow of films, television and radio programmes, records, cassettes and printed materials from centre to periphery, all of which carry cultural messages in persuasive formats (Varis, 1974, 1976; Guback, 1974; de Cardona, 1975; Gould and Johnson, 1980). The United States 'communications complex' has been described as a 'powerful mechanism [which] now directly impinges on people's lives everywhere' carrying 'a vision of a way of life. The image is of a mountain of material artifacts privately furnished and individually acquired and consumed' (Schiller, 1969, pp. 3, 17; Schiller, 1978). People in the periphery have been shown to receive their news about the periphery via the centre (Harris, 1974, 1976; Masmondi, 1979). The effect of tourism on West Indian culture has been described in terms of art, music, dance and literature becoming 'the patrimony of an expanding tourist economy. In the process, artistic expression in the West Indies loses its integrity and, indeed, its relevance to the West Indian experience' (Perez, 1975, p. 140). These studies conclude that present relations between centre and periphery can accurately be characterized in terms of 'cultural imperialism by the capitalist centre'.

Beyond this kind of empirical work, however, lies the need to construct a geographic theory of culture. Such a theory must address two main topics: what is culture, and how is it formed; and what gives capitalist culture its extraordinary powers of diffusion and destruction? This chapter attempts to answer these questions, mainly via an analysis of certain ideas developed in Marx's writings – particularly *Capital* and *Grundrisse*. However, the chapter can only provide an outline of certain aspects of such a theory and these aspects must be bluntly and briefly stated, without the usual academic qualifications, and without extensive exemplification. A complete Marxian–geographic theory of culture, adequately supported by empirical research, is still years away.

One aspect of culture is emphasized – what Marx called the 'entire superstructure of distinct and peculiarly formed sentiments, illusions, modes of thought and views of life' which arises as the basis of the 'social conditions of existence' (Marx, 1969); that is, emphasis is placed on the consciousness dimension of culture. By consciousness we mean, quite simply, 'the way people think' – not about each specific thing which crosses their minds, but about 'things in general'. Consciousness refers to the patterns and modes of thought, seeing these as conditioned by the whole way a people live. In turn, consciousness guides all aspects of cultural production – thought is materialized as art and literature. The central idea is that different human experiences in different environments yield different regional consciousnesses and cultures. World capitalism is a new order and scale of experience, represented as a powerful culture, which overwhelms local and regional experience. As a result, the mass of the world's people become adherents to one global culture system.

This new world system, however, shares certain attributes with previous regional cultures, especially those aspects of consciousness prescribed by domination by forces beyond human control.

Human domination is traced here to two main sources: domination by natural forces in the early stages of human development; and domination by a spontaneous, uncontrollable mode of production in the later period. The chapter concentrates on one main effect of domination, the assumption by consciousness of a religious, mystical form. Thus the idea is to follow one connecting strand from environment, through mode of production, to culture and religious consciousness. Other aspects of the geography of consciousness are considered by the author elsewhere (Peet, 1980, 1982).

THE SOCIOLOGY OF CULTURE

We can approach an understanding of the geography of culture through the more developed concepts of its sociology as outlined by Williams (1980, 1981). There is a problem in defining the 'exceptionally complex term' culture. Williams traces this to two different kinds of understanding. The earlier, idealist emphasis, dating from the eighteenth century, lay on the 'informing spirit' of a whole way of life, most evidently its language, styles of art, and kinds of intellectual work. The later, materialist emphasis was on culture as the direct or indirect product of a whole social order. Williams accepts the second, with the proviso that 'cultural practice' and 'cultural production' are not simply derived, but are also constitutive, of the social order. Phrasing this a little differently, culture is seen as the '*signifying system* through which necessarily (though among other means) a social order is communicated, reproduced, experienced and explored' (Williams, 1981, p. 13). Any social system has a distinguishable signifying system – as a language, as a system of thought or consciousness, as a body of specifically signifying works of art. While this signifying system is essentially involved in all forms of social activity, Williams retains the more specialized use of the term 'culture' to refer particularly to artistic and intellectual activities, interpreting these broadly to include all 'signifying practices . . . from language, through the arts and philosophy to journalism, fashion and advertising' (p. 13).

Sociology focuses on the forms of culture resulting from the social process of cultural production. Hence Williams is interested in social institutions (feudal households, the market, the corporation), cultural institutions (craft guilds, academies, professional societies), and means of culture production (speech, dance, writing, amplificatory systems), all seen in relation to art forms and products. While accepting the general determination of form by social process, Williams argues that art forms can never be reduced to mere anticipations or reflections of social processes. Cultural processes are always relatively autonomous. Some cultural practices, for example those occurring within conditions of wage labour, are effectively inseparable from their determining social relations; others are only indirectly determined, or perhaps not determined at all, for example poetry and sculpture where there seems to be absolute autonomy.

For Williams, there are a number of tendencies in cultural development of significant importance which are also pertinent to the theme of this chapter. The first tendency is the transformation of 'popular culture'. In capitalist society this is increasingly mass-produced, both privately under market conditions and by state educational and political systems. This movement is paralleled by a major expansion of the cultural and educational bureaucracies, interlocked with the more general political, economic, and administrative bureaucracies. Williams's conclusion is that while there is innovative work in many forms of art and thought, the genuinely emergent in art has to be defined primarily in terms of its contribution to alternatives to this dominant general system.

The second tendency is the institution of an international, even a world, market. Except in some closed or subsistence societies, the processes of cultural import and export have always been important. But changes in the means of cultural production and distribution, especially cinema and television, have led beyond such simple processes to more general processes of cultural dominance and dependence. These have radical effects on national signifying systems, like languages, and lead to new forms of multinational cultural combine.

The third tendency is fundamental changes in the labour process, which have radically affected the definition of cultural production. In advanced industrial societies, direct cultural production now often involves a small and declining proportion of the working population, while the number involved in information processing and handling has increased, in the case of the United States to as much as 50 per cent of the working population. While many of the older types of determination – state power or economic property and command – are still decisive, there are quite new complexities in the whole system of cultural production and reproduction (Williams, 1981, p. 233).

The sociology of culture thus investigates the aesthetic forms, institutions and relations of society's artistic and intellectual life. A materialist explanation understands culture as the realized signifying system of a social order, which Marxism usually interprets in terms of a mode of production – i.e. a determinate combination of the physical and social forces and relations of production. The main contribution of Williams is his articulation of the social order and the system of social reproduction, the latter understood as the various types of cultural practice. Williams's articulation does not withdraw from the essential Marxist position – that there is a process of determination in any social totality – but rather attempts to 'revalue "determination" towards the setting of limits and the exertion of pressure, and away from a predicted, prefigured and controlled content' (Williams, 1980, p. 34). Williams's work is the most successful account of the multiple interactions between determination and autonomy so far developed in the broad tradition of Marxian cultural analysis.

THE GEOGRAPHY OF CULTURE

Having briefly explored the sociology of culture, we are now in a position to investigate its geography. This will be carried out from a materialist perspective similar enough to Williams's to employ his useful analytical categories.

What is the role of geography in the academic division of labour? Geography investigates two of the relations which all humans must enter: the relation with the natural environment, ultimate source of material existence; and the relation with other humans across space, usually seen as relations between localized human groups. A historical materialism which incorporates the geographic dimension thus includes relations with nature and relations between societies across space. In particular, the structure of determination, inherent in a Marxian understanding, is deepened to include determination by the natural world. Thus for the Italian Marxist Timpanaro:

> By materialism we understand above all acknowledgement of the priority of nature over 'mind', or if you like, of the physical level over the biological level, and of the biological level over the socio-economic and cultural level; both in the sense of chronological priority (the very long time which supervened before life appeared on earth, and between the origin of life and the origin of man), and in the sense of the conditioning which nature still exercises on man and will continue to exercise at least for the foreseeable future. (Timpanaro, 1975, p. 34)

Not only the social relations between humans, but also relations between humans and nature, give rise to scientific and philosophical reflection and to artistic expression. Relations with nature are not eternal, but nevertheless are long lasting, providing a continuity of cultural theme through history. Thus religion is always an illusory compensation for the fear of death and the oppression in general which nature exercises on humans (pp. 48–52).

Nature, however, does not exercise the same kind, or level, of determination in all places and at all times. Place-specific natural determination is the fertile ground for geographical investigation. There are several dimensions to this place-specificity. First, the nature of nature varies between different regional, and even local, environments – if reflection on nature is a primary source of intellectual life, then reflection on a particular nature can be seen as a primary source of regional consciousnesses and art forms. Second, humans encounter not only local nature, but a wider natural environment, through many kinds of spatial interactions, from migration to the diffusion of cultural traits – hence the aspect of relative location is significant. Third, the relation with nature is always mediated by socioeconomic forces and institutions, of which the forces of production applied to natural resources are an extremely important component. As the level of the productive forces available to any regional-social group increases, determination by nature decreases. Space thus becomes a mosaic of different levels of determination, similar to the different levels of economic development. This takes a centre (low natural determination) and periphery (high natural determination) geographic shape under capitalism. New forms of cultural practice, developed in the centre, then diffuse over space, even into areas for which they are inappropriate in terms of the (low) level of indigenous productive development. This last aspect of the geography of culture will be investigated below.

Cultural geography thus extends material determination back into the relations between society and nature. It investigates the particular, local forms taken by culture in response to particular environments, locations and levels of development; and it looks at the spatial interactions between these local cultural forms. Far from separating geography from sociology, this perspective integrates the two into a holistic understanding of the totality of cultural practice.

NATURE AND CULTURE IN PRE-CAPITALIST SOCIETIES

Even when investigating such relatively autonomous dimensions of life as human culture, Marxists insist on founding their analysis in the material production process. This is particularly the case for geographically oriented Marxists, whose scientific function involves deliberately stressing the geo-material aspects of the reproduction of life. Marx's analysis of labour and production, outlined in *Capital*, provides an introduction.

For Marx, labour is first of all a process in which natural materials are appropriated in forms adapted to human needs. Through acting on nature humans not only transform the external environment, but also find and develop their own inner (human) nature – the difference from other animals being that humans increasingly regulate and control their metabolism with nature. 'Man not only effects a change of form in the materials of nature; he also realizes his own purpose in those materials. And this is a purpose he is conscious of' (Marx, 1976, p. 284). The land is the universal material for human labour, both objects of labour spontaneously provided – fish, timber and ores – and objects of labour filtered through previous labour – raw materials. Similarly an instrument of labour is an originally natural thing interposed between the worker and the object of labour. With only the slightest development of the labour process, specially prepared instruments are required. For Marx, the use and construction of instruments is characteristic of the specifically *human* labour process – instruments are the means by which the relation with nature is regulated. 'It is not what is made but how, and by what instruments of labour, that distinguishes different economic epochs. Instruments of labour not only supply a standard of the degree of development which human labour has attained, but they also indicate the social relations within which men work' (p. 286). Thus mechanical instruments of labour offer the most decisive evidence of the economic character of the present social epoch of production.

For Marx, therefore, the productive forces – instruments and objects of labour (means of production) and productive living labour – are the underlying determinants of the overall character of a historical epoch. Different social relations between producers, and between producers and environment, are generally appropriate to different levels in the development of the forces of production. When humans rely mainly on spontaneous natural products, and instruments of labour, as in hunting and gathering societies, the natural environment is regarded as the extended body of the individual, and the private ownership of nature is absent. With the development of specially prepared instruments of labour and the use of raw materials, private ownership appears. This eventually extends, from pieces of nature owned by individuals, to the labour power of other human beings from outside the community (slavery), and then inside the community (feudalism) (Peet, 1981). The achievement of minority class control over all the productive forces of a society, as under capitalism, enables nature to be conquered. Nature is increasingly transformed into useful objects (use-values) and a 'second nature' (i.e. a humanly altered environment).

For Marx: 'The mode of production of material life conditions the general process of social, political and intellectual life' (1970, p. 21). More generally, social existence determines consciousness. When social existence is characterized by dominance and servitude, including an immediate reliance on nature, human consciousness is restricted, the forces which control existence are deified, and thought clouded by religious suppositions. As Marx says, the 'ancient social organisms of production':

> are founded either on the immaturity of man as an individual, when he has not yet torn himself loose from the umbilical cord of his natural-species connection with other men, or in direct relations of dominance and servitude. They are conditioned by a low stage of development of the productive powers of labour and correspondingly limited relations between men within the process of creating and reproducing their material life, hence also limited relations between man and nature. These real limitations are reflected in the ancient worship of nature, and in other elements of tribal religions. (1976, p. 173)

This pre-scientific understanding of the natural and social conditions of existence pervades consciousness and culture at low levels of productive development. It is characterized particularly by the transposition of will, from humans just beginning to realize they have it, to a nature which continually contradicts it.

While for Marx 'not what is made but how . . . distinguishes different economic epochs' in history, for Marxist geographers both *what* is made and *how* it is made distinguish different regional social formations in space. The different regional social formations are characterized by different levels of productive development ('how things are made') and thus different levels of the development of consciousness. Regional social formations are also located in entirely different environmental settings, transform different kinds of natural resources into varying useful objects ('what is made'), and are subject to the varying control of dissimilar natural forces.

There is a number of approaches to this conception of regional differences in the type of society. Most profoundly, Wittfogel argues that because different social organisms find different *means* of production in their local environments, their *modes* of production are different, development being channelled in certain definite directions, leading to various kinds of states and politics. Hence the need for control over water resources in arid and semi-arid Asiatic regions led to hydraulic civilizations dominated by strong centralized state bureaucracies, and thus to 'oriental despotism' (Wittfogel, 1929, 1957).

At a more immediate level, different natural environments provide varying physical opportunities for different kinds of specialized production, in terms of climate, natural soil fertility, resources and the presence of such natural instruments of labour as energy sources. Culture is thereby influenced in two main ways: productive complexes structure cultural development in general – industrial districts have different cultural emphases from agricultural districts; and cultural production itself finds different materials with which to work in the local natural environment. Thus the different economic and cultural productive forces, in combination with different natural materials, yield an array of regional socio-*cultural* formations across geographic space.

Perhaps the most significant aspects of regional socio-cultural formation in response to environment is the kind of consciousness produced. In the discipline of geography, the most prominent proponent of this idea was the environmental determinist Ellen Churchill Semple. For Semple, the 'physical effects of geographic environment . . . are reflected in man's religion and his literature, in his modes of thought and figures of speech' (1911, p. 40). Thus habitat influences the legal structure of a social group. The effect of environment, acting through the type of economic activity, enriches the language in one direction but restricts it in others. The mythology of a people echoes the surrounding natural environment. The cosmography of primitive people – what she calls 'their first crude effort in the science of the universe' – also bears the impress of the local habitat (pp. 40–1). The problem with Semple's version of determinism, however, is the directness of the relation between environment and culture. Thus in discussing world climatic zones as determinants of the 'girdles of culture around the earth', she passes straight from heat and moisture to the natural qualities of 'human temperament' (pp. 633–5). Missing from her explanation is an elaborated theory of the social mediation between the natural environment and a people's 'spirit', which would result from a structural – materialist analysis. We can, however, admire her willingness to take bold leaps where other geographers have feared to tread.

Nature and Religious Consciousness in Pre-capitalist Societies

Let us isolate one aspect of this complex issue, the influence of environment on religious consciousness, for detailed consideration. First we must ask: what is the origin of religion, and how has religious understanding changed over time?

Religion is an attempt to understand and influence the great forces on which life depends: religion is a 'set of symbolic forms and acts which relate man to the ultimate conditions of his existence' (Bellah, 1969, p. 67). These 'ultimate conditions' are such matters as the origin of human existence, in terms of descent from a line of ancestors, and the continuation of existence, in terms of the social relation with nature. But as the eighteenth-century philosopher David Hume, one of the first to subject the concept of religion to scientific scepticism, argued:

> We are placed in this world, as in a great theatre, where the true springs and causes of every event are entirely concealed from us; nor have we either sufficient wisdom to foresee, or power to prevent, those ills with which we are continually threatened. . . . These *unknown causes*, then, become the constant object of our hope and fear; and while the passions are kept in perpetual alarm by an anxious expectation of the events, the imagination is equally employed informing ideas of those powers on which we have so entire a dependence. (Hume, 1968, p. 21)

Religion, therefore, results from contemplation under circumstances of existential threat, and the desperate search for control over the possibility of continued existence. Hence primitive religion has two recurrent themes: the worship of the dead, under the assumption that they retain consciousness and can influence the fortunes of the living; and the worship of natural phenomena, conceived as animated, conscious and endowed with the power and the will to benefit, or injure, humankind. The most universal phenomena of nature, the sky and the earth, have been most universally worshipped. Other phenomena enjoy more restricted, regional deification – the sun, moon, stars, fire, water, plants and animals (Frazer, 1926).

At a low level of productive development, and a low level of control over nature, the religious practices of simple ethnic (tribal) systems are quite directly related to local physical environments and the way these are used:

> In the simple ethnic systems, religion often seems to be almost entirely a ritualization of ecology. Religion is the medium whereby nature and natural processes are placated, cajoled, entreated, or manipulated in order to secure the best results for man. Even at a very primitive technological level, however, every culture operates selectively in taking its sacred 'resources' from its ecological milieu. The religious behaviour of such societies becomes an extended commentary on selected, usually dominant, features of their economies. (Sopher, 1967, pp. 17–18)

Archaic myths and rituals, however, persist long after the ecological elements around which they have crystallized have passed out of the focus of particular interest. Hence broad regional religions appear, based on the sanctification of different economies through ritual, and the differential persistence of archaic ecologies in ritual forms (p. 19).

Universalizing religious systems (Buddhism, Christianity and Islam) break through the restriction of a special relationship to particular places and human groups, to appeal to all humankind: 'As society and economy become more complex, symbolization and abstraction of ecological matter increase, the process becoming intensified in the transition from ethnic to universalizing systems' (p. 19). Thus the religious calendar of Judaism reflects the ecological characteristics of the Mediterranean; Christianity preserves some of these elements but incorporates also aspects of earlier pagan religions, such as celebration of the winter solstice (Christmas); and the Islamic calendar is more completely liberated from ecological ties – perhaps because Islam was, from the beginning, a religion of the mercantile town (p. 22).

In the pre-capitalist world, therefore, people thought (and still think) about the origins and purpose of life in ways broadly similar (roughly the same things are being thought about), but particularly different (there are different natural circumstances and levels of control over circumstances). The resulting map of religious consciousness is characterized by both broad spatial order (the universalizing religions) and spatial specificity (ethnic and tribal religious systems). It is the product of multilinear historical development, based originally on greatly different physical environments, with these different historical pasts differentially preserved into the present. Environment has thus acted to produce a mosaic of regional forms of consciousness in the traditional world.

EXCHANGE AND THE DISSOLUTION OF PRE-CAPITALIST SOCIETY

The pre-capitalist cultural world was thus made up of a series of regional socio-cultural formations, each with its own kind of consciousness, as in the case of different religions. The capitalist mode of production, founded on the production and exchange of commodities and wage-labour relations, originates a new kind of socio-cultural order, universal in scope. The growth of this new order breaks down the old geography of society and culture through various means. One such means – the growth of commodity exchange – is examined here.

Economic contact between capitalist and non-capitalist societies usually begins with the occasional trading of commodities. Exchange between the two kinds of society – the one resting on exchange, the other on direct use – has effects which transcend the commodity, acting to dissolve all the social relations of non-capitalist societies. This process of dissolution, part of an articulation between capitalist and non-capitalist modes of production, is analogous to the original development of the capitalist mode of production out of pre-capitalist modes. We can approach an understanding through Marx's analysis of this historical process.

In pre-capitalist societies, each productive individual had a presupposed access to land, the main means of production, guaranteed by the occupation of a certain territory by a communal group, and protected by warfare from surrounding or invading communities. The several forms of pre-capitalist society were differentiated mainly on the basis of the control of land and soil, whether this was communally owned ('primitive communism'), diffused throughout the community ('Germanic mode of production'), locally centralized ('feudal mode of production'), or centralized ('Asiatic mode of production') (Peet, 1981). In all pre-capitalist modes, most production was primarily for the immediate satisfaction of the needs of the family and community. Surpluses were transferred within the pre-capitalist class structure to the controllers of the communal territory (the warrior class and/or the state) and the guarantors of favourable natural conditions (the priests). Relations of immediate dependence on nature were paralleled by relations of personal dependence in production, individuals being 'imprisoned within a certain definition, as feudal lord and vassal, landlord and serf, etc., or as members of a caste etc. or as members of an estate etc.' (Marx, 1973, p. 163). Generalizing, Marx regards all societies characterized by these kinds of dependence as the 'first social forms, in which human productive capacity develops only to a slight extent and at isolated points' (p. 158).

The second great historical form, personal independence founded on real dependence, begins with the exchange of surplus products at boundaries between communities. As products became commodities in the external relations of a community they also, by reaction, became products in its internal relations. Now, for Marx, 'the characters who appear on the economic stage are merely personifications of economic relations; it is as bearers of these economic relations that they come into contact with each other' (1976, p. 179). The exchange of commodities means that the 'guardians' of products must recognize each other as owners of private, alienable property, persons who are independent of each other. This 'relationship of reciprocal isolation and foreignness does not exist for members of a primitive community of natural origin, whether it takes the form of a partriarchal family, an ancient Indian commune or an Inca state' (p. 182). Exchange thus produces a new kind of human personality and new social relations. As more and more products become exchanged commodities, the traditional relations between people in pre-capitalist societies disintegrate – 'in the developed system of exchange . . . the ties of personal dependence, of distinctions of blood, education, etc. are in fact exploded, ripped up . . . and individuals *seem* independent (this is an independence which is at bottom merely an illusion, and it is more correctly called indifference), free to collide with one another and to engage in exchange within this freedom' (Marx, 1973, pp. 163–4).

Whereas in the natural community the reproduction of the individual as a member of the community is the objective of production, with exchange the pursuit of individual wealth becomes the main objective. In pre-capitalist society, Marx argues, natural wealth supposed an essential relation between the individual and the objects which form that wealth; but with money a world of things becomes accessible and greed limitless. 'Monetary greed, or mania for wealth, necessarily brings with it the decline and fall of the ancient communities . . . it is the antithesis to them. It is itself the community, and can tolerate no other standing above it' (p. 223). This process is completed when, as a result of the decay of pre-capitalist communal relations, land and labour are separated and become purchasable on the market. With this, money directly becomes the 'real community' since it is the general substance of survival, and social product, of all. Furthermore, Marx concludes:

> in money the community is at the same time a mere abstraction, a mere external, accidental thing for the individual, and at the same time merely a means for his satisfaction as an isolated individual. The community of antiquity presupposes a quite different relation to, and on the part of, the individual. The development of money in [this] role therefore smashes this community. All production is an objectification of the individual. In money (exchange value), however, the individual is not objectified in his natural quality, but a social quality (relation) which is, at the same time, external to him. (p. 226)

Thus for Marx one form of compulsion, the domination of the individual by nature and other individuals in pre-capitalist societies, is replaced by 'an objective restriction of the individual by relations independent of him and sufficient unto themselves', conditions which 'although created by society, appear as if they were *natural conditions*, not controllable by individuals' (p. 164). This is far from the abolition of relations of dependence. It is, instead, 'the dissolution of these relations into a general form' (p. 164). This idea will be discussed in more detail shortly.

Marx does not mourn the passing of early society. He regards it as just as 'ridiculous to yearn for [the] original fullness' of the historic individual, as it is to 'believe that with this complete emptiness [capitalism] history has come to a stand still' (p. 162). Instead he anticipates a third epoch in the history of humanity, for which capitalism, with its formation of 'a system of general social metabollism, of universal relations, of all-round needs and universal capacities', creates the preconditions: 'Free individuality, based on the universal development of individuals and on their subordination of their communal, social productivity as their social wealth, is the third stage' (p. 158). In this discussion, there are strong implications of historical inevitability, capitalism being the necessary creator of universal relations between people: 'Universally developed individuals, whose social relations, as their own communal relations, are hence also subordinated to their own communal control, are no product of nature, but of history' (pp. 161–2).

NEW FORMS FOR OLD IN THE DEVELOPMENT OF CONSCIOUSNESS

Although there are broad similarities, the dissolution of pre-capitalist societies, through the development within them of embryonic capitalist relations, differs from the destruction of contemporary non-capitalist societies, through exchange and other external relations with an advanced capitalism. In particular, sophisticated and powerful institutions, forms of culture and modes of consciousness have now developed which make the process of dissolution more rapid and totally effective. The periphery of the world capitalist system, where non-capitalist relations of production still prevail, is therefore subjected to attack at a number of levels simultaneously: the economic level, through exchange; the political level, through colonial control; and the cultural level, through the penetration of capitalist cultural products and ideas. But the ideas capitalism exports to the periphery lead merely to the replacement of one kind of mysticism by another. How does this come about?

The way in which humans produce their lives determines the way in which they conceptualize life. Under capitalism, the productive forces are privately owned, with antagonistic relations between wage labour and capital, and competitive relations within the class of capitalist owners. Wage-labour relations channel economic surplus into the few hands of the private owners of the means of production, while competition between owners forces the reinvestment of surplus in improved, efficient means of production. The social relations of production are thus exactly the source of the rapid development of the productive forces. In turn, productive development reduces the domination of nature, eventually reversing the main direction of determination in the capitalist centre, in the sense that nature can now be altered and controlled by advanced societies armed with more powerful productive means. Increasingly, also, nature is rationally understood via a science which develops as part of the development of the productive forces. Nature need no longer be feared as a destructive god, although at times of natural catastrophe the ancient ritual of prayer immediately surfaces again. As continued human existence comes to depend on human productive effort, rather than the whim of nature, religious mysticism tends to be replaced by scientific rationalism. This is what Marx calls the 'great civilizing influence of capital', that is:

> its production of a stage of society in comparison to which all earlier ones appear as mere *local* developments of humanity, and as *nature idolatry*. For the first time, nature becomes purely an object for humankind, purely a matter of utility; ceases to be recognized as a power for itself; and the theoretical discovery of its autonomous laws appears merely as a ruse so as to subjugate it under human needs, whether as an object of consumption or as a means of production. In accord with this tendency, capital drives beyond national barriers and prejudices as much as beyond nature worship, as well as all traditional, confined, complacent, encrusted satisfactions of present needs and reproductions of old ways of life. It is destructive towards all of this, and constantly revolutionizes it, tearing down all barriers which hem in the development of the forces of production, the expansion of needs, the all-sided development of production, and the exploitation and exchange of natural and mental forces. (Marx, 1973, pp. 409–10)

Civilization as a whole is thus transformed by the development of the productive forces. But consciousness does not break through, from religion to science, in *all* aspects of this more civilized life. Instead new mysticisms develop, or old ones are updated, particularly in the realm of social explanation. The means for understanding and controlling nature (natural science and technology) outstrip the means for understanding and controlling society (social science and politics). To gain comprehension of this we have to draw out more fully the implications for consciousness of the development of capitalist relations of production. Again we will rely on Marx for the direction the analysis should take.

Under capitalism, each person's survival is made to depend on the pursuit of self-interest by all others. Common interest is not the motive of production and exchange, but proceeds 'behind the back of these self-reflected particular interests, behind the back of the individual's interest in opposition to that of the other' (p. 244). Production and consumption are thus organized through a network of spontaneous relations between reciprocally independent and indifferent individuals. These relations confront the individuals not as their relations with another, but as their common subordination to relations which exist independently of them: 'The general exchange of activities and products, which has become a vital condition for each individual – their mutual interconnection – here appears as something alien to them, autonomous, as a thing' (p. 157).

More concretely, the allocation of the society's labour power is not achieved directly, through social planning, but via the collision on the market of products made by quantities of labour:

> In other words the labour of the private individual manifests itself as an element of the total labour of society only through the relations which the act of exchange establishes between the products, and, through their mediation, between the producers. To the producers, therefore, the social relations between their private labours appear as what they are, i.e. they do not appear as direct social relations between persons in their work, but rather as material relations between persons and social relations between things. (Marx, 1976, pp. 165–6)

The commodity, in reality merely a sensuous thing, is at the same time suprasensible, or social. What are, in fact, definite social relations between humans assume the fantastic form of a relation between things. To find an analogy:

> We must take flight into the misty realm of religion. There the products of the human brain appear as autonomous figures endowed with a life of their own, which enter into relations both with each other and with the human race. So it is in the world of commodities with the products of men's hands. I call this the fetishism which attaches itself to the products of labour as soon as they are produced as commodities, and is therefore inseparable from the production of commodities. (p. 165)

Commodity fetishism inevitably arises from the social character of the labour which produces commodities, that is labour organized indirectly through the exchange of products on the market. It results in a mode of thought analogous to the natural religion of pre-capitalist times.

Reflection on social forms of human life begins later, after they have already assumed the fixed quality of natural forms. Thus the economic formulae of bourgeois economics 'which bear the unmistakable stamp of belonging to a social formation in which the process of production has mastery over man, instead of the opposite, appear to the political economists' bourgeois consciousness to be as much a self-evident and nature-imposed necessity as productive labour itself' (p. 175). Hence the idea that it is 'natural' for society to be organized for the benefit of a minority class of individuals who pursue their own self-interest. (Capitalism corresponds to an eternally and exclusively selfish human nature.) Taking this social form for granted, science is misled, its categories incapable of explaining the structure and movement of society.

A society which does not scientifically understand itself – whose economists, for example, cannot predict the autonomous course of economic change – requires some other general theory, some other account of the essential causes of things. Religion served this function in the past, when humans were dominated by nature. Religion continues to serve this function in the present, when humans are dominated by the form taken by their own society:

> For a society of commodity producers, whose general social relation of production consists in the fact that they treat their products as commodities, hence as values, and in this material form bring their individual, private labours into relation with each other as homogeneous human labour, Christianity with its religious cult of man in the abstract, more particularly in its bourgeois development, i.e. in Protestantism, Deism, etc., is the most fitting form of religion. (p. 172)

In other words, instead of understanding themselves as individuals connected to each other in the production of their existence (which would occur in a co-operative, planned society), capitalist individuals understand their necessary connecting relationship to occur indirectly – 'man in the abstract', rather than humans directly, controls the course of history. Instead of society being understood scientifically, as would be possible if humanly created laws guided its development, society is understood religiously, as a power outside human control, controlling individuals rather than being controlled by them. (Hence the president of the world's most powerful nation prays for economic guidance.) Finally, instead of morality being a set of principles observed in the everyday practice of economic life, it is abstracted from this life and observed only on Sundays, in special places, and with dubious real intent. Social consciousness thus remains religiously mystical in capitalist society. As this society becomes increasingly unstable and uncontrollable, as during crisis periods, social consciousness is increasingly mystified. Religious revival occurs in a situation demanding social-scientific understanding.

CONTRADICTION, CRISIS AND CONSCIOUSNESS

On the basis of the general statements made above about the relation between economic structure and consciousness, we can outline some features of contemporary systemic development at the centre of world capitalism. The centre is the region where capitalist social relations prevail. This means not only that all economic functions are dominated by wage labour, all products made for, and exchanged via, the market, but also that commodification has proceeded deep into culture, so that ideas are thought for sale, and beauty aesthetically defined by market criteria. The main tendencies in cultural production and the movement of consciousness, however, still fundamentally respond to the dynamic of the economic base of capitalist society. Once initiated, cultural tendencies may have an autonomy of movement, but this occurs within limits set by their necessary and continuing connections with social production. The uncontrolled movement of the economy continues to determine the dynamic of society as a whole. The implications for consciousness are profound.

Under capitalism the relations which tie together the main elements of production are inherently contradictory, making society prone to repeated crises. Competitive market relations oppose one capitalist to another, one segment of production to another, one region to another. Antagonistic relations within each segment of production oppose capitalist to workers. As an example of just one crisis result of such relations of production, in the case of unemployment crises, competition forces employers to relocate production from unionized areas where wages are high, to non-unionized areas where wages are low. Such movements cause regional unemployment directly, and also general unemployment indirectly via a reduction in worker incomes, a lack of mass markets, a lower overall rate of economic growth, and thus a lack of demand for workers (Peet, 1983). Widespread and persistently high unemployment rates call for a co-operative response at the level of the society in general. But what is society under capitalism? The captains of industry 'related' through competition? Share-owners interested only in higher dividends no matter where these come from? The most realistic answer is the national state. Yet under capitalism, the state does not control the investment of capital, the fundamental process through which employment is generated. The capitalist state can ameliorate the effects of unemployment, but it cannot eradicate its causes, which lie in the very way capitalism operates. As it cannot be the function of the capitalist state to destroy the basis of the capitalist system, there are limits to state policy. These limits preclude social action aimed at the *systemic roots* of crises. The result is the escalation of the level of crises of all kinds at the centre of the world capitalist system. Consciousness responds to an environment of perpetual crisis.

Past social crises were precipitated by natural causes which were worshipped as gods. Present social crises are precipitated mainly by social causes, equally uncontrollable, and equally worshipped as gods. Hence people pray for salvation from the effects of crises. 'God' is entreated to act to save humankind from social and political disasters. If scientifically understood by a people in collective control of their own destiny, the causes of crises could be eradicated by concerted human action. As it is, however, the social causes of crises are not understood, nor do they change ('God refuses to act'). Culture and consciousness are forced into a number of more particular forms.

One form is the perpetuation of diverse kinds of mysticism, beyond formal religion, each with a dubious claim on the future course of events. Hence astrology, which makes the human personality and historical events a function of the arrangement of the stars! Yet astrological tables and forecasts are printed in virtually all mass-communications media. A second form is a perverse fascination with partial or implausible 'solutions' to earthly problems, like high technology, super-human beings, or discoveries in outer space. A third form involves revelling in the dramatic *effects* of crises while ignoring, or vastly simplifying, the causes (forces of evil cause problems, forces of good solve them). Hence the continual production of art forms which depend on an escalating level of violence and destruction for their appeal, even reaching the point where people are really killed, rather than 'merely' seen to be, in the 'video nasties' rented nightly to pre-teenagers by kindly village storekeepers who 'only supply what people want'. A fourth form involves the propagation of individual super-hero images before a people desperate for someone, something, to admire, to be comforted by, to live their lives via – hence the royalty in Britain, film and sports stars in the United States, etc. Super-heroes are symbols of society's good intentions, when the reality is that capitalism is driven only by selfish intent. The important point here is that such culture forms respond to the structural needs of the system rather than simply to the perversion of their immediate producers.

These forms of culture and thought need a mode of expression also suited to the social-structural origins of crisis, a mode which allows problems to be aired, but not taken seriously. This need is met by 'entertainment'. Hence even the news media, the main form by which problems are communicated, are now embedded in the entertainment industry. Entertainment is the opium of the people. Culture becomes the aesthetics of anaesthesia.

Cultural production increasingly involves the production of entertaining commodities, using the same techniques as material commodity production – indeed pioneering these techniques. But the links between commodity production and culture production transcend technique. The development of mass commodity-production techniques requires a mass market, people 'habituated to respond to the demands of the productive machinery' (Ewan, 1976, p. 25). The function of the 'culture industry' thus became the mass-production of 'ready-made clichés' which overpower the consumer, stunting her powers of imagination, turning participants into listeners and observers amenable to control (Horkheimer and Adorno, 1972). The 'consciousness industry' (radio, television, cinema, recording, advertising, etc.), one extremely important part of the culture industry, does more even than this. Enzensberger

(1974, p. 11) argues that beyond selling products, it sells the existing social order: 'The few cannot go on accumulating wealth unless they accumulate the power to manipulate the minds of the many.' More generally, the consciousness industry operates to proscribe information and explanation, limiting the range of thought while making its consumers dependent on the industry for those thoughts which they do have.

The theoretical difficulty here lies in the question of 'deliberate intention' – that is, explaining 'consciousness manipulation' without resorting to the naive idea that the heads of corporations meet to decide what to allow people to think. It must be remembered that under capitalism the 'general interest is precisely the generality of self-seeking interests' (Marx, 1973, p. 245). Corporations pursue their own special interest first, and the interests of all corporations second. Thus while propaganda deliberately manufactured in the general interest of capital is not unknown (see, for example, most British newspapers), this is not the main way minds are reproduced in advanced capitalist countries.

The 'consciousness industry' holds a central position in advanced capitalism. It can use the attractions of high monetary reward and mass adulation to employ the most creative minds, the most beautiful bodies, the most convincing voices, the most appealing personalities, the latest technology, to mass-produce technicoloured, stereophonic, edited pieces of exaggerated 'experience', which the modern mind has come to prefer over real experience, just as the addict prefers drug-induced fantasy over mundane reality.

The ideas produced at the capitalist centre, together with the cultural forms taken by these ideas, are infused with a convincing power. They take their strength from the levels of contradiction and crisis which produce intense experiences in the First World. These experiences are then sifted through, images intensified, and these images strung together to form 'entertainment'. Entertaining programmes are then projected with all the might of high technology into the minds of a world of people. Yet such entertainment, dealing only with effects and not causes, is not satisfying. Failure to find satisfaction in consumer culture, however, only leads to more powerful, technologized forms of that culture. The end result of this process might be called 'super-culture', had the description 'super' not already been overtaken by the very normalization of the extraordinary we seek to describe. We shall call the resulting product by its own favourite description – hence we are now in the phase of 'ultra-culture'.

Ultra-culture is differentiated from its predecessors by its distance from the topics which inform its content and by its highly technological manufacture, not as a whole, planned culture, but as carefully prepared individual components launched on the market of minds in the pursuit of individual profit. It is relatively autonomous in that it limits the minds of its *producers*, as well as its consumers, creating thereby the mental conditions for its own more exaggerated continuation.

The resulting consciousness is driven by social crisis but remains fundamentally unconnected with the *origins* of crisis. In this way, capitalist consciousness can become increasingly false, yet increasingly persuasive, both at the centre of crisis (the First World) and in the periphery (the Third World).

CENTRE AND PERIPHERY IN THE GEOGRAPHY OF CONSCIOUSNESS

The economic grounds for the penetration of capitalist ultra-culture into the minds and lives of the people of the periphery have long been prepared. There are few areas of the world which have not been involved in the production of commodities for the world capitalist market and which, therefore, have been subject to the dissolving effects of exchange. Involvement in exchange opens the non-capitalist community to outside influences: first by its effect on the traditional relations and purposes of production (as discussed previously) and thus on the economic basis of culture; second by the implantation of foreign elements directly into local culture, via individuals and institutions oriented to the outside world, and via the communications media. The last of these may initially be connected with commodity exchange, but cannot be restricted to purely economic functions. Indeed in the subsequent cultural invasion, the 'communications media' play a central role. The medium itself (radio, television, etc.) is destructive of local culture, apart from the messages it carries. Advanced communications media overwhelm those of a technically less developed society – thus in India, the cinema is presently obliterating village and street theatre.

Beyond the influence of technical superiority, however, lie the messages carried from centre to periphery. The argument has been made earlier that centre culture signifies the contradictions of advanced capitalism, but only by dwelling on effects, 'solutions', etc. A culture which endlessly revolves around effects cannot be fundamentally satisfying; yet one which plunges into causes will be threatening, not only to authority and the established institutions, but also to the normal lives of a comfort-seeking populace. The result is an ultra-culture with intense powers of visual and aural stimulation, but little real content, which provides mesmerizing diversion at the flick of a switch. Under the desperate economic conditions of the Third World, where 'solutions' appear to flow from the centre countries in the form of aid, loans, etc., rather than from the efforts of Third World people themselves, the need for diversion is equally, if not more, pervasive. The dreams presented by the Hollywood factories, reflecting the intense contradictions of the centre, invested with all the technical and economic power of the centre, combining intense stimulation with tranquilization, are more effective diversions than those locally produced – thus 'Hollywood' keeps half the cinemas in the non-socialist world supplied with films (Varis, 1976).

This is not to argue that peripheral–regional cultural production has disappeared. The Indian film industry, for example, draws on regional folklore ('it's what village life would be like if dreams came true') for its predominant themes. Film then becomes so powerful that traditional cultural forms are relegated to an adjunct status – hence puppeteers are forced to mimic the Bombay studios to draw a crowd, while snake charmers serenade with tunes borrowed from musical films (Channel 4, 1984). But in the interaction between centre culture and local culture, there can be little doubt which is more dynamic, and what direction cultural synthesis is taking. The tendency is towards the production of one world mind, one world culture, and the consequent disappearance of regional consciousness flowing from the local specificities of the human past.

The people of the periphery are thus subjected to three kinds of domination. Where the forces of production remain undeveloped, they remain the victims of uncontrollable forces of nature. They are increasingly and especially subject to the vagaries of world commodity markets. And their minds are captured by forms of consciousness evolved at the centre of contradiction in the world capitalist system.

Consciousness in the periphery retains its religious nature. Hence the universalizing religions, especially Christianity, linked with Euro-American economic superiority, become ever more universal. Peripheral people thus seek to control local nature by praying to the gods of the powerful centre. This was dramatically exemplified, as these words were being written, when the Pope visited Papua New Guinea. Villagers in red-feathered head-dresses and painted faces welcomed him in a ceremony that had required abstinence from meat and sex for the previous month; at the same ceremony they took snapshots with miniature cameras. Meanwhile: 'The Pope prayed in pidgin English that the threatening volcanoes on a neighbouring island would be stilled. He told the tribesmen: "May God's peace . . . descend upon your volcanoes"' (*Guardian*, 8 May 1984, p. 1). Victory of the religious ceremony of the centre over that of the periphery!

Mystical consciousness in the periphery is also enhanced by the diffusion of the whole congeries of more modern ideas carried by a persuasive ultra-culture. Thus the new gods of entertainment are worshipped around a globe which assumes all the characteristics of one big fan-club.

Either way, through formal or informal mysticism, the result is a consciousness alienated from the real and desperate conditions which Third World people must face in the reproduction of their lives.

CONCLUSION

Human history is the history of domination by forces beyond human control. During most of history, the main source of domination was the rest of nature, or rather 'Nature' as it was conceived – that is, natural forces endowed with conscousness and will, whose capriciousness alternately favoured, then eliminated, human life. The very means by which this form of domination was destroyed (capitalist relations of production) became the main source of new kinds of domination. Thus capitalism likewise capriciously favours or eliminates human life, creates or destroys employment, makes some rich, others poor. What humans have thought about these determining conditions of their existence is the basis of consciousness, in the sense of Marx's formula that social existence determines consciousness. Likewise the practices and institutions built around experiences of domination constitute the core of culture, in the sense of Marx's statement that the mode of production of material life conditions the general process of social, political and intellectual life. Ways of thinking and living have arisen under definite conditions which are not chosen but inherited, not understood but fundamentally mystified, not controlled but controlling. Religion is the main way of understanding events emanating from causes beyond human understanding and control, events which are interpreted as the material results of an almighty conscious force ('God'). Prayer is the only salvation when the human individual is confronted by an otherwise unalterable force. Human liberation within an accurate structure of consciousness is possible only when these forces are socially and communally controlled. As Marx said:

> The religious reflections of the real world can in any case, vanish only when the practical relations of everyday life between man and man, and man and nature, generally present themselves to him in a transparent and rational form. The veil is not removed from the countenance of the social life-process, i.e. the process of material production, until it becomes production by freely associated men, and stands under their conscious and planned control. This, however, requires that society passes a material foundation, or a series of material conditions of existence, which in their turn are the natural and spontaneous product of a long and tormented historical development. (Marx, 1976, p. 173)

This long and tormented development can be shortened by using the fragments of accurate understanding so far achieved to pierce the veil shrouding the countenance of the social life-process. This is the essentially political purpose behind radical intellectual labour, both in the centre and, especially, in the periphery.

Geography is that part of a whole knowledge which specializes in the relation with natural environment and relations with others across space. These relations also are characterized by dominance and human servitude, although a transition has occurred from an early domination by local nature, to the more recent domination of local events by world-wide forces. Determination by nature has been replaced by determination from world space. What little local control over life there was, at a low level of development of the productive forces, is lost not primarily to centralized control, although elements of this exist, but more profoundly to a lack of control. That is, a world capitalist system which moves under the power of its unfolding contradictions, which reduces human action to a series of short-term protective reactions not amounting, even in total, to anything resembling social control. Common ways of misunderstanding this world system, and common forms of escape from its consequences, are the basis of a world culture which overwhelms and destroys local cultures.

It may be argued that all that is lost in the process is a litany of past mysticisms, little deserving lament (see the opening quote from Fanon). But regional and local cultures represent the sum total of past experience under a vast range of environmental conditions. The selective incorporation of a reinterpreted past into a liberated future cannot occur if the memory of that past has been obliterated, or if its cultural products are known only as museum pieces. This is one danger inherent in the spread of world homogeneous culture. The other danger is that everyone, including the peoples of the peripheries, becomes caught in a way of life and thought unsuited to the solution of the problems thrown up by an inherently contradictory way of life. This is particularly dangerous when the technical devices used to 'solve' problems become capable of widespread destruction. Hence the urgent need for a science of society and a revolutionary praxis based on this liberative science.

References

Bellah, Roberts N. 1969: Religious evolution. In N. Birnbaum and G. Lenzer (eds), *Sociology and Religion*. Englewood Cliffs: Prentice-Hall, 67–83.

de Cardona, E. 1975: Multinational television. *Journal of Communication*, 25, 122–7.

Channel 4 (British television) 1984: There'll always be stars in the sky. Documentary programme, 25 March.

Enzensberger, H. M. 1974: *The Consciousness Industry: On Literature, Politics and the Media.* New York: Continuum.

Ewan, S. 1976: *Captains of Consciousness: Advertising and the Social Roots of the Consumer Culture*. New York: McGraw-Hill.

Fanon, Frantz 1963: *The Wretched of the Earth.* New York: Grove Press.

Frazer, J. G. 1926: *The Worship of Nature*. London: Macmillan.

Golding, P. 1978: The international media and the political economy of publishing. *Library Trends*, 26, 453–66.

Gould, P. and J. Johnson, 1980: The content and structure of international television flows. *Communication*, 5, 43–63.

Guback, T. H. 1974: Film as international business. *Journal of Communication*, 24, 90–101.

Harris, P. 1974: Hierarchy and concentration in international news flow. *Politics*, 9, 159–65.

Harris, P. 1976: International news media authority and dependence. *Instant Research on Peace and Violence*, 6, 148–59.

Horkheimer, M. and T. W. Adorno, 1972: *Dialectic of Enlightenment*. New York: Herder & Herder.

Hume, D. (ed.) 1968: Origin of religion. In N. Birnbaum and G. Lenzer (eds), *Sociology and Religion*, Englewood Cliffs: Prentice-Hall, 19–22.

Janus, N. and R. Roncaglio, 1979: Advertising, mass media and dependency. *Development Dialogue*, 1, 81–97.

Marx, K. 1969: The Eighteenth Brumaire of Louis Bonaparte. In K. Marx and F. Engels, *Selected Works*, vol. 1. Moscow: Progress Publishers, 16–30.

Marx, K. 1970: *A Contribution to the Critique of Political Economy*. New York: International Publishers.

Marx, K. 1973: *Grundrisse: Foundations of the Critique of Political Economy*. Harmondsworth: Penguin.

Marx, K. 1976: *Capital*, vol. 1. Harmondsworth: Penguin.

Marx, K. and Engels, F. 1957: *On Religion*. Moscow: Progress Publishers.

Masmondi, M. 1979: The new world information order. *Journal of Communication*, 29, 172–85.

Peet, R. 1980: The consciousness dimension of Fiji's integration into world capitalism. *Pacific Viewpoint*, 21, 91–115.

Peet, R. 1981: Historical forms of the property relation: a reconstruction of Marx's theory. *Antipode*, 13, (3), 13–25.

Peet, R. 1982: International capital, international culture. In M. Taylor and N. Thrift (eds), *The Geography of Multinationals*. London: Croom Helm, 275–302.

Peet, R. 1983: Relations of production and the relocation of United States manufacturing industry since 1960. *Economic Geography*, 59, 112–43.

Perez, L. A. 1975: Tourism in the West Indies. *Journal of Communication*, 25, 136–43.

Schiller, H. I. 1969: *Mass Communications and American Empire*. Boston: Beacon Press.

Schiller, H. I. 1978: Decolonization of information: efforts toward a new international order. *Latin American Perspectives*, Special Issue on Culture in the Age of Mass Media, 9, 35–48.

Semple, E. C. 1911: *Influences of Geographic Environment on the Basis of Ratzel's System of Anthropo-geography*. New York: Russell & Russell.

Sopher, D. E. 1967; *Geography of Religions*. Englewood Cliffs: Prentice-Hall.

Timpanaro, S. 1975: *On Materialism*. London: New Left Books.

Varis, T. 1974: Global traffic in television. *Journal of Communications*, 24, 102–9.

Varis, T. 1976: Aspects of the impact of transnational corporations on communication. *International Social Science Journal*, 28, 808–30.

Williams, R. 1980: *Problems in Materialism and Culture*. London: Verso Editions and New Left Books.

Williams, R. 1981: *Culture*. Glasgow: Fontana.

Wittfogel, K. 1929: Geopolitik, geographischer Materialismus und Marxismus. *Unter den Banner des Marxismus*, 3, 17–51; 4, 485–522, 698–735.

Wittfogel, K. 1957: *Oriental Despotism: A Comparative Study of Total Power*. New Haven: Yale University Press.

8

Individual Freedom and the World-Economy

R. J. JOHNSTON

We hold these truths to be self-evident, that all men are created equal, that they are endowed by their Creator with certain unalienable Rights, that among these are Life, Liberty and the pursuit of Happiness.

These ringing phrases, which introduced the American Declaration of Independence, provided the context for framing the Constitution of the United States, a document which became the model for many later exercises in the writing of constitutions and bills of rights. The American Constitution, especially the first ten Amendments plus the three (13–15) passed with the abolition of slavery after the Civil War, presents an image of American society in which individual control over life and livelihood is paramount. When collective action is taken, by the state on behalf of the people, this is done for the general welfare and so for the long-term good of every individual. The ideology is one of individual freedom and self-control. But what is the reality?

This chapter focuses on the position of the individual in the capitalist world-economy. Its starting-point is Marx's concept of alienation, which provides the context for appreciating the function of the individual within the capitalist mode of production. Because of alienation, which is inevitable under capitalism, individuals lack control over their own lives – whether they are members of the bourgeoisie or of the proletariat. The empirical reality of this lack of control is the labour market and the maldistribution of economic and political power within society. These become the focus of protest, especially from the relatively powerless among the alienated – i.e. the proletariat. It is countering that protest, creating a consensus within society, that legitimizes such an alienating mode of production, which forms a major role of the state under capitalism (Clark and Dear, 1984). The concessions that have been provided include the granting of democracy and human rights.

Democracy and human rights are concepts which are widely accepted in the contemporary world, by both capitalist and non-capitalist governments. Thus the United Nations Universal Declaration of Human Rights was unanimously adopted in 1948. With regard to democracy, this includes the statements (in Article 21), that:

> Everyone has the right to take part in the government of his country, directly or through freely chosen representatives,

and:

> The will of the people shall be the basis of the authority of government; this will shall be expressed in periodic and genuine elections which shall be by universal and equal suffrage.

In this context, Berg (1978, p. 156) has defined *democracy* as 'an ideal type of national decision-making system whose members (above some minimum age level) enjoy equality of self-determination', and *self-determination* is defined (p. 167) thus: 'An individual has self-determination to the extent that he is not excluded from making decisions that are relevant to him and to the extent that he makes or effectively participates in the making of such decisions.'

Such concepts and definitions are open to a variety of interpretations. In particular, there is a clear division between liberal (or bourgeois) democracy and popular democracy (Hindess, 1980). The former is defined within the context of the capitalist mode of production and the capitalist state. Democracy in such a situation involves competition to manage a capitalist social formation. Certain parties in such competition may wish to manipulate the social formation towards certain interests (the proletariat's, for example), but, as shown by British and French 'socialist' administrations in recent years, the constraints of the system prevent them steering it far from what is in the short-run, let alone the long-run, interests of capital. (Capitalism as a mode of production is relatively robust, however, and can bring into line local attempts to create alternative modes of production, as in Chile in the early 1970s. This raises major doubts as to the possibility of achieving socialism via liberal democratic means: Hunt, 1980.) Popular democracy, on the other hand, can only take place in a classless society, produced via the dictatorship of the proletariat. It involves individuals in all aspects of the control of their lives, the achievement of which leads to the withering away of the state (Luard, 1978).

The concepts of liberal democracy are part of the ideology of the capitalist mode of production, used by the state to mystify the real nature of alienation. The goal of this chapter is to unravel some of this mystification, particularly as it relates to the situation during the present crisis and the geography of liberal democracy. It begins with an outline of the concept of alienation. The geography of liberal democracy is then analysed, followed by a discussion of the geography of human rights.

ALIENATION

The concept of alienation was the starting-point of Marx's analysis of the capitalist mode of production. Capitalism alienates the individual from him-or herself; individuals are taken over by their own works, which have an independent existence. In a non-alienated condition, the individual is at one with nature, interacting with it in order to reproduce; humanity involves physical commerce with nature, the only influences on which are the individual and the caprices of the environment. In an alienated condition, on the other hand, the physical commerce with nature is organized and institutionalized. The individual loses control over it, and therefore over his or her reproduction, and instead can only survive either through the sale of labour power (the proletariat in a capitalist society) or by the purchase of labour (the bourgeoisie); in either case, the individual is no longer a 'being-for-himself' and is depersonalized in the commerce, becoming a 'being-for-another'. Thus, according to Kolakowski (1978, p. 222), 'Marx's starting point . . . is . . . the fact that individuals are alienated from their own labour and its material, spiritual, and social consequences in the form of goods, ideas, and political institutions, and not only from these but from their fellow beings and, ultimately, from themselves.'

The capitalist mode of production is dehumanizing, therefore: instead of the individual controlling the means of production, the means of production control the individual. Those means (land in the traditional trilogy of land, labour and capital) have been captured by the bourgeoisie, and within the proletariat the individual can only survive by agreeing to sell his or her sole resource – labour – on terms very largely dictated by the purchaser.

Under the capitalist mode of production, therefore, the individual is captured by the system, and becomes subordinate to it. (This is true of individuals in both proletariat and bourgeoisie, for survival of the latter is just as much dependent on their acceptance of the dictates of the mode of production as is survival of the former. The classes differ, of course, in the unequal division of the material gains, which very much favours the bourgeoisie.) Thus as capitalism spread through the world, so its particular form of alienation took over. For most of those involved, there was no alternative. They were forced to give up their pre-capitalist mode of existence, notably through the expropriation of their land resources and the pressures on them to move to urban areas where the commodification of their labour power was complete. Today, as economic power is increasingly centralized so the processes of alienation (or dehumanization of life and livelihood) are extended.

The causes and consequences of this alienation are readily apparent in capitalist societies. The individual has no control over the basic means of reproduction – food, water, shelter, etc. – but can gain access to these only by selling labour and using the proceeds to bargain with those who are selling what is needed. In selling labour, the individual is usually bargaining in an unfairly structured labour market, in which the powers of the individual are constrained by political, institutional and other factors. Similarly, in seeking access to the means of reproduction, individuals operate in environments structured by others.

Alienation involves the removal of self-control from individuals; they are manipulated by others, because of the dictates of the mode of production. There is potential within capitalism for alienation to be carried to such extremes that individuals will collectively revolt against it. To counter this threat, and the possibility of the demise of capitalism, the state has been established as a separate (but not independent, see Clark and Dear, 1984) body which legitimizes capitalism and maintains social cohesion. One of the strategies that may be pursued is to grant concessions to the proletariat, thereby 'buying' their acceptance of the capitalist system. Such concessions include liberal democracy, the 'apparent' involvement of individuals in the control of the economic system. Liberal democracy is not universally practised within the contemporary capitalist world, however, for reasons outlined in the next section.

THE GEOGRAPHY OF LIBERAL DEMOCRACY

Democracy is generally conceived as 'government of the people, by the people, and for the people'; all adult individuals have the right to decide what are matters of general concern and how they should be tackled, and the consensus view prevails. Ideally, this implies a mode of socio-political organization in which every member of society is an equal participant. In practice, because of the scale problem, it implies representative democracy, whereby every individual has an equal part to play in both electing a body to organize the society and calling the representatives to account. In popular rhetoric, especially in western Europe and North America, democracy is equated with individual freedom.

If liberal democracy is defined as government by an elected body (or individual), with that body accountable to the electorate regularly and frequently, with no constraints on the choice of representatives available to the electorate, and with no constraints on who can vote (other than age), then it is a system operated in only a minority of countries at the present time, and available to only a minority of the world's population. Figure 8.1 shows all those countries identified by Butler, Penniman and Ranney (1981) – excluding those with populations of less than 3 million (a list that contains several clearly democratic states, notably Costa Rica, Iceland, Jamaica, Luxemburg and Malta) – which satisfy the following six conditions: (a) universal or near-universal adult franchise; (b) a regular timetable for elections that is adhered to; (c) no substantial group is denied the opportunity to form parties and nominate candidates; (d) all seats in the major legislature can be, and are, contested; (e) campaigns are reasonably fair without violence or intimidation; and (f) votes are cast freely and secretly. Only 28 states met these criteria; as

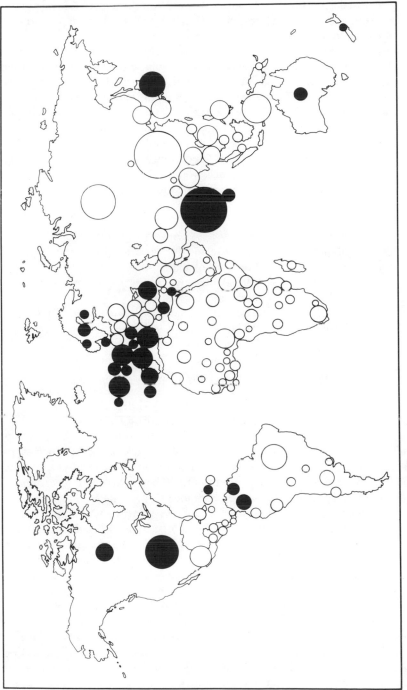

Figure 8.1 Countries which hold 'free' elections
Source: Butler, Penniman and Ranney, 1981

the map, figure 8.1, shows, nearly all are in western Europe. (In this and other world maps in this chapter, the size of the symbol for each country is proportional to its population.)

Democracy is more than holding elections, however. In many countries, frequent elections are held, but the choice available to the electorate is either constrained (certain individuals are prevented from standing as candidates, or certain parties are precluded from fielding candidates, for example, as in Turkey in 1983) or nil (a one-party state is the goal of the Prime Minister of Zimbabwe, Robert Mugabe, for example). In others, only a minority are allowed to register as electors and to vote. Dahl (1978) has argued that democracy should give all citizens the opportunity to formulate and signify preferences and to have those preferences weighted equally in the conduct of government. For this to occur, a set of institutional guarantees is required, as laid out below:

Necessary condition	*Institutional guarantees required*
The formulation of preferences	Freedom to form and to join organizations
	Freedom of expression
	The availability of alternative information sources
	The right to vote and to compete for votes
Signifying preferences	All the above, plus:
	Free and fair elections
	Freedom to stand for public office
Equal weighting of preferences	All the above, plus:
	Institutions which ensure that government policies depend on voting and other popularly expressed preferences

Study of the geography of liberal democracy should take all of these necessary conditions into account. This has been done annually for several years in the publication *Freedom in the World*. Countries have been classified according to their level of political rights into seven categories, from the freest to the least free. The criteria used are described as follows (Gastil, 1981, pp. 13–17). Countries in the top category 'have a fully competitive electoral process and those elected clearly rule'. Those in the second category have some constraints to the effectiveness of this policy, and the equality that it implies; the factors involved include 'extreme economic inequality, illiteracy or intimidating violence' which can weaken effective competition. The next three categories imply increasingly less effective popular control, and most countries in category 5 may have no elections. In category 6, no competitive electoral processes are allowed: 'The rulers of states at this level assume that one person or small group has the right to decide what is best for a nation, and that no one should be allowed to challenge that right', but such rulers do respond to popular desire and operate within the context of local culture. In category 7, the 'least free',

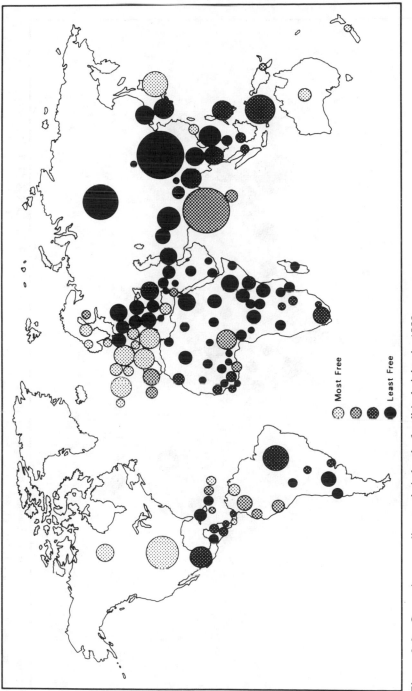

Figure 8.2 Countries according to their level of political rights in 1980

Source: ratings from Gastil, 1981; categories 3–4–5 and 6–7 have been combined

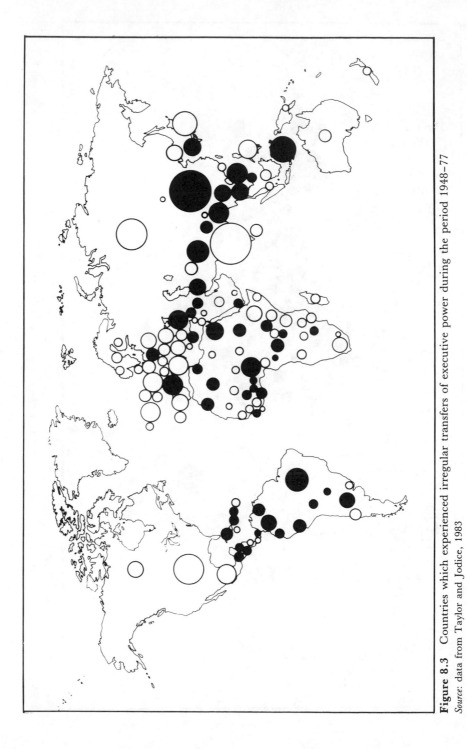

Figure 8.3 Countries which experienced irregular transfers of executive power during the period 1948–77

Source: data from Taylor and Jodice, 1983

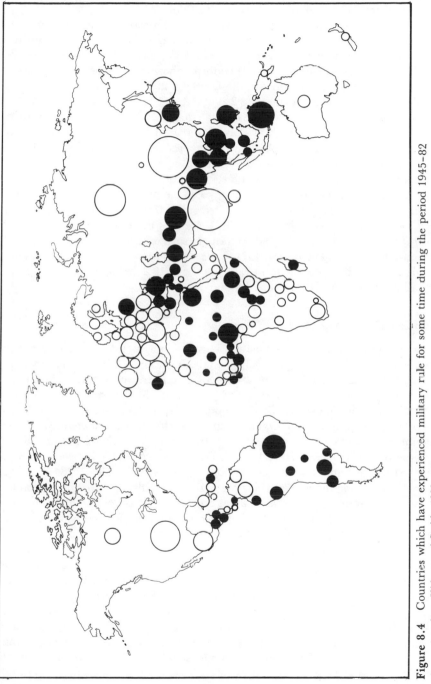

Figure 8.4 Countries which have experienced military rule for some time during the period 1945–82

Source: data from Kidron and Smith, 1983

'the political despots at the top appear by their actions to feel little constraint from either public opinion or popular tradition.'

Clearly there is some element of subjectivity in this categorization of countries, although the outcome accords with general beliefs – at least in those countries in category 1, where the ideal of democracy is proclaimed. The map of the 1980 categorization (see figure 8.2) confirms those general beliefs. Countries such as the United Kingdom and the United States are in category 1, India, Israel and Jamaica are in category 2, Poland and Yugoslavia are in category 6, and East Germany and Haiti are in category 7. (For some of the countries in the lower categories – such as Poland and East Germany – the concept of liberal democracy is not accepted: such countries are being classified on criteria that are irrelevant to *their* interpretations of democracy.)

Liberal democracy implies popularly elected governments. A corollary of this is that governments will only change at the popularly expressed behest. In many countries, however, there are 'irregular' transfers of power, that occur without popular consent (see figure 8.3). Most of these involve some form of *coup d'état*, and very many (including the only such transfers in western Europe – France in 1958 and Portugal in 1974) have some form of military involvement. Rule by the military is far from rare (see figure 8.4), providing a particular type of government in categories 6 and 7.

Economic Development and Liberal Democracy

The 'geographies of liberal democracy' outlined in figures 8.2–8.4 suggest clear correlations with what we generally term the 'geography of economic develop-ment'. In broad terms, liberal democracy is associated with the most industrial-ized and prosperous countries of the world, whereas the absence of political freedom is associated with underdevelopment, especially in the so-called 'Third World'. This suggests, in line with Rostow's (1960) classic, if discredited, model of the processes of economic development, that as countries become more prosperous so democracy is established. Democracy, it seems, is associated with a particular economic and social condition (see also Chaffee, 1984).

Several authors have tested this proposition. Coulter (1975), for example, conducted a series of statistical analyses regressing indices of liberal democracy against measures of economic development and social structure – what he called 'social mobilization'. Democracy was defined by three concepts – political competitiveness, participation and public liberties – which were combined into an index of liberal democracy. The Netherlands had the highest index value (the data refer to the period 1948–69), followed by Belgium, West Germany and Iceland. The bottom five positions (of the 85 countries studied) were occupied by Pakistan, Kenya, Sudan, Iraq and the United Arab Republic. Social mobilization was measured by a composite index, comprising variables relating to urbanization, education, communication, industrialization and GNP. Coulter found that level of social mobilization accounted for 48 per cent of the variation between countries in their level of liberal democracy, and changes in the level of social mobilization accounted for exactly half of the variation in level of liberal democracy.

A slightly more sophisticated statistical analysis was conducted by Bollen (1983), to test the hypothesis that 'economic development . . . increases the likelihood of political democracy' (p. 468). This was modified, however, in the recognition that in the contemporary world-economy 'economic development' in peripheral countries does not bring as much autonomous power to local elites as it does in core countries, because powerful groups in the latter (including multinational companies) have a great deal of influence over those in the former. Using a measure of liberal democracy similar to Coulter's but only a single measure – energy consumption per capita – of economic development, his basic equation for a sample of 100 countries accounted for 47 per cent of the variation: the greater the level of development, the greater the level of democracy, but at any level of development the level of democracy was significantly lower in peripheral than in core countries.

An Alternative View

The above analyses describe the geography of liberal democracy in terms of the geography of economic development, but provide no understanding of the mechanism whereby such democracy develops. The implication is that it comes about 'naturally' as a consequence of some mechanistic process embodied in economic development: with industrialization, urbanization and prosperity come elections, a wider franchise and freedom of choice. Alternative views suggest that the process is far from automatic, that democratic gains are usually the consequence of long struggles by alienated labour, and that victories gained are frequently overturned. To understand why the observed correlations occur, we need a model of the fight for democracy.

Liberal democracy focuses on the state, so to understand its operations we require an appreciation of the nature and role of the state. In any society, it has three basic roles – to maintain cohesion, to promote the mode of production, and to legitimate it. It is an institution empirically separate from, but totally interlinked with, the powerful class within the mode of production. (For full discussions, see Johnston, 1982, 1984a; Clark and Dear, 1984.) By promoting the mode of production it promotes the interests of that class. Under the capitalist mode of production, therefore, the state by promoting capitalism promotes the interests of the bourgeoisie; as a consequence, it is acting against the interests of the proletariat, the alienated labour being exploited by the capitalist class. But capitalism is founded on inter-class tension. Promotion of capitalism can exacerbate the tension, creating the conditions for conflict which will damage the mode of production and hence the interests of the bourgeoisie. Thus the state is also involved in ameliorating that tension, by containing proletarian disquiet. It must obtain support.

Support is generally won by granting concessions. But what if it cannot, if legitimation cannot be achieved because the victories would undermine the interests of the capitalist class? In such a case, coercion is the usual alternative pursued, and legitimation is achieved rather than agreed.

The capitalist state, then, is involved in the promotion and legitimation of the mode of production. As that mode is built on alienation, the state must both promote and legitimate it, either by offering concessions to the alienated labour in return for their (grudging) support or by imposing a regime on labour, by coercing it. (Because the state is empirically independent, it appears to be coercing all, in the 'national good'. That coercion, however, will almost invariably benefit the bourgeoisie more than the proletariat.)

These complementary roles are made difficult for the state by general tendencies within capitalist economic systems. Over the last two centuries, capitalist economies have not displayed unbroken economic progress. Rather, they have been characterized by a series of long waves (generally known as Kondratieff cycles) comprising a boom followed by a slump (see Taylor, 1985a). Each wave has been about 50 years long (i.e. the gap between the nadir of two adjacent slumps is about 50 years; shorter, less severe cycles have taken place within these long waves). The slumps are brought about by a combination of factors which are seemingly endemic to capitalism: investment in productivity increases means that the ability to produce outruns the ability to consume; markets are saturated; sales and profits fall; investment declines; new investments are sought in sectors where profits are more likely; and so on (see Harvey 1982, 1984). During such slumps, both classes in capitalist society suffer, the bourgeoisie from a lack of wealth accumulation, and the proletariat from low demand for labour. Of the two, the proletariat suffers most, because it lacks the accumulated wealth on which to live until there is an upturn in the economy and the demand for labour increases.

The state is fully implicated in these crises of capitalism because its twin roles are to promote and sustain the mode of production. It faces three sets of crises (Habermas, 1976). The first are rationality crises. The state is supposed to promote accumulation, so it is judged to be failing its supporters in the bourgeoisie. The second are legitimation crises, which focus on the proletariat, who find that the system legitimated by the state is failing them. Together, these generate motivation crises; the state is failing both classes, who will withdraw support (not necessarily immediately or completely).

In order to maintain cohesion within society and avoid motivation crises, the state must ameliorate the impacts of rationality and legitimation crises, and create an environment within which they will be removed by a further cycle of prosperity. It must take steps to promote accumulation, without which it has nothing to legitimate. This provides the basis for understanding the changing geography of liberal democracy in the world.

The world-economy, as pointed out several times in this book, comprises three 'zones': core, semi-periphery and periphery. Countries in the core are distinguished by their nodal position within the economic system, in terms of control and the repatriation of profits. Wealth (i.e. surplus value) created in the periphery has been expropriated to the core. This has provided the foundation for the major international inequalities, and has allowed the states within the core to legitimate the capitalist mode of production by granting concessions to their proletariats. Such concessions can be 'afforded' because they have been paid for by the peripheral countries. One of the concessions has been liberal democracy (Johnston, 1984b). In response to proletarian demands, the state has granted a near-universal franchise (eventually), allowing widespread participation in the government of the state, which inevitably means that to some extent the state has granted further concessions to the proletariat. As long as the core country is prosperous, this has been affordable. Further, an ideology of democracy linked to that of capitalism has been promoted by the state, which reduces proletarian demand for radical restructuring and thereby retains the grudging support of the bourgeoisie. Thus in major crises the proletariat has largely accepted pro-capitalist arguments in order to counter the rationality crisis (as with the 1931 National Government in the United Kingdom: see Taylor, 1983).

The situation in peripheral countries within the world-economy is very different, because they lack the accumulated wealth with which to tackle crises. Such countries are almost impotent in their attempts to influence the operations of the mode of production. They are used by outside interests as sources of cheap resources and labour, and because there is an abundance of most resources, certainly of cheap, unskilled labour, those outside interests can play off one country against another. Investors want guaranteed, cheap commodities, plus guaranteed, cheap, disciplined labour. If the guarantees are not forthcoming, or if they are doubted, the investment will go elsewhere. To win investment, the state operates policies designed to ensure 'order and stability' (Osei-Kwame and Taylor, 1984).

A state within a peripheral country may face a motivation crisis, therefore. It has to tackle a rationality crisis by creating an environment within which capitalist profits can be made; without this, investment will not take place, jobs will not be created, and legitimation will be threatened. It can only create such an environment, it feels, by 'disciplining' the proletariat. Democracy creates instability – governments may fall, or be forced to yield concessions that threaten profits – and so, in the national interest, cannot be afforded. Coercion is necessary, to provide the stability that will attract investment and prepare the path to prosperity. Thus non-democratic rule is promoted as being in the national interest, and the state is 'taken over' by groups – often military – pursuing such policies. But what if it fails – relatively, at least? Some investment is attracted (including, perhaps, some locally generated capital). But it has little multiplier effect, and creates insufficient jobs and prosperity to satisfy the demands of the local proletariat. Their judgement of the state will be that its policies have failed, and this will generate a legitimation crisis. It can be tackled by further coercion and oppression – which is expensive in its demands on well-paid 'safe' manpower (for the police and military apparatus) – or the controllers of the state can yield and 'return the country to democracy'. The former solution is a totalitarian, unfree regime. The latter is liable to promote a further rationality crisis. Neither is likely to counter the problems of alienation. This, then, is the politics of failure.

This scenario suggests an ideal-type situation whereby a peripheral country passes through a continuing cycle of democracy (to counter a legitimation crisis), non-democratic rule (to counter a rationality crisis), democracy again, and so on (see Johnston, 1984b). A number of countries (e.g. Argentina, Brazil, Chile, Ghana, Nigeria) have recent political histories that display these characteristics. As an ideal-type scenario, it is not a predictive model. Some countries may not change their form of government: not all states facing legitimation crises have created liberal democracy, and not all states facing rationality crises have abandoned it (e.g. Jamaica). Alternative strategies may be pursued by those in power within the state apparatus, although this may strain their abilities to build coalitions of support (e.g. Osei-Kwame and Taylor, 1984; Taylor, 1984). And it may be that a strategy works, that a country rises out of the peripheral status and achieves the level of permanent, general prosperity which allows it to afford the luxury of permanent democracy.

And the Core Countries?

The above discussion has suggested that liberal democracy is a form of political organization which, in general, will only be possible in the prosperous core countries of the world. This implies that, within the latter, proletarian participation in and numerical dominance of government means that policies are followed which are very largely in proletarian interests. Investigation of this proposition indicates that it is not the case, in absolute terms; in relative terms, however, the proletariat is much more prosperous in the core democracies than elsewhere in the world.

Representative government has developed into government by parties. These are not only organizations which allow for some efficiency in government – a party or a coalition of parties with a majority virtually ensures that agreed policies are enacted; they also structure the agenda on which elections are fought. The parties can thus determine the issues, and can organize the political agenda (Riker, 1983). To the extent that they control the political system, they control the content of political debate. In this way, many issues salient to the electors may never become salient within the political system (see Schattschneider, 1962).

The strength of this organizational bias depends on the ease with which the electorate can influence the number and nature of the parties. It is, of course, possible for new parties to be established which promote issues ignored by those already established. They face major problems, however. In order to win support, they must promote themselves. This requires money and access to the main channels of information – the media. Political campaigning is extremely expensive. To afford lengthy campaigns and permanent organizations, parties must attract funds – either from the proletariat at large (in general very difficult, especially over long periods) or from sectors of the bourgeoisie. Thus only parties, or individuals, which do not threaten the established order have much chance of support – and if they don't threaten the established order they have little base on which to seek support. Further, in most countries the media are in private ownership (i.e. they are owned and controlled by the bourgeoisie). These are also firmly committed to the established order, and so are unlikely to give much positive support to new, 'threatening', political movements.

This does not mean, of course, that such political movements will not attract support in some situations; the successes of the 'Green Party' in West Germany in the 1980s, Mogens Glistrup in Denmark in the 1970s, and Pierre Poujade in France in the 1950s illustrate this. But very few are likely to survive for long, unless they promote policies acceptable to the established order. The state is not independent of the mode of production, and if parties in control of the state act in ways perceived by the bourgeoisie as harmful to capitalist interests, then they can be 'disciplined' through the creation of a rationality crisis. A consequence of such rationality crises for many governments has been an inability to service overseas debts, and they have only been 'rescued' from a fiscal crisis by the IMF on terms favourable to outside capitalist interests, and not to the local proletariat's (Johnston, 1982); core countries have been forced to call on the IMF, too, as a British Labour government did in the 1970s.

Parties structure the political agenda, then, and are themselves constrained in their actions by the imperatives of the capitalist system. Their degrees of freedom of action are limited by the 'penalties' that can be imposed upon them by capitalist interests. This is more the case now than ever before. The hypermobility of capital and the control of the world-economy by multinational corporations means that rationality crises can be stimulated very rapidly by the threat to withdraw investment. The crisis of the state is potentially deeper than ever before – in the core countries as much as in the periphery: its ability to react positively to the demands of the proletariat is increasingly constrained (Johnston, 1984a).

This situation is apparent in the United Kingdom in the 1980s. The rationality crisis associated with a major depression in the Kondratieff cycle has produced unemployment at well over 10 per cent nationally, well over 20 per cent in some areas (including major cities) and well over 40 per cent among some disadvantaged groups. Those in control of the state have identified the only route out of this crisis as a reduction of the democratic luxuries that they believe can no longer be afforded. Thus local government – in some places operated by parties with different prescriptions – has been curtailed by fiscal policies, democratic control over local service provision has been replaced by administrative centralism, and participation in elections is to be curtailed by raising the deposit to be paid by each candidate ('to discourage frivolous candidates'). Such policies could stimulate a legitimation crisis, but this has in part been forestalled by transferring large sections of the proletariat into a petty property-owning bourgeoisie through the promotion of, for example, owner-occupancy of housing and ownership of shares in formerly nationalized concerns. In this way, the ideology of capitalism – the promotion of individual self-interest – can be promoted as the ideology of the majority, and members of the proletariat are less likely to take action – striking, for example – which would deepen the rationality crisis. (The control of their assets by this transferred proletariat is slight, however. The pension funds established by trade unions are controlled by capitalist interests, which may mean investments that are against the union members' own interests.) The labour force is being disciplined by a process that in effect involves some erosion of democratic rights, and yet its support for such authoritarian policies is being 'bought' in other ways (Hall, 1980), in part by the ideology of the contemporary state.

This method of tackling the rationality and legitimation crises has been criticized in Britain by groups which argue that its potential success is threatened by the existence of a political opposition which, if it gained power, would initiate major shifts in policy. The mere possibility of this happening after the next general election – never more than five years away – creates an unstable environment within which investment in long-term development plans by capitalists is not encouraged (Finer, 1975). The rationality crisis in Britain is at least in part a function of the political system, it is claimed.

Most countries have a range of parties offering alternative policies. In Britain, however, there is a much greater chance of a fundamental change of government after an election than in many other countries, because of the electoral system. The 'first-past-the-post' method means that a party with minority support among the voters can obtain a majority in Parliament, and it magnifies changing preferences within the electorate so that two parties with approximately equal voter support can both have reasonable hopes of electoral victory. If those parties differ fundamentally, then outside interests face possible major switches of policy after every election. This, it is claimed, has been the case in Britain since about 1960 as the two main parties (Conservative and Labour) have become more polarized, creating the unstable situation termed 'adversary politics' (Finer, 1975).

The solution offered to the problems of adversary politics and their impact on the rationality crisis is electoral reform. An electoral system based on proportional representation would, it is claimed, virtually ensure a permanent 'government of the centre' and remove the possibility of major policy shifts after elections. This would create stability (and so tackle the problems of the rationality crisis) and be more representative of the electorate's views (thus insuring against a possible legitimation crisis). To some, this would be more democratic. To others it would be less, because it would concentrate power in the parties of the centre who will structure the political agenda in the interests of the bourgeoisie; real choice is diminished and politics has been 'depoliticized' – without actually doing away with democracy (Johnston, 1985; Taylor, 1985b).

CIVIL AND HUMAN RIGHTS

This chapter has focused mainly on liberal democracy because it is widely regarded as the foundation of all civil liberties. If individuals lack control of their governments, it is probable that they will be denied many of the other

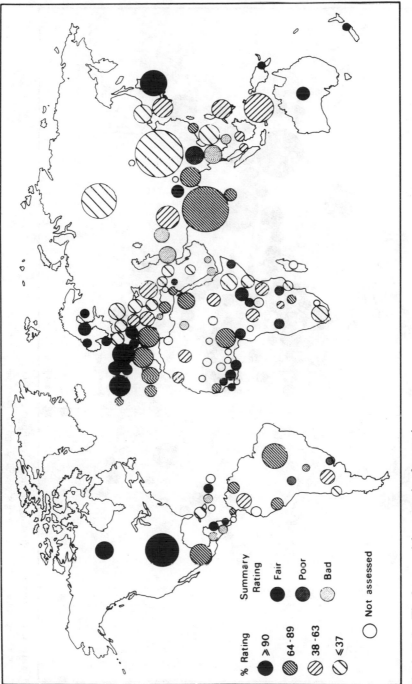

Figure 8.5 The human rights records of countries
Source: data from Humana, 1984

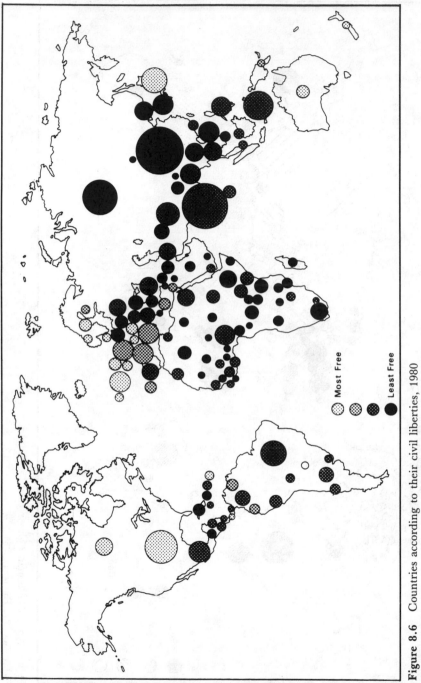

Figure 8.6 Countries according to their civil liberties, 1980

Source: ratings from Gastil, 1981; categories 3–4–5 and 6–7 have been combined

Most Free

Least Free

fundamental civil and human rights. In 1948 those rights were defined by the General Assembly of the United Nations which adopted, without a single dissenting vote, a 'Universal Declaration of Human Rights' comprising 30 articles setting out the rights and freedoms to which everyone is entitled. Twenty-eight years later this Declaration, which was no more than a statement of principles, was translated into an 'International Covenant on Civil and Political Rights', which established legal obligations on each state ratifying the covenant: 77 had ratified it by 1983.

A recent survey has assessed the countries of the world according to their performance on human rights in the context of the Covenant (Humana, 1984). For 75 countries, it was possible to make a comprehensive assessment, and these were rated on a scale from 0 to 100; the higher the value, the better the human rights record. The average score was 64, the lowest 17 (Ethiopia), and the highest 96 (Denmark, Finland and New Zealand). For the countries (49) which had ratified the Covenant, the average was 70. Thirty-two other countries were assessed on a three-point scale only, because of the lack of information: four had a 'fair' human rights record (two had ratified the Covenant – Dominican Republic and Honduras); 16 had a 'poor' record (including five ratifiers); and 12 had a 'bad' record (including El Salvador, Iran and Libya, which had all ratified the Covenant).

A map showing this categorization of countries according to their human rights records correlates very closely with that of political rights (see figure 8.5). A clearer statement of this correlation is provided by comparing Gastil's (1981) seven-fold categorization of countries according to their political-rights situation in 1980 (see figure 8.2) to a comparable categorization on civil liberties (see figure 8.6). For the latter, in countries rated in the top class:

> publications are not closed because of the expression of rational political opinion, especially when the intent of the expression is to affect the legitimate political process. No major media are simply conduits for government propaganda. The courts protect the individual; persons are not imprisoned for their opinions; private rights and desires – education, occupation, religion, residence, and so on, are generally respected; law-abiding persons do not fear for their lives because of their rational political activities. (pp. 17–19)

As one moves through the classes, so these freedoms are restricted. Courts are more authoritarian in class 2; political prisoners are common in 3, as is censorship, and torture is practised. By class 6 'the legitimate media are completely under government supervision; there is no right of assembly; and, often, travel, residence, and occupation are narrowly restricted' (pp. 19–22). By class 7, political terror is common: 'there is pervading fear, little independent expression takes place even in private, almost no public expressions of opposition emerge in the police-state environment, and imprisonment or execution is often swift and sure' (p. 22).

Table 8.1   Cross-classification of countries according to their ratings on political rights and civil liberties

Political rights	Civil liberties							Total
	1 (Most free)	2	3	4	5	6	7 (Least free)	
1 (Most free)	18	5	–	–	–	–	–	23
2	–	14	13	–	–	–	–	27
3	–	–	2	7	–	–	–	9
4	–	–	3	5	1	–	–	9
5	–	–	1	2	21	4	1	29
6	–	–	–	2	8	18	5	33
7 (Least free)	–	–	–	–	4	13	14	31
Total	18	19	19	16	34	35	20	161

Source: ratings from Gastil, 1981

The extent of agreement between the two classifications is shown in table 8.1. Because of different class sizes, complete agreement is not possible. Of the 161 a maximum of 137 could fall on the main diagonal of the table: 92 did. The greatest agreement is in the top left-hand corner: the countries with the best records on political rights also have the best on civil liberties. Towards the lower ends of the classifications, there are some disparities: four countries (Bolivia, Central African Republic, Pakistan and Surinam) are in class 5 for civil liberties but 7 for political rights, whereas one (Syria) rates 7 on civil liberties but 5 on political rights. Overall, however, the correlation is clear. A good record on political rights is usually consistent with one on civil liberties: liberal democracy and human rights go hand in hand.

Even in the countries with good records, however, it must be recognized that there are flaws, that 'these flaws are significant when measured against the standards these states set themselves' (Gastil, 1981, p. 19), and that the interpretation of their standards may be far from ideal. The United States, for example, gets positive ratings from Humana (1984) on the 'freedom to seek information and teach ideas' and on the 'freedom of movement in own country', and racial discrimination is constitutionally outlawed. Yet the interpretation of these freedoms by the courts suggests inequality of treatment (Johnston, 1984c). The United Kingdom has similar provisions, but movement between Great Britain and Northern Ireland is politically restricted (Taylor and Johnston, 1984), as is the right to join an independent trade union in certain occupations. (And in 1984, during the National Union of Mineworkers' strike, miners were prevented by the police from travelling to other coalfields, on the ground that they might be intending to commit an offence against the anti-picketing laws.)

CONCLUSIONS

Alienation has a variety of forms and appearances. To some analysts, for example, it involves the alienation of individuals from nature, from other individuals, from the product of their hands and minds, and from themselves; to others, it leads to powerlessness, meaninglessness and self-estrangement. All of these conditions stem from the organizational nexus of the mode of production, which requires alienation in order to promote the interests of the ruling class. Under capitalism, those interests involve accumulation by the bourgeoisie, which is achieved through the materialist focus of life, all elements of which are commodified and marketed.

Part of the ideology of capitalism, especially in the core countries of the world-economy, is its association with individual freedom: according to Friedman and Friedman (1980), the market economy of the United States provides freedom and an opportunity for individuals to make the most of their talents, 'through hard work, ingenuity, thrift and luck' (p. 19). Linked to this ideology of economic freedom is the ideology of democracy: according to the Friedmans (p. 21), 'economic freedom is an essential requisite for political freedom', and Macpherson (1973, p. 4) shows that the justification for western liberal democracy lies in two claims – 'the claim to maximize individual utilities, and the claim to maximize individual powers'. Whereas the Friedmans are passionate advocates of the ideologies, however, Macpherson's conclusion is that 'Neither claim has stood up very well' (p. 6). The present chapter has upheld that conclusion, isolating geographical variations in the provision of liberal democracy but arguing that even where 'freedom and democracy' are supposed to reign this does not imply individual self-control.

Under the capitalist mode of production, individuals are required to behave, and to organize their lives, in certain ways, otherwise their reproduction cannot be guaranteed. (Some societies punish 'deviants' from this rule. Others are more tolerant – of hippie communes, for example – in the belief that the market economy will soon 'discipline' them.) Such behaviour and organization is alienating. Some people prosper because of it – absolutely and relatively – but many are degraded. They are treated not as individuals but as commodities, to be used and discarded as the market economy dictates. Many are categorized according to their race, religion, gender or membership of some definable group, and are discriminated against because of what they are rather than who they are.

Resentment against this exploitative alienation has generated political movements which have demanded greater participation by individuals in control over their lives and livelihoods. The liberal democratic system of government has evolved as a response to these demands, as 'safer' than anarchism in the bourgeoisie's interests, making concessions to the alienated but within the context of the capitalist mode of production. The concessions granted to some have, as demonstrated here, largely been won at the cost of others: liberal democracy and the ability to 'reward' the proletariat is only affordable, it seems, in the core countries of the world-economy, and if the concessions are too great, crisis will ensue and they will have to be retracted – even to the extent of reducing, if not removing, democracy.

There is a strong correlation between the geography of liberal democracy and the geography of human rights and civil liberties, and also a correlation between both of these and the geography of economic development. This can lead to a crude, Rostovian hypothesis, that economic development is dealienating. From this, it is inferred that human dignity is best advanced by programmes of capitalist economic development. Four arguments have been assembled here against such a view. First, the Rostow model is wrong and ignores the organization of the world-economy into core and periphery. Secondly, the liberties and freedoms associated with economic development are fragile. Thirdly, there is little evidence that the democratic freedoms of the core countries are dealienating – though the personal freedoms are clearly much greater, with regard to, for example, physical abuse. Finally, the current crisis of the world-economy appears to be increasing alienation, with a reduction of democratic freedoms even in the core countries.

Alienation is an inherent condition of the capitalist mode of production, based on materialism. All individuals are subject to the dictates of the market economy and lack control over their own lives as a consequence: some prosper in a material sense, but all are exploited and degraded. The ideology of capitalism has been linked to the ideology of liberal democracy as a form of political organization: this, too, has brought benefits to some, but the condition of alienation has not been dented and the practice of democracy remains constrained by the dictates of the market place.

References

Berg, E. 1978: Democracy and self-determination. In P. Birnbaum, J. Lively and G. Parry (eds), *Democracy, Consensus and Social Contract*, London: Sage Publications, 149–72.

Bollen, K. 1983: World system position, dependency and democracy: the cross-national evidence. *American Sociological Review*, 48, 458–79.

Butler, D., Penniman, H. R. and Ranney, A. (eds) 1981: *Democracy at the Polls*. Washington DC: American Enterprise Institute.

Chaffee, W. A. 1984: The political economy of revolution and democracy: toward a theory of Latin American politics. *American Journal of Economics and Sociology*, 43, 385–98.

Clark, G. L. and Dear, M. J. 1984: *State Apparatus*. London: Allen & Unwin.

Coulter, P. 1975: *Social Mobilization and Liberal Democracy*. Lexington: Lexington Books.

Dahl, R. A. 1978: Democracy as polyarchy. In R. D. Gastil, *Freedom in the World: Political Rights and Civil Liberties 1978*. Boston: G. K. Hall, 134–46.

Finer, S. E. (ed.) 1975: *Adversary Politics and Electoral Reform*. London: Anthony Wigram.

Friedman, M. and Friedman, R. 1980: *Free to Choose*. Harmondsworth: Penguin.

Gastil, R. D. 1981: *Freedom in the World: Political Rights and Civil Liberties, 1981*. Oxford: Clio Press.

Habermas, J. 1976: *Legitimation Crisis*. London: Heinemann.

Hall, S. 1980: Popular-democratic vs authoritarian populism. In A. Hunt (ed.), *Marxism and Democracy*, London: Lawrence & Wishart, 157–85.

Harvey, D. 1982: *The Limits to Capital*. Oxford: Blackwell.

Harvey, D. 1985: The geopolitics of capitalism. In D. Gregory and J. Urry (eds), *Space and Social Structures*, London: Macmillan.

Hindess, B. 1980: Marxism and parliamentary democracy. In A. Hunt (ed.), *Marxism and Democracy*, London: Lawrence & Wishart, 21–54.

Humana, C. 1984: *World Human Rights Guide*. London: Hutchinson.

Hunt, A. 1980: Introduction: taking democracy seriously. In A. Hunt (ed.), *Marxism and Democracy*, London: Lawrence & Wishart, 7–20.

Johnston, R. J. 1982: *Geography and the State*. London: Macmillan.

Johnston, R. J. 1984a: Marxist political economy, the state and political geography. *Progress in Human Geography*, 8, 473–92.

Johnston, R. J. 1984b: The political geography of electoral geography. In P. J. Taylor and J. W. House (eds), *Political Geography: Recent Advances and Future Directions*, London: Croom Helm, 133–48.

Johnston, R. J. 1984c: *Residential Segregation, the State, and Constitutional Conflict in American Urban Areas*. London: Academic Press.

Johnston, R. J. 1985: People, places, parties and parliaments: a geographical perspective in electoral reform in Great Britain. *The Geographical Journal*, 151.

Kidron, M. and Smith, D. 1983: *The War Atlas*. London: Pan Books.

Kolakowski, L. 1978: *Main Currents of Marxist Thought*, vol. 1. Oxford: Oxford University Press.

Luard, E. 1978: *Socialism Without the State*. London: Macmillan.

Macpherson, C. B. 1973: *Democratic Theory*. Oxford: Clarendon Press.

Osei-Kwame, P. and Taylor, P. J. 1984: A politics of failure: the political geography of Ghanaian elections 1954–1979. *Annals of the Association of American Geographers*, 74, 574–89.

Riker, W. H. 1983: Political theory and the art of heresthetics. In A. W. Finifer (ed.), *Political Science: The State of the Discipline*, Washington DC: American Political Science Association, 47–68.

Rostow, W. W. 1960: *Stages of Economic Growth*. Cambridge: Cambridge University Press.

Schattschneider, E. E. 1962: *The Semi-Sovereign People*. Hinsdale Ill.: Dryden.

Taylor, C. J. and Jodice, D. A. 1983: *World Handbook of Political and Social Indicators*, vol. 2, 3rd edn. New Haven: Yale University Press.

Taylor, P. J. 1983: The changing political map. In R. J. Johnston and J. C. Doornkamp (eds), *The Changing Geography of the United Kingdom*, London: Methuen, 275–90.

Taylor, P. J. 1984: Accumulation, legitimation and the electoral geographies within liberal democracy. In P. J. Taylor and J. W. House (eds), *Political Geography: Recent Advances and Future Directions*, London: Croom Helm, 117–32.

Taylor, P. J. 1985a: *Political Geography*. London: Longman.

Taylor, P. J. 1985b: All organization is bias: the political geography of electoral reform. *The Geographical Journal*, 151.

Taylor, P. J. and Johnston, R. J. 1984: The geography of the British state. In A. M. Kirby and J. R. Short (eds), *The Human Geography of Contemporary Britain*, London: Macmillan, 23–40.

9

The Question of National Congruence

COLIN H. WILLIAMS

The inherent tension between state nationalism and ethnic nationalism within the world system has already contributed to two major catastrophes this century. At times their interaction has created powerful, dynamic socioeconomic structures. At other times the clash of interests represented by these two forces has produced open conflict reflecting a sustained rivalry between striving participants in the developing state system. There is little reason to believe that violence will be eradicated in this relationship, for 'Despite the attempts of capital to tame and rationalise social relations, to subordinate them to its much more coldly destructive logic, violence will always occur' (Shaw, 1984, p. 4).

The pattern of state formation is abundant testimony to the influence of conflict and warfare in the development of national territories. The size and shape of contemporary states are as much a product of international rivalry as they are reflections of the settlement pattern of constituent 'national' populations. Indeed, the quest for national congruence, defined as the attempt to make both national community and territorial state into coextensive entities, has been a major feature of modern history, particularly in Europe. This 'western model' of state formation has been so influential that Williams and Smith (1983, p. 510) claim that the quest for its constituents, authenticity, legitimacy and equality, 'bedevils interstate and intrastate relations all over the world'. The emergence of the 'territorial–bureaucratic state' has had profound consequences for the political organization and structure of the interstate system, especially in those territories carved out of former colonial dynastic rule. For:

> The central point . . . of the Western experience for contemporary African and Asian social and political change has been the primacy and dominance of the specialised, territorially defined and coercively monopolistic state, operating within a broader system of similar states bent on fulfilling their

dual functions of internal regulation and external defence (or aggression). (Smith, 1983, p. 17)

My intention in this chapter is to examine the quest for national congruence within an interdependent world system and to illustrate the manner in which several political movements have sought to change the system of sovereign states so as to effect a more 'representative' distribution of national states.

Taylor (1982) argues that both statism and nationalism, being expressions of the search for ideological legitimacy, are related to specific epochs in modern capitalist development. I want to examine the relationship between these ideologies and the modern world system, taking Wallerstein's work on the effects of the uneven development of capitalism as representative of the central thread of a world-systems argument.

EXPANSIVE CAPITALISM

Wallerstein's influential analysis of the European-centred world-economy, comprising core, semi-periphery and periphery, is central to the analysis of the modern world-system animated by capitalism. The emerging world-economy encouraged spatial interdependence and a recognizable international division of labour whose profitability was a 'function of the proper functioning of the system as a whole' (Wallerstein, 1979, p. 38). A two-way interaction was initiated between the specialist role of a state's economy within the system, and a corresponding set of pressures imposed on domestic political developments by changes within the emerging world-system. Taylor (1982) and Smith (1983) draw attention to the consequences of a state system facilitating the expansion of capitalism. They include the various dynastic and structural changes witnessed in the period 1500–1648, and legitimized in the Treaties of Westphalia, 1648, which established the state system of Europe.

> Since that date, long wars ended by congresses and treaties have become the accepted European norm for state-creation and state-consolidation: witness the treaties of Vienna, Versailles and Yalta. Each new agreement limited the number and extent of new states which could participate in the system; and the later the period, the more did wars and ensuing treaties *create* the recent states. (Smith, 1983, p. 16)

The state system became a framework which facilitated the integrative capacity of capitalism to link previously disparate regions and interest groups into an evolving world-system. Wallerstein's original argument runs as follows:

> Capitalism is based on the constant absorption of economic loss by political entities, while economic gain is distributed to 'private' hands. What I am arguing . . . is that capitalism as an economic mode is based upon the fact that the economic factors operate within an area larger than that

which any political entity can totally control. This gives capitalism a freedom of manoeuvre that is structurally based. It has made possible the constant economic expansion of a world-system, albeit a very skewed distribution of its rewards. (Wallerstein, 1974, p. 348)

The details of how capitalism influenced the development of status-groups, national bureaucracies, bourgeois ideology and state boundaries are beyond the scope of this chapter (see Wallerstein, 1974; Rich and Wilson, 1967; Anderson, 1974a). But undoubtedly the evolving state structures owed much to regional and trans-frontier economic performance. The early integration of Spain, Portugal, France and southern Britain (see figure 9.1) stemmed from the superior capacity of the local bourgeoisie and state apparatus to control and influence internal economic arrangements while also pursuing vigorous foreign trade and revenue campaigns. Core states were thus more able than

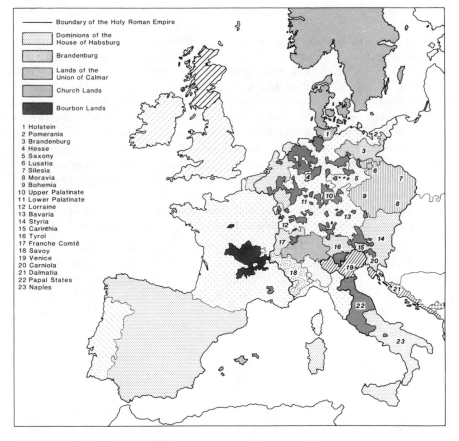

Figure 9.1 Europe in 1519
Source: Treharne and Fullard, 1976, p. 34

peripheral ones to influence the patterns of commodity flow, and hence to realize a greater share of the surplus value (Wallerstein, 1979, p. 292). Wallerstein argues that this initial advantage was translated into a semi-permanent structure wherein the bourgeoisie of the core states were better placed than were their counterparts within peripheral states. This influenced their specific relationship with the core-state proletariat, a relationship which may have been quite different in kind from that between the peripheral bourgeoisie and proletariat. The argument then turns on the differential character of this relationship, mediated through the emergence of the state as the locus of conflict. He writes: 'Since states are the primary arena of political conflict in a capitalist world-economy, and since the functioning of the world-economy is such that national class composition varies widely, it is easy to perceive why the politics of states differentially located in relation to the world-economy should be so dissimilar' (p. 293).

The state is conceived of as a particular kind of social organization which seeks to perpetrate its advantage through intervention, force and economic manipulation. For Wallerstein, this advantage is institutionalized in the concept of a state's 'sovereignty':

> a notion of the modern world, is the claim to the monopolization (regulation) of the legitimate use of force within its boundaries, and it is in a relatively strong position to interfere effectively with the flow of factors of production. Obviously also it is possible for particular social groups to alter advantage by altering state boundaries; hence both movements for secession (or autonomy) and movements for annexation (or federation). (p. 292)

While individual states and factions may seek to challenge the existing pattern, it is the state system itself which 'encrusts, enforces, and exaggerates the patterns, and it has regularly required the use of state machinery to revise the pattern of the world-wide division of labour' (p. 292).

Though capitalism is encouraged in part by the regulations of a stable state system, Wallerstein argues that the unequal exchange in the appropriation of its surplus value is spatially differentiated, producing regionally variable effects. At its crudest his argument rests on the inherent unevenness of the patterns of exchange such that, in summary:

> Capitalism is a system in which the surplus value of the proletarian is appropriated by the bourgeois. When this proletarian is located in a different country from this bourgeois, one of the mechanisms that has affected the process of appropriation is the manipulation of controlling flows over state boundaries. This results in patterns of 'uneven development' which are *summarized* in the concepts of core, semiperiphery and periphery. (p. 293)

We may accept Wallerstein's characterization of the long sixteenth century as a period within which a multi-layered world-system developed, without necessarily accepting his interpretation of this system as a world-empire. Neither need we accept the claim that it was, above all, the economic processes inherent in capitalism which produced this world-system. For our purposes the critical feature of this perspective is its recognition of the European state system as the superstructure, whose transformations influenced the differential occurrence and subsequent modification of the process of national congruence. Wallerstein's contribution, in articulating these structural transformations, is well recognized by his critics (Zolberg, 1981; Skocpol, 1977; Modelski, 1978), but they would remind us that he pays too little attention to the 'politico-strategic' linkages between parts of the world-system (Zolberg, 1981, p. 262) and underemphasizes non-economic factors in the genesis of early modern states.

Skocpol (1979) is particularly sensitive to an economic reductionist argument that would 'assume that individual nation-states are instruments used by economically dominant groups to pursue world-market orientated development at home and international economic advantages abroad' (p. 22). She argues that the state system, as 'a transnational structure of military competition was not originally created by capitalism' (p. 22), but rather, quoting Hintze, that 'the affairs of the state and of capitalism are inextricably interrelated . . . they are only two sides, or aspects, of one and the same historical development' (Hintze, 1975, p. 452, quoted in Skocpol, 1979, p. 299). Her analysis of both the structures of the capitalist world-economy and of individual national responses to that structure is comparative macro-analysis at its best because it allows for the relative autonomy of several layers or scales of analysis in her work. The international state system, for example, 'represents an analytically autonomous level of transnational reality – *interdependent* in its structure and dynamics with world capitalism, but not reducible to it' (p. 22).

In addition to domestic economic performance and comparative international economic position, she recognizes, what Wallerstein underplays, the relevance of factors such as 'state administrative efficiency, political capacities for mass mobilization and international geographical position' (p. 22). In this context the advantage of the world-system approach is that it offers an integrated holistic perspective on an admittedly complex process of global development.

Interstate competition over the past four centuries has animated the ever fluctuating capitalist system. It has also produced the inexorable integration of diverse culture groups into a 'national population' as part of the process of national congruence. The state has sought to harness the potential of such 'nations' and control their productivity to enhance its own resource base. In consequence, state activity has created a new set of geographies for incorporated peoples, influencing their socio-economic opportunities and political representation. Superordinate 'nations' came to dominate 'unrepresented nationalities' and used the power of the state to buttress their own cultural apparatus as the orthodox, legitimized value system. The new opportunities and freedoms were those sanctioned by the state and woe betide dissident minorities who questioned the verity of state regulations. Indeed much of the resurgent nationalism of contemporary Europe is but a playing out of minority aspirations unsatisfied during the critical period of state formation.

THE EUROPEAN ORIGINS OF NATIONAL CONGRUENCE

During the two centuries after Charles V's disastrous attempt to revive the Holy Roman Empire as a world monarchy, Europe's fulcrum lurched westward, away from the declining periphery of the eastern territories towards the maritime powers and the promise of the New World beyond. It was a period which saw the political unification of each of three formidable states, Spain, France and Great Britain, the core areas of the expanding European colonial enterprise. State unification necessitated uniform legislation, taxation, conscription, defence and, to an increasing extent, cultural compliance. International exploration and conflict, the search for raw materials and new markets, required internal administrative reform. But domestic stability also required the settlement of religious conflict. The principle of *cujus regio, ejus religio* transferred power from the universal claims of pope or emperor to those of monarch or prince, and focused attention on the individuality of emergent states. Further devolution of power into the hands of representative assemblies in much of Protestant Europe during the period also reflected the search for national congruence, anticipated in the eighteenth century and only realized in the nineteenth.

By 1740 maritime Europe had been consolidated into a pattern of core states whose approximate boundaries have survived to the present (see figure 9.2). Central Europe, still severely fragmented, witnessed the expansion of Austrian dominions and the consolidation of the Brandenburg – Prussia territories. Eastern Europe, dominated in the past by the regional competition between Sweden and Russia, and between Austria and the Turks, was preoccupied by the drive towards territorial expansion to finance the development of Muscovy's absolute monarchy and Austria's 'defence of Christendom'. For these were frontier regions still, studded with pockets of modernization set in sharp contrast to the overwhelming feudal context of the vast and sprawling multi-ethnic empires.

To the west the Enlightenment in '*Aufklärung* Europe' accelerated the development of national communities, not only through its liberalizing ideology but also through major technical changes in social communication, principally the transmission of the written word. As Anderson (1983) reminds us, print capitalism's search for ever-expanding markets influenced national consciousness in three ways. First, it 'created unified fields of exchange and communications below Latin and above the spoken vernaculars'. Standard literary forms transcended often mutually unintelligible local dialects, and provided, through print, the 'embryos of the nationally imagined community' (p. 47). Second, print capitalism provided a permanent written record, a ready repository of learning, debate and dissent. History could be rewritten,

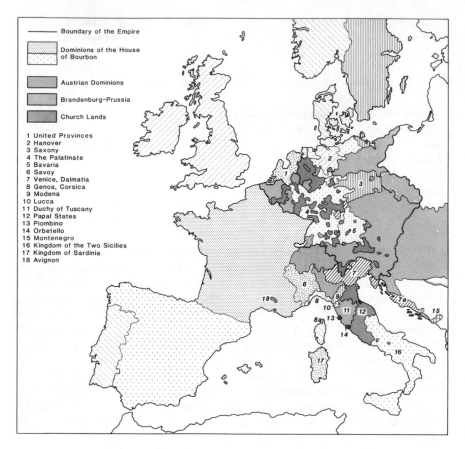

Boundary of the Empire

Dominions of the House
of Bourbon

Austrian Dominions

Brandenburg-Prussia

Church Lands

1 United Provinces
2 Hanover
3 Saxony
4 The Palatinate
5 Bavaria
6 Savoy
7 Venice, Dalmatia
8 Genoa, Corsica
9 Modena
10 Lucca
11 Duchy of Tuscany
12 Papal States
13 Piombino
14 Orbetello
15 Montenegro
16 Kingdom of the Two Sicilies
17 Kingdom of Sardinia
18 Avignon

Figure 9.2   Europe in 1740
Source: Treharne and Fullard, 1976, p. 54

rerecorded and reproduced, to correspond with the political needs of the present, particularly in creating, often from mythology, 'that image of antiquity so central to the subjective idea of the nation' (p. 47). Third, it produced new 'languages of power', conferring economic advantage, social position and political privilege. On this basis, Anderson argues that the convergence of capitalism and print technology created the 'possibility of a new form of imagined community, which in its basic morphology set the stage for the modern nation' (p. 49). Called unto liberty by the power of the printed word, whole peoples could set their political aspirations beyond the confines of class, region and even history itself, if the potency of history could now be channelled to serve the will of the masses.

It is now commonplace to attribute the genesis of political nationalism to the French Revolution's insistence on human freedom and the selfhood of both state and citizen. But it was the violent, passionate exportation of these ideas, via the French revolutionary armies, which, often by default, spawned reactive nationalism in Europe. Snyder (1978, p. 58) put it thus: 'When Napoleon decided to spread his ideas of the French Revolution as he interpreted them into other countries by military force, he invariably ignited the fires of nationalism.'

While many acknowledge the force of democratic ideas crystallized in the French Revolution (Ronen, 1979), others have argued that the Revolution symbolized a people's conflict which had a profound effect on French collective identity. Warfare was central to this process, because it emphasized the centralizing tendencies of the previous two centuries and bound people's destiny together more firmly than ever before. Anthony Smith argues that conflict became a mobilizing agent of national significance:

> Within France, the Revolution reduced the long-standing gulf between state and army, and society, and so could release the tide of patriotic sentiment. In the great *fêtes*, the tricolour, anthem and *levées en masse* under the Jacobins, French national consciousness gained classic expression. The need to defend and export the Revolution threw up a whole new patriotic imagery of France as the home of republican virtue and liberty, and later, under Napoleon, of the great nation in arms, an imperial liberator and civiliser. (Smith, 1981b, p. 386)

Smith does not claim that warfare, by itself, shapes ethnic or national identity, but rather that the 'historical consciousness', fundamental to ethnic community reproduction, is often a 'product of warfare or the recurrent threat therefore' (p. 379). Imminent fear for collective survival maximizes the internal similarities of a people and serves to distinguish more critically the 'we' from the 'they' in any shared territory.

Preparation for war and resultant post-war settlements also have a key bearing on shaping collective consciousness: the former by mass mobilization, propaganda and heightened loyalty to the state, the latter by population transfer, boundary adjustment and new resource development. But Smith observes that warfare is also a salient test of the character of the emergent bureaucratic state to act efficiently to defend its own interests in the world-system. The cutting edge of this trend is the development of a professional army, especially after 1792. Prior to this, the effect of warfare on ethnic consciousness was indirect; after 1792, and particularly after the Napoleonic era, 'by strengthening a stable network of territorial states, the professional army indirectly fostered a loyalty and cohesion in the demarcated population, which helped to erode local allegiances and encouraged the belief in an all-powerful bureaucratic state and its standardised culture' (pp. 385–6).

The medium-sized states of the Atlantic seaboard used their military might, together with their mass taxation systems, developing educational institutions and social communication networks, to enforce their effective sovereignty throughout their territory. Ethnocentrism was forged in the citizenry as a response to repeated and incessant warfare. Each successive generation was charged with the solemn duty to protect 'the state' and to honour the sacrifice of previous generations' yielding to the call of war in defence of their national liberties. Over the centuries the process, whereby ethnic consciousness is mobilized through interstate conflict, has had profound effects, it:

> tended to 'harden' national space, to eliminate all twilight zones and interstices between compact, clearly bounded national states, and so to present to other comparable units a fully mobilized and nationally conscious population wielding military power through its political apparatus. These wars have determined not only the extent and shape of a national territory; they have often hammered the resident population into a community and created potent associations between it and the territory it came to occupy. (Williams and Smith, 1983, p. 515)

Nowhere was this process more evident than in the great unification nationalisms of nineteenth-century Germany and Italy. Under the twin influences of the romantic idealists and the aggressive military and economic impulses of the Prussian elite, German speakers were to be partially united under the umbrella of organic nationhood. Snyder (1978, p. 59), among others, has argued that the special romanticism so prevalent in Germany during the last century was a desperate attempt to hide the ignominy and shame of Napoleonic defeats by focusing on a mythical folk tradition lost since the middle ages. The stress on land, language, lore and loyalty was an expression of original historicism; an attempt to reuse traditional values in a changing context, against the universal principles, inspired by the French Revolution, which sought to negate the distinctiveness of folk communities in favour of rational individualism. This great clash of ideals, between revolutionary liberalism and conservative nationalism, was to forge a dynamic political tension which reverberated in the domestic socio-economic issues and factions of most European societies.

If, in general, the nineteenth century may be characterized as a century of national unification, reaching three peaks in 1848, the 1870s and the 1890s, it was also a period of enormous changes in the political boundaries of several European states. Connor, commenting on this wholesale change, says, 'In the one hundred and thirty year period separating the Napoleonic Wars from the end of the World War II, all but three of Europe's states had either lost extensive territory and population because of ethnonational movements or were themselves newly created self-determined states' (Connor, 1981, p. 210). (The three in question were Portugal, Spain and Switzerland.) Comparison of figures 9.3 and 9.4 reveals the effect of the wholesale dismantling of multinational empires in central and eastern Europe under the impulse of nationalism. Most historians are agreed that the motivations underlying nationalist movements are a complex interplay of religious and economic factors, expressing deep-rooted social discontent. In central and eastern Europe these elements were skilfully welded primarily in defence of language rights, whose denial was interpreted as a symbol of oppression, historic domination and conquest.

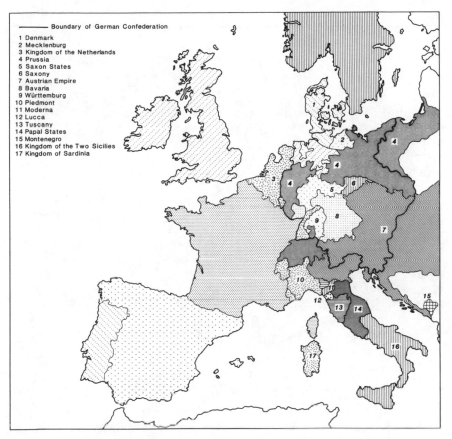

Figure 9.3   Europe in 1815
Source: Treharne and Fullard, 1976, p. 64

Language agitation proved extremely virulent in its capacity to mobilize previously disparate peoples.

Under the banner of liberal nationalism (which so often turned into a conservative force by the end of the century), the struggling nationalities of the east revolted against their former rulers. Some clung to their institutional distinctiveness and sought to reassert their former independence, as did Hungary. Others, such as the Croats, fearful of Magyar intolerance towards minorities, stressed their special institutional and legal relationships, guaranteed by the Nagodba concession of 1868. Still others, deprived of institutional or legal distinctiveness, sought their legitimacy in the 'natural rights' of 'the people' and adopted a Fichtean version of a linguistically defined nationhood as the supreme locus of their loyalty, as happened in Romania and Czechoslovakia.

The attraction of language as a badge of nationality was twofold. First it gave authenticity to the putative claims of the nationalist intelligentsia that they

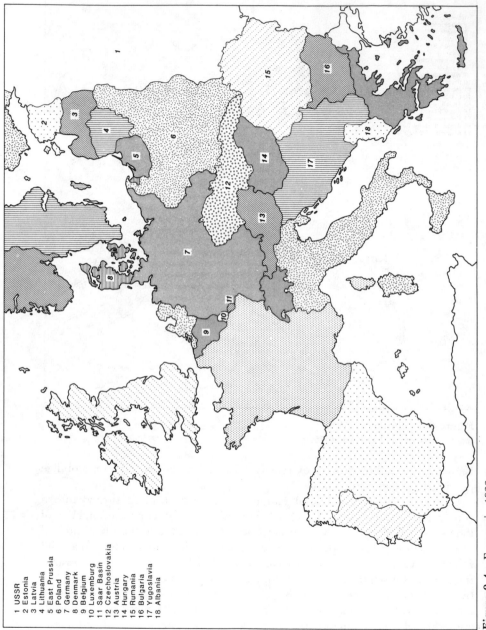

Figure 9.4 Europe in 1923

Source: Treharne and Fullard, 1976, p. 84

represented the real conscience and destiny of their people, i.e. it legitimized their corporate political aspirations. But in the view of some historians this insistence on a conservative organic nationalism stifled the liberalizing individualism derived from transatlantic ideological developments. Kitromilides suggests that:

> The idea of Herder appeared especially relevant to these concerns and reinforced the trends of historicism and folklorism that became the primary characteristics of Southeastern European thought in the nineteenth century. In the political sphere, these trends sustained an organicist conception of the national community that allowed an eventual compromise with the corporatism of traditional culture – a compromise that made modern nationalism acceptable to entrenched social elites but at the price of sacrificing the liberal impulse of the Enlightenment. (1983, p. 59)

Second, language nationalism gave an inclusivity to the target group and excluded the nobility and 'foreign intrusive' merchant class, who found themselves categorized as enemies of the people on both class and national lines. As Orridge and Williams (1982, p. 29) argue, an ethnically distinct landlord and capital-owning strata superimposed on a peasantry speaking a different language is a situation especially conducive to autonomist nationalism, as in late-nineteenth-century Wales. However, one must also cite variant examples, as in Croatia, where the nobility and the intelligentsia, who formed the nucleus of the nationalist movement, both spoke Croatian, in contrast to the Hungarian aristocracy, who demonstrated greater loyalty to the emperor than to Hungary, especially at the beginning of the process.

Two further factors need consideration. The frontier position of the eastern European multinational empires so bedevilled their drive for political stability and establishment of institutional structures that few resources were available for the administrative centralization and cultural assimilation practised in the west (p. 29). The struggle with the Ottoman Turks to defend disputed territory delayed the implementation of any effective homogenizing policies, which may have led to the establishment of nation-states along the European frontier with Islam. Secondly, because of great-power rivalry, cross-frontier intrigue and religious and linguistic conflict, this region witnessed a continuously changing population settlement pattern which exasperated any attempts at socializing a settled population into a permanent patriotic citizenry. In short, the state structures of the multinational empires were maintained by force, fear and foreign ordinances. In consequence the region lagged behind the economic, social and political developments of western Europe and preserved feudal elements, such as the 'second serfdom', which reinforced already existing cultural divisions (p. 32). More importantly the south-east was subject to the first impulses of westernization, whereby in resisting the foreign domination of empires nationalist leaders sought to imitate the equally foreign model of the nation-state, developed on the Atlantic seaboard and offered as an epitome of all that was rational, democratic and uplifting in modern civilization. In consequence one may recognize here many of the classic features of a European periphery identified earlier by Wallerstein: the east was fragmented, dependent and 'underdeveloped', and its economic and political rhythms were reactions to impulses generated, either by the core of the modern world-system or by the last vestiges of medieval Christendom and Islam.

Poland's Unequal Struggle for National Survival

Illustration of the impact of nationalism and warfare on national sovereignty and state boundaries in this region can best be undertaken by reference to Poland and its neighbours over the past two centuries.

We have seen that a country's geopolitical context is a vital factor in shaping its 'national history'. Nowhere is this more evident than in modern Poland. The search for Polish national congruence is one of the most tragic elements of European history, and still suggests resonant lessons for aspiring nationalists elsewhere in the world. Since the eighteenth century at least, great-power intervention, annexation and forced assimilation have characterized Polish political life. Initially sparked off by Catherine II's concern for the treatment of its Orthodox population, the three partitions of Poland – in 1772, 1793 and 1795 – were a grand display of great-power prerogative. By these partitions Poland was divided between the Russian Empire, the Hapsburg Monarchy and the Prussian Kingdom. Polish hopes of liberation were realized within 11 years, when in 1806 Napoleon's army entered Poland en route for the Russian frontier. The Treaty of Tilsit, July 1807, had re-established a semi-autonomous Polish state as the grand duchy of Warsaw, placed under the sovereignty of the King of Saxony (Seton-Watson, 1977, p. 123), and neutralized, *pro tempore*, the Russians' threat, who now busied themselves in a half-hearted continental blockade. In 1809 the duchy's territory was further increased after Napoleon had, once again, subdued the Austrians and ceded many of their former territories as tribute to the fidelity of the many thousand Polish volunteers in his armies. Poland's characteristically brief period of liberty ended on the defeat of Napoleon in 1812, when the partitions were restored, with Russia the net beneficiary of Poland's demise.

For the remainder of the century, though Poles were active in European nationalist movements and revolutionary societies as far flung as Paris, Sicily, Piedmont and Hungary, at home they failed to win any more than a limited regional autonomy for Galicia and representation in the Viennese *Reichsrat*, from their most sympathetic occupying power, Austria (p. 128). Policies of systematic Russification and, after 1880, of forced Germanization, as part of Bismarck's *Kulturkampf*, brought limited assimilation and a more general strengthening of Polish national consciousness. However, the international climate did not favour mass mobilization in the cause of freedom, as it had done to the south and east, and therefore various factions sought to negotiate with the occupying powers with the aim of isolating and removing one of them from Polish territory. Russia was the most likely victim (despite the efforts of national democrats to seal an alliance), Austria the willing instrument for the eviction, and on the eve of the first world war Pilsudski's Polish Patriots mustered to the Austrian ranks and in due course expelled the Russians.

But centuries of ethnic intermingling and post-war refugee movements were to confound the rational logic of the Wilsonian principle of 'national self-determination' embodied in the Versailles Treaty of 1919. Here, as Seton-Watson observes, 'the difference between the Polish nation and the historical Polish state emerged in acute form,' as indeed it was to do in the boundary delimitation of most central European states legitimized by the Versailles deliberations (see figure 9.4). The three common problems of establishing a sovereign territory, respecting the rights of newly disenfranchised ethnic minorities and creating a buffer zone between rival continental powers took on extra significance as the west sought to overcompensate for Poland's suffering at the hands of voracious neighbours.

> In the West, the victorious great powers gave the benefit of the doubt to the Poles at the expense of the Germans in drawing the frontiers in Pomerania and Silesia – though they gave a good deal less than Polish nationalists would have liked, and created an awkward problem through the separation of East Prussia from Brandenburg by a belt of Polish territory, the so-called 'Polish Corridor'. (Seton-Watson, 1977, p. 129)

Post-war readjustments provided Poland with several gains, specified in the 1919 peace treaty, e.g. the industrialized coalfield of Upper Silesia, Posen's rich agricultural hinterland, a Baltic coastline, a well-developed communication system and a primary-educated population in the new territories (Tägil, 1977, p. 138). However, long-established trading patterns and communication links were abruptly broken in the new areas as they transferred from the pre-existent east–west patterns of trade and commerce and stagnated before a comprehensive north–south rail and road link could be instituted. Old markets, resource areas and rules of trade were abandoned wholesale. This fragmentation was compounded by the mass emigration of German-speaking professionals, urban artisans and rural workers, only some of whom were replaced by Polish migrants from Galicia and Congress Poland (p. 139).

Both sides of the new German–Polish borders contained substantial minorities, an inflammatory element in subsequent Nazi propaganda and a lasting grievance for irredentist organizations determined to undo the post-Versailles settlement. To the east, the government determined to assimilate its Belorussian and Ukrainian minorities, but met with only limited success in the inter-war period. Resistance to state integration had been a characteristic feature of eastern European society for well over 50 years, and the 'unsatisfied nationalism' of the Ukraine in particular was not about to yield its cause, especially as the principle of self-determination had the most radical effect on the dismantling of empires, producing a mosaic of nation-states for almost all of the Ukraine's neighbours and confederates in the nationalist struggle (see figure 9.4).

The clearest evidence of the influence of warfare on delimiting national boundaries is provided by the several territorial changes in eastern Europe following the second world war. The question of Polish boundary adjustments had been determined at the Yalta conference as part of the agreement on administering occupied German territory. At the Potsdam conference, 17 July to 2 August 1945, the Allies sought to minimize the extent of the Soviet zone of occupation in Germany, by reluctantly acknowledging that the disputed western frontiers, portions of East Prussia not occupied by the Soviet Union, and the Free City of Danzig should be under the administration of the Polish state, pending a final peace settlement. By a strange paradox of fate Poland had reverted to occupying territory it had not held for nearly two centuries

Figure 9.5 Territorial changes in eastern Europe following the second world war
Source: Day, 1982, p. 31

(see figure 9.5), but the restoration, like its previous dismemberment, was largely determined by external forces, not by an application of national will in the form of self-determination.

CONTEMPORARY CURRENTS OF ETHNICITY

In many ways the boundary problems of Poland and its neighbours reflect the invention of nation-ness, for, despite their putative ethnic origin, successive populations were socialized *in situ* to identify themselves as Poles. The architects of national consciousness were the intelligentsia (who spread their ideological hold over the masses) and reluctant nobility alike, for the inclusivity of nationalism would brook no class antagonism, in its rhetoric if not always in its actions. Literacy in the vernacular was the key to the unleashing of popular support. Throughout eastern Europe independence movements preached the sovereignty of the people, with all its principled implications for the abolition of serfdom, the emancipation of the proletariat and the drive towards an ethnically determined 'universal suffrage' for all co-nationals. Liberation from the shackles of the colonial empires promised a glorious future for peoples who barely two generations earlier had no right to expect a future at all as a nation among nations. Their liberation came via conflict and warfare, for the dismantling of empires in the east was the product of revolution and post-war settlements producing a different European order after both 1919 and 1945.

In the west, however, a different pattern emerged. Previously strong nation-states emerged from the cataclysmic conflict to face both domestic reconstruction and the challenge of decolonization of their far-flung empires. The 'descent from empire' not only produced a new set of international actors but also a questioning of the very basis of state legitimacy and popular representation at home. The myriad forms of discontent prompted new approaches to old problems. Government commissions inquired into popular democracy, central–peripheral relations, and the form and function of government itself. Alternatives to class-related politics were canvassed throughout western Europe, chief of which were the ethnically inspired inheritors of nineteenth-century liberal nationalism.

The post-war 'ethnic revival' in western Europe has been interpreted in at least four different ways: first, as the continuation of a historic struggle between superordinate 'states' and subordinate 'nations' (Foueré, 1980); secondly, as a response to the decolonization processes and the visible success of liberation movements in overthrowing their imperial shackles; thirdly, as a realization on behalf of local ethnic activists that their socioeconomic position is a direct result of systematic discrimination by the core majority – such discrimination structures the individual's life-chances in employment, educational opportunity and general standards of living, and also determines the limits of political activity superimposed upon the peripheral minority by the host state's majority (Hechter, 1975); and, lastly, as a direct response to the uneven spread of capitalism, operating as a transcendent force in the world-system. For Nairn (1981), capitalism's uneven development is necessarily 'nationalism producing' because development always comes to the less advanced peoples within the 'fetters of the more advanced nations', as with France or England (Smith, 1981a, p. 37). The latter two interpretations of ethno-nationalism have aroused great interest, particularly among social scientists and ethnic activists concerned to portray their cause within both historic and an academically respectable framework. The force of Nairn's account is that he sets the nationalist reaction within the operation of a global division of labour and provides a holistic interpretation for the scope and the timing of the current round of nationalist resurgence.

Central to this relationship between uneven capitalist development and reactive nationalism is exploitation at the national, regional, collective and individual level. In other words, it is an all-encompassing relationship. Orthodox modernization theory would argue that it is only by being transformed to resemble 'modern' majority cultures that minority 'dependent' cultures can escape the pejorative connotations of this unequal relationship. But as Glyn Williams forcefully stresses, in so doing they cease to exist, so that the 'ideological or hegemonic nature of this argument should be evident' (Williams, 1980, p. 364).

Smith argues that Nairn is correct when he suggests a close relationship between foreign domination and nationalism, and has shown the significance of conflict and warfare in heightening national consciousness (Smith, 1983). But conflict and exploitation have been the stuff of inter-group relations since time immemorial; why should capitalism *per se* generate a particularly ethnic, as opposed to a class, religious or territorial reaction? The most revealing answer is Smith's explanation of the rise of the bureaucratic state and its role in the formation of 'national culture' (Smith, 1981a). Because the state apparatus and traditional institutions are barred to them, the ethnic intelligentsia resort to the one resource they have access to – the people and their own unique history, which they can rewrite in accordance with a nationalist view of global history, and disseminate through print capitalism (Anderson, 1983). In stressing the historicism of the intelligentsia, scholars such as Smith, Berry (1981) and G. A. Williams (1982) point to the utility of language, religion, territory, oppression and myths as agencies for group mobilization. Critically, these are factors independent of the state, whose legitimacy is internally derived not externally imposed, and may often be the only 'political' resource not fully controlled by a powerful state machinery.

In an earlier phase of capitalist development, though the peripheral regions of western Europe may have been characterized by an imbalanced economic structure, there was nevertheless sufficient mobility and growth in the system to promote state integration. For ethnic aspirants in colonial motherlands, blocked in the upper echelons of government and commerce, there was always the release valve of serving in the colonial territories (Smith, 1982). But with the run-down of empire many of the repatriated ethnic professional classes failed to secure positions commensurate with their talent and expectations. In consequence 'exclusion breeds "failed assimilation" and reawakens an ethnic consciousness among the professional elites, at exactly the moment when the intellectuals are beginning to explore the historic roots of the community' (p. 31). When historicism and reawakening combine, argues Smith, the ethnic revival can 'blossom and assume full political form' (p. 32). This trend may be exacerbated by regional economic decline within the ethnic homelands. For as capital investment transfers from lagging industrial regions to new growth areas, the ethnic intelligentsia interpret such structural manifestations as the inability or unwillingness of the central state agencies to redirect growth into the periphery. Nationalist leaders conclude that the only means of redressing this economic imbalance is by wresting sovereign political control, or at least substantial elements of autonomy, from the constituent state. Very few nationalists have been able to make a strong *a priori* case for an economic revolution and substantial increase in living standards for their homeland on independence. But most conceive foreign rule as the greatest barrier to national development and make autarky (self-sufficiency) the economic counterpart and basis for sovereignty (Williams and Smith, 1983, p. 509).

Ethnic Resurgence in Western Europe: Violence and Reform

Given the overall context of state integration in Europe it is remarkable that current ethnic unrest should be so virulently manifested in the three European states with the longest history of unification and consolidation. France, Spain and the United Kingdom all possess minorities within minorities who seek greater autonomy. Their style of resisting centralization and assimilation varies from the extra-constitutional activities of violent movements in Ulster, Euskadi and Corsica, through non-violent resistance in Catalonia, Wales and Brittany and to party political opposition in all of the above, in Scotland, Galicia and Alsace (see figure 9.6). Obviously we should be wary of generalizing about such movements as if they reflected a single concern for decentralization, for a plethora of factors account for their initial emergence and subsequent developments (Anderson, 1978; Breuilly, 1982; Foster, 1980; Krejci and Velimsky, 1981). Here I concentrate on two case studies which reflect much of the ethnic discontent in contemporary Europe. I have refrained from discussing the nationalist problems of the UK state, preferring to concentrate on the less well understood examples of the Basque country and Corsica.

Basque nationalism. The Basque case illustrates many of the classic features of nationalist opposition to state stability. The Basques enjoyed a long period of autonomy prior to their incorporation into the Spanish state; elements of an institutional framework, the *fueros*, survived until fairly recently and were used as evidence of a prior claim to legitimate statehood. Their language and culture were deemed unique, among the oldest surviving elements of civilization in Europe; but, under the impress of state-building, non-Spanish elements were

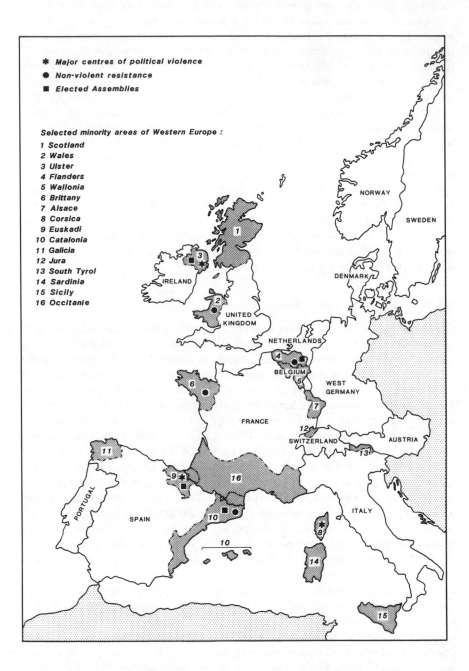

Figure 9.6 Selected minority areas of western Europe

ruthlessly eradicated, producing a deep resentment within the Basque community. State oppression was confirmed during the Spanish Civil War, when many of the Basques, though conscious of the international nature of the conflict against fascism, believed themselves to be engaged in a war of national liberation. Thereafter violence and oppression characterized Basque–Madrid relationships as the Franco regime sought to eradicate local political dissent and to destroy Basque cultural identity.

The amalgamation of previously disparate movements to form ETA, *Euskadi ta Askatasuna* (Basque Homeland and Liberty) in 1957 reinvigorated Basque nationalism. A strategic switch to mount spectacular urban-guerilla operations in the early 1960s produced a government backlash of repression and a new round of 'internal colonial domination' by a police state. Such repression had a profound effect on large sections of Basque society and mobilized previously uncommitted citizens to the cause of liberty. Outside Euskadi, the turmoil precipitated major political crises elsewhere in Spain (Medhurst, 1982), and heralded the return of a socialist government in the post-Franco era.

The crucial struggle revolved around the legitimacy and the character of the Spanish state. Both Basque nationalists and socialists questioned the ideological and material control exercised from Madrid, which effectively negated the Basque identity. Central to this struggle is the control over the agencies of cultural reproduction, since it is culture which serves as the medium for the legitimization of power and structured inequality (Williams, 1980). For nationalists, state education is interpreted as the basis for social control through its legitimizing, ideological function. Thus the struggle over Euskera education involves a struggle for ideological control at whose heart lies the revolutionary potential of a minority language which can be employed to transmit a radical, counter-state position (1980). Evidence of the state's desire to control this potential and expropriate the cultural role within the dominant ideology was provided by the twin threats to Basque identity: the decline of the Basque language, especially among young people; and the post-war influx of workers from other regions. Both trends serve to reduce the ethnic homogeneity of the 'provinces' and have split the nationalist movement in its attempt to devise appropriate measures to counter these deleterious influences. A key result of the large-scale immigration was to strengthen the support base for socialist and communist factions at the expense of the PNV (Partido Nacionalista Vasco).

As working-class resistance increased throughout Spain in the 1960s, workers from the Basque provinces were in the vanguard of the illegal strike movement. ETA was particularly disturbed by this trend, for sections of its elite were Marxist, and their attempt to combine class and ethnic appeals confused the largely immigrant population of urban industrial areas (Clark, 1981; Medhurst, 1982) leading to vacillation on key principles of autonomy. Further divisions concerned the appropriateness of employing violence as a mobilizing strategy, to expose the 'real' character of the Spanish state in its overt repression. The details of ETA's violent campaign are too well known to bear repetition here and it is tendentious as to whether recent reforms would have been inaugurated had it not been for this persistent threat to the stability of the state. However, it is only since 1975 that the government has acknowledged several of the traditional demands of the Basque activists. In May of that year it issued a decree allowing the teaching of Euskera on an optional basis, and in October it issued a second decree providing protection for several regional languages, but took the opportunity to reaffirm that Spanish was still the only official language of governance (Clark, 1981). These concessions were strengthened in May 1979 when the Ministry of Education issued its long-awaited decrees accepting responsibility for programmes of instruction in Euskera at all levels, and providing financial assistance to the private Euskeran *ikastolas* (schools).

The culmination of Sr Suarez's determination to institute liberal democratic principles in Madrid–Basque relations was the approval of the Basque Autonomy Statute in 1979. The first Basque parliament was elected in March 1980. Its earlier deliberations strengthened the autonomous domain of Euskera, a relatively problem-free task compared with the more daunting exercise of improving the economic position of Euskadi vis-à-vis both Spain and Europe. Unlike Brittany or Corsica, one cannot invoke a history of rural underdevelopment as a catalyst for Basque nationalist developments. Quite the contrary, it has long been a leading industrial sector, more akin to South Wales and central Scotland historically. What is at issue though is whether the formal trappings of autonomy can effect real structural changes in Euskadi's economic performance. If they cannot, will this promote separatism or give credence to the socialist argument that a healthy Euskadi can only be realized with increased socioeconomic integration between all constituent parts of Spain?

Whatever the outcome, violence against the state apparatus continues to animate Basque resistance. Clark's (1984) analysis of ETA's strategy examines a number of recent 'explanations' for the persistence of conflict, but concludes that despite the relevance of socio-political factors in inducing a violent political culture, insurgent violence is self-sustaining, 'almost apart from the wishes of the participants or the objective conditions that led to the insurgency' (p. 278).

This observation must be tempered by two significant changes. First the Basque resistance is now directed towards a socialist government which has shown an astonishing readiness to accommodate many of the autonomist demands, yielding concessions which Francoists would have considered tantamount to a denial of the indivisibility of the Spanish state. Secondly, the extradition of wanted insurgents from their relatively safe exile in France casts doubts on the capacity of ETA to sustain a large-scale violent opposition to the current regime, especially when that regime exercises a great deal of leniency in its formal dealings with former 'terrorists' who return voluntarily. Spain's impending membership of the EEC and the recent co-operation between socialist regimes in France and Spain can also work as a counterbalance to 'regionalist' threats within France itself. Extradition orders are a clear signal to neighbours that though decidely more liberal in the treatment of minorities than previous governments, the current French administration does not countenance centres of violent opposition on French soil.

Nationalism Within France. Napoleon's inheritance and the Jacobin centralist tradition continue to influence the manner in which the French state negotiates with its constituent 'dissident' nationalities. Previous attempts at determining a specific regional role for areas such as Brittany, Corsica and Alsace in relation to the needs of the French space economy have been increasingly questioned since 1945. Clear economic differentials between core and periphery, a failure to devise appropriate regional development policies, and a continued stigmatization of 'traditional cultures' are cited as preconditioning grievances for the emergence of reactive nationalist movements. The root of these periodic disturbances is economic exploitation and external control.

In Corsica, after decades of neglect the French state sought both to colonize the island and to develop its natural resources. Kofman (1982) demonstrates the results of state and capitalist penetration for the period 1950–80. Developments in the three most important employment sectors – agriculture, construction and tourism – produced two forms of marginalization: first, a spatial polarization, between coastal development and interior neglect; and secondly, a social polarization consisting of a tripartite stratification. Key positions were reserved for French mainlanders and foreigners, while the Corsicans were squeezed between these spiralists and the influx of North Africans and Iberians imported as semi-skilled labour. Corsicans resented the development of their territory by 'outsiders' and a colonizer–colonized mentality was intensified with the repatriation of some 15,000–17,000 settlers from Algeria and an increase of non-Corsican-born inhabitants from 10 per cent of the population in 1954 to 45 per cent in 1975 (Kofman, 1982, p. 305).

Numerous resistance organizations were formed and reformed, the strongest of which were the Action Régionaliste Corse dating from 1967 and the more vitriolic Front de Libération Nationale de la Corse formed in 1976. The socialist government's *statut particulier* (a devolutionist reform recognizing Corsica as a territory with a regionally elected assembly), announced by Gaston Defferre, the Socialist Minister of the Interior and 'Decentralization', in August 1981, has not assuaged the sporadic violence associated with Corsican autonomists (pp.309–10). But the new interdependent structure of councils, the state–regional employment committee, new agencies for transport, hydro-electric power, agriculture and regional development do provide an innovative institutional framework wherein grievances may be voiced. However, as Mény has demonstrated, if the reforms are limited to institutional changes they will be ineffective; the real transformation would accompany 'the establishment of the rule of law and a respect for universal suffrage' (*Le Monde*, 20 November 1983, quoted in Mény, 1984, p. 74). The Defferre reforms seek to increase local democracy and involvement and have gone a long way to stifling the opposition cries that a diminution of centralist control would threaten the viability of the French state.

Government pronouncements that its decentralist measures will reduce the source of core–periphery conflict in France have been judged premature and overoptimistic. Mény (p. 75) observes that the very creation of new organs of government and the establishment of new relationships may create problems, for they 'constitute a disruption of the system'. But in resolving such problems attention will have been lifted from the activities of the central government to the local-level competition for the exercise of regional power (Mény, 1984; Hirsch, 1981). Such reforms may very well strengthen the central state apparatus in time, by making it an arbiter of local and regional conflicts and by distancing it from events in Brittany, Corsica and Occitania, so 'objectifying' and 'depersonalizing' the role of the state that its legitimacy increases.

The break-up of the state? The French and Spanish examples were selected to reflect the wider structural discontent in contemporary Europe. The expansion of the national territorial state ideal, in the past two centuries in particular, has strained the basic resources which constitute the building-blocks of nation-formation. Yet while materialist approaches often view the state as the unwitting midwife of global capitalism, unable to control the very processes it brought into being, idealist approaches root much of the threat to global stability in the aggrandizing process inherent in the competitive state system itself. Idealist alternatives focus on a return to small historical communities as a panacea for the problems created by the emergence of a world-economy and its concomitant state system.

Leopold Kohr argues that aggression and warfare are a product of a near-critical mass of power which is periodically unleashed as open conflict because of the failure of countervailing pressures. Great size and power, rather than being a positive benefit as theories derived from economies of scale would have us believe, are in fact dangerous attributes producing widespread social misery. Kohr's antidote to this danger is to dismember large states, for he concludes:

> If wars are due to the accumulation of the critical mass of power, and the critical mass of power can accumulate only in social organisms of critical *size*, the problems of aggression, like those of atrocity, can clearly again be solved in only one way – through the reduction of these organisms that have outgrown the proportions of human control. (1957, p. 54)

Small may not necessarily be beautiful, but it is certainly safe; or safer than superpower rivalry! To reduce Europe's states to their constituent historic nations, or, in Kohr's terms, 'Europe's natural and original landscape', would require massive structural changes and would produce a plethora of new polities (see figure 9.7). But he claims the effort would make Europe more peaceful for it would reduce the problem of contested border areas and of non-state national minorities. 'With all states small, they would cease to be mere border regions of ambitious neighbours. Each would be too big to be devoured by the other. The entire system would thus function as an automatic stabilizer' (p. 59). He does not claim that wars would be eliminated in a reconstituted Europe, but they could be contained and made more bearable as periodic events

Figure 9.7 Europe's constituent ethnic territories
Source: Kohr, 1957, p. 233

unlikely to bring the global system to the brink of a world war. Localized peace just as much as localized war is 'divisible' and Kohr's thesis echoes the principles of the middle ages where warfare was divisible not only in space but also in time, according to the controlling institution of Treuga Dei, the Truce of God (p. 63).

Restoration of Europe's old nations in a European federation smacks of romantic idealism from the perspective of power politics, *realpolitik* or integration theory and the fact that Kohr's ideas have lain neglected by mainstream political science for three decades may prove conclusive to the cynic. Analagous proposals have had an interesting, if chequered, career and have deeply influenced both regionalists and federalists. But the works of Heraud (1963), Foueré (1980) and Kohr (1957) now seem both more cogent and also more respectable than they did when such ideas were first mooted. Of particular significance is the attempt by several European institutions to legitimize and channel the growth of ethno-national awareness so as to promote it as a positive force and deflect the potentially disastrous effects of neglect or further repression. Evidence of this may be found in the Council of Europe's proposal to establish a Charter of European Regional and Minority Languages and its long-term promotion of regional-authority responsibility in as many aspects of daily life as possible. Further evidence is the establishment of both public and private agencies, such as the Bureau of Unrepresented Nations in Brussels, the European Bureau of Lesser Used Languages in Dublin and the Federal Union of European Nationalities, while transnational and trans-frontier co-operative ventures continue apace, and are particularly fruitful in the Alto Adige and Friuli-Venezia-Giulia regions.

The international state system, if not its constituent parts, remains intact, virulent and eminently capable of defending itself. That Europe has not witnessed a cataclysmic continent-wide eruption of violence in this generation, contrary to the experience of every generation since 1648, gives cause for much rejoicing. But, as Shaw has warned, we should not grow complacent in our attitude to periodic warfare;

> In the face of the immense evidence that periods of peace are so often periods of preparation for the next war, there are still those who are able to ignore or 'normalise' the relationship. The overwhelming majority of writings about modern capitalism grossly underplay the role of the Second World War in creating the system which has subsequently developed, and underestimate the likelihood that this whole period of capitalist development will culminate in nuclear catastrophe. (1984, p. 3)

National Congruence in Former Colonial Territories

In contrast to the long experience of state formation and national congruence in Europe, Third World societies convinced of the value of the European-derived 'nation-state' have a seemingly impossible task of reconciling divergent interests in the pursuit of state stability and economic development. In many respects nationalism was more virulent in the colonial context, even though the traditional factors which conduce toward nationhood were often but a pale reflection of their European origins. Indeed the very notion of a nation itself, linked intimately to its own state structure for full political expression, was an alien concept to all but a few of the western-educated elite. Let us illustrate the interplay of nationalism, conflict and state formation by reference to the Nigerian experience, conscious, of course, that we are selecting but one of a large number of possible cases.

History permits us to interpret colonialism as a fascinating example of nineteenth-century liberal notions superimposed on the *anciens regimes* of Africa, Asia and Latin America. High ideals, and even higher profit levels, determined the extension of European influence over the newly conquered territories of the far-flung empire, regulating the interaction between a world-system of core, semi-periphery and peripheries. The 'accidents' of imperial Balkanization produced a diverse pattern of multi-ethnic colonies whose transition to independence is one of the most squalid and tragic episodes in world history. Not that the call to liberty was in itself a tragedy, but the passage from servitude to statehood was so often marred by widespread conflict, warfare and subsequently new forms of domination that their effects largely determine the future role and direction of many newly independent states.

The basic political crisis is legitimacy. Principles of national unity are employed in the most unpromising circumstances, to shape a population largely incorporated forcibly into a nation, served by a strong state apparatus. Under the drive of nationalism, post-independence developments have strengthened the process of filling-out of power vacuums, extending the reaches of the bureaucratic–military elite to the furthest periphery. Central to this European-style pattern of nation-building is identity-formation. As we have seen, national integration is a difficult enough process in Europe; it is well-nigh impossible in many African contexts. The basic building-blocks are absent from the national construction of a unified society. Reflect on Azikiwe's statement in 1945: 'Nigeria is not a nation. It is a mere geographic expression. There are no Nigerians in the same sense as there are English, Welsh or French. The word "Nigerian" is merely a distinctive appellation to distinguish those who live within the boundaries of Nigeria from those who do not' (Sklar, 1963, p. 233, quoted in Oberschall, 1973, p. 91).

The interdependent relationship between the professional intelligentsia and varieties of nationalism is crucial in the post-colonial state (Smith, 1983, pp. 90–4). In its search for national pride, economic development, state unity and international recognition, the intelligentsia is uniquely placed to interpret local and global events, and to analyse their effects on the 'nation' which they have helped forge into a self-conscious political community. However, as Smith demonstrates: 'it follows that the chief political struggles in Africa today, including ethnic ones, are at root factional conflicts within the intelligentsia – civilian versus military, liberal versus marxist, regional or ethnic conflicts – and that any involvement on the part of the other strata or classes is at the invitation or behest of one or other faction within the ruling stratum of the intelligentsia' (p. 90). In Nigeria, the scale of the intelligentsia's problems in transmitting its various schemes for the state's future was daunting, a task compounded abroad by the constraints of neo-colonialism and at home by the vast ethnic and regional disparities inherited on independence.

It is now commonplace to attribute to Nigeria's ethnic diversity the seeds of the eventual civil war. But many commentators on the period 1950–66 have argued that certain historical factors, not inevitable elsewhere, have exacerbated these differences. Three are of prime importance: the legacy of colonial administration – direct rule in the south, indirect rule in the north; the internal dynamics of the Nigerian military and of civil–military relations; and federal–regional rivalry with each of the major political parties trying to outmanoeuvre its opponents in gaining access to power, patronage and privilege.

The period prior to independence (1951–9) and just after (1960–6) was one of intense regional and ethnic bargaining between competitive elites and their respective ethnic voting blocks (for details see Luckham, 1971; Young, 1976; Himmelstrand, 1973). It was difficult to develop a sense of national identity, and there were constant threats of secession from disaffected regions and unrepresented minorities. The salient issues were in effect mediated by the regional governments which were controlled by political parties reflecting the majority ethnic group in each of the three regions: the Northern People's Congress (NPC) in the Hausa-Fulani Emirates of the north; the Action Group, led by Chief Akintola, in the west; and the National Council of Nigerian Citizens (NCNC) based upon Ibo dominance in the east. Luckham (1971, p. 209) argues that one reason for the consolidation of political power in the regions was to promote each group's bargaining position at the centre. A number of themes dominated the regional bargaining process, including: (a) the division of power between the federal core and constituent regions; (b) the distribution of revenue allocations and management of scarce economic and natural resources; (c) the allocation of key regional and federal posts in patronage politics; (d) the timing of independence; (e) the status of Lagos as either the chief city of the Yoruba region or the proposed new federal capital; (f) the struggle for political power within the federation; (g) the constitutional provision to be made for ensuring minority-group rights; and (h) the vexing question of the creation of new states after independence to accord more equitably with Nigeria's ethnic groups (Luckham, 1971).

On the eve of independence (1 October 1960) the various expressions of anti-colonial nationalism and regional power were far from being harmonized in the quest for national congruence and statehood. Indeed, the great diversity of available options was itself evidence both of the fragility of the state idea and of the clash of rival sectional groups. Himmelstrand (1973) has outlined five contending nationalist options, each of which was present to some degree, and none of which was sufficiently powerful to command total loyalty when the integrity of the state was threatened. The first was Nigerian nationaism, devoted to the territorial sovereignty of an indivisible Nigeria capable of withstanding regional challenges. The second was regionalism, a policy whereby the federal core is reduced to the status of a manipulated distributor of patronage to the regional ruling elites. This reflected a competition described by Luckham (1971, p. 210) as 'an oligopolistic bargaining' between the three principal parties, two of whom sought to exclude the third from coalition power. The third represents an underlying grievance, ethnic nationalism within multi-ethnic regions. Here Himmelstrand has in mind the demands for redrawing the administrative boundaries to reflect 'ethno-cultural realities', demands for the creation of new states from disaffected minorities, and attempts to build up local ethnic associations tied neither to the dominant regional group nor to the largesse of the federal state. The fourth option is ethnic nationalism between regions, i.e. inter-regional irredentism, which was particularly attractive for Ibos in the mid-west, Yorubas in the north and the middle-belt peoples generally. The final option, secession, was threatened often by the north in its attempt to produce an independence settlement which was entirely favourable to the preservation of the status quo and hence to its dominant position. But it was the Ibo military leadership which in the event precipitated a Nigerian civil war by declaring secession and establishing the Republic of Biafra, on 30 May 1967 (Himmelstrand, 1973).

I do not wish to recount the details of Biafran separatism, merely to illustrate that one can learn much of the improbabilities of ethno-regional secession from this episode. It is scarcely in any state's interest to legitimize a wholesale disintegration of the multi-ethnic state structure; Bangladesh is the only successful separatist attempt of late and provides ample evidence of the international strictures involved. However, it may be useful to analyse the Biafran case in terms of preconditioning factors and triggering events to highlight the fluidity of political competition.

Among the many preconditioning factors none was more powerful than the periodic exclusion from power of the Ibo elite after independence. Among the most ardent of Nigerian nationalists, contributing a disproportionate input to both the civil service and the military, the Ibos saw themselves in the vanguard of Nigerian modernization – a viewpoint inherited from their position as colonial intermediaries, and vigorously put into practice for the first four years of self-government.

However, in 1964–5 the struggle for political power and patronage went outside the established electoral process (Luckham, 1971). The federal elections of 30 December 1964 produced a vitriolic and unconstitutional campaign. The results weakened the position of the NCNC in the coalition, which was now dominated by an NPC–NNDP (Nigerian National Democratic Party) alliance. Realizing that they were heading for the same degree of political exclusion suffered by the Action Group in 1962, the leaders of the east openly threatened secession. Unsupported by any other political party, the east's grievances festered, to be compounded by the increasing conviction that their isolation and insecurity was the result of northern discrimination and western manipulation of the coalition. This was confirmed in the character of the

Western Region's elections of October 1965 which were 'openly rigged by the NNDP' (Luckham, 1971, p. 218). The results were widely challenged and the Action Group refused to recognize them. Outbursts of collective violence characterized the period from October 1965 to January 1966, when the military intervened to restore order. The first *coup* sought to end corruption, nepotism, inefficiency and 'regionalism'. General Ironsi, though head of a unified military structure, sought to maintain a quasi-federal system with military governors replacing regional administrators. But it was clear to most observers that the trend towards a unitary form of government would accelerate after Ironsi's speech on 28 January in which he declared 'all Nigerians want an end to regionalism. Tribal loyalties and activities which promote tribal consciousness and sectional interests must give way to the urgent task of national reconstruction. The Federal Military Government will preserve Nigeria as one strong nation' (quoted in Panter-Brick, 1970, p. 16). In the event Ironsi issued a decree establishing a unitary state on 24 May, which was followed by widespread rioting in the north.

In the context of inter-regional rivalry, Luckham argues that the January *coup* was but one more instance of this 'periodic shifting power between the regions' – isolating the north from the political core – 'though the method of

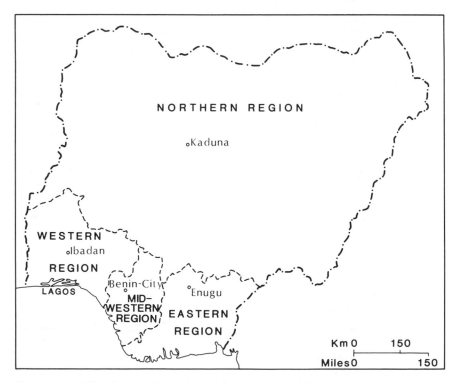

Figure 9.8   Nigeria as a federation of four regions, 1966
Source: Panter-Brick, 1970, p. X

transferring power was new' (Luckham, 1971, p. 219). The July *coup*, when Yakubu Gowon emerged to succeed the assassinated Ironsi, restored the north's pre-eminent position and denied the east access to the centres of political power. It confirmed the awareness of political isolation felt so keenly by the eastern civilian and military elite. Added to this were the fears for survival engendered by the massacres of May and September/October 1966, both of which were directed at Ibos living in the north. In consequence 1.2 million Ibo refugees left, crowding into the eastern heartland of Biafra, bringing with them stories of atrocities, fears of genocide and rumours of imminent northern invasion (Luckham, 1971; Panter-Brick, 1970; Oberschall, 1973). Federal oil revenues were retained in the east for the relief of refugees, a development which troubled non-Ibo tribes who feared being subjugated by an Ibo majority in an independent Biafra.

But if the east were allowed to secede it was feared that the west would also, for it could not withstand the north in an emasculated Nigeria (Oberschall, 1973, p. 99). To forestall such developments the federal military government on 27 May 1967 declared a state of emergency and divided Nigeria's four regions into twelve states (see figures 9.8 and 9.9). This effectively abolished

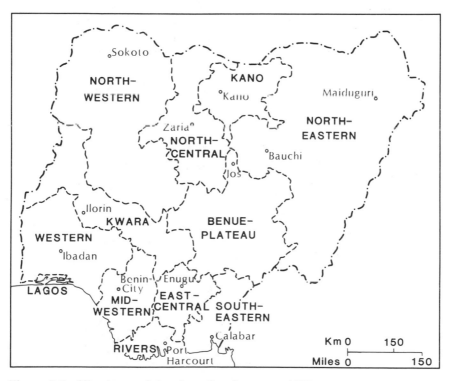

Figure 9.9   Nigeria as a federation of twelve states, 1967
Source: Panter-Brick, 1970, p. X

the three-party oligopoly dominated by the north and allowed the stronger minority groups to play a more independent role (Luckham, 1971). The Ibos interpreted this reform as an attempt to deny them access to their oil supplies and revenues now under the jurisdiction of the Rivers state (see figure 9.10). They also discerned an appeal to non-Ibo easterners in the Ogojo, Calabar and Rivers area to resist Ibo influence with federal support (Oberschall, 1973, p. 100).

Underlying all this, of course, was the key role of the military, examined superbly in Luckham's (1971) book. The triggering factors leading to the secession of the Eastern Region on 30 May 1967 relate as much to the internal military conflict as they do to the wider issues of federalism and ethnoregionalism. The key conflict derived from the fragmentation of the army after July 1966 and the challenge to a hierarchical authority structure induced by two military *coups*. The initial disagreement between Lt-Colonel Gowon, who declared himself Supreme Commander, and Lt-Colonel Ojukwu, leader of the army in the east, was over the rules of precedence and legitimate continuity in the army hierarchy. Subsequently Ojukwu enunciated that the key to legitimacy was effective control and leadership, qualities he claimed he

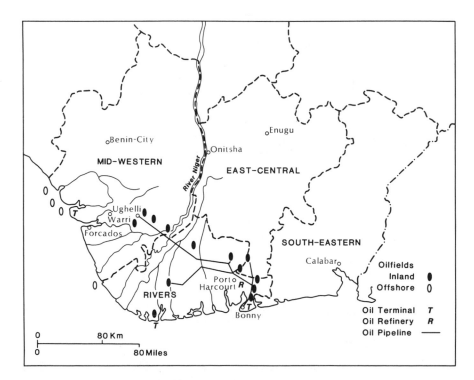

Figure 9.10   Location of oilfields, terminals and pipelines, 1969
Source: Panter-Brick, 1970, p. XI

represented over and above any other contender. In consequence, once the army lost its cohesion 'the nation was on the verge of disintegration' (Luckham, 1971, p. 298, 147–50).

Thirty months of warfare demonstrated that secession would not be tolerated. The civil war ended in January 1970 with the lessons of conflict and the 'unvindictive peace' apparent to all African states (Kirk-Greene and Rimmer, 1981). Gowon's twin challenges of post-war reconstruction and the return to civilian rule were mediated through a comprehensive reform programme designed to induce a 'period of lasting peace and political stability' (p. 4).

The Nigerian experience suggests that though nationalism may be a potent force in the anti-colonial struggle, it by no means offers a blueprint for governance on independence. The constant oscillation between federal core and ethnic–regional homeland called into question the effectiveness of pre-independence negotiations in harmonizing inter-ethnic and inter-regional disparities. Economic autarchy was hindered by the harsh reality of underdevelopment and of the limited scope allowed to Nigeria in its tightly structured role in the international division of labour. Above all, it was the fragility of the state ideal itself, which strained deep-rooted and often bitter rivalries, as citizens fought to defend their new-found freedoms, symbolized in the paradoxical, but nevertheless powerful, sentiments of an indivisible Nigerian 'territorial state'.

CONCLUSION

We have seen that nationalism has become an increasingly influential factor in the emergence of an interstate system. Its enigmatic character is displayed in its utility as an instrument both for nation-building and for state disintegration at various junctures. However, our emphasis on the question of national congruence has sought to highlight an abiding dilemma common to many contemporary societies. In their attempt to represent political and economic developments as essentially populist and communal, the leaders of modern states have to appeal to the 'common ground' of popular involvement in the territorial state. But this appeal presupposes a solidarity of interest and involvement among the populace, which is often lacking, especially in former colonial territories. In order to strengthen this identification states often resort to centralist bureaucratic institutions to buttress the state apparatus. In turn this reinforces the relative advantage of groups already able to control the direction of future state activity and economic development. In consequence, marginalized minorities perceive the state apparatus as the monopoly institution of an opposition group, both unwilling and unable to recognize their legitimate grievances within the framework of state activities. Thus in seeking to incorporate the masses in the national socialization processes, the bureaucratic state often re-emphasizes the very lines of conflict which discriminate against subordinate groups.

Attempts to modify the state structure have often led to conflict, and civil or international warfare is far too common an outcome to treat the issues of this chapter as ephemeral products of an expanding world system. In the mid-seventies commentators spoke of the demise of the nation-state in certain western democratic societies; a decade on we may conclude that the salutary experience of being challenged by ethnic–regional demands (among others) has made a number of states far more sensitive to the needs of their constituent ethnic minorities, while simultaneously strengthening their central agencies of government. There is little imminent fear of the collapse of the nation-state system, though caution should be expressed as to the nature and direction of national identification in selected multi-ethnic societies as we enter a new period of economic and cultural readjustment and redefinition of identity.

We have much to learn before we answer the question 'Why do the nations rage asunder?' If indeed the concerns of this chapter are powerful contributors to a world in crisis, the best we can perhaps hope for is that we recognize it as a permanent crisis, and one that demands permanent tolerance, for fear of something worse.

Acknowledgements

I owe a particular debt to the encouragement of A. D. Smith, Ron Johnston and Peter Taylor. I also wish to thank a number of friends who read the manuscript and offered constructive criticism: Wilbur Zelinsky, Sven Tägil, Kerstin Nyström, Ralf Rönnquist and Rune Johansson. Jane Williams, cartographer at the North Staffordshire Polytechnic, drew the figures with her customary skill and patience.

References

Anderson, B. 1983: *Imagined Communities*. London: Verso Editions.
Anderson, M. 1978: The renaissance of territorial minorities in western Europe. *West European Politics*, 1, 128–43.
Anderson, P. 1974a: *Lineages of the Absolutist State*. London: New Left Books.
Anderson, P. 1974b: *Passages from Antiquity to Feudalism*. London: New Left Books.
Berry, C. J. 1981: Nations and norms, *The Review of Politics*, 20, 75–87.
Best, G. 1980: *Humanity in Warfare*. London: Weidenfeld & Nicolson.
Boal, F. W. and Douglas, N. J. (eds) 1982: *Integration and Division: Geographical Perspectives on the Northern Ireland Problem*. London: Academic Press.
Boyce, G. 1982: *Nationalism in Ireland*. London: Croom Helm.
Breuilly, J. 1982: *Nationalism and the State*, Manchester: Manchester University Press.
Clark, R. P. 1979: *The Basques: The Franco Years and Beyond*. Reno: University of Nevada Press.
Clark, R. P. 1981: Language and politics in Spain's Basque provinces. *West European Politics*, 4, 85–103.
Clark, R. P. 1984: *The Basque Insurgents, ETA, 1952–1980*. Madison: University of Wisconsin Press.

Connor, W. 1981: Nationalism and political illegitimacy. *Canadian Review of Studies in Nationalism*, 8, 201–28.

Day, A. J. (ed.) 1982: *Border and Territorial Disputes*. Burnt Mill: Longman.

Foster, C. R. (ed.) 1980: *Nations Without a State*. New York: Praeger.

Foueré, Y. 1980: *Towards a Federal Europe*. Swansea: Christopher Davies.

Gilbert, F. (ed.) 1975: *The Historical Essays of Otto Hintze*. New York: Oxford University Press.

Hamers, J. F. and Blanc, M. 1984: *Bilingualité et bilingualisme*. Brussels: Pierre Mardaga.

Haugen, E., McClure, J. D. and Thomson, D. S.: 1981: *Minority Languages Today*. Edinburgh: Edinburgh University Press.

Hechter, M. 1975: *Internal Colonialism: The Celtic Fringe in British National Development*. London: Routledge & Kegan Paul.

Heraud, G. 1963: *L'Europe des ethnies*. Paris: Presse d'Europe.

Himmelstrand, U. 1973: Tribalism, regionalism, nationalism and secession in Nigeria. In S. N. Eisenstadt and S. Rokkan (eds) *Building States and Nations*. London: Sage Publications, vol. 2. 427–67.

Hirsch, J. 1981: The apparatus of the state, the reproduction of capital and urban conflicts. In M. Dear and A. J. Scott (eds) *Urbanisation and Urban planning in Capitalist Society*, London: Methuen, 593–607.

Kirk-Greene, A. and Rimmer, D. (eds) 1981: *Nigeria Since 1970*. London: Hodder & Stoughton.

Kitromilides, P. 1983: The Enlightenment east and west: a comparative perspective on the ideological origins of the Balkan political traditions. *Canadian Review of Studies in Nationalism*, 10, 51–70.

Kofman, E. 1982: Differential modernisation, social conflicts and ethno-regionalism in Corsica. *Ethnic and Racial Studies*, 5, 300–13.

Kohr, L. 1957: *The Breakdown of Nations*. Swansea: Christopher Davies.

Krejci, J. and Velimsky, V. 1981: *Ethnic and Political Nations in Europe*. London: Croom Helm.

Luckham, R. 1971: *The Nigerian Military*. Cambridge: Cambridge University Press.

Medhurst, K. 1982: Basques and Basque nationalism. In C. H. Williams (ed.) *National Separatism*, Cardiff: The University of Wales Press, 235–61.

Mény, Y. 1984: Decentralisation in socialist France: the politics of pragmatism. *West European Politics*, 7, 66–79.

Modelski, G. 1978: The long cycle of global politics and the nation state. *Comparative Studies in Society and History*, 20, 214–35.

Nairn, T. 1981: *The Break-Up of Britain*. London: Verso.

Oberschall, A. 1973: *Social Conflict and Social Movements*. Englewood Cliffs: Prentice-Hall.

Orridge, A. W. 1981: Uneven development and nationalism. *Political Studies*, 29, 1–15 and 181–90.

Orridge, A. W. and Williams, C. H. 1982: Autonomist nationalism: a theoretical framework for spatial variations in its genesis and development, *Political Geography Quarterly*, 1, 19–39.

Panter-Brick, K. S. (ed.) 1970: *Nigerian Politics and Military Rule: Prelude to the Civil War*. London: The Athlone Press.

Panter-Brick, K. S. (ed.) 1978: *Soldiers and Oil*. London: Frank Cass.

Pettman, R. 1979: *State and Class*. London: Croom Helm.

Reece, J. E. 1977: *The Bretons Against France*. Chapel Hill: The University of North Carolina Press.

Rich, E. E. and Wilson, C. H. (eds) 1967: *The Economy of Expanding Europe in the 16th and 17th Centuries*, Cambridge: Cambridge University Press.

Rokkan, S. and Urwin, D. W. (eds) 1982: *The Politics of Territorial Identity*. London: Sage.

Ronen, D. 1979: *The Quest for Self-Determination*. New Haven: Yale University Press.

Ros i Garcia, M. and Strubell i Trueta, M. (eds) 1984: Catalan sociolinguistics. *International Journal of the Sociology of Language*, 47.

Rudolph, J. 1982: Belgium: controlling separatist tendencies in a multinational state. In C. H. Williams (ed.), *National Separatism*, Cardiff: The University of Wales Press, 263–97.

Seton-Watson, H. 1977: *Nations and States*. Boulder, Colorado: Westview Press.

Shaw, M. 1984: War: the end of the dialectic? *Journal of Area Studies*, 9, 3–6.

Sklar, R. 1963: *Nigerian Political Parties*. Princeton: Princeton University Press.

Skocpol, T. 1977: Wallerstein's world capitalist system: a theoretical and historical critique. *American Journal of Sociology*, 82, 1075–90.

Skocpol, T. 1979: *States and Social Revolutions*. Cambridge: Cambridge University Press.

Smith, A. D. 1981a: *The Ethnic Revival*, Cambridge: Cambridge University Press.

Smith, A. D. 1981b: War and ethnicity: the role of warfare in the formation, self-images and cohesion of ethnic communities. *Ethnic and Racial Studies*, 4, 375–97.

Smith, A. D. 1982: Nationalism, ethnic separatism and the intelligentsia. In C. H. Williams (ed.), *National Separatism*, Cardiff: The University of Wales Press, 17–41.

Smith, A. D. 1983: *State and Nation in the Third World*. Brighton: Wheatsheaf Books.

Snyder, L. L. 1978: *Roots of German Nationalism*. Bloomington: Indiana University Press.

Tägil, S. (ed.) 1977: *Studying Boundary Conflicts*, Lund: Lund Studies in International History, Esselte Studium.

Tägil, S. 1982: The question of border regions in western Europe: an historical background. *West European Politics*, 5, 18–33.

Taylor, P. J. 1981: Political geography and the world-economy. In A. Burnett and P.J. Taylor (eds), *Political Studies from Spatial Perspectives*, Chichester: Wiley.

Taylor, P. J. 1982: A materialist framework for political geography, *Transactions, Institute of British Geographers*, N.S. 7, 15–34.

Treharne, R. F. and Fullard, H. 1976: *Muir's Historical Atlas*. London: George Philip & Son.

Wallerstein, I. 1974: *The Modern World System*. New York: Academic Press.

Wallerstein, I. 1979: *The Capitalist World Economy*. Cambridge: Cambridge University Press.

Williams, C. H. (ed.) 1982: *National Separatism*. Cardiff: The University of Wales Press.

Williams, C. H. 1984: Ideology and the interpretation of minority cultures. *Political Geography Quarterly*, 3, 105–25.

Williams, C. H. and Smith, A. D. 1983: The national construction of social space, *Progress in Human Geography*, 7, 502–18.

Williams, G. 1980: Review of E. Allardt's *Implications of the Ethnic Revival in Modern Industrial Society, Journal of Multilingual and Multicultural Development*, 1, 363–70.

Williams, G. A. 1982: *The Welsh in their History*. London: Croom Helm.

Wolf, E. 1971: *Peasant Wars of the Twentieth Century*. London: Faber & Faber.

Young, C. 1976: *The Politics of Cultural Pluralism*. Madison: University of Wisconsin Press.

Zolberg, A. R. 1980: Strategic interactions and the formation of modern states: France and England. *International Social Science Journal*, 32, 687–716.

Zolberg, A. R. 1981: Origins of the modern world system: a missing link. *World Politics*, 33, 253–81.

10

World-Power Competition and Local Conflicts in the Third World

JOHN O'LOUGHLIN

Let's not delude ourselves. The Soviet Union underlies all the unrest that is going on. If they weren't engaged in this game of dominoes, there wouldn't be any hot spots in the world. (Ronald Reagan)

Wars are needed only by imperialists to seize the territories of others. American imperialists lay claim to the whole world living under their heel and threaten humanity with a rocket and nuclear war. (Nikita Khrushchev)

In 1977, a simmering and longstanding border dispute between Somalia and Ethiopia erupted into full-scale war, claiming over 25,000 lives by 1980 and resulting in hundreds of thousands of refugees in crowded and miserable conditions along the border of the two countries. The outbreak of the war was only one of a series of disasters and conflicts that had plagued the Horn of Africa since 1968. The great famine of the early 1970s, causing at least 400,000 deaths, the civil wars in the Ethiopian provinces of Eritrea and Tigre, the military coups in Somalia in 1969 and Ethiopia in 1974, and the recurrence of famine throughout the region in the early 1980s have been only the visible elements of endemic economic and political difficulties in the region. Though barely noticed in the west until late 1984, preoccupied with its own economic difficulties and the American–Soviet confrontation of a second cold war, the crisis in the Horn of Africa reveals much about the state of international relations in the late twentieth century. The USA and the USSR became heavily involved in the Somali–Ethiopian conflict as a result of their global rivalry. The second cold war between the superpowers, beginning about 1979, differs fundamentally from the first cold war (1947–53) in the shift of the regional focus of competition from Europe to the 'Arc of Crisis' (Kenya through the Arabian Peninsula to

Pakistan); a diminution of the ideological basis of the differences between the superpowers, replaced by an emphasis on their struggle for influence throughout the world; approximate parity in nuclear weapons is now accompanied by a renewed emphasis on the feasibility of using conventional forces in scattered locations around the globe; a narrowing of the military superiority of the United States over the Soviet Union; a questioning of American foreign policy and military strategy by her western allies; and, perhaps most importantly, a focus on local contests in the Third World (Halliday, 1983).

By some accounts, the contemporary Third World is like the Balkans of the 1900–14 period as great-power tensions are expressed by alliances with local political forces and by pouring large amounts of military and economic aid to their allies. In this scenario, just as Balkans tensions helped create the climate of suspicion, fear and rearmament as well as the spark that set off the first world war, so, too, the deep and growing involvement of the two superpowers in Third World disputes could set off the third world war. The crisis in the Horn of Africa, currently less evident than in 1978 but no closer to resolution, is only one of dozens of regional disputes in which the superpowers have taken sides. Among the major tensions, those in Afghanistan, between Israel and its neighbours, in the Horn of Africa, between Vietnam and its neighbours, in southern Africa (South Africa and neighbouring Angola, Mozambique and Namibia), in Central America, in the Persian Gulf and in the Korean Peninsula spring readily to mind as cases of potential escalation to hemispheric or global conflict. It is difficult to measure if the world in 1985 is a more dangerous place than the world of 1950, or even of 1910, but widespread publicity to the nuclear arms impasse between the USA and the USSR, the near-total abdication of the 1953–78 recognition of spheres of influence and the aggressive foreign policy of the first Reagan administration, the independent and growing importance of Third World states in a bipolar world, the continued downturn in the global economy, and the widening income gap between rich and poor nations, have generated a pervasive sense of global crisis.

In this chapter, I will focus on superpower roles and strategies in the Third World as an important aspect of their hegemonic struggle. Hegemony, as the term is used in this chapter, is a combination of the economic and military superiority achieved by the leading global power. The term is used in a Modelskian sense and hegemony is usually measured by economic indicators (GNP total, percentage of world trade, industrial strength, etc.) and military indexes (number and type of nuclear weapons, number of troops, military expenditures, etc.). Political influence throughout the world is viewed as a logical extension of economic and military pre-eminence. Most observers agree that the United States emerged from the second world war as the hegemonic state. America's hegemony was evident until the late 1960s. Since that date, the Soviet Union on the political–military side and other capitalist states in both the west and the Third World on the economic side have challenged America's hegemony.

Rather than describing the details of the behaviour of the global powers in the 40 or so contemporary wars, I will examine only the conflicts in the Horn of Africa, Afghanistan and Central America, to illustrate the general range of commitment, strategy, doctrine and choice faced by the superpowers in areas perceived vital to both (the Horn) and in their own 'backyards'. Three research perspectives in the fields of international relations and geopolitics are reviewed first for their potential theoretical insights into one of the most critical issues of our day, international conflicts among major powers. The major theme of the chapter, the hegemonic decline of the United States in the late twentieth century and the current efforts by the Reagan administration to reverse it, will be developed from one of the three theoretical perspectives. This theory, with a focus on superpower hegemonic struggle in the Third World, is then applied to three geopolitical struggles: the conflict in the Horn, now involving both superpowers, and the particular threat to Soviet interests in Afghanistan and American interests in the Central American isthmus by indigenous popular movements of liberation. Some conclusions on superpower conflict in the context of a rapidly changing global arrangement of political and economic power and possible geopolitical analyses complete the chapter.

THEORY IN INTERNATIONAL RELATIONS

The field of international relations is characterized by a bewildering array of approaches, models, ideologies, policies, advocacy positions, disciplinary emphases and publication outlets. The global disaster of the first world war promoted an interest in international relations in Europe and North America. Early research was predominantly of an 'idealist' nature, attempting to understand the causes of international disputes and suggesting policies for their solution. After the second world war, a 'realist' or power politics approach, viewing international behaviour as essentially in the national interest and not necessarily motivated by an ideology, replaced early idealist work. All nations, regardless of location, history, size, political orientation, leadership style, government form and military and economic strength, were motivated by the same goal, maintenance of world order according to the logic of power. Forming alliances, balancing a strong power by a coalition of weaker states, viewing war as an instrument of foreign policy, and using international organizations for national goals were considered part of the normal game of power politics. Diplomatic history was the key discipline, teaching modern practitioners of the art of international politics the rules of the game, the strategies for successes and the lessons of failure.

We can view *Geopolitik* (the school of geopolitics) as the geographic contribution to this traditionalist school of international relations, both idealist and realist. A state's location, in both absolute and relative space, was seen as a strong motivating force in its external relations. Going beyond the historical geography of Mackinder's 'Heartland–Rimland' model, the post-first-world-war German geopoliticians advocated a national policy of aggression and conquest to achieve regional and eventual world dominance (Kristof, 1960).

This development points to one of the major problems with the traditional power-politics approach to international relations. Most of its practitioners are strongly motivated by national concerns, adopting a state-centred or ethnocentric policy focus. Henry Kissinger could be considered a classic example in his early academic writings, in his government service in the Nixon and Ford administrations, and in his memoirs. The approach has a strong policy focus; that is not a problem in itself, but in practice it leads to the development of a nationalist, often biased, perspective on international conflicts (Agnew, 1983). In the recent works by Cline (1980) and Gray (1977), we can see the geographic role in foreign affairs raised to new heights. An alliance strategy is advocated for the United States by taking each nation's power status, adding up the totals for friends and adversaries (the Soviet bloc), identifying key global choke-points such as the Straits of Malacca, Cape of Good Hope and the Red Sea, and urging an American commitment to maintaining an aggressive foreign and military policy to ensure the 'Pax Americana'.

A combination of dissatisfaction with the state-centred or unique view of world politics of the traditionalist school and a social-scientific trend towards positivist research in the 1950s and 1960s, with its use of hypothesis-testing, acquisition of large data sets and widespread use of statistical analysis, led to the 'hegemony' of the behavioural approach in the field of international relations. Currently about 70 per cent of the researchers and key works in world politics in North America are classified as belonging to this group (Alker and Bierstecker, 1984). Less than 20 per cent are from the traditional school and the remaining 10 per cent are from the 'dialectical' school (see below). Behaviouralists share a 'neutral', analytic, empirical perspective on interstate relations. Although specific theories have been developed and tested for detailed relationships, such as relating external behavioural to internal domestic politics and the outbreak of war to imperial competition between major powers, the field has been labelled as 'non-theoretical'. One of the major behavioural research efforts, the Correlates of War (COW) project led by J. David Singer, has accumulated a massive data bank on interstate, colonial and civil wars since 1815. In responding to critics, who castigate the project's almost exclusive data orientation, Singer (1981) has defended the work by stating that, because of the complexity of the causes of conflict and the weak knowledge base of the international-relations discipline, the best prospects for the field lie in a 'brush-clearing operation of some magnitude'. Consequently, thousands of correlation analyses of attributes, derived from *realpolitik* (power politics) such as alliance behaviour, geographic contiguity, military and economic capacity and crisis behaviour, and conflict indices, such as war severity or length of conflict, have been produced but no systematic explanation of the causes of conflict seem to be emerging from this inductive approach. Alker and Bierstecker (1984) classify most practitioners of the behavioural approach as 'liberal internationalists' since their research perspective of an interaction matrix of all states in the global system, with conflict and co-operation scores in the matrix cells, lends itself perfectly to an interdependence viewpoint.

The 'dialectical' school of international relations is characterized by a variety of approaches but its practitioners share some key perspectives. While dominant in eastern Europe and China and making major inroads in Third World scholarship, the dialectial view is still poorly represented in North America. 'Typically, dialectical theorists have valued emancipation, favored structural or revolutionary change, and have fundamentally challenged the legitimacy of the existing world-order' (Alker and Bierstecker, 1984, p. 125). The 'dialectical' school has clear internal dissensions between classical Marxists, such as the 'New Left Review school'; world-system theorists such as the *Monthly Review* school; and non-Marxists such as Johan Galtung who use a dialectical approach to advocate a reordering of global priorities. Wallerstein (1983), whose world-systems project is examined in detail in chapter 11 of this book, can be classified as a member of the *Monthly Review* school, with his stress on the integration of the global market for commodities, the competitive interstate system, the economic hierarchy from core through semiperiphery to periphery, the regularity of growth and decline in the world economy, and the geographic diffusion of capitalism from its north-west European core.

Although constantly criticized for his economic fetish, Wallerstein's world-view has produced a profound questioning of the whole field of international relations. Empirical tests of the relationship between cycles of economic growth and decline with global conflict have not produced consistent results but the importance of Wallerstein's work lies in his insertion of the economic factor firmly into the core of the debate on the most appropriate approach for international relations. In the Wallerstein view, a differentiated global economic system with a strong hierarchical form, uneven economic development, regular systemic upheavals through global war and the reluctance of the hegemonic state to create a world-empire since it profits more from a world-economy, results in the survival and reproduction of the multicentric interstate system (Chase-Dunn, 1981; Chase-Dunn and Sokolovsky, 1983). This view has been strongly challenged by Thompson (1983a, b) who finds Wallerstein's model deficient as a *political* – economic explanation of interstate conflicts. As an alternative framework, Modelski's (1978, 1983) long-cycle model of the world-system is gaining rapid notice in the community of scholars in international studies. While it shares many of the characteristics of Wallerstein's model (one world-system, cycles of economic and political growth and decline, core–peripheral relations, world-economy versus world-empires) it is most clearly distinguished by its emphasis on political processes and global wars in shaping the global arrangement of power and prosperity. Modelski's framework has been severely criticized for describing only the surface manifestations of global political change in its historical evolution since 1494 and for not identifying the 'central engine' of change. If this motor is not Wallerstein's core–peripheral economic relation, what is it? Recent work by Modelski (1983), Thompson (1983c) and other long-cycle theorists (Gilpin, 1981; Doran and Parsons, 1980; and Oye, 1983) has elevated the 'hegemonic' explanation to a point that allows academic tests of its propositions using historical data and close examination of the contemporary behaviour of nations in the interstate system. It is the perspective that is adopted in this chapter as offering the best prospects for full explanation of American and Soviet foreign policy and actions in the Third World. The theoretical formulation, historical manifestations, propositions and threshold of evidentiary support are described in the next section and the actions of the superpowers in the Third World, especially in the Horn of Africa, Central America and Afghanistan, are interpreted in light of this model in subsequent sections.

LONG-CYCLE MODELS OF GLOBAL HEGEMONY

While Modelski's long-cycle theory of the world-system is still in the process of conceptualization and refinement, enough details have been provided to identify the core elements of the theory. Like Wallerstein, Modelski believes strongly that the current state of international relations is the product of a half-millennium of changing patterns of interstate linkages and that the behaviour of an individual state is the result not only of domestic (internal) dynamics but also of the role that the state plays in the world-system of nations. A focus on the relative emphasis given to political and economic explanations in both models tend to exaggerate in an artifical manner the differences between Modelski and Wallerstein and to hide the similarity of their basic positions. Both models date the modern world-system from the sixteenth century as the feudal society of Europe was replaced by proto-capitalism and the numerous independent principalities were gradually superseded by larger political units. Modelski nominates 1494 as the critical turning-point. The Italian wars, which led to the first hegemonic power, Portugal, began at that time, and the immutable shift from the Mediterranean to the Atlantic was begun. Modelski's world-system has five long cycles of hegemonic growth and decline, each decline and growth beginning and ending in a global war. The wars (and resulting world powers) are the Italian wars 1494–1516 (Portugal), Spanish wars 1581–1609 (Netherlands), wars of Louis XIV 1688–1713 (Britain), revolutionary and Napoleonic wars 1792–1815 (Britain) and the first and second world wars (United States). Each war involved all of the global powers of the day and each world power faced challenges during the period (consistently about a century) of hegemony.

The phases and dynamics of each long cycle are repetitive. From a global war, a single state emerges with a comparative advantage over its adversaries. In his 1983 work, Modelski stresses the role of seapower, which allows the capacity for global reach to be achieved. Harking back to the nineteenth-century study of Admiral Mahan (1980), he believes that four preconditions related to seapower must be met before the world power can become the global power. The state must have a protected ocean location, such as Britain on an island; it must be able to provide ocean-going power in the form of a large and powerful navy and a shipbuilding industry; it must develop a strong economy based on ocean trade, allowing the state to pay for the naval costs; and it must possess a strong central government. Modelski (1983) would appear to be suggesting that seapower and its economic linkages provides the basis of hegemony, particularly if combined with a strong nation-state. The global power not only possesses the leading economy in the world system but, through control of the treaty arrangements ending the global war, it legitimizes and reinforces its position as the hegemonic power. The global power matches this political dominance by ordering global economic structures in its favour, particularly through money and trade mechanisms. After about a generation, the relative advantage of the global power begins to erode as the growing relative capability of its adversaries allows them to formulate challenges to the existing power arrangement. The globe is gradually transformed into a multicentric power division. In this second generation, the phase of delegitimation, while the leading power is still ahead of its international competitors, the struggle for hegemony begins which will eventually deteriorate to global war. The third generation, the phase of deconcentration, is marked by oligopolistic competition and since the major challengers are not ready to press their claims for a rearrangement of global power, this quarter-century is the lull before the storm. The last period of the cycle is again a generation of global war from which a new global power or a reconstituted global power, such as Britain in the early nineteenth century, emerges. In Modelski's (1978, p. 232) memorable phrase; 'We might say that one generation builds, the next consolidates, and the third loses control.'

Given that the primary concern of this chapter is to explicate a model of international conflicts based on hegemonic struggles, the relationship between hegemonic growth/decline and the outbreak of war in Modelski's long-cycle model is of particular interest. Following a guns-versus-butter argument, Modelski and his model's advocates argue that, in times of war, less resources are available to promote economic growth. A trade-off between political (including military) spending and economic development funding is expected. In the second (delegitimation) and fourth (global war) phases of the cycle, we see rising prices, resource scarcity and general economic stagnation. Conversely, we see falling prices, ready and cheap access to resources, and a rapidly expanding economic sector in the first (world power) and third (deconcentration) phases of the cycle. Interestingly, territorial expansion of the hegemonic state is seen not as an indicator of growth and prosperity, but as a despairing effort to shore up a faltering position. 'Territoriality is the final nemesis of global power. It is a defensive response to the challenge of oligopolistic rivalry' (Modelski, 1978, pp. 229–30). The hegemonic power, on the verge of decline, can ill afford the additional burden of defence costs associated with colonial aggrandisement. Modelski clearly sees a message for American foreign policy-makers from a close inspection of previous long cycles and the external dynamics of growth and decline. By most accounts, the cycle of American power has now entered the third or deconcentration phase. Whether America's leaders, benefiting from the lessons of history, can postpone the inevitable dénouement, remains to be seen.

In the Wallerstein model, as elaborated by Chase-Dunn (1981), 'world wars may be understood as violent reorganizations of production relations which allow the accumulation process to adjust to its contradictions and to expand on a larger scale' (Thompson, 1983d, p. 351). Specific tests of this economic interpretation of outbreaks have not yet produced consistent support for the hypothesis (Thompson, 1983c). Thompson (1983a) claims that, while global wars 'reorganize' the world political and economic structure, the changes are not necessarily due to the challenger's effort to restructure the world-economic system in its favour. Chase-Dunn and Sokolovsky (1983), following Wallerstein's logic, have argued that wars reflect an effort to convert politico-military strength into a greater share of world-economic surplus. Since wars in general and global wars in particular are critical to the long-cycle interpretation of hegemonic rises and falls, Thompson (1983a–d) has devoted considerable effort to reinterpretation of war studies in the light of long-cycle theory. He has concluded that wars resolve ambiguities in the world-system caused by confusion over the relative capabilities of a declining global power and ascending challengers. Cycles of global war and peace are related to cycles of hegemonic growth and decline, resulting in cycles of power concentration and deconcentration.

A focus on Wallerstein's and Modelski's models in this chapter should not obscure the fact that other models of power growth and decline are widely discussed in the literature of interstate relations. Among the explanations, those of Gilpin (1981) and Doran and Parsons (1980) bear closest relation to the long-cycle interpretation of global power changes. Examining the Athenian, Roman, Dutch, British and American empires, Gilpin (1981) attributed their decline to a consistent set of three factors; external burdens of leadership resulting in costly and consistent military expenditures; internal secular tendency towards rising consumption, thereby reducing infrastructural investment; and the international diffusion of technology which bridges the gap between the initial advantage accruing to the leading state and its lagging competitors. Using a military-versus-civilian-expenditure logic (guns versus butter), Oye (1983) found evidence to support this interpretation of American hegemonic decline in the past two decades. Doran's cyclical view is somewhat at odds with other views because, unlike Wallerstein and Modelski, he adopts a state-centric approach. By focusing on individual states, he attributes attempts to establish hegemony to the aspiring global power's position on the relative cycle of power, that is, rising, cresting, falling or in decline. Movement through those four phases of the state's cycle of relative power affects the state's propensity to become entangled in major wars. The Doran approach, though accurate in its description of the rise and fall of individual states, lacks the systemic base, with its stress on international links and effects, of the world-system or long-cycle perspectives. Therefore, we must see it as an addendum to the long-cycle model rather than as an alternative framework of analysis.

Common to all cyclical models is the designation of the post-second-world-war period as that of the 'American hegemony'. Unlike earlier global powers, whose leading position endured for over half a century, most observers believe that American dominance of the world economic, military and political scene began to erode by the middle 1960s (Oye, 1983; Halliday, 1983; Barnet, 1971; Senghaas, 1983; Frank, 1981; Harris, 1982). The erosion was not caused by the Vietnam war or by the 'weakness' displayed by American leaders in dealing with foreign powers, as right-wing commentators have claimed. Rather, it was caused by a combination of global economic and political circumstances which the United States could not control. To a certain extent, the US was a victim of global developments. Between 1960 and 1979, the average annual growth rate in GNP in the United States was 3.6 per cent compared to 3.9 per cent in West Germany and 8.5 per cent in Japan. Between 1950 and 1980, America's share of the world's total GNP dropped from 40 per cent to 25 per cent, as developing nations and America's capitalist competitors increased their share. On the politico-military front, the American share of world military spending dropped from 51 per cent in 1960 to 28 per cent in 1980 and its share of armed forces personnel from 13 per cent to 8.3 per cent. (All data are from Oye, 1983.)

Explaining these trends has become a major national, as well as academic, problem. It is clear that competition from abroad in the form of rapid economic growth in capitalist nations and military growth in socialist and some Third World nations, rather than absolute American decline, explains the declining American shares. Oye (1983) provides a strong case for using Gilpin's (1981) trichotomy of the causes of hegemonic decline for interpreting the relative American decline since 1960. Essentially, the argument states that the United States cannot compete successfully with Japan, western Europe and the newly industrializing countries (NICs) on the economic front and with the Soviet Union on the military front, at the same time. Ironically, the Reagan administration, pledged to restore American hegemony, has made matters worse by ignoring Gilpin's causal factors of decline. The administration's expansive military policy has substituted the appearance of strength for deeply rooted growth. The basic problem remains that 'American policy, alone, cannot arrest or reverse structural tendencies toward cyclical hegemonic decline' (Oye, 1983, p. 16). Investment in fixed capital formation is much higher in Japan, West Germany and the NICs than in the US, while spending on the military and private consumption is much lower. Until these underlying causes of decline are questioned and changed, a reversal in declining American fortunes in the near future cannot be expected.

HEGEMONIC COMPETITION IN THE SECOND COLD WAR

The issue of declining American hegemony has been projected into the consciousness of the American voters. While President Carter had talked about 'national malaise', President Reagan, in his 1984 re-election campaign, stressed that America was again number one, both economically and militarily. Whether this statement was accurate mattered little; the public perception of a resurgent nation which less than five years previously was reduced to a supine position (hostages were held in Teheran, and the US was suffering a deep economic recession and was victimized by excessive dependence on imported oil) was turned into political profit by re-election-candidate Reagan. But political campaign rhetoric will not dismiss the reality of the international competition that the United States, the leading global economic and military power, continues to face. Unlike earlier hegemonic rivalries which were essentially confined to a handful of major states who offered both political and economic challenges to the existing global power, the contemporary global situation is characterized by multi-dimensional rivalries. In the politico-military dimension, the United States faces a strong challenge from the USSR, a 'rising hegemonic power' (Senghaas, 1983). Ideological differences only serve to reinforce, but not cause, the rivalry which, in historical terms, is classically hegemonic. On a less well-known level, the US is challenged by 'Third Worldism', particularly in its Moslem transnational guise, rejecting American (and Soviet) dominance of the world's trade, economic, political, military and cultural relations (Alker, 1981). The interaction between the two superpowers and Third World states provides one of the major conflict arenas in contemporary world politics.

On the economic front, the United States also faces two sets of challenges. As discussed earlier, two of America's major capitalist competitors, West Germany and Japan, have had higher investment and GNP growth rate since 1960. In Wallerstein's (1983) view, this major capitalist state competition is expected to intensify over the next 20 years as the post-war global economic structure, arranged and dominated by the United States, enters a stage of crisis. In periods of recession, such as that since 1974, this competition becomes intense. One feature of this intra-capitalist competition has been a renewed reluctance of America's allies to support US political strategy when it contradicts their own economic interests. The embargo placed on the European suppliers to the Siberian gas pipeline by the Reagan administration and the refusal of European states to comply provides a perfect illustration of this intra-capitalist tension. Unlike the first cold war, this second cold war between the superpowers has seen an end of the European–American consensus on an anti-Soviet strategy (Mujah-Leon, 1984).

Another competitive front has emerged in the past decade. Some Third World countries, the NICs, have provided a strong challenge to the world market shares held by the older capitalist states, a challenge that continued unabated during the recession of the 1970s. While the United States, western Europe and Japan together had an average annual growth rate between 1970 and 1978 of 3.3 per cent, the NICs grew by 8.6 per cent yearly and eight nations (Hong Kong, Taiwan, South Korea, Spain, Mexico, Singapore, Yuglosavia, Brazil and Portugal) had an annual rate over 15 per cent (Edwards, 1979). Domestic American producers of steel, textiles, electronic goods, ships, cars and other consumer goods demanded tariff restrictions against cheaper imports from the NICs. Though the governments of the NICs are almost uniformly authoritarian right-wing regimes and though they remain generally supportive of the United

States in the second cold war, they nevertheless chafe under American market dominance, demand ready access to western markets and are willing to pursue strongly their capitalist development strategy, even if it involves an economic war with western Europe and the United States.

A convenient summary of the global dual competition (east versus west, north versus south) has been provided by Alker (1981). The interactions among the opposing systems dialectically produce social, political, economic and cultural conflicts among the members of the world-system at different points in time. Alker does not accept the Wallerstein core–periphery dichotomy of nations; instead, he sees the globe as comprised of 'competing world order systems' and predicts major shifts in the arrangement of power relations in (heretofore) unexpected ways. Although none of the four geopolitical blocs identified by their ranking on the two axes – Soviet socialist, corporatist–authoritarian (NICs), capitalist power-balancing, and collective self-reliance – is coherent, the blocs identify preferred major world-order or idealist arrangements. Obviously the importance of the ten possible tensions (four blocs with inter- and intra-group tension) will vary spatially and temporally.

In this chapter our major focus is on east-versus-west tension (or capitalist power-balancing versus Soviet socialism in Alker's term) in the Third World. That tension has military, political, economic and cultural elements, with the military domain divided into nuclear and conventional weapons. Most observers agree that an early American lead in nuclear arms had evaporated by the middle 1970s and that a situation of rough parity currently exists between the superpowers. The Reagan administration's discovery of a 'window of vulnerability' in the nuclear weapons capability of the United States was used effectively to generate domestic political support for the largest military build-up in peacetime. One key element of the build-up was the expansion of non-nuclear forces designed for rapid intervention, costing about 25 per cent of the military budget. It is evident from Reagan's speeches and actions that he regards the cold war as a multifaceted battleground, and that with nuclear stalemate the greatest opportunities for American successes lie in the non-nuclear arena.

The post-war division of the globe into a hierarchic, bipolar arrangement of spheres of influence lingers on in the 1980s (see figure 10.1). At the heart of each sphere lies the superpower. Allied politically, militarily, culturally and economically to the superpowers are the core nations of each bloc, such as the NATO countries of western Europe and the Warsaw Pact countries of eastern Europe. The ecumene of each bloc designates those countries not allied formally to a superpower but supportive of its position in cold-war disputes: most Latin American nations for the US, and socialist Third World states, such as Vietnam, Ethiopia, South Yemen and Nicaragua, for the USSR. The remaining area constitutes the group of truly non-aligned nations, which is much smaller than the 'non-aligned' group of over 100 states in the UN General Assembly. Barring a drastic and unexpected shift in post-war trends, the superpowers can rely on the core of their support. Their general geostrategy, then is (a) to preserve

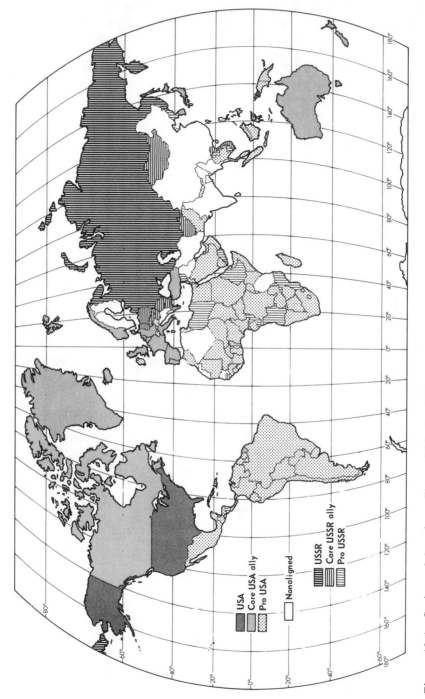

Figure 10.1 Soviet and American allies and friends, 1982

USA
Core USA ally
Pro USA

Nonaligned

USSR
Core USSR ally
Pro USSR

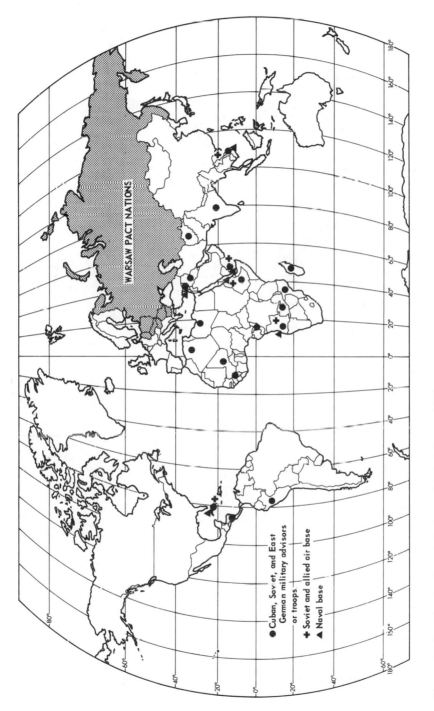

Figure 10.2 Distribution of Soviet and Allied Bases, 1982

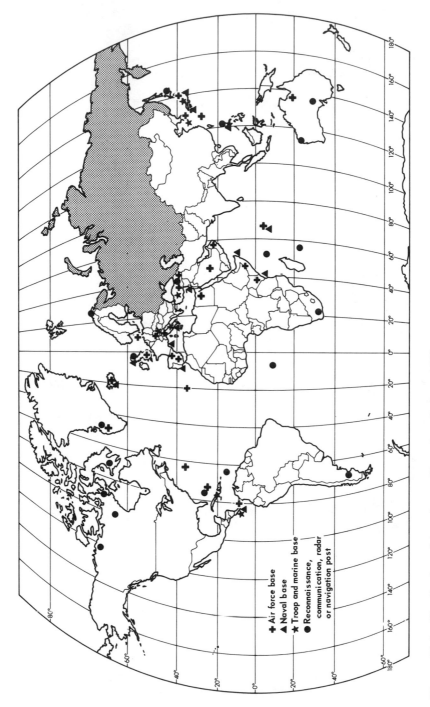

Figure 10.3 Distribution of American military installations, 1982

+ Air force base

▲ Naval base

★ Troop and marine base

● Reconnaissance, communication, radar or navigation post

their support in allied nations, (b) to make inroads into the allied bloc of their adversary, through supporting 'progressive forces' (Soviet Union) or helping to 'defend liberty' (United States), and (c) to woo non-aligned nations into their allied bloc, or, at the least, to counter adversary efforts in the opposite direction. A wide range of military, economic, diplomatic, trade, even sport, weapons are used to pursue these general strategies (see figure 10.2 and 10.3) which, with modest deviations, have remained in place since the Yalta Conference at the end of the second world war.

It is not possible in the space available to discuss in detail the doctrines and geostrategies of the two superpowers since the second world war. (Excellent recent reviews include Gaddis, 1982; Oye, Lieber and Rothchild, 1983; Wolfe, 1979; Barnet, 1980.) Halliday (1983) distinguishes four periods in post-war Soviet–American relations: the first cold war, 1946–53; oscillatory antagonism, 1953–69; detente, 1969–79; and the second cold war, 1979 to the present. Each superpower has an evolving foreign policy, modified by ideology, domestic circumstances, international developments and past commitments. For the United States, the Truman Doctrine of 1947 marked the openly stated willingness of that superpower to support potential allies in the 'fight against communism' anywhere in the world. A string of regional alliances advocated and supported by the United States ringed the Soviet Union and China from NATO in western Europe through CENTO in the Arc of Crisis to SEATO in south-east Asia. American military forces were committed to Lebanon, Berlin, Korea and Vietnam, and economic aid was provided by the Marshall Plan. While the strategy of containment ebbed and flowed from presidency to presidency, the basic doctrine has remained the centrepiece of American foreign policy. Although in basic agreement with this general containment strategy, the 'globalists' and 'regionalists' in the American foreign-policy establishment have debated changes in the world political map and the most appropriate response to these changes (Ambrose, 1983). The regionalists stress the diversity of the globe, the uniqueness of each nation and political circumstance, and maintain a generally sympathetic view of the problems facing Third World nations in achieving economic development and political freedoms. Jimmy Carter and his foreign-policy advisers epitomized this 'regionalist' perspective, and in the political–geographic field Saul Cohen's recent writings (1982) develop a geostrategy for the United States based on the notion that interregional variation precludes the application of an unbending global strategy.

Ronald Reagan's election changed accepted post-war doctrines of US foreign policy. Reagan has moved beyond containment to 'win back' some of the nations 'lost to communism'. This aggressive stance demands a huge investment in military and economic weapons. Reagan believes that 'communist subversion is not an irreversible tide. We have seen it rolled back in Venezuela and, most recently, in Grenada . . . the tide of the future can be a freedom tide. All it takes is the will and resources to get the job done' (Ronald Reagan, 9 May, 1984). The second major change since 1980 has been a return to the 'globalist' view of world politics. In his early presidential statements, Reagan castigated the Soviet Union and its allies, the Cubans, for instigating revolution in Africa and Latin America. Most recently, he accepts that conditions of extreme poverty and deprivation may have rendered these nations susceptible to 'communist subversion' and, consequently, has argued that economic aid be part of the foreign-policy package. But he continues to believe 'the simple fact that we were not deterring [before 1980], as events from Angola and Afghanistan made clear. Today we are, and that fact has fundamentally altered the future for millions of human beings. . . . American leadership is back. Peace through strength is not a slogan; it's a fact of life' (Ronald Reagan, 5 April, 1984). While Reaganism is still in the ascendancy and the globalist, aggressive, anti-Soviet policy predominates, America will not live with Third World revolutions, as urged by the late Senator Frank Church (1984). In Reagan's view, regional disputes in the Third World are basically east–west conflicts with no neutral parties (Rothchild and Ravenhill, 1983). Soviet involvement must be opposed by American assistance, and in the case of Africa 'the question for U.S. strategies is not how does America fit into Africa's perspective but rather how does Africa fit into ours' (Thompson, 1982, p. 1015).

While the national debate over foreign policy in the United States is accompanied by widespread scrutiny by Congress, the media and the public, it is much more difficult to discern the consistent elements of Soviet geostrategy. While professional Sovietologists waste mountains of paper and rivers of ink trying to gauge Soviet strategy from the nuanced behaviour of members of the Politburo, it appears that Soviet foreign policy has been remarkably consistent since Stalin. The Soviets share many of the same international perspectives as the Americans, such as near-paranoia about 'national security', promoting a buffer zone of client states, stability in contiguous regions (especially in the Arc of Crisis) and a general wish to help progressive forces. As Halliday (1982, p. 27) shows, the two main pillars of Soviet foreign policy are written into the 1977 Soviet constitution: 'ensuring international conditions favourable for building communism in the USSR' and 'supporting the struggle of peoples for national liberation and social progress'. From Moscow's perspective, the global deck of cards is stacked against them. In the UN General Assembly vote requesting the removal of Soviet troops from Afghanistan, only 18 non-Soviet states voted against the resolution. By any economic measure, the American bloc is between five and ten times greater than the Soviet bloc, and even militarily the gap is much larger than Pentagon analysts would suggest (Cline, 1980). Sticking to the argument that superpower negotiations on matters of mutual benefit such as nuclear arms control should not be linked to other political issues, such as human rights or support for Third World regimes, the USSR has consistently advocated the building of a working relationship with the United States. In contradistinction to the 'linkage' policy of American administrations, the Soviet Union argues that events in Poland, Afghanistan or Nicaragua should not interfere with stable and peaceful relations between the superpowers.

Soviet attitudes toward developments in the Third World have shifted over the past decade. No doubt hampered by domestic economic weakness and an inability to project military power past a narrow range along its international border, the Soviet Union was essentially a bystander during the decolonialization period. In the 1970s, the Soviet Union, while adhering to the Brezhnev Doctrine of protecting its national interests in bordering states, appeared more willing to become active in African affairs (Gavshon, 1981; Rothchild and Ravenhill, 1983). Active in the Horn of Africa, Zimbabwe, Angola, Mozambique, Guinea-Bissau and Libya, the Soviet Union generally acted in accordance with the principle of providing aid within its limited resources to 'progressive governments'. But it should be stressed that compared to western involvement in African affairs, Soviet efforts are indeed modest. Most of the Soviet attention to Third World politics is concentrated in the Arc of Crisis for the most basic of reasons; it shares a long border with one of the world's most unstable regions, from Turkey to Afghanistan (Dawisha and Dawisha, 1982). Just as the Americans express strong opinions about instability in their 'backyard' of Central America, so the Soviet Union is alarmed by events that it cannot control in Afghanistan, Iran and the Arabian Peninsula and in the extended Arab–Israeli conflict. The actions of the Soviet Union in Afghanistan since 1978 must be interpreted in this geopolitcal vein.

From the preceding paragraphs discussing Soviet and American geostrategies and deepening rivalry in the Third World, it should not be assumed that the states of the Third World have been passive and pliant in their relations with the superpowers. One of the main features distinguishing the second from the first cold war has been the independent role played by Third World states, many of whom were still colonies in the early 1950s. By inviting the major powers, including Britain and France, to help them suppress regional separatist movements, repel incursions, launch invasions, defeat domestic opponents, win political victories at home through careful distribution of outside aid, and hide their own inadequacy, the leaders of scores of Third World states have drawn their nations and regions closer to the front of the major ideological split in world politics. Both superpowers know from bitter experience that their stay in a Third World country may be curtailed at a moment's notice and major investments over an extended period yield nothing. The Soviet expulsion from Egypt in 1972 and the American expulsion from Iran in 1979 are only two, through major, examples of the uncertainties of First, Second and Third World relations. Despite the enormous differences in power-ranking, the smaller Third World states can often persuade the superpower to accede to regional policies that yield little geopolitical benefit for the superpower while meeting the most salient of the Third World state's local objectives. Thus Soviet and Cuban aid has been used to suppress the Eritrean revolt and American arms were used by Iran to defeat the Kurds in north-west Iran. The dilemmas of great-power involvement in geographically contiguous zones of instability is perhaps illustrated best by both superpowers' involvement in the Horn of Africa, the Soviet involvement in Afghanistan and by American involvement in Central America. It is to these regional troublespots that we now turn our attention.

CONFLICT IN THE HORN OF AFRICA

A glance at a location map of north-east Africa and south-west Asia clearly indicates the strategic location of the Horn of Africa at the entrance to the Red Sea and straddling the Persian Gulf/East African coast axis (see figure 10.4). In recent years, the Indian Ocean and its littoral have become an area of concentration of naval and interventionary forces from Britain, France, the Soviet Union and, particularly, the United States (House, 1984). The perceived threat to western oil supplies from the Persian Gulf region (15 per cent of America's supply, 60 per cent of western Europe's and 90 per cent of Japan's), was viewed by the Carter administration as a 'threat to America's security' and used to justify a deployment of troops to the region. Zbigniew Brzezinski, Carter's National Security Advisor, coined the phrase 'the Arc of Crisis' for the Pakistan to Kenya semicircle. The region contains five major conflicts, Afghanistan, South Yemen and its neighbours, the Horn of Africa, the Iran–Iraq conflict, and the unresolved question of a Palestinian homeland and its wider Arab–Israeli setting. In the 1970s, the region was the world leader in arms imports with the Soviet Union supplying Afghanistan, Iraq, Syria, South Yemen, and Somalia (to 1978). It is estimated that between 1975 and 1982 the USSR supplied more than 7,000 tanks and self-propelled guns, 2,330 supersonic combat aircraft, and 15,000 surface-to-air missiles to its clients in the region (including India), while the US supplied its clients with 4,933 tanks and self-propelled guns, 785 aircraft and 6,311 surface-to-air missiles (Manning, 1983). About 60 per cent of all arms purchases in the Third World were in the Arc of Crisis between 1977 and 1980, with Syria, Libya, Saudi Arabia, Egypt, Iraq and Israel occupying six of the top seven positions on the world list of arms importers (SIPRI, 1983). The region possesses all the elements of a 'Shatterbelt', where 'internal, geographical, cultural, religious and political fragmentation is compounded by pressures from external major powers attracted by the region's strategic location and economic resources' (Cohen, 1982, p. 226).

From remaining essentially peripheral to the struggle between European powers in the nineteenth century and between the US and USSR in the first cold war, the Horn of Africa today occupies a pivotal position in the second cold war. In less than a decade, post-colonial north-east Africa has disintegrated into continued turmoil and a significant breakdown of traditional alliances. The most important American ally of the 1960s in sub-Saharan Africa, Ethiopia, has become the most important Soviet ally in the 1980s. The combination of civil strife, internal regional dynamics and superpower strategy producing this drastic shift in the Horn is repeated in other regions of the Third World. Beyond arms sales, military advisers and general economic aid, it is difficult to estimate

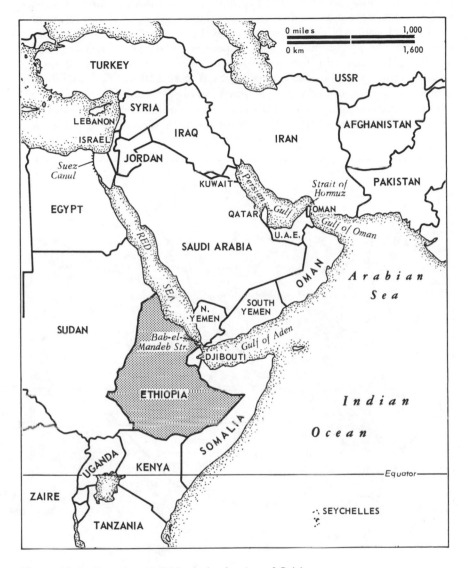

Figure 10.4 Location of Ethiopia in the Arc of Crisis

the escalating effects of superpower involvement in local disputes. Frequently, the major power acts as a restraining force on its ally. Both of the great powers were invited to intervene in the Horn's conflict by regimes seeking to inflict a knockout blow on traditional enemies, and both the US and the USSR complied for strategic, as opposed to economic, reasons (Ottaway, 1982; Shaw, 1983). While the stage was set in the late nineteenth century, the plot thickened after Somali independence in 1960 and the showdown occurred in the mid-1970s. We are still awaiting the eventual resolution of the protracted play.

Modern Ethiopia is generally regarded as the creation of Emperor Menelik, who reached an agreement with the European colonial powers, Britain, France and Italy, that ensured Ethiopia's expansion from its traditional highland out to its contemporary boundaries (see figures 10.5 and 10.6). This doubling of Ethiopian territory brought large Moslem populations into the same state as Coptic Christians, although Eritrea was only relinquished by the British to Emperor Haile Selassie in the 1950s. While the population of the Ogaden were

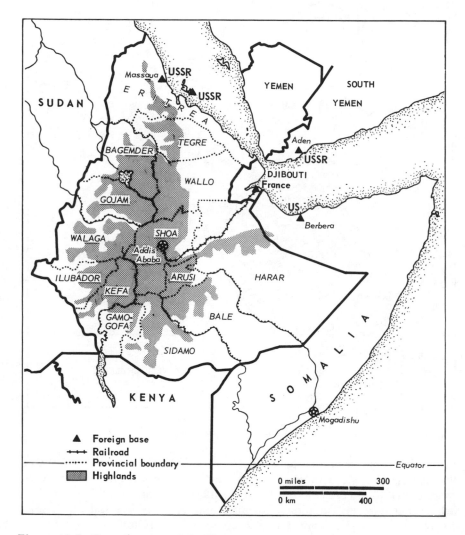

Figure 10.5   Location map of the Horn of Africa

ethnic Somalis, nomadic and Moslem, the population of Eritrea, now in federation with Ethiopia, was about equally divided between Moslem separatists and Ethiopian unionists (see figure 10.7). The three European states subdivided the coastal area of the Horn, their major interest in the region until Italy began oil exploration in the interior in the 1930s (see figure 10.6). Somalia was granted independence in 1960 from the old Italian protectorate (administered by Britain until 1950 and by Italy again from 1950 to 1960) and British Somaliland. The French Territory of the Afars and the Issas became the independent state of Djibouti in 1977 but retained a French garrison, ostensibly to protect the tiny

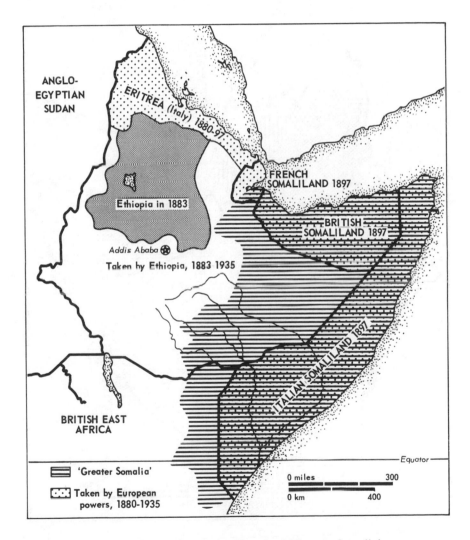

Figure 10.6   Colonial territories in the Horn and 'Greater Somalia'

state from Somali irredentist claims and Ethiopian expansionism. (For full details of the colonial period and its aftermath see Halliday and Molyneux, 1981; Ottaway, 1982; Abate, 1978; Wiberg, 1979.)

As is clear from figures 10.5 to 10.7, the international borders designated by a series of treaties between 1890 and 1910 bear little relationship to the distribution of ethnic or religious groups. The achievement of 'Greater Somalia', incorporating Somalia and parts of Ethiopia, Kenya and Djibouti, has been the goal of Somali foreign policy since independence, resulting in unsuccessful invasions of Kenya in 1962 and Ethiopia in 1977. The Organization of African

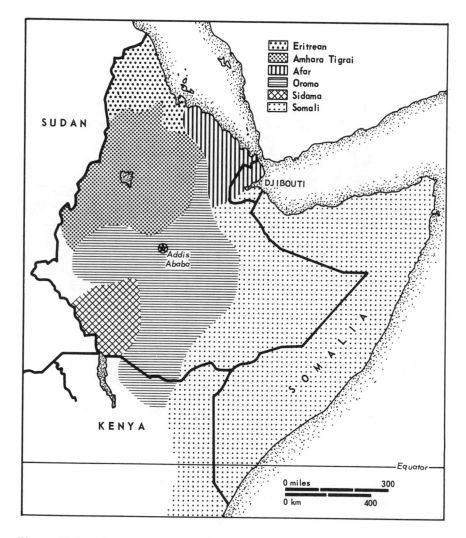

Figure 10.7   Distribution of ethnic groups in the Horn

Unity (OAU) has consistently denied Somali irredentist claims, fearing that granting such a precedent would open a Pandora's box of similar claims and counterclaims across the continent. Ironically, the large majority of African states insist on respect of colonial borders; the nineteenth-century demarcations are today's international boundaries. Somalia, one of the five poorest African countries after independence and two-thirds nomadic, accepted a Soviet offer in 1963 to form, equip and train its army. By 1969, the Somali armed forces were among the best-equipped and largest in the continent. Somali clearly initiated the military build-up, expecting to pursue its pan-Somali aims throughout the Horn and to act as a counter to the large military and economic aid that the United States was providing its traditional enemy, the Ethiopia of Emperor Haile Selassie. A military *coup* in 1969 brought General Siad Barre to power, determined to pursue vigorously the Somali claim to the Ogaden area of eastern Ethiopia. Siad Barre intensified ties with the Soviet Union, advocated 'scientific socialism' and allowed the Soviet military the use of a strategic base at Berbera (see figure 10.5). From 1963 to 1978, although Soviet involvement in Somalia intensified, there is no evidence that the Soviets instigated events – but they clearly benefited strategically from Somali civil politics and regional rivalries.

In Ethiopia, Haile Selassie had consolidated his position since returning to power in 1941 after Italy's defeat in the Horn by the British. Regional breakaway movements in Eritrea and Tigre (see figure 10.5) were contained and the emperor built up a professional army with American aid after 1953, encouraged commercial agriculture, allowed an American base at Kagnew in Eritrea, and in general tried to 'westernize' the country using western technology and American money and advisers. Ethiopia received about half of all US aid to Africa and had the largest number of Peace Corps volunteers. The emperor pressed the US for more military aid in the early 1970s when it became clear that Somalia was receiving greater amounts of Soviet weapons and equipment. Like the USSR in Somalia, the Americans essentially reacted to Ethiopian requests and were content to allow Haile Selassie to pursue his strong 'pro-western' policies. Both countries of the Horn were deeply divided along ethnic and class lines, with political (pro- and anti-Emperor) divisions in Ethiopia and geographic (north versus south) divisions in Somalia also present (Ottaway, 1982, pp. 53–6).

In early 1974, revolution broke out in Ethiopia in the wake of the major drought and resulting famine in the eastern provinces and of the attempted cover-up of the disaster by Haile Selassie. In September 1974 Haile Selassie was replaced as the governing authority by the Derg, a loose group of 120 members, many of them junior and non-commissioned officers. Land reforms were instituted, local peasant organizations were established, and by May 1976 a split in the Derg resulted in the eventual victory of Major (now Colonel) Mengistu Haile Mariam, in 1977. With a Marxist student and urban base, Mengistu had to deal with strained relations with the United States (who first rejected a request in February 1975 for military aid but later acceded), with a revived autonomous movement in Eritrea and with a resurgent Somali nationalism laying a renewed claim to the Ogaden. The US was in a dilemma.

To counter growing Soviet influence in the Horn through Somalia, the US had to rely on Ethiopia, yet the Derg had nationalized US property, continually denounced 'US imperialism', and looked the other way as attacks began on US civilian and military personnel still in the country. The Soviet Union was also caught in a dilemma. Despite a marked shift to the left by the Derg and its supporters and Soviet military aid to Ethiopia of $200 million in 1976, the Soviet Union continued to support Somalia because of their long and close relationship with that country and because of the importance of the base at Berbera. After Mengistu's final triumph in February 1977 and the expulsion of all remaining American institutions and personnel in April of that year, close ties between the Derg and the USSR quickly developed. It was apparent that the Soviets thought that they could maintain their presence in Somalia while developing new ties in Ethiopia, hoping to use their influence in both countries to suppress ancient local rivalries.

Confusion in Addis Ababa was the opportunity that the Eritrean People's Liberation Forces (EPLF), the Western Somalia Liberation Front (WSLF) and other separatist movements had been awaiting (see figure 10.5). The Derg could do little to tackle these problems because of the internal power struggle in the capital. The Soviet Union tried to get all the 'Marxist–Leninist' movements on both sides of the Red Sea (Ethiopia, Somalia, South Yemen and the EPLF in Eritrea) to form a confederation but failed due to the (mistaken) belief by the Eritreans and the Somali-backed WSLF that they were close to victory. The Soviet Union was also unsuccessful in persuading Somalia to refrain from invading the Ogaden (Harar province) in 1977. Soviet indecision on whether to give full support to Ethiopia was ended when Siad Barre of Somalia repudiated this Treaty of Friendship and Co-operation with the Soviet Union in November 1977. All Soviet technicians and advisers were expelled from Somalia, and immediately the Soviet Union began a massive airlift of supplies to Ethiopia (Ottaway, 1982, p. 116). Since then, total Soviet aid to Ethiopia is estimated at more than $3 billion. Up to 16,000 Cuban troops assisted in the defeat of the Somalis and WSLF in the Ogaden (Harar province). Somalia withdrew from Ethiopia in March 1978, and the Ethiopians then proceeded to reinstate their authority over most of Eritrea. The circle was completed when Brzezinski, President Carter's adviser, declaring that 'SALT [Strategic Arms Limitation Talks between Washington and Moscow] lies buried in the sands of the Ogaden', advocated strong US support for Somalia, and military and economic aid began to trickle into Somalia. Berbera became an American base in 1980, an ideal node in the network of Indian Ocean and Persian Gulf installations set up after the Iran crisis of 1978–9. US support for Somalia is still reduced somewhat by the American insistence that the military equipment should not be used to attack Somalia's neighbours and by pressure on Siad Barre to reduce support for the WSLF and to stop continued Somali incursions into the Ogaden.

Since 1978, events in the Horn and the adjoining north-east African states have emphasized the continued fluidity of the situation. Sudan, strongly allied to Egypt, has complained that Libya and Ethiopia are trying to promote a split in Sudan based on the north–south, Moslem–animist division. It seems clear that both Ethiopia and Sudan are trying to encourage separatism in each other's territory. Both countries harbour refugees from the other's secessionist regions. Border skirmishes between Ethiopian and Somali troops, together with their various allies, persist. In 1981, Ethiopia formed a pact with South Yemen and Libya, the source of its oil supplies.

The past two decades of great-power involvement in the Horn have established consistent behaviour of the four powers directly involved. First, the exchange of military and economic aid for military bases has been the basis of the relationships between the two local and two global powers. Second, both Somalia and Ethiopia actively encouraged outside involvement in their regional disputes. Both superpowers were more than willing to respond. Third, Somalia is clearly the consolation prize in the fight for regional influence. The Soviet Union from 1963 to 1977 and the United States from 1977 on looked to Somalia to balance the other superpower's efforts in Ethiopia. Given the huge difference in population size (Ethiopia has 32 million and Somalia only 4 million) and the long history of Ethiopian geopolitical importance in the Horn/Arabian Peninusla region, it is not surprising that both superpowers should consider Ethiopia the greater prize. Fourth, both local powers have managed quite successfully to maintain their independence from superpower pressure. By making overtures to Moscow, Haile Selassie consistently pressured the US into greater generosity. Siad Barre, by joining the Arab League, succeeded in avoiding excessive dependence on Soviet supplies. Ethiopia has expelled Soviet diplomats for inter-fering in domestic Ethiopian politics and has refused to allow the Soviet Navy better facilities in Eritrea. Somalia has placed the Americans in a quandary by insisting on a domestic policy of 'scientific socialism' and maintaining its aggres-sion toward Djibouti, Kenya and Ethiopia without support from any other African state. It must be concluded that 'the great powers considered them [Ethiopia and Somalia] important enough to provide but not important enough to make a major effort to force them to comply when reluctant to do so' (Ottaway, 1982, p. 167). Finally, the Horn has become one of a score of regional (border) conflicts in Africa and the Arc of Crisis in which the superpowers have accelerated their involvement in the second cold war. Although the exact location and chronology of events are unique to the Horn, the pattern of aid for bases and influence has been repeated in other tension zones as part of evolving superpower geostrategies. We clearly need a general model of international relations that would help us to understand the complexity of dyadic super–local power links, superpower aims in diverse geographic locales and the expected future behaviour of the actors based on historical trends and evolving geostrategies.

THE SOVIET UNION IN AFGHANISTAN

Numerous American commentators have pointed to the Soviet invasion of Afghanistan as the beginning of the second cold war. More accurately, the

Afghan invasion should be viewed as the death-knell of detente between the superpowers since the second cold war had already begun with the failure of the US Senate to ratify the Salt II agreement on nuclear weapons. Whatever its timing with respect to the breakdown in Soviet–American relations, the Afghan invasion has become a rallying cry for anti-Soviet feeling through the Moslem and western worlds. Views on the invasion range widely. Indira Gandhi, then Prime Minister of India, described it as a defensive, rather than offensive, move motivated by Soviet fears of the loyalty of its own Moslem population, comprising 25 per cent of the USSR total. In this view, unrest in Afghanistan, fermented by fundamentalist Moslem leaders, might spread across the border into Soviet Central Asia to the Moslem population. The other extreme is represented by many in the west, including a French foreign-policy analyst who wrote that 'the Soviet invasion of Afghanistan is the most serious and dangerous demonstration of Soviet Marxist imperialism since the end of the Second World War' (de Riencourt, 1983, p. 437). To a large extent, one's analysis of the invasion depends on whether one has a deductive model of Soviet foreign policy (Halliday, 1983). President Reagan, as quoted at the beginning of this chapter, expresses the theory that Soviet foreign policy is essentially expansionist. This deductive approach leads one to an interpretation of all Soviet actions in this framework. The accuracy of this view must be tested by a close examination of the chronology of Soviet–Afghan relations and internal Afghan politics before the invasion.

Until the events of 1978–9, Afghanistan was far removed from the centre of western foreign policy (Poulluda, 1981). Beginning in the 1950s, this landlocked mountainous state with 90 per cent illiteracy developed a close military and economic dependence upon the Soviet Union. US aid and interest in Afghanistan was minimal, focusing instead on Afghanistan's two large Moslem neighbours, Iran to the west and Pakistan to the south. Apart from its shared border with the Soviet Union, Afghanistan seemed to be insignificant in the post-war hegemonic world-view of the Americans. The Soviet Union was Afghanistan's main trading partner and, as long as the government and society remained near-feudal and non-communist, the west was content to ignore the Soviet influence. In Afghanistan, the PDPA (People's Democratic Party of Afghanistan) grew out of a small underground urban communist movement and throughout the 1960s and 1970s had been on the verge of power in Kabul. In 1973 Mohammed Daoud, as leader of a PDPA faction, became president, and by 1974 he had formed an unsigned alliance with the Shah of Iran. The Shah was intent on exerting influence on his weaker Moslem neighbour as part of a strategy to establish Iran as the regional power in the eastern half of the Arc of Crisis. Savak, the Shah's secret police, operated openly in Afghanistan, and Iranian military and economic aid flowed in. In April 1978, the PDPA staged a successful *coup* under eventual Prime Minister Hafizullah Amin; Nur Mohammed Taraki was installed as president. Some have seen Soviet involvement in the *coup* but, according to one newspaper account, it was the Shah and not the Kremlin who precipitated the *coup* by urging Daoud to purge the PDPA from Afghanistan (Harrison, 1979). The new regime asked the USSR for increased aid, partly to replace Iranian aid. Soviet concern over events in Afghanistan mounted as the PDPA was unable to achieve stability in Kabul or extend its rule over the countryside.

By early 1979, it was clear that Amin and Taraki were alienating rather than gaining support. In a strongly fundamentalist Moslem state, the regime tried to introduce state control of a traditionally tribal way of life. Within the PDPA, factional fights made a difficult situation worse and there is no doubt that throughout 1979 the USSR was active behind the scenes in trying to promote a strong and stable regime in Kabul. By December 1979 the situation of the Amin regime became untenable as the Moslem counter-revolution in the countryside went from strength to strength, with backing from Pakistan and post-Shah Iran. Amin invited the Soviet troops into Afghanistan to help Afghan troops repel the counter-revolution, but within a few hours he was dead and Babrak Karmal, leader of an anti-Amin PDPA faction, was installed in power. The presence of over 100,000 Soviet troops seemed to galvanize the mujahaddin, and with widespread defections from the Afghan army, support from Pakistan, Iran and the US, an ideal terrain for guerilla war and general popular support, they have waged a generally successful war against the Soviet troops and the Karmal regime. In late 1984, the Kabul government controlled only a few major cities and routeways and its yearly spring offensive against the guerillas was reduced to nothing by the autumn retreat to Kabul and environs. After more than five years of war, the military and political situation in Afghanistan has hardly changed from that of December 1979, despite periodic Soviet pushes and the improved organization and equipment of the factionalized mujahaddin (*Economist*, 8 January 1983; 14 July 1984).

This description of events in Afghanistan would suggest that the Soviet Union did not control events but, until spring 1979, reacted to internal changes in Kabul. A comparison of the Afghan events with those in Ethiopia described earlier indicates two similarities and two differences. Neither the regime in Addis Ababa nor that in Kabul managed to generate popular support. Both looked to outside powers for assistance in maintaining their position, to the US in the case of Haile Selassie and to the USSR in the case of Amin. The revolutionary movement was centred initially in urban areas, but whereas the Ethiopian revolution managed to gain the support of the mass of the rural poor, the Afghan regime failed and found itself under pressure from a relentless counter-revolution. The Soviet Union, invited in by both revolutionary regimes, found itself welcomed by the Ethiopian population and attacked by the Afghans. Assuming Soviet intelligence was fully aware of the unpopularity of the Amin regime, the question remains, Why did the Soviet Union send troops into Afghanistan in December 1979, risking world-wide opprobrium (only 18 states supported the USSR in the UN General Assembly vote which followed), the total collapse of detente, a revitalized anti-Soviet feeling throughout the Moslem world, possible defections from the Red Army by Soviet Moslems and the prospect of an unending and ultimately unsuccessful guerrila war?

From Tass reports and a Leonid Brezhnev interview with *Pravda* (*Beijing Review*, 17 January 1983; Medvedev, 1980), the official Soviet explanation of the Afghan invasion consists of three points. First, in accordance with the Soviet-Afghan Treaty of Friendship and Co-operation signed earlier, the USSR sent troops at the request of the Afghan government. Second, the Afghan government requested the troops because the Amin regime was in a critical state as a result of the successes of the counter-revolutionaries: the Afghan army simply could not cope. Third, the counter-revolution in Afghanistan is supported by the US, China and Pakistan and, in line with Soviet principles, the USSR will support progressive forces against counter-revolutionaries. While this justification adequately describes surface reality, it does not explain the motivation for such an enormous commitment, nor does it explain how and why Amin, who invited the Soviets, was removed within hours. It is clear that the USSR wavered for a year before it eventually acted in December 1979. It faced a Hobson's choice – either withdraw all civilian and military personnel, resulting in the replacement of Amin by a fundamentalist Moslem regime hostile to the USSR, or plunge in with troops and a permanent commitment to control events in Kabul. The latter was chosen as the lesser of two evils (Medvedev, 1980).

Two views, the defensive reaction and the aggressive geostrategic, on the Soviet invasion of Afghanistan were outlined earlier. Clearly, it is impossible to estimate precisely to what extent either view is accurate. Some western analysts think that events in Afghanistan made possible the Czarist dream of a warm-water port on the Indian Ocean. The south-western province of Pakistan, Baluchistan, has seen periodic attempts at secession and some strategists believe Soviet encouragement of this separatist movement will bring dividends in the form of a pro-Soviet state on the Indian Ocean. 'The eventual prize is remarkably attractive; a 200-mile coastline along the Indian Ocean, naval and air bases at Gwadar, Pasni and Ormara, from which Soviet fleets could operate at the mouth of the Gulf and linking up with their existing bases in Aden, Socotra and Ethiopia at the entrance to the Red Sea – in effect, the Soviets would have the potential to interdict entrance or exits from both the Gulf and the Red Sea' (de Riencourt, 1983, p. 433). In this general view, which at its most liberal sees the Soviet Union taking advantages of geopolitical opportunities, events in Afghanistan provided an ideal pretext for Soviet expansion to the south and for pressure on Iran from a second side. The USSR is perceived as possessing a grand design to impose its will on post-Khomeni Iran and events in Afghanistan and Baluchistan are simply the first act of the larger south-west Asian drama.

For the defensive-reaction school, Soviet actions were rendered essential by the rapid deterioration in Kabul after the April 1978 coup. Just as the Soviet Union interfered militarily in Hungary in 1956 and Czechoslovakia in 1968, and politically in Poland in 1981–2 to retain a pro-Moscow communist party in power, so it installed Karmal in Kabul. In each case, the country involved bordered on the Soviet homeland. In a corollary of this model, if pro-Soviet governments in other parts of the world were overthrown, the Soviet Union would not interfere militarily, either because it chose not to, the threat being far removed, or because of a lack of military capability, in the face of western opposition or the tyranny of distance. The demise of generally pro-Moscow governments in Mali (1968), Ghana (1966), Zanzibar (1963), Iran (1953), Guatemala (1954), Chile (1973), Grenada (1983) and of pro-Soviet movements in Iraq (1978), Sudan (1971) and Oman (1975), to the accompaniment of Soviet inaction, lends credence to this view. The Soviet Union, adhering firmly to a principle of a *cordon sanitaire* of states on its frontiers, will plunge if the perceived costs of inaction are greater than the costs of military action. In this respect, Soviet geopolicy has not changed much since the 1940s. Close parallels exist with American policy in the Central American isthmus, to which we now turn.

CENTRAL AMERICA: AMERICA'S AFGHANISTAN

Before he even took office, President Reagan signalled to the world that he viewed Central and Latin America as a special geopolitical challenge. The 1980 Republican Party platform condemned the 'Marxist Sandinista takeover of Nicaragua and the Marxist attempts to destabilize El Salvador, Guatemala and Honduras'. As the new US ambassador to the United nations, Jeane Kirkpatrick, said, 'Central America is the most important place in the world for the United States today.' In dozens of speeches, Reagan and his top policy-makers attempted to emphasize the proximity of the Central American isthmus to the US, referring to the region as 'our backyard' or stating that San Salvador is closer to San Diego and Houston than either American city is to Washington, DC. Every new American president of the twentieth century had started his term with an initial strong interest in Latin America, but Reagan seemed to go beyond this historic commitment. In speech and in action, he made it plain that Central America was a special case for American foreign policy; that the new cold war would be fought out in El Salvador and Nicaragua, without directly involving American troops; that the Soviet Union and its surrogates, Cuba and Nicaragua, were responsible for the unrest in the region; that military, rather than economic, solutions must be found to the region's problems; that the Carter administration had erred grievously in its withdrawal of support for Somoza, the Nicaraguan dictator, and in its cool relations with pro-American right-wing regimes in Chile, Argentina, Brazil, Guatemala, Honduras and Paraguay; and that domestic American public opinion would be convinced of the seriousness of his commitment to restoring American dominance, after the malaise of the Carter years, by recreating the 1920s American hegemony in Latin America (Feinberg, 1982; Pearce, 1982; Black, 1982; Lafeber, 1984).

Apologists for US imperialism in Latin America point to the Monroe Doctrine of 1823 as the guiding document and historical–legal justification for their position, though why a statement that any interference by an outside power in Latin America would be viewed as 'the manifestation of an unfriendly disposition toward the United States' should gain near-biblical reverence is not clear. By 1900, the expanding economic imperialism of the United States had swelled south across the international border in search of new markets, resources, investments and opportunities (Hoffman, 1982). European, particularly British and German, interests were swamped. US military force was used over 135 times between 1823 and 1983 (Congressional Record, 1969, quoted in Conway, 1984) to ensure quiescence in the region, including Cuba in 1898, Puerto Rico 1901, Honduras 1905, Cuba 1906–9, Panama 1908, Nicaragua 1909, Honduras 1910, Panama 1912, Cuba 1912, Honduras and Nicaragua 1912, Haiti 1914–34, Dominican Republic 1916–24, Cuba 1917–23, Panama 1918, Honduras 1919, Nicaragua 1916–33, Honduras 1924, Dominican Republic 1965 and Grenada 1983. In addition to these direct military actions, the United States was active in undermining reformist or leftist governments such as Arbenz in Guatemala in 1954 and Allende in Chile in 1973.

In the 1930s the so-called 'Good Neighbor' policy of Franklin Roosevelt became the US strategy in place of the military option, with a shift to using US economic power to provide the support system necessary for capitalism to develop in the undeveloped economies of the hemisphere. The Alliance of Progress 1961 continued this 'liberal' notion of promoting economic progress but unexpectedly mild economic progress 'weakened the system by raising both the expectations of the masses and the wealth and power of the oligarchs. Revolutionary groups multiplied, the United States responded with increased military commitments' (Lafeber, 1984, p. 24). By responding to these movements with military force, the US has precipitated further violence. In each term, the new president, starting with a 'good neighbour' policy and reform ideals, reacted with surprise and then anger at their failure and eventually came round to unilateral use of force and boycott to re-establish American dominance. Carter was the latest of this line of erstwhile reformists.

Central America (Honduras, El Salvador, Nicaragua and Guatemala) became the focus of Reagan's 'aggressive globalism' in Latin America. The situation is complex but basically unchanged from the beginning of Reagan's term in 1981. Nine battlefronts, including both civil and clandestine interstate wars, have American involvement to a greater or lesser extent (*Economist*, 29 October 1983). In Guatemala, a right-wing military regime faced small, though growing, opposition with pockets of the country controlled by left-wing guerillas with significant Indian support. Because of the human rights provisions attached by liberals in Congress to American military aid, Guatemala has not been able to receive open American aid since 1977. El Salvador experienced a massive civil war since 1979, with three sets of actors. The extreme right, strongly entrenched in the upper class, the army and the National Guard and led by Major Roberto d'Aubisson, was supported by 46 per cent of the voters in the May 1984 presidential election. Their only support in the US came from the Republican right-wing led by Senator Jesse Helms of North Carolina. The Reagan administration, following in Carter's steps, supported the titular head of state, President Napoleon Jose Duarte, the centrist candidate, pressured by both left and right. His power base was suspect, the moderates having been eliminated or forced to choose between left and right in the civil war. Duarte managed to obtain a large increase in US economic and military aid, now up to $200 million in 1984, and made tentative steps toward land reform, though without any real success. His goal is to establish himself so that he does not fall victim once again to a right-wing *coup*, as he did in 1972. The left-wing guerillas control one-third of El Salvador's provinces and strike at will everywhere. Without strong American support for the government, the guerillas would have repeated the 1979 Sandinista success in Nicaragua. Civil war looks like a long-term probability in El Salvador.

In Honduras, over 2,000 American troops remained after the well-publicized joint military operations with Honduran forces in 1982 and 1983. Honduras, with a right-wing strongly pro-American government and no organized opposition, became the central staging ground for American military efforts in the whole region as well as the base for the most important Contra (anti-Sandinista) group, National Democratic front, mostly comprised of Somozan ex-supporters. Nicaragua became the biggest thorn in America's foot. There in 1979, the Sandinista guerillas, after winning the support of the majority of the population, replaced Somoza, whose father had been installed by the Americans in the 1930s. The Carter administration adopted a generally passive stance and sent some economic aid to war-torn Nicaragua. The European socialists were particularly supportive of the Sandinistas in the 1979–81 period through aid and political support in the Socialist International. Reagan, immediately upon taking office, withdrew all American aid and proceeded to help organize and arm the anti-Sandinistas, now mostly in Honduras. Faced with an outside threat and economic sabotage at home, the Sandinistan government became more repressive and began to lose European and American liberal support. By 1982, former members of the Sandinista junta had left and formed a second Contra front in Costa Rica, alleging that the junta had sabotaged the revolution by adopting a strong Marxist–Leninist line with close ties to Cuba (Cruz, 1983). The Sandinistas then managed to win back much of their outside support by holding open elections in November 1984, curtailing their support for El Salvador's guerillas, and maintaining a mixed economy and an uncensored press; world opinion shifted against the Reagan administration as it stepped up its efforts to destabilize the Sandinista government.

Within the United States and the western community in general, two dominant and one subordinate interpretations are used to analyse the Central American conflicts. The conservative or Reaganite stand, as exemplified by the report of the (Kissinger) National Bipartisan Commission on Central America (1983) and recent Reagan administration official statements, has become more sophisticated than the earlier anti-Soviet statements (Toal, 1984): 'We can and must help Central America. It's in our national interest to do so,' and 'if we do nothing or if we continue to provide too little help, our choice will be a communist Central America with additional communist military bases on the mainland of this hemisphere and communist subversion spreading southward and northward. . . . There is a way to avoid these risks. It requires long-term American support for democratic development, economic and security assistance and strong-willed diplomacy' (Ronald Reagan, 9 May 1984). Current US policy sees the Soviet Union and its ally, Cuba, like thiefs in a hotel corridor, checking doors to see if one is unlocked and then stealing from the room (Halliday, 1982). The administration claims that economic underdevelopment presents the opportunity for Soviet exploitation of the resentment against local elites and American interests. To remove this economic cause of the conflict, the administration proposed spending $8 billion over five years in the region and continued strong military aid to governments in El Salvador and Honduras and covert support for the Contras (or 'freedom-fighters,' as Reagan prefers) in Nicaragua.

The liberal view, shared by European socialists and liberal Democrats in the US Congress, sees conflicts in the Third World as locally generated, resulting from indigenous social and economic causes. Further, they believe that bringing the east–west competition to the Third World, as the Carter and Reagan administrations have done, will hurt agreement on other issues such as nuclear arms control, and reflects an effort by the US to restore its hegemony, particularly in Central America (Mujah-Leon, 1984). As a US foreign policy, the liberals wish to implement a true 'good neighbour' policy with acceptance of Latin American political independence, granting of significant economic development aid and ready access to US markets, diplomatic negotiation to end current conflicts, and encouragement of leftist regimes to move towards the centre through economic subsidy. The difficulty that the liberal approach faces is that 'reformism' had died in Central America by 1982 (Fagen and Pellica, 1983) and the only choices remaining are essentially right or left. It is not clear to what extent the liberal viewpoint is supported in the US. A consistent majority of the electorate does not want American troops committed to the conflict in Central America, but President Reagan has also generated a majority in support of his analysis of the causes and solutions of the conflict.

The Marxist views are varied but generally based on an economic interpretation of American involvement in Central America. The 'political economy of late imperial America' is in decline, so that an 'ultra-imperialist military and economic order' around the globe is threatened by the kinds of political and economic forces described earlier in the chapter. American economic interests in Central America and the Caribbean are substantial (Barry, Wood and Preusch, 1983) but direct US investment in the area is only 2 per cent of the Latin American total, so a simple equation of economic interest and military intervention is not accurate. The large foreign-policy bureaucracy in the US responds to the 'national interest', which is some combination of strategic, political and economic interests (Krasner, 1978). While in general this establishment works to protect and promote American economic interests, the individual policy-makers are motivated to act in a particular fashion by mainly non-economic realities such as balance-of-power strategy, geopolitical rationales and historical and ideological commitments; as seen earlier, they are controlled by, as much as they control, events in the Third World.

As phrased by the *Economist*, the Reagan administration faces three choices in Central America; flinge, plunge or stick. Withdrawal (flinge) is unlikely given the political commitment of the Reagan administration to prevent the Nicaraguan revolution from spreading and to take an aggressive stand against the Sandinistas. Plunging, or sending in American troops, is unlikely given the undoubted political damage this would cause at home. Reagan has repeatedly denied having any plans to commit American troops but the widespread public approval of the Grenadian invasion of October 1983 suggests that Americans would support a quick and successful strike. The implausibility of this kind of operation in Nicaragua probably precludes an American invasion. The third option, sticking, is most likely, continuing current commitments at a higher level to American friends in the region. El Salvador received about $200 million in military aid in 1984, and if the Kissinger Commission recommendations are implemented the country will receive over $1 billion in economic aid in the next five years. The only regional peace effort, that of the Contadora Group (Mexico, Venezuela, Panama and Colombia), is stalled as the Sandinists and the Reagan administration cannot agree on even the negotiating principles. The dual recommendations by America's European allies that El Salvador's government be forced to negotiate with the guerillas and that the Reagan administration accept the continued presence of the Sandinistas in Nicaragua has received a cool reception in Washington. Peace in Central America looks as remote as ever.

The constant use of the term 'geopolitical relationship' by the Reagan administration to describe the connection of the United States to Central America has propelled the geographic element in foreign policy to national attention. Reagan has projected an 'aggressive confrontationism' with the USSR in American foreign policy. Central America is literally the front line in the confrontation. For practical and analytical purposes it matters little if Soviet and Cuban involvement in the region is much less than the administration asserts. In this instance, regional geostrategy responds to image, a part of a global picture. Reagan not only wants stability in Central America on America's terms but he wishes to reassert American hegemony by denying the legitimacy of claims for social reform, an economic redistribution and a growing independence from American economic dominance. The combination of the north–south and east–west global political and economic divisions is nowhere more clearly illustrated than in the US/Central American conflicts.

CONCLUSIONS

Four conclusions seemed warranted on the basis of this wide-ranging review of international conflicts. It is clear that a purely American, Soviet or Third World perspective lacks the objectivity that is so desperately needed in international politics. There is enough blame for causing present and previous conflicts to be spread around all the participants, both local and non-local. Leaders in Third World states, anxious to defeat external enemies or score internal political victories, blithely invite the superpowers to help achieve success and draw their state on to the front line of global competition. It would not be going too far to say that they make themselves pawns on the chessboard of hegemonic struggles.

The first major conclusion of this chapter relates to the declining hegemony of the United States. Economic and military evidence abounds of the US's declining share of the world's capacity. Even the Reagan administration accepts that this trend was characteristic of the late 1960s and 1970s. They see it as a challenge to which they must respond. This aggressive position places the challengers, the Soviet Union politically and the western and non-western capitalist nations economically, in an unattractive position, with little option except to respond in turn. The United States political establishment seems unable to adjust to the realities of the late-twentieth-century globe, with the growing diversity of the Third World and the increasing numbers of power centres, especially on the economic front. Locked in a 1940s cold-war mentality, the United States in the early 1980s cannot accommodate the new economic demands of newly industrializing countries. The US 'should pay more attention to Brazil, Mexico, and Venezuela than to Cuba, Nicaragua, and Grenada' (Lowenthal, 1983, p. 333).

The second conclusion concerns the argument that both superpowers are waging 'gangster diplomacy' (Barnet, 1984a). As we have seen in three case-studies, the superpowers are willingly dragged into local disputes. Though not initiating the disputes, they exacerbate the problem through wholesale commitment to one local actor. 'Yet while each self-styled peace-loving country permits itself anything that it can get away with, each holds its ideological enemy to the strictest ethical standards' (p. 53). Still more worrisome is the evidence that even in times of detente, such as the 1969–79 decade, the superpowers continued to compete aggressively in the arena outside their immediate spheres of influence. The future looks as bleak in this regard as the period since decolonialization has been.

Although this chapter has focused on political competition and conflict, that is the east–west dimension in world politics, the north–south conflict looms as the most destabilizing element in world affairs. Despite pleas from international bodies (Brandt Commission, 1980) and from two-thirds of the world's nations for a new arrangement of economic power, including immediate access to western markets, there has been no progress toward reducing global inequities. In advanced capitalist nations, demands for trade barriers to restrict imports of cheaper products from non-western nations are growing rapidly. The current global debt crisis has concentrated the world's attention on the fragility of the global economy and the threat posed to western capitalism by widespread defaults. While this debt crisis can be resolved, or at least postponed, the structural causes of the crisis remain untackled. The Soviet Union sees this crisis as essentially one caused by capitalism and itself as an interested by-stander, but there is little doubt that world-economic crisis would affect even the socialist economies of eastern Europe. An international conference, involving east, west and south nations, to arrange a new economic and financial system along the lines of the Bretton Woods Conference of 1944, is desperately needed.

The final conclusion of this chapter is more a proselytizing message to the geographic community. The renaissance in political geography over the past decade in Anglo-Saxon nations has left the traditional interest of the discipline, geopolitics, by the wayside. John House (1984) has recently shown the way for political geographers to engage in regional analysis of global conflicts. Regional conflicts are numerous, complex, growing and interwoven with events elsewhere in the world. Continued neglect of those conflicts, the major research interest of the field, places the whole renaissance of political geography in jeopardy. This chapter is only a small step in the long march of political geography to a respected position in the social sciences.

References

Abate, Y. 1978: Africa's troubled Horn: background to conflict. *Focus*, 28, 1–16.

Agnew, J. A. 1983: An excess of 'national exceptionalism': towards a new political geography of American foreign policy. *Political Geography Quarterly*, 2, 151–66.

Alker, H. R., Jr 1981: Dialectical foundations of global disparities. *International Studies Quarterly*, 25, 69–98.

Alker, H. R., Jr and Biersteker, T. J., 1984: The dialectics of world order: notes for a future archeologist of international savoir faire. *International Studies Quarterly*, 28, 121–42.

Ambrose, S. E. 1983: *Rise to Globalism: American Foreign Policy, 1938–1980*, 2nd rev. edn. New York: Penguin.

Barnet, R. J. 1971: *The Roots of War*. Harmondsworth: Penguin.

Barnet, R. J. 1980: *The Lean Years: Politics in the Age of Scarcity*. Washington DC: Institute for Policy Studies.

Barnet, R. J. 1984a: Beyond gangster diplomacy. *Mother Jones*, February–March, 53–5.

Barnet, R. J. 1984b: Why trust the Soviets? *World Policy Journal*, 1, 461–82.

Barry, T., Wood, B. and Preusch, D., 1983: *Dollars and Dictators: A Guide to Central America*, 2nd edn. New York: Grove.

Black, G. 1982: Central America: crisis in the backyard. *New Left Review*, 135, 5–34.

Blatch, G. S. 1982: Im Horn von Afrika ist die Zukunft nie gewiss: Anmerkungen zur Ogaden-Frage. *Beiträge zur Konfliktforschung*, 12, 69–90.

Bradsher, H. S. 1983: *Afghanistan and the Soviet Union*: Durham, N.C.: Duke University Press.

Brandt Commission 1980: *North–South: A Program for Survival*. Cambridge, Mass.: MIT Press.

Brock, L. 1982: World power intervention and conflict potentials in the Third World. *Bulletin of Peace Proposals*, 13, 335–42.

Chaliand, G. and Rageau, J.-P., 1983: *Atlas stratégique: Géopolitique des rapports de forces dans le monde*. Paris: Fayard.

Chase-Dunn, C. 1981: Interstate system and capitalist world-economy: one logic or two? *International Studies Quarterly*, 25, 19–42.

Chase-Dunn, C. and Sokolovsky, J. 1983: Interstate systems, world-empires and the capitalist world-economy: a response to Thompson. *International Studies Quarterly*, 27, 357–67.

Church, F. 1984: It's time we learned to live with Third World revolutions. *Washington Post Weekly Edition*, 26 March, 21.

Cline, R. S. 1980: *World Power Trends and U.S. Foreign Policy for the 1980s*. Boulder, Colorado: Westview.

Cockburn, A. 1983: *The Threat: Inside the Soviet Military Machine*. New York: Random House.

Cohen, S. B. 1982: A new map of global geopolitical equilibrium: a developmental approach. *Political Geography Quarterly*, 1, 223–42.

Conway, D. 1984: Grenada–United States relations: Part I: 1979–1983, prelude to invasion. *USFI Reports*, 39, 1–9.

Cruz, A. J. 1983: Nicaragua's imperilled revolution. *Foreign Affairs*, 61, 1031–47.

Davis, M. 1984: The political economy of late imperial America. *New Left Review*, 143, 6–38.

Dawisha, K. and Dawisha, A. (eds) 1982: *USSR and the Middle East: Policies and Perspectives*. New York: Holmes & Meier.

Dickey, C. 1984: Central America: from quagmire to cauldron. *Foreign Affairs*, 62, 659–94.

Doran, C. F. and Parsons, W. 1980: War and the cycle of relative power. *American Political Science Review*, 74, 947–65.

Edwards, A. 1979: *The New Industrial Countries and their Impact on Western Manufacturing*. London: Economist Intelligence Unit.

Fagen, R. R. and Pellica, O. 1983: *The Future of Central America: Policy Choices for the U.S. and Mexico*. Palo Alto: Stanford University Press.

Feinberg, R. E. (ed.) 1982: *Central Amercia: International Dimensions of the Crisis*. New York: Holmes & Meier.

Frank, A. G. 1981: *Reflections on the World Economic Crisis*. New York: Monthly Review Press.

Gaddis, J. L. 1982: *Strategies of Containment: A Critical Appraisal of Postwar American National Security Policy*. New York: Oxford University Press.

Gavshon, A. 1981: *Crisis in Africa: Battleground of East and West*. Harmondsworth: Penguin.

Gilpin, R. 1981: *War and Change in the International System*. New York: Cambridge University Press.

Gray, C. S. 1977: *The Geopolitics of the Nuclear Era*. New York: Crane Russek.

Halliday, F. 1982: *Soviet Policy in the Arc of Crisis*. Washington DC: Institute for Policy Studies.

Halliday, F. 1983: *The Making of the Second Cold War*. London: Verso.

Halliday, F. and Molyneux, M. 1981: *The Ethiopian Revolution*. London: Verso.

Harris, N. 1982: *Of Bread and Guns*. Harmondsworth: Penguin.

Harrison, S. 1979: The Shah, not Kremlin, touched off Afghan coup. *Washington Post*, 13 May, p. C1.

Hoffman, G. W. 1982: Nineteenth-century roots of American world power relations. *Political Geography Quarterly*, 1, 279–92.

House, J. 1984: War, peace and conflict resolution: towards an Indian Ocean model. *Transactions, Institute of British Geographers*, N.S. 9, 3–21.

Howard, M. 1983: *The Causes of War*. Cambridge, Mass.: Harvard University Press.

Keal, P. 1983: Contemporary understanding about spheres of influence. *Review of International Studies*, 9, 155–72.

Kissinger, H. 1984: *National Bipartisan Commission on Central America Report*. Washington DC: Government Printing Office.

Klare, M. T. 1981: *Beyond the Vietnam Syndrome: U.S. Interventionism in the 1980s*. Washington DC: Institute for Policy Studies.

Krasner, S. 1978: *Defending the National Interest*. Princeton: Princeton University Press.

Kristof, L. K. D. 1960: The origins and evolution of geopolitics. *Journal of Conflict Resolution*, 4, 632–45.

Kurth, J. R. 1982: The United States and Central America: hegemony in historical and comparative perspective. In R. E. Feinberg (ed.), *Central America: International Dimensions of the Crisis*, New York: Holmes & Meier, 39–57.

Lafeber, W. 1984: The Reagan administration and revolutions in Central America. *Political Science Quarterly*, 99, 1–26.

Lowenthal, A. E. 1983: Ronald Reagan and Latin America: coping with hegemony in decline. In K. A. Oye, R. J. Lieber and D. Rothchild (eds), *Eagle Defiant: United States Foreign Policy in the 1980s*, Boston: Little Brown, 311–35.

Mahan, A. 1980: *The Influence of Sea Power upon History, 1660–1783*. New York: Hill & Wang.

Manning, R. 1983: Superpowers as suppliers. *South*, August, 14.

Medvedev, R. 1980: The Afghan crisis. *New Left Review*, 121, 91–6.

Modelski, G. 1978: The long cycle of global politics and the nation-state. *Comparative Studies in Society and History*, 20, 214–35.

Modelski, G. 1983: Long cycles of world leadership. In W. R. Thompson (ed.), *Contending Approaches to World System Analysis*, Beverly Hills: Sage, 115–39.

Mujah-Leon, E. 1984: European Socialism and the crisis in Central America. *Orbis*, 20, 53–82.

Ottaway, M. 1982: *Soviet and American Influence in the Horn of Africa*. New York: Praeger.

Oye, K. A. 1983: International systems structure and American foreign policy. In K. A. Oye, R. J. Lieber and D. Rothchild (eds), *Eagle Defiant: United States Foreign Policy in the 1980s*, Boston: Little Brown, 3–32.

Oye, K. A., Lieber, R. J., and Rothchild, D. 1983: *Eagle Defiant: United States Foreign Policy in the 1980s*. Boston: Little Brown.

Parboni, R. 1981: *The Dollar and its Rivals: Recession, Inflation and International Finance*. London: Verso.

Pearce, J. 1982: *Under the Eagle: U.S. Intervention in Central America and the Caribbean*. Boston: South End.

Poulluda, L. B. 1981: Afghanistan and the United States: the crucial years. *Middle East Journal*, 35, 178–90.

de Riencourt, A. 1983: India and Pakistan in the shadow of Afghanistan. *Foreign Affairs*, 61, 416–37.

Rothchild, D. and Ravenhill, J. 1983: From Carter to Reagan: the global perspective on Africa becomes ascendant. In K. A. Oye, R. J. Lieber and D. Rothchild (eds), *Eagle Defiant: United States Foreign Policy in the 1980s*, Boston: Little Brown, 337–65.

Senghaas, D. 1983: The cycles of war and peace. *Bulletin of Peace Proposals*, 14, 119–24.

Shaw, T. M. 1983: The future of the great powers in Africa: toward a political economy of intervention. *Journal of Modern African Studies*, 21, 555–86.

Singer, J. D. 1981: Accounting for international war: the state of the discipline. *Journal of Peace Research*, 18, 1–18.

SIPRI 1983: *Yearbook 1983*. Stockholm: Stockholm International Peace Research Institute.

Thompson, W. R. 1982: U.S. policy toward Africa: at America's service. *Orbis*, 25, 1011–24.

Thompson, W. R. 1983a: Cycles, capabilities, and war: an ecumenical view. In W. R. Thompson (ed.), *Contending Approaches to World System Analysis*, Beverly Hills: Sage, 141–63.

Thompson, W. R. (ed.) 1983b: *Contending Approaches to World System Analysis*. Beverly Hills: Sage.

Thompson, W. R. 1983c: The world-economy, the long cycle, and the question of world-system time. In P. McGowan and C. W. Kegley Jr (eds), *Foreign Policy and the Modern World-System*, Beverly Hills: Sage, 35–62.

Thompson, W. R. 1983d: Uneven economic growth, systemic challenges, and global wars. *International Studies Quarterly*, 27, 341–55.

Thompson, W. R. 1983e: World wars, global wars, and the Cool-Hand-Luke syndrome: a reply to Chase-Dunn and Sokolovsky. *International Studies Quarterly*, 27, 369–79.

Toal, G. 1984: Exploring the nature and form of contemporary geopolitics: a case study of the U.S. and El Salvador. Paper for Master's Degree, University of Illinois, Department of Geography.

Wallerstein, I. 1983: *Historical Capitalism*. London: Verso.

Wiberg, H. 1979: The Horn of Africa. *Journal of Peace Research*, 16, 189–96.

Wolfe, A. 1979: *The Rise and Fall of the 'Soviet Threat': Domestic Sources of the Cold War Consensus*. Washington DC: Institute for Policy Studies.

Yapp, M. 1982: Soviet relations with the countries of the Northern tier. In K. Dawisha and A. Dawisha (eds), *USSR and the Middle East: Policies and Perspectives*, New York: Holmes & Meier, 24–44.

11

The World-Systems Project

PETER J. TAYLOR

'That's another fine mess you've got me into,' says Oliver Hardy to Stan Laurel again and again. Although an unlikely analogy, modern capitalism does seem to display a level of competence on a par with Stan Laurel. The world is in a mess once again. And yet modern capitalism would seem to be better run than ever before. Business schools are turning out the best-ever trained managers, while university economics and commerce departments are providing financial advisers with the best-ever technical models. Furthermore, governments employ more social scientists than ever before to provide the best-ever advice on economic, political and social issues. And yet the world is in a mess. It seems that all these modern experts have Laurel's incompetence without his endearing innocence. For, to make matters worse, it is not a matter of the world being accident-prone. The current situation is not an unfortunate random event. The mess is cyclical. Whereas Laurel and Hardy were a product and symbol of the last mess, this time Hollywood has come up with a president. And it's no longer a joke. In the nuclear age the question of who has the last laugh is macabre.

The most obvious lesson of the current situation is that we need a rethink in politics and in academia. And this is of course happening. Cycles of growth and stagnation on a global scale are of practical and academic concern throughout the world. For instance, in 1978 two books appeared on precisely this topic. W. W. Rostow's *The World Economy: History and Prospect* introduces long cycles into his familiar non-communist manifesto of economic stages, and V. V. Rymalov's *The World Capitalist Economy: Structural Changes, Trends and Problems* brings cycles and trends back to the centre of official communist thinking. How far these two books represent a rethink is of course disputable. Despite their intellectual elegance they don't fool anyone – they are bringing the cold war in academia up to date. Most 'western' academics deplore this political intrusion and choose instead to remain in their ivory tower, which separates them from the politics. But this is the route that leads to just the sort of 'neutral' technical knowledge that produced the Stan Laurel 'experts' of the recent past. If we really only had to choose between a pseudo-neutrality or cold-war mentality the future would be bleak indeed. In this chapter I hope to show that there is another way.

A rethink does not, of course, mean making a completely new start. Past ideas, concepts and theories may be used but only after they are understood in the context in which they were produced. All theories are the products of their time and place, and their need for revision or rejection varies accordingly. The world-system project centring on the work of Immanuel Wallerstein is a product of the current world recession. It is a reaction to the optimistic social sciences of the early post-war era especially in their predictions for 'Third World' countries 'catching up'. They got it wrong, horrendously so. They must be replaced. I will argue that their replacement should look something like the world-systems project.

This project has been a highly controversial production assailed on all sides. Most criticism has been the result of misunderstanding of the nature and purpose of the project. I will show that it is actually more controversial, that is more dangerous to existing ideas, than even its critics realize. They say that it is not history; they say that it is not social-scientific; they say that it is not Marxist; and, the most cardinal of all sins, they say it is not objective. I agree, it is not all of these and more, at least on their terms. That is what makes the project so interesting and why liberals and Marxists, historians and social scientists have all misunderstood it. On each of their criteria it is inadequate; but that is not surprising, since it is built on new combinations of criteria. It is, in the real sense of the word, an alternative.

THE MODERN WORLD-SYSTEM

The core of Wallerstein's project is a set of four volumes in which he is attempting nothing less than a description of the dynamic capitalist world-economy from its inception in about 1500 through to the present day. Only the first two volumes have been published so far (Wallerstein, 1974a, 1980a) but the overall framework has been presented (Wallerstein, 1974b). The story Wallerstein is telling goes as follows. A capitalist world-economy emerged out of the crisis of feudalism based on agricultural production in the 'long' sixteenth century (volume I). This world-system is consolidated in the stagnant seventeenth century to 1750 (volume II). In the late eighteenth and nineteenth centuries the world-system expands again as industrial capitalism to cover the whole world (volume III). The crisis of capitalism begins in the twentieth century (from 1917) so that we are currently living through a transition from capitalism to, possibly, socialism (volume IV). What Wallerstein is talking about therefore is the rise and fall of an entity he calls the capitalist world-economy. This entity maintains certain characteristics through its different phases. First, there is a world market for commodities. Second, there is a competitive state system so that no one political unit can control that market. Third, there is an economic hierarchy of spaces from core through semi-periphery to periphery. Fourth, there are economic classes and social status groups which interact with one another and with the spatial hierarchy. Fifth, the dynamics of the entity are cyclic in terms of long economic waves. Sixth, there are secular trends in the system which are asymptotic, such as the geographical spread of the entity. Wallerstein uses a massive quantity of secondary historical sources to weave together the story of his world-system in terms of these basic characteristics.

As the above suggests, this 'empirical core' of the project is not divorced from 'world-systems theory'. A holistic structuralism transcending history and the individual social sciences is proclaimed in the above works. This is explicitly treated by Wallerstein (1976 and in many other papers brought together as *The Capitalist World-Economy*, 1979; and, with others, in *World-Systems Analysis* – Hopkins and Wallerstein, 1982). Other empirical 'examples', and theoretical issues are to be found in the quarterly journal *Review* and the series *Political Economy of the World-System Annals*, both edited by Wallerstein. There are numerous other books related to the project, notably Bergeson (1980), Chase-Dunn (1982), and Amin et al. (1982). Most importantly Wallerstein (1983a) brings together his main ideas in a short and very readable essay, and his political essays have been collected as *The Politics of the World-Economy* (1984a). This covers most of the literature which makes up the project but unfortunately its quantity and quality has not prevented misunderstanding. My main purpose in this chapter is to dispel some of this misunderstanding.

Wallerstein's work has been used by others in one of two ways. First, it can be seen as an alternative temporal framework for describing the evolution of the modern world. Some economic historians have treated it this way but the main group here are the international-relations researchers. Wallerstein's 'world-systems theory' is described as one of three approaches (Hollist and Rosenau, 1981) or even as part of 'the menu of choice' (Russett and Starr, 1981). Thompson (1983), for example, explicitly compares it with Modelski's (1978) alternative temporal framework on the assumption that they are equivalents, that is 'contending approaches'. Wallerstein does, of course, provide a temporal framework for empirical studies, but to treat his work as only that is to miss the whole point of the project. Second, other social scientists, especially sociologists, have emphasized the 'theory' in the project. Wallerstein provides an alternative to the Parsonian equilibrium system and one which moreover seems to be necessary for transcending comparative sociology. World classes, world status-groups and even the replacement of sociology (about social formations) by globology (about global formations) can be found here (Bergeson, 1980). One aim is to develop the theory to produce 'falsifiable predictions' (Chase-Dunn, 1983). These studies also miss the point of the project. Wallerstein is not trying to create a better and more 'accurate' sociology (or even globology).

What is the point of the world-systems project therefore? Briefly, Wallerstein's purpose is to contribute to the transition from capitalism to something more humane and democratic which we may wish to call socialism. The empirical and historical framework of the world-systems theory is only part of the project in so far as it provides tools to that end. People may wish to use the framework for other purposes but they are not then contributing to the project. Hence Wallerstein's work is probably bad economic history, bad international relations and bad sociology as conceived by the practitioners of those disciplines. The test of his work lies elsewhere, however. It leads to alternative modes of theorizing and ultimately to new methodologies. In fact, Wallerstein (1983b, p. 306) has gone as far as suggesting that 'the crucial terrain of struggle may well turn out to be that of methodology.' In the remainder of this chapter I will attempt further to elucidate the project's purpose as another attempt 'to turn the world upside down'.

'TRUTH AS OPIUM'

Wallerstein (1983b), perhaps surprisingly, refers to the historiography he is creating in the four-volume core of the project as a myth. This is not self-criticism since he considers all history as the creation of myths. What Wallerstein claims is that he is providing an alternative organizing myth to that which has dominated history since the nineteenth century. Organizing myths are important because they incorporate as virtually unexamined assumptions the nature of the *present*. The dominant organizing myth that Wallerstein is attempting to replace, for instance, may be termed the progressive myth, since it produces a historiography of conflicts between 'pre-modern' and 'modern' forces which delineates a path from traditional feudalism to our modern affluent society. Obviously the progress organizing myth celebrates the achievements of present. For Wallerstein it fails utterly to explain historical regression, and this is central to the world-system project. We deal with this important topic separately in some detail below. The key point here is that since recounting the past is always a social act of the present (Wallerstein, 1974a, p. 8) – it cannot logically be otherwise – all history must be merely 'transitory' knowledge.

The progress organizing myth is more than a matter of history, of course. In academia the task of building, illustrating and proving the myth has been divided between two groups. The particularists, mainly historians, beavered away at filling in the details, while the generalists, who eventually became known as social scientists, attempted to provide the models and theories of how progress came about. For Wallerstein, since both groups operated within the same overall myth, the 'grand debate' of ideographic versus nomothetic knowledge is beside the point (Wallerstein, 1976). History and social science are one subject-matter, which he terms *historical social science*. Quite simply all historical descriptions of particular events must use concepts that imply 'generalizations about recurrent phenomena', while all social-science theories must be ultimately 'a set of inductions from history' (Wallerstein, 1979, p. ix). The separation of social science from history has enabled the progress organizing myth of history to be transformed into assertions of universal generalizations. Whereas historians have retreated from the Victorian view that cumulation of enough facts will eventually lead to 'ultimate history' (Carr, 1961), positivist social scientists have maintained the idea that further refinements of their theories will eventually unmask reality and produce the truth. But if all history is a myth and social science is history then all social science is myth. We have now reached the very heart of Wallerstein's position.

Modern science is based on a belief that nature and society can be described by universal statements and it is the task of science to search for such generalizations. This is an epistemology which proclaims a faith in 'truth' as a *real* phenomenon, the goal of science. As such it has become self-evident that truth is a disinterested virtue for which we must strive. But if all history is transitory, a product of the fleeting present, and all social science is history, it follows that 'truth' changes as society changes. Truth is a variable not an absolute. 'Absolute truth' has, therefore, an ideological role. It is a cultural idea which has operated as the opiate of the modern world (Wallerstein, 1983a, p. 81). Traditional societies and their myths have been vanquished by our truth. It is this arrogant 'modernization' which has produced a rationality upon which economic efficiency can be developed. As such the rationality of scientific activity has been able to hide the ultimate irrationality of endless capital accumulation (p. 85). It has socialized the cadres who operate the world-economy into a recognizable common stratum just below the apex of the social hierarchy. Their role in the world division of labour has been vital as the emphasis on meritocracy through education reinforces the hierarchical structure. Universalism, therefore, has been nothing less than 'the keystone of the ideological arch' of capitalism (p. 81).

If truth is transitory so too must be our theories and organizing myths in historical social science. They will depend on our particular window on the past and the lenses through which we view. Where does all this leave the basic concept of the objectivity of scientist and scholar? To begin with we can note that every choice of conceptual framework is a political one. There is no such thing as an uncommitted historian or social scientist. This is because all assertions of truth are based on assumptions which ultimately involve a metaphysics of values. The 'disengaged' scientist or scholar who claims objectivity by remaining in his ivory tower is merely drawing up the ramparts to hide his or her premises. This does not mean that there can be no objectivity, however. The first step towards objectivity is to admit commitment. It is the lack of this basic honesty which makes conventional objectivity such a sham. The current production of knowledge, for instance, represents a social investment which reflects the current structure of power. Objective knowledge on the other hand will only be produced when all major groups in the world-system are equitably represented. Since knowledge can never be produced separately from the society that brings it forth it follows that at present we can only aim for a more balanced creation within our given society. This is a route towards a collective notion of objectivity which we can all work along (Wallerstein, 1974a, pp. 9–10).

Let us return to the politics. Not only does Wallerstein bridge the gap between history and social science but it obviously follows from the above argument that historical social science cannot be meaningfully separated from politics. Wallerstein (p. 9) distinguishes between scientist/scholar and apologist/advocate. Both are committed but they have different roles within their chosen framework. It is the duty of the scientist/scholar to describe and interpret the present in the light of the past in order to aid in the construction of the future. Although the work may seem at times to be quite esoteric it is all 'relevant' in that its *raison d'être* can only be application. The choice of organizing myth, the filling in of the particulars or the development of more general notions, will all be part of a larger social movement. The testing of the ideas will ultimately be in political practice: does this particular organization of knowledge generate ideas which can usefully contribute to our manipulation of reality. Or as Wallerstein (1983b, p. 307) puts it: 'as we become more political we become more scientific; as we become more scientific we become more political'. Scientists and scholars are part of political practice, they must theorize it so that it can be constructively criticized and improved. This is what the world-systems project is trying to do for what is generally termed 'socialism'. The products are heuristic theories and since 'truth' is merely 'an interpretation meaningful for our times' (Wallerstein, 1979, p. xii) they must be essentially transitory.

Finally, how do we produce these heuristic theories? What is this methodology which Wallerstein feels may be so crucial? If we return to his organizing myth we find that we are provided with a single entity, the capitalist world-economy, which is by definition unique. This is fundamental to the question of methodology. O'Brien (1982), for instance, has tried to show how unimportant the periphery was to the economic development of Europe in the period covered by Wallerstein's (1974a, 1980a) first two historical volumes. But as Wallerstein (1983d, p. 550) replies, 'How much is a lot? That is the question,' for the fact is that western Europe did not develop in isolation. It was part of a wider system and it did benefit from that membership. We cannot construct an experiment rerunning European history without the Atlantic, Baltic and Indian trade. We can never know what would have happened. Experimental design and comparative statistical methodology are just not an option. Let us make this clear: quantitative techniques may be useful as descriptive devices if harnessed to meaningful categories, but the notion of testing empirical data to produce general theory is simply meaningless in this context. Although they are intimately intertwined, it is the *methods* and not the *techniques* which are the crux of the matter.

Current methodology involves moving from the complexity of empirical description to generate general statements about that reality. The implication of heuristic theorizing is to reverse the order. We start with general statements of the operation of the complex entity we call the world-economy and then observe their conjunction in specific events or groups of events until we can produce a set of 'utilizable concrete descriptions of historical structures' (Wallerstein, 1983b, p. 307). But what are these structures? The entity we are dealing with is not the ahistorical system of modern sociology with its equilibrium structures, but a much less familiar dissipative structure where disequilibrium is the normal state of affairs. Order is not a final outcome of the system but is a constantly changing pattern as initial conditions and new conditions continually interact in the evolving totality. Wallerstein (1983c, p. 33) talks of 'this scientific–metaphysical–ideological transition' which will be linked to political practice but of which we know little as yet; he quotes Prigogine: 'We are only in the beginning at the prehistory of our insights' (p. 36).

THE SPIRIT OF MARX

Although liberal scientists and scholars will find the previous discussion quite distasteful, Marxists will find much of it familiar. The connection of theory with political practice is, of course, central to Marx's own work. In short, Wallerstein's epistemology is not basically different from that of Marx. They are both part of a tradition of scholars who have challenged the universalism of the social sciences. Wallerstein's departure from orthodox Marxism relates, therefore, to the new historiography he is creating. For Wallerstein, Marxists and other radical critics of liberal theory have made 'a fundamental error of judgement' because 'by surrendering the historiographical domain, they undermined fatally their resistance in the epistemological realm' (1984a, p. 180). In fact, Wallerstein (1983b, p. 302) describes the dominant organizing myth in such a way that *both* liberals and Marxists can identify with the historical sequence: Marx's conception of history is a progressive one. The distinctive terminology – the succession of modes of production – cannot hide the fact that orthodox Marxists hold the same basic progress organizing myth as their liberal opponents: 'For Rostow's stages, substitute Stalin's' (Wallerstein, 1984a, p. 181). Since Wallerstein provides an alternative organizing myth it is not surprising that he has been criticized as much by Marxists as by liberals.

Whether we consider Wallerstein to be a Marxist is itself not a particularly important question since it merely rests upon definitions of Marxism. Wallerstein (1974a, p. 396) talks of following the 'spirit of Marx if not the letter'. I think the position is best summed up by Lefebvre:

> To attack this person or that, and to say that this one is a Marxist and that one isn't, seems to me bad methodology, a bad line of thought. The correct line of thought is to situate the works and the theoretical or political propositions within the global movement of the transformation of the modern world. (1980, p. 23)

Marx must be seen as 'a man of the nineteenth century, whose vision was inevitably circumscribed by that reality' (Wallerstein, 1983a, p. 9). His great legacy must not be left to 'dead Marxists' (controlled by nineteenth-century texts or twentieth-century governments) but must be seen as part of 'a much vaster global movement' (Lefebvre, 1980, p. 22), a living movement incorporating a 'living Marxism'. Wallerstein terms this movement the anti-systemic movement of the world-economy which has historically included two components: socialist challenge initially concentrated in the core and nationalist challenge in the periphery. The former has been the traditional arena of Marxism but in the post-war era the two have come to be merged in the national liberation struggles of the periphery. It is in the interpretation of the nature of the periphery and its political struggles that Wallerstein's project differs most from more orthodox Marxist interpretations. This theoretical debate is known as 'the modes of production controversy' (Foster-Carter, 1978) and its relevance for the political practice of the anti-systemic movement is fundamental.

For Marx a mode of production is defined by the forces and relations of production. From this it follows that a capitalist mode of production exists when the means of production are appropriated by the dominant class leaving the dominated class only their labour power to sell to the highest bidder. Hence the existence of 'free' labour is the key requirement for identifying capitalism. If this definition is applied strictly in the contemporary world we find that 'capitalism' has yet to reach many parts of the periphery. Hence other 'pre-capitalist' modes of production must exist alongside capitalism. Much modern Marxist theory (e.g. Taylor, 1979) has been about the 'articulation' that occurs between these contemporary modes of production. Basically it is agreed that, as long as the reproduction requirements of two modes of production are compatible, they may exist side by side and may in fact reinforce one another.

If modes of production 'interact' it follows that there must be some 'entity' larger than the individual modes themselves. Here the terminology varies. For Laclau (1971) different modes of production can exist together within a single 'economic system', for Rey the articulation occurs within a particular 'social formation' (Brewer, 1980). In both cases mode of production is treated as an abstract concept and the containing entity is a concrete occurrence of the modes. Sfia (1983), on the other hand, identifies two 'modes of disposition': a non-market mode based on a dominance of use values and a market mode based on a dominance of exchange values. In this scheme the modern world has several modes of production but there presently exists only one mode of disposition, the market one. But the market means the domination of capital so that this mode of disposition integrates capitalist and non-capitalist spaces into one entity, the 'world system' whose logic is capitalist.

Clearly Sfia's approach seems to be closest to Wallerstein's, but mode of disposition, economic system or social formation are all equally distinct from the world-economy of the world-system project. Wallerstein (1976, p. 348) uses a much broader definition of mode of production: 'the way in which decisions are made about dividing up productive tasks, about quantities of goods to be produced and labour time to be invested, about quantities of goods to be consumed or accumulated, about the distribution of the goods produced'. Hence he breaks from 'the sterile assertion of the analytical priority of relations of production over those of exchange and indeed all else' (Foster-Carter, 1978, p. 76). Wallerstein defines the capitalist mode of production as 'one in which production is for exchange, that is, it is determined by its profitability on a market' (1976, p. 351) or 'production for sale in a market in which the object is to realize the maximum profit' (1974b, p. 13). Perhaps under pressure of criticism from Marxists, Wallerstein has more recently expressed his definition differently – 'The primary desideratum, the defining characteristic, of a capitalist system, is the drive for ceaseless accumulation' (1983b, p. 15) and 'endless accumulation of capital' is the 'economic objective' (1983a, p. 18). This alternative notion of capitalism, focusing on 'ceaseless accumulation' rather than 'free labour', has been, of course, a major concern of orthodox Marxists in their criticism of Wallerstein. Before we discuss this debate however we need to consider the more general historical implications of Wallerstein's broader concept of mode of production.

The primary reason for identifying modes of production for both orthodox Marxists and Wallerstein is to challenge the universalism of social thought within capitalism: the social institutions and individual motivations found in capitalism have not existed from time immemorial. But if the past was not 'naturally' capitalist, how then should it be conceptualized? Enter modes of production to classify past societies and so link the modes-of-production controversy to the historiographical realm. Marx himself proposed a progression of modes with the following sequence: primitive communism – classical slave – feudal – capitalist – socialist (Peet, 1980). In addition Marx also refers to an Asiatic mode of production outside the European sequence. This notion of alternative sequences outside Europe has been developed as a set of multilinear sequences (Peet, 1980). In contrast Wallerstein, using his broader definition of mode of production identifies only three historical modes of production: a reciprocal-lineage mode which roughly coincides with primitive communism; a redistributive-tributary mode which incorporates all the various categories between primitive communism and capitalism; and finally the capitalist mode, which currently covers the whole world as the capitalist world-economy. Only two class societies are identified, those based on political control, which are termed world-empires, and those based on markets, termed world-economies. Hence classical, feudal and Asiatic systems are all interpreted as identical modes of *production* with merely alternative political superstructures. Marx's identification of an Asiatic mode is then seen as based on inadequate sources and Eurocentrism: 'Since Asian societies were not like those of Ancient Greece or Rome or feudal Europe, they must constitute something else. The very geographical characterization of the category indicates its residual nature' (Chandra, 1981, p. 18). Although Marx used the term 'Asiatic mode of production' only once (p. 17), the idea of a distinct 'timeless' Asia was important for his subsequent identification of British colonialism in India as being 'progressive'. It is doubtful whether this interpretation remains useful.

Similar specific modes of production continue to be generated. For instance, colonial and African modes of production have been proposed as modern concepts for describing India and parts of Africa respectively (Foster-Carter, 1978; Cooper, 1981). But as Cooper (1981, p. 14) states, 'If every way of catching an antelope or growing a banana defines a mode of production, the concept blends into an empiricism that Marxists scorn.' Foster-Carter (1978, p. 74) makes exactly the same point but feels that Wallerstein's solution of just three historical modes is 'an extreme way of resolving' the modes-of-production controversy. Extreme, yes, but surely preferable to a devaluing of the concept by multiplication. The test of Wallerstein's parsimony is in the fresh insights it provides.

THE SMITHIAN TWIST

Let us return to the question of defining the particular mode of production known as capitalism, since this reaches to the very heart of Marxist criticisms of Wallerstein. If Wallerstein is not to be a Marxist then some other label derived from a lesser, and preferably non-revolutionary, intellectual figure seems to be required. Aronowitz (1981, p. 520) finds this task difficult but nevertheless purports to detect 'the spirit of Weber' in Wallerstein. The main derogatory label attached to Wallerstein, however, is that he is a 'neo-Smithian', that is his emphasis on the market rather than production makes him closer to Adam Smith than to Karl Marx. It is not our task here to get into labelling games (beyond suggesting Wallerstein is a Wallersteinian!) but there is a tangle of ideas that requires unknotting. Some of the criticism is based on simple misunderstanding of Wallerstein's work, some relates to ambiguities and even changes of emphasis in his work (Agnew, 1982), and part of the problem is that the two most compelling criticisms where the Smithian label is justified (Aronwitz, 1981; Brenner, 1977) review only the first volume of *Modern World System*. We will make use of some of Wallerstein's more recent writings to challenge these criticisms.

We can begin by describing Wallerstein's position on the labour question. 'Capitalism thus means labour as a commodity to be sure. But wage labour is only one of the modes in which labour is recruited and recompensed in the labour market' (Wallerstein, 1974b, p. 17). Hence labour may be used and controlled in different ways in different parts of the capitalist world-economy but this does not indicate different modes of production. In fact one of the characteristics of the world-economy throughout its history is for more free labour to exist in the core with various forms of unfree labour occurring in the periphery. There are different forms of labour control suitable for the different circumstances in different zones of the world-economy. American slavery, the 'serfs' of eastern Europe, industrial proletarians and peasant households are all examples of direct producers in the capitalist world-economy. For Wallerstein 'capitalist world-economy' and 'capitalist mode of production' are just two ways of saying the same thing.

At first sight this new schema seems to be merely an alternative set of terms – 'much of the debate over modes of production has been about the use of words and no more' (Brewer, 1980, p. 273). Instead of economic system or social formation over different modes of production we have a single mode of production imposed over different forms of labour control. But is much more than a semantic point. Brenner (1977) emphasizes the unique characteristic of the capitalist mode of production as defined by Marx in its generation of new technologies. Hence in order to understand the dynamics of our modern world we must deal with relations of production which produce the economic change upon which the whole system pivots. Emphasis on the world-level therefore misses the vital processes of production which are unique to capitalism. It is at this point that Brenner dismisses Wallerstein's definition of the capitalist mode of production as neo-Smithian rather than Marxist. In a similar vein Aronowitz (1981, p. 520) states that 'What Wallerstein has given us is a theory of the forms of appearance of capitalism. The core of the system remains unseen.' Brewer (1980, p. 181) goes even further: 'What is lacking is real theory.'

Essentially Wallerstein provides two forms of defence against the criticism. First, he provides a reinterpretation of the relations between the ideas of Smith, Marx and Weber. Second, he locates his own work as a product of the late twentieth century which has more heuristic value than past 'truths', however eminent the purveyors of those truths. These two defences are very closely related but we will disentangle them and present them consecutively.

With Arrighi and Hopkins, Wallerstein has sketched out his ideas on classes and status groups from a world-systems perspective (Arrighi et al., 1983). They begin by defining the political economy paradigm as initiated by Adam Smith. Two particular assumptions are highlighted: classes are defined in terms of their relation to the market, and society is assumed to be coterminous with the state. Marx's critique of this political economy overturns both of these assumptions involving two basic shifts – from the market place to the work place and from state-defined economic spaces to world-economic space. However, Wallerstein and his colleagues note that in his studies of current events Marx did 'retreat into political economy' (p. 291) by dealing with state-defined economic spaces. This may be acceptable for concrete studies for short-term purposes. Similarly the increasing importance of the state at the beginning of the twentieth century required similar concrete analyses to highlight state-defined economic spaces. But this cannot be extended to *theoretical* revisions of the monopoly capital/imperialism variety, especially when developed as stages of capitalism. By identifying stages as occurring in state-defined economic spaces the Leninist position represents 'the theoretical retreat of Marxists back into political economy' (p. 291). In short, it is the orthodox Marxists who are the neo-Smithians! And so our task now is to break out of this old political economy straitjacket once again so as to understand features such as imperialism as cyclical properties of the world-economy as a whole (Wallerstein, 1980d). This point is also important for defining class. Weber's concepts of classes *an sich* and *für sich* are used, but again Wallerstein breaks away from their simple application to particular political communities and states. For Wallerstein class *an sich* can only be defined at the level of production processes which in his scheme are organized at the world scale. The problem for socialism is that classes *für sich* have been created at the national level. This is one of the basic antinomies of capitalism (Wallerstein, 1984a, p. 36) but one which is lost in political economy. Hence the need to abandon political economy and return to Marx's critique of that paradigm. Wallerstein's historical social science is not another political economy – it is a replacement of political economy.

The emphasis on state-defined spaces from the Second International to the present day has had enormous practical significance. Concepts such as the permanent revolution (skipping stages) and making alliances with 'progressive' bourgeois forces against 'feudal' forces in peripheral countries all fall before this definition of classes and hence of transition (or revolution) as world-scale processes. Such political-economy concepts may have had important roles in their time but they are no longer adequate – in fact they are quite dangerous – if applied to current political situations. Of course, like political economy in its various formulations, Wallerstein's historical social science is a product of its time. It is an attempt to review and revise anti-systemic thought to make it relevant to the period of declining US hegemony in the world-economy. Wallerstein does not deny the importance of production for defining capitalism. His pre-industrial-revolution capitalism is not the 'mercantile capitalism' of many Marxist writers but a fully fledged agricultural capitalism based on agro-industrial production, for instance. But Wallerstein does not limit the key processes of change to one particular social relation within this production system. The bourgeois–proletarian relation is integrated with a core–periphery relation to produce world classes, as we have seen. In doing this Wallerstein's critics believe that he over-looks or at least devalues the fundamental process of change within capitalism. The key word here is 'believe'. The issue of the importance of 'core' or 'periphery' in the development of the modern world-system is untestable, as we have previously pointed out. What we have are alternative organizing myths producing their very different 'metahistories' (Wallerstein, 1983c). Aronowitz (1981) comes close to recognizing this when he describes his critique as 'metatheoretical'. Hence the clash between Wallerstein and his Marxist critics is one of 'opposing faiths' (Wallerstein, 1983a, p. 20). Wallerstein's (1983e, p. 24) second defence is thus quite pragmatic:

> The justification therefore for our metahistory comes neither from the data it generates nor from the null hypotheses it supports nor from the analyses it provokes. Its justification derives from its ability to respond comprehensively to the existing continuing real social puzzles that people encounter and of which they have become conscious. It is, in fact, precisely the reality of the ever-increasing historical disparities of development that has called into question the old organizing myths . . . and which has been pushing world scholarship to the construction of an alternative metahistory.

Ultimately, therefore, Wallerstein is asserting that his world-systems project will produce better heuristic theory to interpret the past, to understand the present and to guide future practice.

We can glimpse what Wallerstein is getting at with such grand assertions by showing how the 'theoretical disappearance' of pre-capitalist modes of production in the periphery provides fresh insights. Defining pre-capitalist modes of production in the modern world has never been an easy task, as Cooper (1981, p. 14), a critic of Wallerstein, admits. This is because of the problem of coming 'to grips with the evident domination of capitalism in a situation where the essence of capitalism, the alienation of means of production and wage labour, is only sometimes relevant' (p. 16). In the world-system project this problem just does not exist. In fact by avoiding identifying capitalism with the existence of proletarian labour new and more interesting problems emerge. If wage labour is so advantageous to capital, 'what is surprising is not that there has been so much proletarianization, but that there has been so little' (Wallerstein, 1983b, p. 23). After centuries of capitalism, probably less than half the world's labour are proletarian. Why? This is not, of course, due to any resistance of pre-capitalist modes of production but because non-proletarian households are integral and fundamental elements of the capitalist world-economy. At all times in the history of the world-economy a large proportion of the world's labour force have lived in 'semi-proletarian households' where wage labour and subsistence labour are combined. These households are particularly advantageous for capital since it does not have to shoulder the main costs of reproduction. Hence the minimum acceptance wage threshold is that much lower. It is not surprising, therefore, that 'one of the major forces behind proletarianization has been the world's work forces themselves' (Wallerstein, 1983a, p. 36). Wallerstein (1984b) has only recently been developing the implication of these ideas. In the world-systems project the increase in proletarianization in the core and elsewhere has always been matched by incorporations of semi-proletarian households from external or internal zones. It is ultimately tied up with cycles of growth and stagnation of the world-economy (Wallerstein, 1984c) and the secular asymptote of proletarianization approaching its limit as the 'compensatory' semi-proletarian households are 'used up'. This brings us to the dynamics of crisis in the world-systems project and perhaps its most revolutionary aspects.

BLASPHEMY ON PROGRESS

Let us return again to the concept of progress and the historiographical domain. As will be clear by now, this is where the world-system project's challenge to orthodox Marxism is most fundamental:

> The Marxist embrace of an evolutionary model of progress has been an enormous trap. . . . It is simply not true that capitalism as an historical system has represented progress over the various previous historical systems that it destroyed or transformed. Even as I write this, I feel the tremor that accompanies the sense of blasphemy. (Wallerstein, 1983a, p. 98)

It depends of course upon how we measure progress. Wallerstein complains that our measures are all inevitably one-sided – progress is measured in terms laid down by capitalist logic which produces emphasis on technical achievement. Well, capitalism is best at accumulating capital, of course, but that is beside the point. Any socialist project should measure progress in terms of equality and democracy, not capital. Wallerstein is not arguing for some earlier 'golden age' of democracy or equality – there was precious little of either in any world-empires – but he is resurrecting the largely discarded Marxist thesis – the *absolute* immiseration of the world's population. Despite the technological achievements of capitalism and the resulting immense accumulation of capital, polarization of rewards has made most people less well off. Although modern politics has achieved some redistribution among the top 10 to 15 per cent of the world's population, for the rest incorporation into the capitalist world-economy has meant providing more labour per annum for less reward. Capitalism is not and never has been progressive, either in early modern England, in India under the British, in Latin America today, or anywhere else.

The organizing myth of the world-system is a non-progress myth, as we have seen. What, in concrete terms, does this mean? To begin with there was no bourgeois revolution. In the progress myth traditional landowners have their power undermined by urban merchant capital and are eventually overthrown by the new progressive dominant class, the bourgeoisie. In the non-progress myth the great landowning families of feudal Europe are slowly transformed into a different sort of dominant class in the long sixteenth century. The crisis of feudalism incorporated ecological, political and economic problems which the dominant class were finding very difficult to handle. Shortage of labour and interclass conflict seemed to be producing a more equal society – perhaps an evolving pattern of small agricultural landowners. But between 1450 and 1650 a transition occurred. Two things stand out: 'the trend towards egalitarianization of reward had been drastically reversed' and there was 'a reasonably high level of continuity between families' in the dominant class (Wallerstein, 1983a, p. 42). Hence, 'far from the bourgeoisie having overthrown the aristocracy, we have instead the aristocracy becoming the bourgeoisie' (Wallerstein, 1983e, p. 22). The new system was never progressive; in fact it arose precisely to prevent progress!

If we accept this conception of history it makes us radically reconsider the classical notion of the transition to socialism. Our view on the latter has been inevitably coloured by the notion of a bourgeois revolution. But if there was no bourgeois revolution, what does this mean for the proletarians, the heirs of bourgeois progressiveness? It means that we have to rethink our theory of revolution, and as we look around us at the states that are products of that theory such a rethink does not seem to be such a bad thing after all.

The anti-systemic movements that have evolved since the nineteenth century are themselves products of the capitalist world-economy. Their theories and ideas, their ideologies and practice, are derivative of capitalism. It could be no other way. Despite the explicit internationalism of socialist rhetoric the political arena in which most anti-systemic political activity has taken place is the state. This state-centred politics is a strategy set in the nineteenth century but one which continues to dominate us today. It is responsible for the tragic element in the story of socialism – the continuous roll-call of traitors, revisionists of all colours and hues. 'Betrayers' have defeated 'pure' socialists time and time again in the realm of practical politics. That obviously suggests that this is more than the weakness or motivation of individual socialists, it is a structural effect of the world-economy itself (Wallerstein, 1983a, p. 69). By taking state power, socialists have to play by the rules of world capitalist games. They may promote important reforms, but these will be easily accommodated and may even strengthen the world-economy. Revolutionary governments have to organize to survive. In Wallerstein's scheme nationalizing the means of production does not make a fundamental change in the nature of the society. Countries where this has occurred remain part of the capitalist world-economy. In practice their main preoccupation has been the traditional mercantilist concern for 'catching up'. The resulting regimes have become an embarrassment to the world anti-systemic movement; they are the albatross we have to bear in any serious discussion of Marxism today (Wallerstein, 1982b, p. 298). As Wallerstein plaintively asks:

> Can survival in state power be, after a certain point, counterproductive – that is counterproductive for revolutionary objectives? To be honest I hesitate to put forward such a heretical notion. . . . But is it not the case that sometimes – not at every moment or in every place – the retention of state power holds greater risks? Must the leadership of popular forces in socialist states be handed over to the ideologues of the traditional right? (p. 298)

Quite simply the anti-systemic movement cannot be bound by the institutions created by capitalism. The seizing and holding of state power must return to being a tactic not a goal for which everything is sacrificed. After all the current socialist states are only products of our current system; they in no way indicate the nature of the transition to socialism.

Wallerstein (1980b, p. 179) has announced that 'we are living in the historic world transition from capitalism to socialism,' although he adds the rider, 'of course the outcome is not inevitable.' What he means by this statement is that the *crisis* of capitalism has begun. He dates this from 1917 when the Russian revolution confirmed for all to see that the historic system of capitalism was not eternal (1982b, p. 31). This must be distinguished from the current stagnation of the world-economy which is merely a cyclic expression of the operation of the system. The world economy can survive a down-turn, it cannot survive its crisis. Paradoxically this reflects the 'success' of the system using up its options as the secular asymptotic processes grind ceaselessly on (1980b). Hence for Wallerstein the future is not about capitalism versus socialism, for the former is a spent force. The question is What follows the capitalist world-economy?

Wallerstein's (1976) use of the phrase 'socialist world government' to describe his preferred successor mode of production has been misunderstood. Any movement towards a more equal and democratic system must involve control of the market, hence Wallerstein's use of the word 'government'. But this is not 'some sort of super Gosplan under the eye of a super-Brezhnev,' as critics seem to fear (Tylecote and Lonsdale-Brown, 1982, p. 283). In fact we are in no better a position to predict the outcome of the crisis of capitalism than a king or peasant could predict capitalism from the crisis they found themselves in about 1450. As Wallerstein (1982a, p. 51) is only too willing to concede, 'I believe history reserves its surprises.'

Nevertheless, we can begin to make intelligent use of historical experience. This does not mean a resurrection of the bourgeois-revolution myth; rather it requires us to consider a non-progressive interpretation of transition. Here Wallerstein (1983a and c) uses Samir Amin's notion of two types of transition: controlled transition as between successive Chinese world-empires and distintegration as between the classical Roman system and its successors. In the former the ruling strata maintain their position, in the latter they are replaced. The new organizing myth reinterprets the transition from feudalism to capitalism from disintegration to controlled transition. Both options are available today. The transition from capitalism may be controlled to produce a new hierarchical system, perhaps under the guise of socialist rhetoric. Alternatively, capitalism may truly disintegrate and a new more equitable and democratic system may take its place. It is the role of the anti-systemic movement to ensure disintegration to a truly classless society and not to succumb to the temptations of further co-option along the road to a new class society beyond capitalism. This is why the anti-systemic movement must separate itself from the constraints of state-centred politics to construct some form of trans-state organization (Wallerstein, 1982b, pp. 48–9). The search for such structures is part of the world-systems project.

THE GEOGRAPHICAL PERSPECTIVE

For Wallerstein (1983b, p. 304) the current division of intellectual labour in social inquiry is absurd and ambiguous, and this is a position he has stated clearly on several occasions (e.g. introductions to Wallerstein, 1974a and 1979). Hence his 'exasperated' response, as Thompson (1983, p. 21) calls it, to the debate about whether Wallerstein's scheme over-emphasizes economic factors or Modelski's scheme over-emphasizes political factors. In Wallerstein's holistic framework such a debate 'largely misses the point of the world-systems perspective' (Wallerstein, 1983b, p. 299).

Hence to talk of two 'logics', a political one and an economic one, is meaningless. More generally he states: 'I do not believe that the various recognized social sciences – in alphabetical order, anthropology, economics, geography, political science and sociology – are separate disciplines, that is, coherent bodies of subject matter organized around separate levels of generalization or separate meaningful units of analysis' (1979, p. ix). There is just one discipline of social inquiry, 'historical social science', which stands alongside other coherent disciplines such as psychology and biology. Of course in all of these disciplines the subject-matter is vast, so that 'it might be convenient to subdivide it for heuristic or organizational purposes, though not for epistemological or theoretical purposes' (p. ix). I read this to mean that since the 'totality' cannot be empirically handled in every inquiry we must devise 'perspectives' on the system as a whole which will guide selection of material. These perspectives will be defined heuristically and will be discarded as the system changes: they are tactical decisions not intellectual ones. I will consider the geographical perspective in this light.

Wallerstein (1983b, p. 300) states that there is no such thing as 'geography', but this does not preclude the development of a geographical perspective whose purpose is not to produce 'geographic theory' but to inform the world-systems project. Clearly this means that we must drop the idea of geography as a modern social science (Cox, 1976) but we can point out that this tendency within 'geography' is only fairly recent anyway (Taylor, 1985). Whereas the other social sciences reflect the tendency towards specialization in social inquiry, this was resisted in geography until the middle of this century. Instead geography maintained a holistic philosophy inherited from the first half of the nineteenth century. Hence geography belonged to that small group of social inquiries which maintained the 'grand' traditions of theorizing which predate modern social science. The most famous was, of course, the *Annales* School from which the world-systems theory, in part, derives (Wallerstein, 1977). It is not surprising, therefore, that some of the basic research tasks on Wallerstein's (1983e) agenda are closely related to aspects of traditional (that is pre-social-science) geography.

Geography developed as an empirical project to describe the content of the earth's surface. This essentially descriptive purpose was shared in the early nineteenth century with 'statistics', as geographical and statistical societies were formed, sometimes in conjunction (Berry and Marble, 1968). But whereas the very term 'statistics' gives away its state-centred bias, in geography a genuine attempt was made to break away from the constraints of the interstate political framework by constructing regional geography (Hartshorne, 1939). This attempted to describe the earth's surface, not state by state but in terms of 'regions' designated on environmental criteria. Although this project was based on what is now a discredited environmental deterministic theory, it does provide a distinct contrast to the state-centred assumptions of the systematic social sciences evolving at the same time. Hence when Wallerstein (1983e, p. 24) bemoans the fact that the data bases of existing literature are 'grossly distorted' and that 'we need, first of all, a new cartography and a new statistics,' regional geography does provide an unlikely precedent for carrying out such a task.

Of course, we cannot resurrect traditional regional geography, any more than we can use the specialist 'spatial social science' as our new geographical perspective. But we do need a geographical perspective in the original sense of describing the earth's surface. The new historical myth undermines much of our existing social knowledge and requires a new 'geography'. This is part of Wallerstein's (1983c, p. 35) agenda for redoing much of the work of the social sciences of the last 200 years. Wallerstein (1980c) has hinted as much in his review of *The Times History of the World Atlas*. The historical geography of progress must be replaced by the geography of the waxing and waning of different historical systems until about 1500, when the exorable spread of the world-economy, gradually, slowly and in spurts, eliminated all its rivals. This is an immense task involving many important new empirical treatments of what currently exist only as theoretical statements. We need to be able to delineate the bounds of historical systems, for example. For the world-economy this will involve precise specification of the locations and timing of incorporations into its division of labour. Within this particular system the variations in intensity of exploitation of labour over time and place will require careful description. A series of maps at any scale showing the distribution of proletarian and semi-proletarian households have never to my knowledge been produced. Quite simply, the new categories of the world-systems project require a 'new geography' as a necessary perspective, a building-block of historical social science.

If the above agenda seems to suggest a 'new historical geography' then the categories we are dealing with have been misunderstood. If we cannot separate history and social science it follows that all geography is historical geography. But this does not, of course, diminish our interest in the transient present (instant history in the making) nor our concern for the future. Our heuristic position means that the *only* reason we will produce a 'new geography' is to help create a future more to our liking. And this is where regional geography is so important. The world-systems project has been criticized as neglecting social forces at less than the world scale. To some it is 'Parsonianism on a world scale': 'The insistence that analysis takes place on the world scale and no other as well as the functionalist nature of the theory has reduced action to triviality' (Cooper, 1981, pp. 10–11). A misunderstanding of the world-systems project of this magnitude is a very serious matter. That intelligent reviewers can make such an error illustrates the difficulties of devising or reconstituting a new discipline when critics, both sympathetic and antagonistic, are all thinking in the old categories. In Wallerstein's totality, 'scale of analysis' is as indivisible as economics and politics. The choice to analyse at any scale is a heuristic not a theoretical one. Just because we are dealing with a world-economy does not mean that local forces are any less important (Taylor, 1981, 1982). What it does mean is that they must be seen in a new light, as part of a larger unfolding system. Such fresh interpretation is imposed on all aspects of historical social science, of course, but this geographical scale problem does seem to be acute. What is required is some sound empirical regional geography illustrating the variety of structural effects and local responses throughout the world-economy. From the making of new 'capitalist spaces' by transition or incorporation through to effects of the current recession and its meaning for the future, regional geographies can provide one springboard for historical social science. After all the world-systems project will culminate in the mobilization of peoples in regions.

References

Agnew, J. A. 1982: Sociologizing the geographic imagination. *Political Geography Quarterly*, 1, 155–66.

Amin, S., Arrighi, G., Frank, A. G. and Wallerstein, I. 1982: *Dynamics of Global Crisis*. New York: Monthly Review Press.

Aronowitz, S. 1981: A metatheoretical critique of Immanuel Wallerstein's *The Modern World System. Theory and Society*, 10, 503–20.

Arrighi, G., Hopkins, T. K. and Wallerstein, I. 1983: Rethinking the concepts of class and status group in a world-system perspective. *Review*, 6, 283–304.

Bergeson, A. (ed.) 1980: *Studies of the Modern World-System*. New York: Academic Press.

Berry, B. J. L. and Marble, D. F. 1968: *Spatial Analysis*. Englewood Cliffs: Prentice-Hall.

Brenner, R. 1977: The origins of capitalist development: a critique of neo-Smithian Marxism. *New Left Review*, 104, 25–92.

Brewer, A., 1980: *Marxist Theories of Imperialism*. London: Routledge & Kegan Paul.

Carr, E. H. 1961: *What is History?* London: Macmillan.

Chandra, B. 1981: Karl Marx, his theories of Asian Societies and colonial rule. *Review*, 5, 13–94.

Chase-Dunn, C. K. (ed.) 1982: *Socialist States in the World-System*. Beverly Hills: Sage.

Chase-Dunn, C. K. 1983: The kernel of the capitalist world-economy: three approaches. In W. R. Thompson (ed.), *Contending Approaches to World System Analysis*, Beverly Hills: Sage, 55–78.

Cooper, F. 1981: Africa and the world economy. *African Studies Review*, 14, 1–86.

Cox, K. R. 1976: American geography: social science emergent. *Social Science Quarterly*, 57, 182–207.

Foster-Carter, A. 1978: The modes of production controversy. *New Left Review*, 107, 47–77.

Hartshorne, R. 1939: *The Nature of Geography*. Washington DC: Association of American Geographers.

Hollist, W. L. and Rosenau, J. N. (eds) 1981: *World System Structure*. Beverly Hills: Sage.

Hopkins, T. K. and Wallerstein, I. 1982: *World-Systems Analysis*. Beverly Hills: Sage.

Laclau, E. 1971: Feudalism and capitalism in Latin America. *New Left Review*, 67, 19–38.

Lefebvre, H. 1980: Marxism exploded. *Review*, 4, 19–32.

Modelski, G. 1978: The long cycle of global politics and the nation state. *Comparative Studies in Society and History*, 20, 214–35.

O'Brien, P. 1982: European economic development: the contribution of the periphery. *Economic History Review*, 35, 1–18.

Peet, R. 1980: Historical materialism and mode of production: a note on Marx's perspective and method. In R. Peet (ed.), *An Introduction to Marxist Theories of Development*, Canberra: Australian National University, 9–26.

Rostow, W. W. 1978: *The World Economy History and Prospect*. London: Macmillan.

Russett, B. M. and Starr, H. 1981: *Global Politics. The Menu for Choice*. San Francisco: Freeman.

Rymalov, V. V. 1978: *The World Capitalist Economy: Structural Changes, Trends and Problems*. Moscow: Progress Publishers.

Sfia, M. S. 1983: The world capitalist system and the transition to socialism. *Review*, 7, 3–14.

Taylor, J. G. 1979: *From Modernization to Modes of Production*. London: Macmillan.

Taylor, P. J. 1981: Geographical scales within the world-economy approach. *Review*, 5, 1–12.

Taylor, P. J. 1982: A materialist framework for political geography. *Transactions, Institute of British Geographers*, N.S. 7, 15–34.

Taylor, P. J. 1985: The value of a geographical perspective. In R. J. Johnston (ed.), *The Future of Geography*, London: Methuen, 92–110.

Thompson, W. R. 1983: World system analysis with and without the hyphen. In W. R. Thompson (ed.), *Contending Approaches to World System Analysis*, Beverly Hills: Sage, 7–26.

Tylecote, A. B. and Lonsdale-Brown, M. L. 1982: State socialism and development: why Russian and Chinese ascent halted. In E. Friedman (ed.), *Ascent and Decline in the World-System*, Beverly Hills: Sage, 255–88.

Wallerstein, I. 1974a: *The Modern World-System. Capitalist Agriculture and the Origins of the European World-Economy in the Sixteenth Century*, New York: Academic Press.

Wallerstein, I. 1974b; The rise and future demise of the capitalist world-system. *Comparative Studies in Society and History*, 16, 387–418.

Wallerstein, I. 1976: A world-system perspective on the social sciences. *British Journal of Sociology*, 27, 345–54.

Wallerstein, I. 1977: The tasks of historical social science: an editorial. *Review*, 1, 3–8.

Wallerstein, I. 1979: *The Capitalist World-Economy*. Cambridge: Cambridge University Press.

Wallerstein, I. 1980a: *The Modern World-System*, vol. II: *Mercantilism and the Consolidation of the European World-Economy 1600–1750*. New York: Academic Press, 11–54.

Wallerstein, I. 1980b: The future of the world-economy. In T. K. Hopkins and I. Wallerstein (eds), *Processes of the World-System*, Beverly Hills: Sage, 167–80.

Wallerstein, I. 1980c: Maps, maps, maps. *Radical History Review*, 24, 155–9.

Wallerstein, I. 1980d: Imperialism and development. In A. Bergesen (ed.), *Studies of the Modern World System*. New York: Academic Press, 13–24.

Wallerstein, I. 1982a: Crisis as transition. In S. Amin, G. Arrighi, A. G. Frank and I. Wallerstein, *Dynamics of Global Crisis*, New York: Monthly Review Press.

Wallerstein, I. 1982b: Socialist states: mercantilist strategies and revolutionary objectives. In E. Friedman (ed.), *Ascent and Decline in the World System*, Beverly Hills: Sage, 289–300.

Wallerstein, I. 1983a: *Historical Capitalism*. London: Verso.

Wallerstein, I. 1983b: An agenda for world-systems analysis. In W. R. Thompson (ed.), *Contending Approaches to World System Analysis*, Beverly Hills: Sage, 299–308.

Wallerstein, I. 1983c: Crises: the world-economy, the movements and the ideologies. In A. Bergesen (ed.), *Crises in the World System*, Beverly Hills: Sage, 21–36.

Wallerstein, I. 1983d: European economic development: a comment on O'Brien. *Economic History Review*, 34, 580–5.

Wallerstein, I. 1983e: Economic theories and historical disparities of development. In International Economic History Congress Bl, *Economic Theory and History*, Budapest: Akademiai Kiado.

Wallerstein, I. 1984a: *The Politics of the World-Economy*. Cambridge: Cambridge University Press.

Wallerstein, I. 1984b: Cities in socialist theory and capitalist praxis. *International Journal of Urban and Regional Research*, 8, 64–72.

Wallerstein, I. 1984c: Long waves as capitalist process. *Review*, 7, 559–75.

12

Epilogue: Our Planet is Big Enough for Peace but Too Small for War

W. BUNGE

THE CREATION OF HUMAN SPACE

Humankind began life on planet earth somewhere in East Africa, and from
that Garden of Eden slowly spread out across the planet, taking 40,000 years
to reach the tip of South America. During this slow colonization of the earth's
surface, the characteristics of the human race were adapted to the environmental
variety. We created a geography of environmental adaptation and use in a vast
mosaic of separate places, with relatively few contacts between the members
of each. The races lived lives apart.

After colonization of the land we shifted onto the earth's water surface,
increasing the average rate of travel and mixing the races up as a consequence.
In doing this we created the foundation for many of our social problems – those
of racism and of starvation, for example. And then we moved into the earth's
atmosphere, again increasing the rate of travel so that the earth is rapidly
shrinking to a dot. We created geography, and now we are eliminating it.

We are told that there are too many people in our human space, that we
are experiencing a population explosion whose consequence is that there will
be insufficient resources to support everybody: put bluntly, there isn't enough
living space for all the babies, especially in all of Africa and most of Asia and
Latin America, where children aged under 15 make up more than 40 per cent
of the population.

But in truth the population explosion is a one-generation phenomenon. It
began with the industrial revolution in Britain when, as a consequence of the
invention of potable water, infant mortality rates plunged. A generation later,
there was a corresponding drop in the birth rate and the population explosion
was over; a new equilibrium was reached. The birth control involved is universal

in the second generation, regardless of public policy, and clearly has nothing to do with abortion or contraception. A universal cut, which seems to have been biologically triggered, occurred in the explosion, and continues to do so. The explosion itself has spread out from Britain, engulfing the rest of human space. Africa is now experiencing the explosive generation.

Even after this worldwide explosion, all of the population – some 5 billion – could have a comfortable family picnic in one average-sized American county, a large grassy park some 25 miles square. So is the world overpopulated? Is the planet now a lifeboat from which we must jettison some people so that the others can survive? Are we short of resources? No: we *invent* natural resources by thinking them up, at a much faster rate than we deplete them.

Then why all the starvation and the mega-famines, especially of black babies in Africa? Colonialism created those famines, replacing local subsistence crops by commercial production for export; and then drought is blamed, just as the potato blight was blamed for the Irish famine of the 1840s while the British were shipping out wheat in armed convoys. We have created a Third World wherever infant mortality rates are high – as they are in America's black ghettos, where the rate is higher than in 57 per cent of the world's countries. Social and economic change would alter the situation. We could create societies where children bloom like little flowers, rather than die like flies – as the Chinese are demonstrating. But to achieve this we must keep our planet human.

THE DESTRUCTION OF HUMAN SPACE

But we face an even bigger threat. The next war will literally overwhelm planet earth. It will not be a finite war, like those of the past; it will be infinite relative to the space occupied by humankind. The qualitative leap from the wars of the past to the next war is analogous to the difference between the effects of a fire-cracker inside a tin can and one released harmlessly in the open. The tin can that we occupy is too small, so that no part of it could avoid the impact of the war; indeed, for some part of the human race to survive, the earth would need to be at least as large as the sun, and growing every day – such is the explosive power available. The earth is a natural lens, so the waves from a large explosion spread out, becoming increasingly thinner, until they recombine and concentrate again at the antipode. This is what happened after the 1883 explosion of Krakatoa, and is the certain consequence of a nuclear conflict somewhere on the earth's surface or in its atmosphere.

That the earth is too small to contain such a war is invariably missed by most strategists, who nibble away at it by concentrating on issues such as the national effects or the capability of a civil defence programme. They look at the war at a scale below its true one – which is the planet itself; and they come up with conclusions that the human species will not be completely destroyed. Study at the global scale denies that conclusion, so geography is the most compelling of sciences for survival because of its holistic focus. The chapters of this book have demonstrated, in their many different ways, the strength of that compulsion.

The shrinking of the world is such that no place on the surface of the earth or in its atmosphere is safe from the nuclear holocaust. The only space still not shrunk to practically nothing is the earth's interior. What if this too became the preferred space, as in the past have the oceans and outer space? If this inner space became easier to penetrate then missiles – or 'moles' – could be sent through the surface, down into the interior and out the other side. As the speed of these moles increased, as undoubtedly would be the case, then a further shrinking of the earth would have been achieved. Already, national sovereignty over the earth's surface and atmosphere has been lost – the United States with its satellites knows more about what is happening in Canada than do the Canadians. Loss of sovereignty over the earth below would be the final destruction of geography.

The Soviet Union and China are now building massive shelters within the earth's interior, and their commitment of significant sums of money proves that they believe that there is still some safety under the earth's surface. But if humankind learns to penetrate the earth's interior, and it is getting better at this all the time, then there would be no safe places left in which to shelter the children. We would have to drop what are fatal illusions that some still have about surviving the third world war.

THE CHOICE

The geography of the heavenly planet is within reach. It is one in which people will be at peace with each other and with nature; machines will be caged and children free to roam; there will be an explosion of variety and free choice; and there will be a stable population living in great abundance with balanced restraint among people, nature and machines. Yet with all this wonder clearly within our reach, there are many – individuals, groups, whole societies even – apparently dedicated to their own suicide and the murder of everybody else. This collective death-wish has been automated into the hair-triggered computers that control the missiles. They may prevail. We can have heaven; or we may choose hell. In geographical terms, this planet is not too small for peace but it is too small for war.

Contributors

PIERS BLAIKIE   School of Development Studies, University of East Anglia, Norwich

P. N. BRADLEY   Beijer Institute, International Centre for Energy and Development in Africa, Nairobi, Kenya

W. BUNGE   Société pour l'Exploration Humaine, Athabaska, Quebec

R. J. JOHNSTON   Department of Geography, University of Sheffield

PETER R. ODELL   Centre for International Energy Studies, Erasmus University, Rotterdam

JOHN O'LOUGHLIN   Department of Geography, University of Illinois, Urbana, Illinois

RICHARD PEET   Graduate School of Geography, Clark University, Worcester, Massachusetts

PETER J. TAYLOR   Department of Geography, University of Newcastle upon Tyne

NIGEL THRIFT   Centre for the Study of Britain and the World Economy, St David's University College, Lampeter

COLIN H. WILLIAMS   Department of Geography and Recreation Studies, North Staffordshire Polytechnic, Stoke on Trent

ROBERT WOODS   Department of Geography, University of Sheffield

Index